BIBLICAL THEOLOGY
AND
THE SPIRITUAL EXERCISES

*This book is
No. 7 in Series II: Modern Scholarly Studies
about the Jesuits,
in English Translations*

Gilles Cusson, S.J.

BIBLICAL THEOLOGY

AND

THE SPIRITUAL EXERCISES

A Method Toward
A Personal Experience of God
As Accomplishing Within Us
His Plan of Salvation

Translated by
Mary Angela Roduit, R.C., and
George E. Ganss, S.J.

THE INSTITUTE OF JESUIT SOURCES
Saint Louis, 1994

This book is an authorized translation of *Pédagogie de l'expérience spirituelle personelle: Bible et Exercices Spirituels,* by Gilles Cusson, S.J. (3rd ed., 1986), published by Les Editions Bellarmin, Montréal. The first French edition of this title, published in 1968, is itself a revision of the original work which bore the title *L'expérience biblique du salut dans les Exercises de saint Ignace.*

THE COVER: fishermen ply their trade
at sunrise on the Lake of Galilee,
in the Holy Land, where
God so graciously communicated
himself,
his illuminating doctrine,
and his loving plan
for the salvation of the human race.

First printing: 1988
Second printing: 1994

©1988 The Institute of Jesuit Sources
3700 West Pine Boulevard
Saint Louis, Missouri, 63108

Library of Congress Catalogue Card Number: 87-81796
ISBN 0-912422-00-9

TABLE OF CONTENTS
(For a detailed table of contents, see page 379)

Father Gilles Cusson's *Pédagogie de l'expérience spirituelle personelle: Bible et Exercices,* presented here in a translation from its third edition in French, is an application of modern biblical theology to the study of the *Spiritual Exercises* of St. Ignatius of Loyola. It is, therefore, a biblical interpretation of these *Exercises* and a commentary on them in that light. In many respects it is the most extensive and best-documented commentary on the *Exercises* presently available in English.

The Gist of the Book

Like other commentaries, it discusses the possible meanings of Ignatius' phrases and the function of individual exercises in the context of the whole. But beyond that it also shows, more forcefully than perhaps any other commentary, how the main thrust of the *Exercises* is a transmission of the central theme which runs through the entire Bible and unifies all its books: God's plan of creation and of redemptive salvation of humankind through Christ, as that plan is revealed in its applications to human beings in the ongoing history of salvation. Ignatius' book, when coupled with the retreatant's activities guided by the book, presents a pedagogical method or channel through which God communicates himself and accomplishes his plan within individual persons for their salvation and rich spiritual development.[1]

This pedagogical method functions on two planes. On the objective level, it presents, as a guide for everything else, God as communicating through his deeds and words in salvation history the main guiding and inspiring truths of Christianity: for example, the Trinity, God's purpose in creating the universe and his supremacy over it, humanity's fall from grace through sin, the remedy for this sin through the Incarnation, life, death, and resurrection of Christ and, through human beings in the beatific vision, the achievement of the purpose of the whole created universe: the praise or glorification of God. On the subjective level of personal experience is the activity of the exercitant. By prayerful interaction with God, his revealed truths, and his graces, he or she applies the divine communications to himself or herself here and now in one's own daily life at this precise moment in the history of salvation.

1 Ephes. 1:9, and many parallel texts, e.g., Col. 2:2, Rom. 16:25; Ephes. 3:1–4:7.

Through this presentation Cusson helps a retreat director or a retreatant to see that Ignatius' book of *Exercises* is focused on that central biblical message which is the chief object of God's inspiration: "that truth which God, for the sake of our salvation, wished to see confided to the sacred Scriptures."[2] It was because of that inspiration that the words of the biblical author became also the words of God.

Cusson sets the scene for his interpretation in his first chapter, by presenting Ignatius' own experience of the divine salvific plan. Already at Loyola in 1521, through his reading of Ludolph's *Life of Christ* and the "book of the lives of the saints" by Jacopo de Voragine, Ignatius began to form his own vibrant personal concept of that divine plan of salvation through Christ—a concept which matured through the rest of his life. Ignatius' prayerful interaction with that plan and with God as its author is what led to his own rich spiritual development. He was endeavoring to fit himself cooperatively into that divine plan at the moment allotted to him in the history of salvation. The matured result in his later life was a spirituality based firmly on God's saving plan and will, and also on the chief truths of his revelation, such as the Trinity, the Incarnation, and "the events and mysteries of the life, death, resurrection, and ascension of Christ our Lord."[3] These chief elements from God's revelation furnish our strongest motivation for carrying our Christian faith energetically into practice.

Ignatius' spontaneous urge to guide others to similar experiences deep in their hearts is what led him to devise the procedures and write the notes which gradually became his *Exercises*. His little book, consequently, contains a compressed reflection of God's plan unfolding in the history of salvation; and it can be a handbook guiding a pedagogical exercise through which a retreatant can discover that to fit himself or herself cooperatively into that plan and its history is his or her chief purpose in life, opportunity, and ultimate fulfillment. To view Ignatius' *Exercises* in this way is a key to an accurate interpretation and an inspiring spiritual experience.

Cusson's book also transmits to us the fruit of his wide consultation of the most important early and modern commentators on the *Exercises*. He draws extensively from them, gives us useful references to them, and shows himself a safe guide as we in his company view and weigh their multifaceted opinions.

Fortunately, since the encyclical *Divino afflante Spiritu* of Pope Pius XII in 1943, and particularly since Vatican Council II, Catholic spirituality has

2 Vatican Council II, "On Divine Revelation," no. 11, (trans. A. Flannery, O.P.).
3 St. Ignatius, in his *Constitutions of the Society of Jesus,* [65].

been growing more and more biblical. Individuals, study groups, and theological or spiritual writings have been focusing ever increasing attention on God's plan of creation and redemption, and its unfolding in salvation history. In our current atmosphere, therefore, the timeliness of Cusson's book is obvious. The Institute of Jesuit Sources is happy to make it available in this English translation produced cooperatively by Sister Mary Angela Roduit, R.C., Treasurer General in Rome of the Religious of the Cenacle until 1986, and the undersigned second translator, who was also the editor. Sister Mary Angela received and gratefully acknowledges the valuable aid she received from Sister Mary Milligan, R.S.H.M., of Los Angeles, California, who from 1980 to 1985 was Superior General of the Religious of the Sacred Heart of Mary.

The Translation

The work of translation and publication has been unfortunately but unavoidably long delayed. Both Sister Mary Angela, the first translator, and the present writer, the second translator, had to ply their work alongside other pressing duties. The delay, however, brought one advantage which softens our regret. New complexities were discovered as the editing progressed, and remedies had time to mature. They had so great a bearing on the nature of the present translation, and of the readers' understanding of it, that they seem to require some explanation here.

Sister Mary Angela produced the first draft in Rome. It was fluent, accurate, and properly but not unduly literal—faithfully turning French technical terms such as *pédagogie* by pedagogy, *mystère* by mystery, *dialectique* by dialectic, *ontologique* by ontological, and the like. This led to discovery of a difficulty. Occasions arose for this editor to show the draft to others interested in the theory of the *Spiritual Exercises*. Some understood the terminology well. However, a majority of others, he found, frequently attached obscure or erroneous meanings to many words used in technical senses which were rightly presupposed as known in the Roman university environment in which the French original was composed. However, many of our local readers, while thinking they understood them, were in reality misunderstanding them and missing the true spiritual message of the book. This experience, coupled with many consultations, led this editor to think that a faithful but literal translation would not be correctly understood or perseveringly read by all too many. If the message and inspiration of the original was to be communicated effectively to them, adaptations would be necessary: clarifying paraphrases and adjustments to the thought patterns of our prospective English-speaking readers.

Hence, with approval from Father Cusson and Sister Mary Angela, this second translator set out to rewrite phrases or passages where he deemed it necessary, and thus to produce a version better adapted to the thought patterns of these readers. He aimed to do this in such a way that they would be able to grasp the correct meanings readily and accurately, usually on the first reading.

Therefore the respective roles of the two translators becomes clear. Sister Mary Angela produced the basic translation, and this second translator and editor the adaptations. He highly esteems Father Cusson's thought for its depth and timeliness, and he has tried to be faithful to it. But there is, of course, danger of human error. If on some occasions he has missed the right meaning or nuance, he alone is responsible. In the footnotes an effort was made to convert references to French works to English translations when they exist; but this was not always possible. To the original bibliography also, in which French works are naturally predominant, has been added a supplementary bibliography of works on biblical theology in English.

Cusson's *Pédagogie* was first published in 1968. Since it was composed before the present concerns about discriminatory language arose, problems in this area were numerous in the translating, especially in the sections of chapter 2 dealing with "l'homme." Both translators tried to handle them with sympathy for the opinions of the many men and women whom they consulted—in conversations in which this editor experienced vividly how widely viewpoints on this topic now differ. In these problems, particularly concerning the use of "man" in the generic sense, and of pronouns in the third person singular which refer back to antecedents such as person, human being, or who, meaning a member of the human race whether male or female, this editor often found helpful models in the recent 1986 edition of the New Testament of the New American Bible. He is especially grateful for the three paragraphs on pages [6] and [7] of its Preface, where he found much guiding light. He drew much consolation, too, from the revising committee's statement on page [5]: "In all these areas the present translation attempts to display a sensitivity appropriate to the present state of the questions under discussion, which are not yet resolved and in regard to which it is impossible to please everyone, since intelligent and sincere participants in the debate hold mutually contradictory views."

The Appendix on the "Mystery of Christ" and God's Plan of Salvation

In the experiences described above, two main sources of difficulty came to light: (1) the many meanings of the word "mystery," and (2) some unfamiliarity with the divine salvific plan which St. Paul named by this term with many varying nuances, and which has become increasingly frequent in recent theological or spiritual writing. Some readers, of course, know this terminology well. But for others it was vague or imperfectly remembered; and unless they have this knowledge fresh in mind, they are likely to miss much of the inspiration offered by Cusson's book. To help them to a more satisfying grasp of its rich message, the editor thought it desirable to provide the overview contained in the Appendix, below on pages 335–344.

Acknowledgments

The Texts of Scripture are quoted from the Revised Standard Version throughout the book; but those on the divider pages introducing Parts I and II are from the Jerusalem Bible. Citations from Ignatius' *Exercises* are taken from *The Spiritual Exercises of St. Ignatius: A New Translation* by Louis J. Puhl, S.J.

Extensive help which much improved the final product has been received from many persons. To name them all is impossible here, but special thanks are due to colleagues who, after reading the typescript in whole or in part, made corrections and suggestions of great value: Sisters Mary Angela Roduit, R.C., and Frances Krumpelman, S.C.N.; and my fellow Jesuits, Fathers Philip C. Fischer, Edward J. Malatesta, Martin Palmer, and Linus J. Thro; finally, for extensive help of different kinds to Fathers Daniel F.X. Meenan, editor of the *Review for Religious,* and John W. Padberg, Director of the Institute of Jesuit Sources.

George E. Ganss, S.J., Editor
Director Emeritus
The Institute of Jesuit Sources
July 31, 1987

Christian tradition, always sensitive to human needs, has put much emphasis on the prayer of petition. But by doing this it has tended to direct our attention to the benefits we beg for, and thereby leave in obscurity the great "gift of God" and its permanence within us. "If you knew the gift of God, . . . he would have given you living water" (John 4:1). Our faith in the gift of God to man needs to be enlightened. We must become aware of its presence and its significance. Otherwise we understand it only poorly; and if we are unaware of its true worth, we allow our most precious talent to lie dormant, and it fails to produce the fruit it could have borne. In our ignorance we may limit our prayer to begging for gifts which do not seem to come.

Through the sacrament of Christian initiation we are born anew into the life of God. Henceforth we are animated by the Spirit of the Father and the Son. The Father ceaselessly maintains in us the interior gift of his Word of knowledge and of his Spirit of love. St. Paul asks: How do we, who are reborn of the Holy Spirit and co-heirs with Christ, live out the reality of this Spirit who is the active presence of the Father and the Son within us? "We will come to him make our home with him" (John 14:23).

We do not lose this gift of God without serious consequences. It is something infinitely bigger than ourselves. It is God himself. We are loved by a God whose presence we can forget, ignore, or pretend to ignore. However, he stands at the door and knocks, awaiting with that patience so characteristic of him the moment of our cooperation, to draw us effectively to himself and to be our happiness through the supreme fulfillment of our being.

Genuine spiritual formation awakens us to this gift of God, disposes us to receive the divine action within us, and teaches us to correspond with this efficacious presence of the Holy Spirit who is moving our own spirit in its journey toward the Life. In this enriched situation our prayer of petition is seen as having new importance: It expresses our desire to be faithful to God and humbly begs for the capacity of a greater, more supple openness—a receptivity which is based on a spiritual knowledge of God's covenants and on our generosity of heart to respond to the human and divine exigencies of life.

It is from this vantage point of a renewed interior light that we now wish to present St. Ignatius' *Spiritual Exercises,* even though already for four centuries they have been applied in practice and been the object of reflective study. We want to view them now as an intelligent transmission of the divine message and as a conscious effort on our part to cultivate the dispositions necessary to be open to "the mystery of God," his efficacious plan for our salvation and spiritual growth. "The *Exercises,*" declared Nadal, a commissioned interpreter of Ignatius, "owe their efficacy to the fact that they teach us a method of preparing ourselves to receive the Word of God, the Good News." We hope to prove this in the book which follows.

To achieve this end we have chosen a method which places the *Exercises* back into the broad spiritual framework in which they were born. For if a study of the parallel between the message of the Bible and that of the *Exercises* does not explain this historical foundation which makes the similarity credible, the reader might regard the study as a gratuitous assertion. But if certain elements in the Ignatian text confirm its relation to the Scriptures, can we not for that reason form in advance a judgment that such was the intention of its author? A detailed analysis of this first problem in Part I of our book will enable us to extract the principles which will guide our interpretation; and then in Part II we shall apply them to the interpretation of the *Exercises.*

Hence, in Part I (chapters 1 through 3), we shall analyze the biblical origins and implications of Ignatius' spiritual experience at Loyola and Manresa where the *Exercises* arose, and also the similar implications of his conception of Christian life which he expressed in his later writings. In this light we shall show with greater precision in what way the *Exercises* proclaim and interpret God's revealed message, and by what steps they dispose the exercitant to receive it.

In Part II, chapters 4 through 8, we shall apply this method of biblical interpretation, the result of our preceding analysis, to the four Weeks of the *Exercises.* However, the reader should not expect a presentation in the form of "points-for-meditation" all ready to be proposed to the exercitant. We hope instead to furnish a working-tool which will enable a director or an exercitant to orient his or her practice of the Exercises along the line of their becoming an experience of the life of faith and of correspondence with the "gift of God"—a deepening of that experience of Christian salvation in which the central message of the Bible is directly sought and utilized. For this purpose we shall also furnish numerous biblical and bibliographical references. These will help the reader to apply in detail to the *Exercises* the principles of interpretation which pertain to the principal stages of the journey we propose.

In this study I have been greatly helped by many authors, theologians, spiritual writers and exegetes. I desire to express my gratitude to them all, and especially my fellow Jesuits, Fathers Gervais Dumeige, Ignacio Iparraguirre, Jacques Lewis, François Bourassa, Ignace de la Potterie, and Jean-Louis d'Aragón.

Gilles Cusson, S.J.

PART I

THE FOUNDATIONS,

IN ST. IGNATIUS' OWN EXPERIENCE,

FOR A BIBLICAL INTERPRETATION
OF THE SPIRITUAL EXERCISES

God destined us . . . to win salvation through our Lord Jesus Christ,
who died for us so that, alive or dead,
we should still live united to him.
(1 Thessalonians, 5:9)

I want you to . . . have knowledge of
the mystery of God, of Christ,
in which all the jewels of wisdom and knowledge are hidden.
(Colossians, 2:1–2)

For He has made known to us in all wisdom and insight . . .
the mystery . . . which he set forth in Christ,
as a plan for the fullness of time,
to unite all things in him.
This mystery . . . has *now been revealed,* . . .
that the pagans now share the same inheritance,
that they are parts of the same Body.
(Ephesians 1:9–10; 3:5–6)

ABBREVIATIONS

---

used in the footnotes

NOTE; For a COMPLETE LIST, see pages 345–347 below.
Only those most frequently used are listed here.

AHSJ	*Archivum Historicum Societatis Iesu.* Periodical, Rome
Autobiog	The *Autobiography* of St. Ignatius
Chr	*Christus.* Periodical, Paris
Cons	*The Constitutions of the Society of Jesus,* by St. Ignatius
ConsSJComm	*The Constitutions,* Translated with Commentary by G. E. Ganss
CyF	*Ciencia y Fe.* Periodical, Buenos Aires
DBTh	Léon-Dufour, *Dictionary of Biblical Theology*
DeGuiJes	De Guibert, *The Jesuits: Their Spiritual Doctrine and Practice*
DirSpEx	*Directoria Exercitiorum Spiritualium (1540–1599* (1955). In MHSJ
EppIgn	*S. Ignatii Epistolae,* 12 volumes in MHSJ
FN	*Fontes Narrativi,* 4 volumes in MHSJ
LettersIgn	*Letters of St. Ignatius,* translated by W. J. Young
Mnr	*Manresa.* Periodical, Madrid
MHSJ	Monumenta Historica Societatis Iesu, the series of critically edited historical sources of the Jesuits, 124 volumes
SpEx	The *Spiritual Exercises* of St. Ignatius
SpExMHSJ	*Exercitia Spiritualia S. Ignatii . . . et Directoria* (1919), in MHSJ
RAM	*Revue d'ascétique et de mystique.* Periodical, Toulouse
ScE	*Sciences Ecclésiastiques.* Periodical, Montréal
WL	*Woodstock Letters.* Periodical, Woodstock, Maryland

THE PREEMINENCE OF GOD'S PLAN OF SALVATION THROUGH CHRIST—THE "MYSTERY OF CHRIST"

A. The Divine Influence Which Led to the Composition of the Exercises

From the time when Ignatius was in Salamanca in 1527, hence before his studies in Paris, he was questioned about the origin of his knowledge. Did he speak "from knowledge or through the Holy Spirit"? The "Pilgrim" refused to answer.[1] Later on, as he told his friends the story of his conversion, which was the time when his spiritual knowledge began, he affirmed that "God treated him at this time just as a schoolmaster treats a child whom he is teaching."[2] Little by little Ignatius told about the graces he received. His contemporaries concluded that Father Ignatius had received great lights from God, and that it was from these exceptional graces that the book of the *Exercises*[3] sprang. His secretary Juan Polanco, for example, refers several times to the spiritual formation of Ignatius and to the composition of the *Exercises* as having come from the teaching of God. In his *Chronicon* he writes:

> Thus he was taught by God himself *(a Domino ipso . . . edoctus),* so much so that even if he had never studied Scripture or the Doctors, he would have known enough to be able to instruct others.[4]

---

1 *Autobiog,* no. 65; see also *LettersIgn,* pp. 80–81.
2 *Autobiog,* no. 27.
3 [The term "Spiritual Exercises" gives rise to many editorial problems. Throughout this book, *Spiritual Exercises* (in italic type) is used when the reference is chiefly to St. Ignatius' book, and Spiritual Exercises (in roman type) when it is chiefly to the activities within a retreat. However, since his book usually envisages these activities and vice versa, there are overlappings of emphasis which often make the choice of typeface somewhat arbitrary.

   To make references easier, in editions since 1928 a number in square brackets has been added to each paragraph of Ignatius' text, e.g., [21]. In references run into the text, e.g., "as is stated in *SpEx,* ([91])," the parentheses ( ) indicate that the numbers are a reference and the square brackets that the numbers themselves are an addition to the text. Editor.]
4 *SpEx*MHSJ, p. 37, citing *PolChron,* I, 23.

Regarding the Exercises Polanco is more precise:

At Manresa he began to communicate to many others these Spiritual Exercises which he himself had received, having been instructed by God himself *(a Deo ipso edoctus)*.[5]

In his Directory too he was to repeat:

. . . At the beginning of his conversion Ignatius, who was instructed and enlightened by God *(a Domino edoctus et illustratus)*, benefited much from these exercises.[6]

The books of primary sources about Ignatius, *Fontes Narrativi*, give us this further testimony from Polanco:

Among other things which he "who teaches men knowledge" (Ps. 93:10) taught him in that year [1522] were the meditations that we call the Spiritual Exercises and their method. . . ."[7]

Ignatius, who had so much respect for God's long hidden plan of salvation—which St. Paul termed "the mystery of God" (Rom. 16:25-26; Eph. 1:9-10; Col. 2:2)—would surely have been aware of such statements. The Preface of the Latin version of the *Exercises* called the Vulgate (1548) states that Ignatius "composed these *Exercises* after having learned more from the unction of the Holy Spirit, his own personal experience, and the practice of spiritual direction than from books."[8] This preface is merely repeating the ideas of the pope himself, Paul III, who in the preceding month of July, 1548, had written in his brief of approbation, *Pastoralis officii:*

. . . Our dear son Ignatius of Loyola, superior general of the Society of Jesus, who has composed certain documents or Spiritual Exercises, which are drawn from Holy Scripture and his experience of the spiritual life, and set them up according to an order that could move the souls of the faithful to piety.[9]

In the same vein we have the testimonies of Laínez, Nadal, Ribadeneira, and the depositions for the process of canonization in the "report given to Paul V on the life and miracles of Blessed Father Ignatius."[10]

5 *SpEx*MHSJ, p. 31, citing *PolChron*, I, 25.
6 *SpEx*MHSJ, p. 796.
7 *FN*, I, 163-164; cited by Rouquette in *Chr*, no. 2 (1954), 26, fn. 2.
8 *SpEx*MHSJ, p. 218, in the Preface, attributed to Polanco, to the first printed edition of the *Exercises* in 1548.
9 *SpEx*MHSJ, p. 216.
10 Ibid., pp. 30-34, 37-39; *MonNad*, IV, 666; (concerning Nadal see also *MonNad*, VI, 842; *FN*, I, 103-104; II, 159-160, 1009. See also the Directories in *SpEx*MHSJ, pp. 883, 935, 1008, and 1116).

These numerous statements on the privileged origin of the *Exercises* do not seem to have aroused any astonishment or anxiety at that time when one had to be so attentive to defend oneself against suspicion of the illuminism of the Alumbrados and the Protestant doctrines on free interpretation. Only later were doubts to arise, when discussion would focus directly upon the inspiration[11] of the book of the *Exercises*. Some would soon view the statements above as exaggerations by Ignatius' first companions and would accuse them of fanaticism or pious naiveté. However, in this era itself in which reserve was so necessary, the statements of Nadal, Polanco, and Paul III himself did not stir up any scandal. Furthermore Ignatius, who was so prudent, was aware of them. It seems, therefore, that we should turn our attention back to the more sober truth which they were aiming to express, and again find the light that this truth can throw on the problem of interpretation which is our concern today. Let us remember that without special graces the composition of the *Exercises* remains a mystery,"[12] especially when we consider the fact that, as the historian Ludwig Pastor wrote, "a soldier, who had learned no more than how to read and write and had only just said farewell to a life adrift among the temptations of the world, . . . was able to compose a spiritual work remarkable for inwardness, lucidity, depth, and strength."[13]

What the first companions truly meant by their statements can be summed up thus: Father Ignatius lived through a very profound and exceptional spiritual experience, under God's action upon him through the unction of the Holy Spirit and the power of his grace. As a result he was, in the constantly recurring phrase of his contemporaries, "taught by God himself" *(a Deo ipso edoctus)*. It was from this experience that he drew up the first

---

11 ["Inspiration," as used here, does not mean that influence of God upon the authors of the Bible, through which the words they wrote are God's words universally obligatory; nor does it mean merely some lofty literary inspiration such as that attributed to Vergil, Dante, or Shakespeare. What it does refer to is God's communication of himself to great mystics such as Augustine, Bernard, or Teresa of Avila, among whom Ignatius ranks. When they tried to describe their experience they often found their language inadequate. On some extreme theories of that inspiration commonly rejected today, such as dictation of the *Exercises* by the Blessed Virgin Mary, see P. Dudon, *St. Ignatius of Loyola* (1949), pp. 456–457. Ed.]

12 P. Debuchy, *Introduction à l'étude des Exercices spirituels de saint Ignace,* in CBE, 6 (1909), p. 13.

13 L. von Pastor, *History of the Popes,* XII (St. Louis, 1923), 17, cited in *SpEx-MHSJ,* p. 39. Pius XI also praised the value of the *Exercises* which he knew from experience. In 1929 he called them "a most wise and universal code of laws for the direction of souls in the way of salvation and perfection" (*AAS,* 21 (1929), 698–706; English from *The Catholic Mind,* XXVIII (1930), 41–58.

draft of the *Exercises,* composed on his own initiative, with the aim that "that they might move the souls of the faithful to piety," as Paul III states in his brief of 1548.[14]

Ignatius' companions did not use the phrase "inspiration of the *Exercises,*" but they did know how to relate them to the "source of their inspiration." That well spring was the spiritual experience which Ignatius had in the school of God and the fruits which he carefully gathered from that experience.[15] One of his companions, Jerónimo Nadal, came to this conclusion:

> Our Lord communicated the *Exercises* to him, and *guided him in such a way* that he devoted himself entirely to God's service and to the salvation of souls. The Lord showed this to him especially in two exercises, those on the Kingdom and the Two Standards. Ignatius understood that this was his goal, that he should devote himself to it completely, and keep it as his aim in all his works.[16]

"Taught by God himself." This original experience, lived out by Ignatius from Loyola to Manresa, is the one upon which we want to focus—his experience of the divine plan of salvation and also, as we shall see, of the divine pedagogical method which in its own time produces that Christian salvation and spiritual growth. This experience of Ignatius, if better understood, will put us in position to draw from it some conclusions of great interest for our understanding of the *Exercises.*

B. St. Ignatius' Own Experience of God
As Accomplishing within Him the Divine Plan of Salvation

We do not mean to repeat here the numerous excellent studies about the spiritual journey of Ignatius after his conversion.[17] Our intention is simply to make explicit the relationship between these well-known stages and God's

---

14 We speak of "the first draft of the *Exercises*" because, as we know, from the time Ignatius left Manresa in early 1523 to his departure from Paris in 1535 he gave the Exercises often and continually corrected their growing text, especially in the light of his experiences in Paris and his theological studies. Numerous studies on the "origin of the Exercises" treat this topic. We shall return to this matter soon.

15 *SpEx*MHSJ, p. 93, referring to the explanation proposed by Luis de La Palma in his *Camino espiritual* (1625), pp. 22–23.

16 An exhortation of Nadal, in *FN,* I, 306–307; see also *DirSpEx* (1955), p. 174.

17 On the subject of the relationship between the "origin of the *Exercises*" as tied to Ignatius' experience, abundant documentation will be found in Gilmont and Daman: *Bibliographie Ignatienne (1894–1957),* nos. 1176–1272. See especially nos. 1183–1184 (Hugo Rahner), 1230 (J. Calveras), 1236, 1238 (A. Codina), 1246–1249 (P. Leturia), 1252 (H. Pinard de la Boullaye), 1265 (H. Watrigant), 1267 (H. Bernard-Maître), 1270 (I. Iparraguirre). [See also P. Du-

revealed plan of salvation, spiritual growth, and final beatitude; and by this we aim to emphasize *the biblical character of the Ignatian experience* which is the source of the *Exercises*. To this end we shall examine the two intense periods in the beginning of his spiritual journey: his meditations at Loyola and the events in Manresa.

To guide the reader during this analysis, we give briefly already here several important conclusions which have emerged from our study of these two periods. They can be summed up in three words: distinction, relationship, and continuity. In the Pilgrim's history both at Loyola and at Manresa we should notice, first of all, the distinction between (1), on the objective level, the message which he received and (2), on the subjective level, the experience which the message with God's grace aroused in him. There is, next, the close relationship between these two levels. If the message presented to Ignatius' attention through his readings at Loyola and the graces of Manresa had been of a different nature, his experience would no doubt have been different too. Consequently, we should notice in the message—to use the terminology of scholastic philosophy—a certain causality both efficient and exemplary, especially that of the word of God upon Ignatius. Finally, from the period at Loyola to that at Manresa we should also notice the continuity on both the levels, that of the doctrine received and that of the religious experience it evoked. In regard to the doctrine, we shall see, this continuity coincides with a progress in the exposition which starts out with very simple but precise elements which Ignatius assimilated during his readings at Loyola, and in time reaches a depth strictly ineffable as a result of the mystical graces at Manresa. With respect to Ignatius' subjective experience, there is a similar continuity linking the message and his assimilation of it. However, there is at one stage a notable gap, due principally to his poor interpretation of the message received from the example of the saints in the *Flos sanctorum*.

At the end of this analysis, we shall better understand that the very content of the divine communication, especially the theological content, explains the chief characteristics of the experience which Ignatius had at Manresa between the years 1521 and 1523, and which he later proposed for others, who would be helped by grace, in his book of the *Exercises*.

don, *St. Ignatius of Loyola* (1949), pp. 455-457; J. de Guibert, *The Jesuits: Their Spiritual Doctrine and Practice* (French, 1953; English trans., 1964, hereafter referred to as *DeGuiJes*), pp. 21-73; *SpExMHSJTe* (1969), pp. 4-64; C. de Dalmases, *St. Ignatius of Loyola, Founder of the Jesuits: His Life and Work* (1985), pp. 57-70. Editor.]

1. His Meditations at Loyola

In studying the genesis of the *Exercises,* authors have focused chiefly on the grace of Manresa which played such a determining role in the history of Ignatius' life. But for our own point of interest in this book, the sojourn at Loyola seems no less rich in information. This state, preparatory to the deepening process at Manresa, was not only chronologically first; it also laid a foundation of such a nature that it led the Pilgrim's soul to undergo a salutary experience which was typically gospel-like. A few concrete details will suffice to reveal how important this stage at Loyola was. Ignatius' readings there centered on the only two volumes in the castle,[18] and lasted five to six months, from August or September, 1521, to the end of February, 1522.[19] They were in fact prolonged meditations, as the saint himself stated in his *Autobiography.*[20] The content of the books, especially of the Life of Christ *(Vita Jesu Christi)* by Ludolph the Carthusian, consisted more in topics for prayer than in narratives, as we shall see. We have a striking proof of the keen attention Ignatius paid to the perusal of these texts in the fact that at this time our knight copied "with delight" about 300 pages from them in his own handwriting.[21] Finally, Ignatius stated that he had drawn great spiritual lights from these readings.[22] When we take everything into consideration, we see that Loyola remains the scene of a radical conversion which was genuine and lasting.

To know the objective point of departure in these months of attentive reflections which brought about Ignatius' interior conversion and also his firm determination to enter the service of God as opposed to the service of the world; and to understand the entire world view given to him in these "lessons" from which he drew such great fruit, we must examine these books which gave to the worldly knight of Loyola his first substantial spiritual nourishment.

In his *Estudios ignacianos*[23] Pedro de Leturia remarks that for three

---

18 See *SpEx*MHSJ, p. 49; *FN,* I, 40.
19 See "Chronología de san Ignacio," on p. 38 of *Obras completas de san Ignacio de Loyola* (Madrid: Biblioteca de autores cristianos, 3rd ed., 1963). [To conform to the French text of *Pédagogie,* henceforth references to Ignatius' *Obras completas* will be to this 3rd edition (1963), rather than to the 4th (1982). Ed.]
20 See *Autobiog,* no. 6, "He read these books over many times." *See also* no. 11: "He took great delight in the books he was reading, ... Part of his time he spent in writing and part in prayer."
21 Ibid., no. 11.
22 Ibid., nos. 9, 11, 12.
23 P. Leturia, *Estudios ignacianos.* Ed. rev. by I. Iparraguirre; I, *Estudios biográphicos;* II, *Estudios espirituales* (Rome, 1957).

centuries historians scarcely bothered to examine the objective contents of the books that were at the origin of Ignatius' conversion. The first to study those books were Fita (1872), Joly (1896), Watrigant (1897), Codina (1919), Boehmer (1921), and Creixell (1922).[24] In studying the genesis of the *Exercises* these authors took the texts of Ludolph the Carthusian and Jacobus de Voragine and were concerned merely with the literary dependence of passages of the *Exercises* on these works.[25] Therefore Leturia took these works up again to analyze their content, in order to try to discern what influence they had on the life of Ignatius after his conversion.[26] He applied this approach to the lives of the saints, and of particular ones among them. As a result, the collection of the "Lives of the Saints" entitled *Flos Sanctorum* became the chief object of his investigations.

It is important for us to distinguish a double fruit that Ignatius derived from his sojourn at Loyola. The first benefit is that of his real and definitive conversion which snatched him from the world and firmly attached him to the service of the Lord. This was a fundamental choice or "election," which called for a new style of life. From it flowed the second benefit, another choice. But in this case the election remained open-ended; it did not have the definitive character of the preceding fundamental choice. Ignatius was well aware of this. He hesitated between the Carthusian life, that is, a life of the cloister and obedience, and a life of pilgrimage where one is freer to practice penance and is subject to the rigors of the highways and of poverty.[27] Ignatius decided in favor of this second style of life, a fact which Leturia elucidates particularly from the example of the saints in the *Flos Sanctorum*. In the case of Francis and Dominic, it was the perspective of great penances and the idea of pilgrimage that attracted Ignatius, much more than the apostolic ideal.[28] However, Nadal affirms that it is the example of St. Onuphrius that offers the greatest resemblance to the solitary life that Ignatius would lead in Manresa.[29]

We desire to adopt the same method of research as Leturia, but to center our attention on the first spiritual stage of Ignatius' conversion, that is, on what we call his "basic election": his profound and definitive conversion which led him to an effective determination to consecrate himself to God. Should we say that it was due solely to an exceptional grace that moved him

---

24   Ibid., I, 97–111, esp. 99–100.
25   Ibid, 99.
26   Ibid., 100.
27   Ibid., 97.
28   Ibid., p. 101.
29   Ibid., pp. 102–111, *FN.* II, 187.

at that moment without human intermediaries, ordinary or extraordinary? According to Ignatius' own affirmation, however, it was not during, but after, his meditative readings that he felt the keen need to amend his life (a first stage), and after this he conceived the idea of imitating the saints (a second stage). Having examined his first conversion, we link it much more to the reading of Ludolph's Life of Christ than to the *Flos Sanctorum,* the role of which we shall also clarify.

a. His Reading of Ludolph's Life of Christ

The studies made on the sources of the *Exercises* have brought to light numerous points of reference to Ludolph's Life of Christ. Many related expressions were found in the *Exercises,* concrete details retained from old, pious traditions, and in some cases similar ways of interpreting the Gospel scenes. These comparisons concern especially these "mysteries," that is, the events in the life of Christ listed in the last three Weeks of the *Exercises.* Though these similarities are not very profound, they nevertheless witness to the fact that Ignatius had a prolonged contact with Ludolph's text. They also give us an idea of the numerous precise details he retained.[30]

By examining the structure, the organization, and the perspective of the ensemble of considerations which Ludolph's Life of Christ presents, and upon which Ignatius meditated for months, we can form some idea of the nature of this contact. We can also deduce—and this is of vital importance for our study—the directly biblical character of the spiritual world into which Ignatius was introduced, with attention and delight. This contact was the intermediary through which Ignatius opened himself to God' plan to save and sanctify all humankind, Jews and gentiles, through Christ—St. Paul's "mystery of God" or "mystery of Christ."

This, therefore, is what makes the meditations of Loyola so important. They laid the basis for a spiritual life that was solidly structured around three principal realities: the Trinity, Christ, and our condition as creatures. Thus they prepared the way for the experiences of Manresa in which, as always, grace built upon the gifts of nature.

For our purpose of showing that the preceding affirmations are well founded, it will suffice, we think, to examine successively the contents of the

---

30 See *SpEx*MHSJ, where the comparative study of the *Vita Christi* and of the *Exercises* goes from page 57 to page 94; also H. Watrigant, "La gènèse des Exercices de saint Ignace," *Et,* 71 (1897), especially pp. 521–522; E. Raitz von Frentz, "Ludolphe le Chartreux et les Exercices de saint Ignace de Loyola," *RAM,* 25 (1949), 375–388; R.M. de Hornedo, "Algunos rasgos comunes entre la contemplación ignaciana y la del Cartujano," *Mnr,* 36 (1964), 337–342.

Introduction and of the first two chapters of Ludolph's book. Then we shall end by presenting a brief overview of its remaining chapters.

The Introduction

The Introduction *(Prooemium)* of Ludolph's book contains a rich doctrine based on Scripture and the Fathers of the Church. To the theological truths, which are set forth briefly, is added a simple pressing exhortation on the manner of assimilating them in order to live them out in practice. This is a concrete exhortation of which the *Exercises* will retain several precise details. In a word, the Introduction proposes a kind of foundation for a comprehensive concept of the Christian life. It seems evident that Ignatius meditated on it at length, since so many elements proper to Ludolph became familiar to the author of the *Exercises* as a result of his reading. That is why we feel we should spend some time on this first text, before examining what characterizes the subsequent meditations on the life of Christ.[31]

The first affirmation of the Introduction—and hence of Ludolph's whole book—sets forth Christ as "the foundation of salvation" *(salutis fundamentum Christus)*. This truth is soberly developed. First of all, man is placed in a situation before God, a fact which poses the problem of his radical powerlessness to effect his own salvation: "Since Augustine states that God is a being supremely sufficient, and man is supremely deficient, . . ." It is in bringing this perspective of "deficient" human existence that Christ is presented as bringing the only solution to the problem, "the remedy for our needs."

> That is why whoever wishes to overcome his faults and to renew himself in spirit, should be careful not to detach himself from the foundation mentioned above, because in it he will find every remedy to his needs *(in eo omnimoda remedia suis necessitatibus inveniet).*[32]

Such is the first point of the Introduction—so brief, so rich in theological content, and so direct in its appeal to a man in the clutches of sin. This first

---

31 Leturia, who did not use his method in the study of the *Vita Christi,* nevertheless had an intuition concerning the influence of the *content* of the book on the life of Ignatius. Indeed he states this without developing his thought: "The prologue of the Carthusian Life of Christ which had brought about his conversion. . . ." *(Estudios,* II, 401).

32 *Prooemium* (Preface), no. 1. We quote from the following Latin edition of the *Vita Christi, ex Evangelio et approbatis ab Ecclesia catholica doctoribus sedule collecta.* Editio novissima, curante L. M. Rigolot, saec., Parisiis, apud Victorem Palme, Bibliopolam; Romae, Libraria S. Cong. de Propaganda Fide, 1870.

point carries the title "Christ the Foundation of Salvation" *(Salutis fundamentum Christus),* and it begins its treatment by a quotation from St. Paul which explicitly links it here with the problem of salvation: "For no other foundation can any one lay than that which has been laid, which is Jesus Christ."[33]

The second point specifies the two stages which are necessary for the person who desires to respond to the call: "The sinner is invited to *forgiveness* and to the *imitation* of Christ." Here we have two complementary stages, that of Purification and that of commitment to the following of Christ, as the only way of salvation. The development which follows distinguishes these two periods. The first is briefly set forth in a classical manner: "through profound contrition" and "the zealous proposal always to refrain from evil and to do good." This movement of conversion is, however, placed under direct dependence upon Christ, the "compassionate and solicitous physician" who alone can relieve and cure.[34] The second period, the imitation of Christ, is expressed in language perhaps more original which emphasizes the personal, intelligent adhesion of the faithful person to his Lord. This characteristic of a faith desirous of being enlightened and deepened will inspire the subsequent work of meditation on the Gospel which Ludolph proposes to his reader. He writes:

> Secondly, let the sinner, who has now become "faithful" in Christ, apply himself with great diligence to cling to the physician who cured him *(studeat diligentissime medico suo adherere)* and to acquire familiarity with him, by meditating on his very holy life with all the devotion he can. Let him be careful, however, not to go through that life by a merely cursory reading; but let him take the parts one after another through the day.

Ludolph then explains how this reading ought to become a prayer which includes all the other actions of the day. He adds certain remarks in which we see his outline of the method which he will later make more precise, and which Ignatius will to a large extent adopt, no doubt after he had himself experienced it fruitfully:

> Let him more often return to the principal mysteries *(memorialia)* of Christ, namely, the Incarnation, the Nativity, the Circumcision, the Epiphany, . . . which are all topics for special recall, and exercise, and spiritual remembrance, and consolation. Let him read the life of Christ in such a manner that he

33 See 1 Cor. 3:11.
34 This entire first development centers on Matt. 11:28: "Come to me, all you . . . and I will give you rest."

endeavors to imitate him as far as he can. For it profits him little to read unless he also imitates.

In support of this doctrine Ludolph cites the testimonies of St. Bernard and of St. John Chrysostom on the prayerful or "divine reading" *(lectio divina).*[35]

The Introduction then sets forth, in a manner customary of old, seven motives for practicing such meditation, and the numerous fruits which can be drawn from it. Then he proposes a compendium of the Savior's life insisting (as Ignatius will do in the *Exercises*) on the necessity of being fully present to the scenes being contemplated: "Make yourself present at his nativity. . . . Journey with the Magi, adore with them. . . . Help the child's parents to carry him. . . . With the apostles, accompany this good shepherd. . . , and the like." He extends this exercise of presence to Christ to every moment in the life of the Christian—something which we find again in what the *Exercises* propose for putting "due order in the use of food." But Ludolph insists above all on the necessity, so dear to Ignatius, to stop and "relish interiorly" *(gustar . . . internamente)* Christ's mysteries, words, and actions:

> As for you, if you want to draw fruit from these sayings and deeds of Christ, put aside all other preoccupations; and then, with all the affection of your heart, slowly, diligently, and with relish, make yourself present to what the Lord Jesus has said and done, and to what is being narrated, just as if you were actually there, and heard him with your own ears, and saw him with your own eyes; for all these matters are exceedingly sweet to one who ponders them with desire, and far more so to one who savors them. Although many of these facts are recounted as having taken place in the past, you nevertheless should meditate upon them as if they were taking place now, in the present; for from this you will surely experience great delight.[36]

In the last points of his Introduction the author recalls the example of the saints, in particular that of St. Bernard, who nourished himself on the Scriptures and who gained much fruit from them. He expounds in greater detail his method "by which the life of Christ should be meditated"; and he introduces us to the text of the Gospels, according to the learning of his time. Finally, this first meditation ends with a colloquy in which the penitent asks, as a grace, for the "imitation of Christ." To this end he asks that all his "thoughts, words, and actions" may be directed to God so as to learn how to do "his will in everything" and thereby merit his salvation. All these ideas

---

35 *Prooemium,* no. 2.
36 Ibid., no. 11, also no. 13. Compare with *SpEx,* [2, 69, 214].

will nourish Ignatius' prayer. Later, too, they will influence the ideas on it which he expressed in the *Exercises.*

The main ideas of the Introduction are again taken up and expanded throughout Ludolph's long Life of Christ. From this fact we may suppose that during his five or six months of convalescence and meditation Ignatius often came back to these fundamental truths, as well as to the simple counsels that accompanied them; and also that, from all the evidence we have, he put them into practice in order to learn how to contemplate and relish the things of God. Once more, let us not forget that at the end of these months Ignatius resolutely and effectively opted for a new service that would commit his whole life to the following of Christ. That obliged him to tear himself away from a service of the world which had held enough fascination to make him, a short while before, undergo the terrible operations of resetting the broken bones of his right leg—in the "butchery," as he called it.

Besides, we know that what characterized this first spiritual stage, according to his *Autobiography,* was the discovery of the conflict of the spirits which revealed to Ignatius the sense of his condition as a sinner, of his intimate involvement with evil, and of his need of God. He must have read and meditated with greater unction certain words of Ludolph's Introduction, which proposes some fundamental truths as the only way to freedom. They recall the first colloquy of the *Exercises.* Ludolph's words are:

> For your sake the Lord came down to earth from his heavenly throne. For his sake you should flee from earthly things and desire heaven. If the world is pleasing, Christ is even sweeter. If the world is bitter, Christ endured everything for you. Arise, go forward, do not delay like a laggard on the road, lest you lose your place in your fatherland.[37]

The First Chapter

Our examination of the Introduction has already shown by examples some interesting points of comparison between Ludolph's purpose in writing his book along with the method he suggests to achieve it and the dominant ideas in Ignatius' *Exercises.* This parallel continues through the entire Life of Christ, since the order of development of the 181 chapters which the long book contains again takes up the structure suggested by the Introduction and expands it. We have seen, in fact, that at the starting point Christ is presented as the unique foundation of salvation; and this constitutes a call for man to turn toward the Lord, the source of life. This movement to conversion initiates the genuine spiritual journey which is progress in the imitation of Christ.

---

37 *Prooemium,* no. 17. Compare with *SpEx,* [53].

From it arises the determination to meditate the Scripture daily and slowly in order to understand and to achieve the progress proper to the Christian life.

In this perspective of an amplification, the first chapter takes up the initial theme of the Lord, the point of reconciliation between God and man. What is important here, however—more than the idea proposed—is the context of his development, where we find several elements which were completely assimilated into Ignatius' spirituality.

Ludolph sets forth his doctrine in his meditation on the prologue of St. John's Gospel.[38] The vision of Christ he presents to us is, appropriately, the very one which the Evangelist wishes to convey to us; and it will be that of St. Ignatius all through his life: the Majesty of the Lord. Ludolph states his reason: "That the divinity of the Word may be manifested." Christ is at the center of everything, that is, between God and creation; and this is what makes him the "foundation of salvation." Ludolph insists on showing him to us that way. He is the Word rather than the Son, because it is as Word that he reveals his relationship both with the Father, whom he expresses, and with creation, of which he is the author, and which he assumes in his Incarnation.

> . . . Son expresses only relationship *(comparationem)* with the Father, whereas Word expresses relationship, not only with the person speaking it, but also with that which is expressed through the word; and indeed, both in regard to the word it uses and to the doctrine which is produced in someone else by means of the word. That is why the Son of God ought to be described here in his relationship not only with the Father from whom he proceeds, but also with the beings he has created, and with the flesh he has assumed.[39]

For our present purpose it matters little whether this interpretation expresses more or less correctly what the Evangelist meant by his use of "Logos." What we want to keep in mind here is the fact that by means of this commentary Ludolph presents to Ignatius a conception of Christ and his mission centered on the double relationship which, for him, is expressed by the title of Word of God: Word, revealer of the Father and creator of man. And it is this double relationship which Ignatius will long meditate during his reading of this first chapter, a commentary on the Prologue of St. John. This double relationship will become the basis for a rich and unified spiritual vision.

38 *Vita Christi,* ch. I, "On the Divine and Eternal Generation of Christ" *(De divina et aeterna Christi generatione)*," nos. 1–11, which comprises eleven points and a colloquy.
39 Ibid., no. 2.

The first statements in this chapter analyze the relationship of the Son's generation from the Father, a relationship which is happily situated within the totality of the mystery of the Trinity. The divinity of Christ, his attributes of majesty and lordship, cannot be dissociated from the Trinity which they reveal. In commenting on the first verses of the Prologue, Ludolph develops the ideas of "personal distinction" (no. 3), "consubstantiality" (no. 4), "co-eternity" (no. 5), and "undivided operation" (no. 6) in which the relationship to the Holy Spirit is made explicit.

Such were, no doubt, the first lights on the mystery of the Trinity communicated to Ignatius. They came to him through the intermediary of the Person of Christ, better recognized as the revelation of God; and so they are situated within the procedure of revelation through which no one can know the Father unless the Son reveal him.[40] Christ will always be the way for us to reach up to the entire Divine Being, and he himself will never be considered independently of this relation to the Trinity from which his own majesty proceeds.

After this we shall not be surprised to see Ignatius manifest right from the beginning so much attraction to this mystery, and to see him develop such great devotion to the Trinity during the time when he was dedicating his life with love to the following of Christ. At Manresa the mystical graces will also follow along the way of this privileged communication. We know that the first writing he undertook during this year of retreat in the school of Christ was the composition of a treatise on the Most Holy Trinity.[41]

Neither shall we be surprised to observe that during these meditative readings Ignatius was becoming deeply attached to the historical Christ; and further, through the Savior's deeds, words, and places of activity during his sojourn among us, Ignatius was building up his lifelong reverence toward the majesty of this eternal Lord.

But since Christ will ever remain the way by which we reach up to the whole Divine Being, he by that fact reaches down to humankind in a direct and saving manner. Neither Ludolph nor Ignatius will be lost in a pseudo-contemplation which might turn them away from created being, from the concrete situation of every day, from the One who has become incarnate.

In fact, the points of meditation that follow, continuing the commentary on the prologue, immediately reestablish the bridge between God and man-

---

40 We are all called, Ludolph writes, to contemplation of the Creator and His Divine Majesty, "to which no one can attain quickly, unless by advancing through that life of our Redeemer" (*Prooemium*, no. 4).

41 On this point we have the testimony of Nadal, Polanco, and Laínez. This point will come up again below when we treat the events of Manresa.

kind. The heart of the Trinity renews a union with sinful human beings through the Word now become also a man. Ludolph groups his reflections around the verses which proclaim that the Word became "the light of men," and that this light "shone in the darkness." For Ludolph "in the darkness" means "among sinners," the sinful condition of the world which will be meditated upon more at length in the following chapter.

He concludes this meditation, his first chapter, with a prayer, a colloquy addressed to the Trinity, that is, directly to the Father, and through him to the Son and the Spirit. He explicitly sets into relationship with the divine Majesty all created being, through which man wishes to adore, praise, glorify, and ask for pardon. "And among all these other beings you created me, a sinner; I adore you, I praise you, and I glorify you."⁴² If we are familiar with the ideas of Ignatius and his conception of the Christian life, we can see from what is above how faithful he remained to the way that was opened to him during his days at Loyola. He retained especially those principal traits which the graces of Manresa accentuated in an extraordinary manner, and then developed them into a perspective much more clearly apostolic.

The Second Chapter

Instead of continuing the meditation on the life of Christ, the second chapter takes up again the sinful condition of humankind, a subject that was briefly set forth in the Introduction. The title of this chapter, however, reveals its purpose as well as its close liaison with the vision of the whole suggested by the Introduction and the first chapter: "On the Finding of a Remedy toward the Salvation of the Human Race, and on the Birth of the Blessed Virgin Mary." Here the image of the condition of sinful humankind is treated at greater length. The chapter considers evil from its historical and theological origins: "the fall of Lucifer and of our first parent." The sin of Lucifer was "to raise himself up against God the Creator." The case of Adam is considered along the same lines: "At the beginning of our human condition, Adam [was formed from clay] on the plain of Damascus, near Hebron, . . ."⁴³ Against the reality of sin our Lord opposes that of mercy:

42 Ludolph devotes ch. 85 of Part II of his work to the topic of divine praise: It is our purpose in life, it must be rendered to God, our Creator and Redeemer (no. 1); it must rise unceasingly from our created heart, starting from all creatures (no. 2), in union with all creatures (no. 3) and with gratitude for all the good we have received (no. 4). Compare this with the First Principle and Foundation and the Contemplation to Attain the Love of God (*SpEx*, [23, 230–237]).

43 Compare this with *SpEx*, [46–54], on the triple sin as the point of departure for the Exercises.

"the Father of mercies and of all consolation." Thus Ignatius, going beyond his own little personal history in which the battle of the spirits had already enlightened him on the opposition between the world and God within himself, through this contact with Ludolph opens himself up to this universal vision of evil. He now sees it as an insubordination of the creature against his Creator.[44] Christ necessarily becomes the only bridge to union with God ("no other foundation can anyone lay"), and to that peace so desired the troubled soul of the penitent of Loyola. It was such peace that Ignatius will want to teach to others throughout his life "for the good of souls and the glory of God."

The Remaining Chapters

Ignatius makes clear that he "found delight" in the subsequent chapters of Ludolph's book.[45] What value do the meditations which the Carthusian proposed there have for Ignatius' spirituality? What is important here is the nature of the prayer they foster, for the *Exercises* will state that "it is not much knowledge that fills and satisfies the soul, but the intimate understanding and relish of the truth ."[46] Objectively, Ludolph develops the contents of his lengthy book at a slow pace, from the birth of Mary, an event or "mystery" directly connected with the history of salvation, to the consummation of the mission of the Redeemer and the outpouring of the Spirit on Pentecost. As we pointed out in regard to the detailed studies on the subject (in B, 1 above), Ignatius retained many elements from this meditation on the Life of Christ which he later used in the composition of the *Exercises.* Perhaps he especially retained what constitutes the very structural arrangement of the Exercises, their content which consists of this unfolding divine plan of salvation of which he began to experience the efficacious action. Ludolph, in fact, presents him with considerations full of scriptural texts which are well integrated along the general line of the theological development mentioned above. This gave Ignatius the opportunity of a prolonged contact with God's revealed message, and it fostered a type of prayer that would unite him to his Lord and open him to His grace.

In summary we can say that the spiritual views of Ludolph are profoundly Christological and simultaneously Trinitarian, because of the fact

---

44 Ignatius borrowed from Ludolph the terms which express the opposition between Christ and Satan, Jerusalem and Babylon, and their respective tactics. For a comparative study of this question, see *SpEx*MHSJ, pp. 80–85.

45 *Autobiog,* nos. 10, 11.

46 *SpEx,* [2].

that Christ is not abstracted from the center of his divine life nor treated as the God-Man in isolation. These views likewise present a very explicit sense of created being, of evil, and of salvation in their relation to Christ thus understood. As a modern writer has stated of Ludolph's Life of Christ:

> This book, written in the fourteenth century, is an act of adoration. In the considerations and prayers at the end of the chapters there is an accent on piety and love which is moving. It was composed to stir souls to the imitation of the life of the Savior. Already in the prayer in the Introduction this intention is expressed thus: "Lord Jesus, grant me—a weak and miserable sinner—the grace always to keep before the eyes of my heart your life and your virtues and to imitate them as well as I can." Ludolph is not content with this general statement; he indicates the means to make alive the memory of the person of Jesus: "Read the account of the events as if they were actually happening now. Set before your eyes past deeds as if they were present, and thus you will feel great delight and sweetness. That is why I have often noted the places in which such and such deeds were accomplished."[47]

We do not wish to exaggerate the perfection of this spirituality which Ignatius experienced through his readings during the long months at Loyola. For we know that if the convalescent soldier arose as a penitent profoundly determined to follow the Lord, he did so as a man who lacked the experience, the light, and the discernment which the Lord was to teach him later at Manresa. But already now the way he undertakes has a typical character. It is especially close to God's revealed mysteries and the harmony existing among them. That is why we attach so much importance to this initial stage.

b. The Book of the Lives of the Saints, Flos Sanctorum

What shall we say about the influence of the "Book of the Lives of the Saints in Spanish" on the meditations at Loyola? We may perhaps seem to have given it little space. Nevertheless Ignatius' *Autobiography* or "Pilgrim's Story" refers to it more often than it does to Ludolph's Life of Christ. First of all, let us remark that, as a result of the studies we have mentioned (in B, 1 above) about the "external sources" of the *Exercises,* the passages parallel to those in the *Vita Christi* are much more numerous than those which could have been inspired by the *Flos Sanctorum;* there is no comparison. Besides, from Leturia we have seen that the influence which the *Flos Sanctorum* had was of a different nature. The meditations on the life of Christ enlightened

---

47 This is an extract from a thesis (incidentally unfavorable to St. Ignatius) presented to the Faculty of Protestant theology of Paris in 1898 by Maurice Malzac, *Essai de psychologie religieuse,* p. 27.

"the spiritual understanding" of Ignatius, taught him to know Christ in His place within the amplitude of God's plan of salvation, to discover through prayer the demands of Christ's call, and to judge the value of his own life; but the living, heroic, alluring models of the saints—Onuphrius, Francis, and Dominic—more effectively moved his will, by showing him an ideal which he could realize, and by stirring his zeal for the commitment proposed. "The great need he had to do penance" for his past life,[48] which the Pilgrim felt when he contemplated the life of Christ, found concrete stimulation in the living example of the saints whose lives he read. In fact, the influence of the *Flos Sanctorum,* as we retrace it, concerns concrete attitudes—life traits which seem to incarnate the ideal being awakened in the soul of the penitent. Only with time and experience would this ideal assume a more personal form. That is why the Pilgrim, as he describes the movement of his conversion which snatches him from the world to consecrate him to the service of his Lord, insists on the deeds, concrete actions, which manifest this transformation. On the contrary, our purpose, that of ascertaining the qualitative aspect of this spiritual way into which he was introduced, obliges us to insist on the "lessons" that Ignatius received through his meditative readings from which he copied pages with delight, and through the Scriptures with which he was in indirect contact.

We might also remark that there is a very particular harmony between the two books upon which the knight meditated at Loyola. We feel that this is a sign of the benevolence of divine providence. The spiritual atmosphere in which these lives of the saints are narrated by Jacobus de Voragine comes very close to the more explicitly theological conception of the Christian life which Ludolph presents in his book. Whereas Fray Montesino introduces his Spanish translation of the *Vita Christi* with a note addressed to Ferdinand and Isabella in which he invites "the kings of the world to work for the Kingdom of God," Fray Gauberto Vagad, in his preface to the *Flos Sanctorum* (his Spanish translation of Jacobus' *Legenda aurea,* "Golden Things to Be Read"), reproduces an image of the Lord which he himself presents with these words: "At the beginning of this work we have put the image of Christ as the illustrious and marvelous summit of all the virtues. The reader ought to take the crucifix in hand as the royal, powerful, and always victorious standard of the knights of God who are the saints."[49] Thus, far from distract-

---

48 *Autobiog,* no. 9.
49 See Leturia, *Estudios,* II, 57–72, "El Reino de Cristo y los prólogos del Flos Sanctorum"; Hugo Rahner, *The Spirituality of St. Ignatius Loyola,* trans F.J. Smith (Westminster, Md., 1953), pp.39–40; also p, 24.

ing Ignatius from the unique ideal which the Life of Christ presented to him, the example of the saints was really a concrete exemplification of the response of this knight who had chosen "freely, deliberately," and irrevocably to enter the "distinguished service" of his Lord. Further on we shall see how, after Ignatius left Loyola, this influence predominated and became the occasion for errors due to a lack of discernment on his part. For the moment, however, let us consider the content of the *Flos Sanctorum* which so much benefited our convert of Loyola. What was the state of Ignatius' soul at the end of his stay at Loyola? To make a precise statement is a delicate matter. Either we can reduce that state to an ambitious desire which he took away with him to equal and surpass the saints—and then we rightly appraise it as superficial; or we can speak of it as a complete conversion, a new orientation in radical opposition to his previous life—and then we do not explain the lack of discernment that followed[50] and the necessity for the great purifications at Manresa where everything seemed to start from scratch. We think that we should hold on to both terms of this paradox. Loyola is the stage of radical conversion in which the Pilgrim was already given, as he says, "a generous heart on fire with the love of God,"[51] and "an ardent zeal to serve Our Lord,"[52] so that his soul is "animated with a great desire to serve him according to all the lights it could have."[53] However, the way he chooses, attracted by the example of the lives of the saints, manifests a search carried on by human effort and will power, a search still too exterior to be regarded as a profound and interior desire of attachment to the Lord.[54] This desire came to him from his discovery of the genuine Christ of revelation who, through his nature as the Word, brings to us an awareness of the Divine Majesty, and also

---

50 We recall, for example, the episode of the Moor whom he wished to strike with his dagger for what he had said about Our Lady (*Autobiog,* no. 15); of the rather spectacular watch at arms of Montserrat, and of his giving his arms and clothing to the poor, and of the sackcloth habit he chose (nos. 16, 17, 18); of the decision to allow his hair and his nails to grow (no. 19)—all so many exterior gestures that reproduce the exploits of the saints without corresponding to the inner movement of the Spirit that was in them.

51 *Autobiog,* no. 9.

52 Ibid., no. 11.

53 Ibid., no. 13.

54 See Iparraguirre, *Adnotationes initiales de spiritualitate sacerdotali et Exercitiis Sancti Ignatii.* Ad usum privatum auditorum, Rome: Gregorian University, 1964, p. 17. See also *Autobiog,* no. 14, "He did not dwell on any interior thing, nor did he know what humility was or charity or patience or discretion to regulate and mature these virtues. Without considering any more particular circumstance, his very intention was to do these great external works because the saints had done so for the glory of God."

of our sinful condition which we carry with us within a powerful movement toward salvation and sanctification. Ignatius tells us clearly that the feeling of his debt to God *preceded* his desire to imitate the saints. This feeling is deeply interior and bears lasting fruits of penance, while the desire to imitate the saints, which does not spring so much from the depths of his soul, launches him too quickly into exterior manifestations. These, while stirring his ardor, prevent him from directly seeking the unique way in which he should commit himself, and which the Lord reserved for him. "Having derived much light from these readings, he began to reflect more seriously on his past life and the great need he had of doing penance for it. It was *then* that the desire to imitate the saints came to him. He was not paying attention to their particular situation, but he promised himself to do, with the grace of God, what they had done" (italics supplied).[55]

Thus, the message proposed to the mind of Ignatius at Loyola was, in large measure, that of God's revelation, expressed through the multiplicity of the Gospel scenes, and made explicit in its broad lines by the theology of Ludolph the Carthusian. And the experience which this revealed content stirred up in him was already profound and persuasive, even though it was limited to the principal articulations of the religious experience of conversion. Ignatius has truly encountered Christ. The first spiritual effect of this contact was freedom *from one kind of evil* in his life, attachment "to the vanities of the world."[56] Ignatius responded to the great desire of serving God which resulted from this effect by striving too blindly for a material imitation of the saints. He still had another step to take, the hardest one, that which distinguishes Christianity from all other forms of asceticism: to surrender oneself to the workings of grace, something which demands the complete abandonment of self to God, and which is authentic evangelical spiritual poverty. Ignatius, all on fire, still wants to effect his salvation by himself, "to conquer" as he did at Pamplona. But God alone can effect the salvation of man: "No other foundation can anyone lay than that which has been laid, which is Jesus Christ" (1 Cor. 3:11). Thus the divine pedagogy, ever faithful to itself, will through future events teach the convert of Loyola to surrender himself completely to the saving action of God.

2. The Events at Manresa

With Manresa[57] we again focus our attention on the two levels—that of

---

55 *Autobiog,* no. 9.
56 Ibid., no. 1.
57 See *Autobiog,* no. 18. Under this heading we consider the stage of Ignatius' life from February, 1522, until February, 1523, that is, from his departure from

the doctrinal message of which the items of elementary knowledge received at Loyola will grow to an unexpected summit, and that of the parallel religious experience which will deepen his determined commitment by ordering it in accordance with the ways and the will of God.

There is, however, an intermediary period between his conversion at Loyola and his very personalized commitment at Manresa. That is the stage of the purifications, in which the intense subjective experience will be difficult to order, and in which the objective message is reduced to a minimum. It is this period at Manresa which precedes that of the great lights he received on the mysteries of the faith. At this time he was drawing his spiritual nourishment by recalling the examples of the lives of the saints which he delighted in reliving, and by reading the *Imitation of Christ*. No doubt because of its insistence on the purification of the interior life, this latter work greatly sustained the courage of the penitent in the struggles he faced. According to the Pilgrim himself, at this time he also found comfort in reading the story of the Passion and in conversing with spiritual persons. Both must have awakened in him motives for perseverance and sustained his fidelity.[58] Now let us look at the details of these two stages which characterize his stay at Manresa—the stage of the purifications and that of the illuminations.

a. The Purifications

On the day following the famous vigil of arms during the night of the 24th to the 25th of March, 1522, at Montserrat, Ignatius "took a side road leading to a town called Manresa where he wanted to stay for a few days."[59] The fact is that he remained there more than ten months, caught up by God, who taught him the purification of his too ambitious spiritual desires and showed him the way of true Christian commitment—that of evangelical detachment. The *Autobiography* remains the most enlightening testimony concerning this stage at Manresa, and we must examine it attentively.

In his account Ignatius describes himself, at the beginning of this period, as finding great satisfaction in giving himself over to this new life in which

Loyola to the end of his stay at Manresa. Thus it included his stops at Aránzazu, Navarrete, and especially Montserrat. Ignatius arrived at Manresa little less than a month after he had left Loyola.

58 *Autobiog.*, nos. 20-21.
59 For this we have the testimony of Juan Pascual, who told how his mother, while on pilgrimage to Montserrat, brought Ignatius to Manresa. Ignatius asked her if there were a hospital in the town. He wanted to serve there for a few days and note some things in his notebook, since he was unable to go to Barcelona immediately because of the imminent departure of the new Pope Adrian VI. See J. Creixell, *San Ignacio en Manresa* (1914), pp. 7, 8, and 19.

were fulfilled his desires for penances and prayers after the example of the saints, especially Onuphrius. He begged, fasted, and completely neglected his appearance, no longer paying any attention to his person.[60] He scourged himself three times a day.[61] And yet he experienced great happiness and peace of soul.[62]

However, two temptations soon assailed him and are the beginning of the period of "great instability" which followed this time of peace.[63] The first temptation, which he perceived to be a temptation only after he had received the great interior illuminations, is that of "the extraordinarily beautiful thing" in "the form of a serpent." It looked at him with many "things that shone like eyes" and gave him "great delight" but it left him "discontented".[64] The second temptation came to him in the form of an insidious suggestion: "How will you be able to endure this for the seventy years you have yet to live"[65] The first of these temptations might be compared to that of vainglory from which Ignatius will later be freed forever. This temptation indicates a return to self-complacency, a satisfaction quickly spent in seeking exterior things instead of interior self-renunciation, a desire to attract attention, and to be considered somebody.[66] As a result he soon experienced an inevitable lassitude. He did not have sufficient motivation and was fearful of the future because he did not rely enough on God. This caused him to act too much on the natural level. "Sometimes he found himself so disagreeable that he found no joy, either in hearing Mass or in any other prayer. At other times

---

60 *Autobiog,* no. 19. See H. Rahner, *The Spirituality of St. Ignatius,* pp. 30–33.

61 The *Autobiography* merely states that he took the discipline every night. Nadal, in his *Dialogi,* says clearly that he scourged himself three times a day, "mas que regularmente" (*Dialogi,* in *FN,* II, 237, cited by J. Calveras, "El origen de los Ejercicios según el P. Nadal," *Mnr,* 26 [1954], 263–288). Polanco says the same thing in his *Chronicon,* I, 19. Finally on the penances of Ignatius at Manresa, consult the eloquent report of "notas de la casa de Amigant," Fol. 45, no. 7, quoted by J. Creixell, *op. cit.* pp. 79–80.

62 *Autobiog,* no. 20.

63 Calveras, following Nadal (*Acta Patris Ignatii,* in *FN,* I, 388–408), considers these two temptations as a sign of transition from the first stage that Ignatius knew at Manresa, a stage "of tranquility," to the second, one "of great variations in his soul." See "El origen de los Ejercicios según el P. Nadal," *Mnr,* 26 (1954), 263–288.

64 *Autobiog,* nos. 19 and 31.

65 Ibid., no. 20. In the "seventy years" there is an allusion to St. Onuphrius, whose life of penance lasted that long.

66 That such was the meaning of this temptation becomes clear enough when we compare this statement of the *Autobiography* with other passages that treat of vainglory, of the temptation to believe oneself "just"; of the difficulty that for

the opposite of this came over him so suddenly that he had an impression that someone had removed the sadness and desolation just as one snatches a cape from another's shoulders. Here he began to be uneasy about these alternations which he had never experienced before."[67]

Thus the divergence between the ideal and the reality became greater in the experience of Ignatius. He preserved "his great determination to go forward in God's service."[68] This functioned in the manner of an ideal demanding everything; but after these "changed feelings" he felt more and more his own powerlessness to respond with constancy and perfection. At the heart of his uneasiness and the temptation that assailed him, there were two ways he might follow: that of anxiety and of scruples which exaggerates the unfavorable judgment one has of oneself, increases the guilt feeling in the face of one's infidelities (the ideal against the reality), and casts one little by little into despair; or the way of recognition of his absolute poverty, *("summe deficiens")*, and self-surrender to the divine Goodness and Omnipotence, the only source of hope.

But at this time Ignatius did not know how to discern. He found himself in a period when he had no precise direction and his will "to go forward" held him a captive of himself and his own activity. Therefore, before letting go, he underwent the terrible anxiety of scruples, the deep depression which the Pilgrim recounts and which would bring him to the depths of despair, even to the temptation of killing himself.[69] Then with God's grace he held out against himself and against his likes and dislikes, and in the midst of his

Ignatius will last for some years, to free himself from this obsession; and of the final victory that must be attributed to God's grace (see *Autobiog,* nos. 18, 19, 32, 36, and the Preface of Gonçalves da Câmara in *FN,* II, 354–363). See also the letter to Teresa Rejadell, ("a true commentary on the period at Manresa," states P. Silos, *AHSJ,* 33 [1964], 13). In it Ignatius describes Satan's tactics with "beginners"; the first tactic corresponds to the temptation to discouragement which he knew ("how can you continue a life of such great penance") and the second, that of believing oneself good, just, is clearly stated, "pride and vainglory" (see *LettersIgn,* pp. 19–20). On the subject of deliverance from this temptation in Ignatius' life, see *FN,* I, 162–163, no. 22; II, 432, no. 8; 473, no. 6. Also read the article of L. Beirnaert, "Discernement et psychisme," *Chr,* no. 4 (1954), 50–61, esp. 57.

67 *Autobiog,* no. 21.
68 Ibid. This was precisely the grace of his first conversion: conviction and desire.
69 See C. A. Lofy, *The Action of the Holy Spirit in the Autobiography of St. Ignatius of Loyola* (Dissertation, Gregorian University, Rome, 1963), vol. II, Appendix III, pp. 33–74: "The Depression of St. Ignatius in Manresa," a study made from a medical point of view, with the collaboration of Dr. F. J. Ayd, Jr. M.D., Chief of Psychiatry at Franklin Square Hospital in Baltimore, U.S.A.

worst temptations he discovered the humble supplication which he remembered so many years later:

> Help me, O Lord, for I find no remedy among men nor in any creature; yet if I thought I could find it, no labor would be too great for me. Show me, O Lord, where I may find it; even though I should have to follow a little dog so he could help me, I would do it.[70]

However, for all of that, the struggle did not end at once. It continued for a long time and with great intensity. At the same time that Ignatius was inspired with a great "disgust for the life he was leading and the desire to give it up came over him,"[71] he experienced an extraordinary fidelity to prayer and his desire for deliverance.[72] Thus in time, having learned no longer to expect salvation and sanctification from himself and his own efforts, but to trust in God, . . . the penitent of Manresa rediscovered that particular attribute of God which Christ came to reveal to us, and which Ludolph spoke about at the very beginning of his work: God's mercy. He writes: "In this way the Lord wished to awaken him as if from a dream." Enlightened regarding "the diversity of spirits" within himself, "he remained free of those scruples and held it for certain that our Lord through his mercy had wished to deliver him."[73] From all the evidence we have, this "deliverance from evil" came from the grace of God and not from the weakened strength of the penitent.

Moreover, it corresponded to a need he keenly felt to be faithful in his response to the Lord. This was the beginning of a new period for Ignatius, that of the great lights in the school of God. In speaking of this period he states: "God treated him at this time just as a schoolmaster treats a child whom he is teaching. Whether this was on account of his coarseness or his dense intellect or because he had no one to teach him, or because of the strong desire God himself had given him to serve Him, he clearly believed and has always believed that God treated him in this way. Indeed, if he were to doubt this, he thought he would offend His Divine Majesty."[74]

Ignatius has now passed through the experience of the fundamental purifications. In a certain sense he will take it up again in the First Week of the *Exercises*. This experience was centered on the sentiment of his present con-

---

70 *Autobiog,* no. 23.
71 Ibid., no 25.
72 Ibid., nos. 22, 23 (weekly confession and communion, seven hours of prayer on his knees, each day, prayer during the night).
73 Ibid., no. 25.
74 Ibid., no. 27.

dition, felt at the time, as a sinner. The *Autobiography* testifies to this by the reference to his repeated confessions of his whole past life, to scruples, and to the temptations to despair which followed.[75] But this deep feeling of deficiency found its necessary counterpart in the mystery of the God who saves, and who formally reveals the Word made flesh for us. Nadal sums up Ignatius' passage from the stage of purifications to that of the graces of which the *Autobiography* also speaks, as follows: "After he exercised himself on the points of the First Week for some time, the Lord made him progress greatly, and he began to meditate on the life of Christ Our Lord, to draw great consolation from it, and to desire to imitate it. At the same time the desire to help his neighbor was born within him."[76]

b. The Illuminations, on the Objective Level:
The Message Communicated

For this last stage, more than anywhere else, we must distinguish between the lights which were communicated to Ignatius and the positive experience which they stirred up within him.

Having insisted on showing that God, for whatsoever reason, undertook his spiritual formation, the Pilgrim adds: "Something of this can be seen from the five following points."[77] He then enumerates the principal graces received, all of which are lights for "his understanding," and which bear on the Trinity, Creation, Christ's presence in the Eucharist, the humanity of our Lord, and our Lady.[78] All of these graces culminated in the outstanding illumination on the banks of the Cardoner, which virtually all modern authors since Hugo Rahner's study of 1955 consider to be "a synthetic view of the mysteries about which Ignatius had already been enlightened."[79] These lights, which the Pilgrim enumerates, were drawn into their extraordinary unity in

---

75 In his *Vita Patris Ignatii*, Polanco states that such was the object of the experience at Manresa: "From this time he entered into a greater and deeper knowledge of himself; and as he began to understand the sins of his past life more deeply, so he wept over them with greater bitterness of soul and contrition" (*PolChron*, I, 21).

76 *FN*, II, Pláticas de Alcalá, p. 190.

77 *Autobiog*, no. 27.

78 Ibid., nos. 28, 29.

79 Ibid., no. 30. See also R. Cantin, "L'illumination du Cardoner," *ScE*, 7 (1955), 38. [In English on Ignatius' mysticism, see the masterful treatment of De Guibert in 1953, now in *DeGuiJes* (1964), pp. 29–32; 36–67; also, Hugo Rahner's two articles on La Storta in *ZAM*, 10 (1935) 21–35 and 124–139, English trans. *The Vision of St. Ignatius in the Chapel of La Storta*, trans. R.O. Brennan (Rome, 1975); also H. Rahner, *The Spirituality of St. Ignatius*, pp. 46–58. Ed.]

the illumination on the banks of the Cardoner. For our purposes here it is vitally important to notice that they themselves are in continuity with the principal elements of the spiritual world view proposed by Ignatius' meditations at Loyola. We think that this is a continuity in conformity with the manner in which grace ordinarily acts. Ignatius himself has given a rather clear testimony which shows that his devotion to the Trinity was not dependent upon his metaphorical description of the vision which he had later in Manresa. For that devotion had preceded this later vision, and Ludolph had already initiated it at Loyola, as we have seen above (in B, 1 above). Ignatius states that "he had great devotion to the Most Holy Trinity," but that he sometimes wondered needlessly about the rather unimportant question of how his prayer was both one and multiple, which he could not then explain. Then he goes on to say that "One day . . . his understanding began to be elevated," and he had this vision of the Trinity in the form of three [musical] keys which made him understand and relish such harmony in this mystery that with "so many tears and so much sobbing he could not control himself." Neither could he, as a result, "stop talking about the Most Holy Trinity, using many different comparisons and with great joy and consolation."[80] It was at this time that he undertook the composition of a treatise "On the Most Holy Trinity."[81]

Here someone might object by bringing forth Ignatius' other remark which concerns the first period of his stay at Manresa, and which might seem to make us doubt the continuity of the message from the days at Loyola: "Until then he had lived in more or less the same interior state of soul, with great and steady joy, but with no knowledge of interior and spiritual matters."[82] But only if we take this statement too literally and out of context would we find contradictions in Ignatius' account. Regarding the struggle with the spirits which he experienced at the time of his readings at Loyola, we read: "He realized from experience that some thoughts left him sad and others happy"; and later when he put the *Exercises* into writing, "he derived the election from that variety of spirits and thoughts which he had experienced at Loyola when he was still suffering from his leg."[83] Also, he says: "From this reading he gained no little insight, and he began to think seri-

---

80 Ibid., no. 28.
81 He was "so enlightened that at that time he began to write a treatise on the Trinity," Polanco states (*PolChron*, I, 22). Laínez says the same thing (*FN*, I, 82), as well as Nadal (ibid., 306–307).
82 *Autob*iog, no. 20.
83 See *Autobiog*, no. 8; also no. 99: "He told me in particular," wrote Câmara, "that the methods for making an election had been drawn from this diversity of

ously on his past life.''[84] If we press too far this ignorance which Ignatius seems to claim, we do not then explain the serious change which his long reading of the Life of Christ, and which he did "with relish," brought about. When he speaks of his ignorance of spiritual things, Ignatius situated himself precisely at that stage where he really lacked practical discernment in his imitation of the saints.

This reinforces our suggested explanation which distinguishes between the influence of the *Vita Christi* and the *Flos Sanctorum*. And precisely, as we shall presently see, the mystical graces of Manresa—so rich in lights for "his understanding"—will deepen beyond every hope the Trinitarian and Christocentric vision of Loyola; and at the same time they will essentially modify the style of life he embraced in imitation of the saints. Let us not go to an extreme in denouncing the "bad" influence of the *Flos Sanctorum*. On the contrary, it was to his reading of this work that he owed his decision, encouraged by the example of the saints who had chosen that path before him. However, because he still lacked the deep and practical knowledge whereby man is made subject to God rather than to his own desires, no matter how edifying they might be, Ignatius made mistakes in the very use of the good that had been proposed to him. He will acknowledge that he erred, and he will henceforth try to spare others from such deviations. But he will still continue to recommend the reading of the lives of the saints (*SpEx*, [100]).

A final reason for paying special attention to the content of the illuminations of Manresa is this very special characteristic which they have, and which we have already pointed out: They are addressed directly to the spiritual intellect in order to enlighten it, and thus they reduce all support for the imagination to a minimum.[85] If there is question of the Trinity, Ignatius says that "his understanding began to be elevated," and that it was as if he saw the Holy Trinity "in the form of three [musical] keys,"[86] When "the manner in

spirits and thoughts that he had known at Loyola, when he was still suffering from his leg wound." See also the note of A. Thiry on p. 51 of *Le Récit du Pèlerin*.

84 Ibid., no. 9.

85 On this topic see the interesting judgment of De Guibert, in *DeGuiJes*, p. 31, particularly about "the very great poverty of the imaginative element in these visions and the wealth of the content which St. Ignatius still attributed to them thirty years later. . . . The graces which Ignatius received were in reality eminent intellectual lights, directly infused by God into his faculty of understanding; . . . and the images which he recorded were simply the reaction from these lights in his soul—his soul which was by nature imaginative but nevertheless very poor in symbolic images adaptable to this order of understanding."

86 *Autobiog*, no. 28.

which God had created the world was revealed to his understanding" he seemed to see only "something white, from which some rays were coming, and God made light from this." Another day at Mass "he saw with interior eyes something like white rays coming from above" at the elevation, and what "he saw clearly with his understanding was how Jesus Christ our Lord was there in that most holy sacrament." The frequent apparition that he had of Christ in his humanity is itself devoid of any precise figure: "He saw with interior eyes the humanity of Christ," and "the form that appeared to him was like a white body, neither very large nor very small, but he did not see the members distinctly. . . . He also saw our Lady in a similar form, without distinguishing parts."[87] Finally the illumination on the banks of the Cardoner is located exclusively on the plane of the intellect: "The eyes of his understanding began to be opened," the *Autobiography* states. "Though he did not see any vision, he understood and knew many things, both spiritual things and matters of faith and of learning, and this was with so great an enlightenment that everything seemed new to him. . . . He experienced a great clarity in his understanding."[88] What characterizes the fact of these particular graces is now clear, and it could hardly be more explicit: tremendous insights for the understanding of the Pilgrim who, by receiving them "with a very profound modesty and humility,"[89] will be transformed interiorly into a "new man."

We should now turn our attention to a noteworthy feature of these exceptional lights. They are a prolongation, on the objective level, of the spiritual outlook imparted to Ignatius at Loyola. We know that from this first experience he had drawn an attachment to Christ as the center of revelation and the foundation of salvation. Through him Ignatius had been endowed with a reverential sense of the Divine Majesty and had drawn from it "much devotion to the Most Holy Trinity."[90] From this encounter with Christ he also realized his own condition as a sinner, a fact which had enlightened him on

---

87 Ibid., no. 29.

88 Ibid., no. 30.

89 ". . . from this he conceived a profound modesty and humility," according to Nadal's narrative (*FN,* II, 239–240), quoted by Cantin, "L' illumination," *ScE,* 7 (1955), 43. We also have the indirect testimony of Ignatius himself in the letter already quoted, in which he says to Teresa Rejadell that God sometimes communicates Himself to the soul, "speaking within it interiorly and without any din of words, lifting it up wholly to His divine love." "This thought of His," he adds, "which we take, is of necessity in conformity with the commandments, the precepts of the Church, and obedience to our superiors. It will be full of humility because the same divine Spirit is present in all" (*LettersIgn,* p. 22).

90 *Autobiog,* no. 28. See also the *Notes* of A. Thiry (in his French edition), p. 71.

"the great obligation he had of doing penance for his past life,"[91] and which had led to his general confession at Montserrat.[92] All this clearly preceded the experiences of Manresa and shows that there is already an important evolution. These first efficacious elements of an ordered Christian life had been suggested to him especially by the spiritual Christocentric outlook which Ludolph so forcefully expressed in his meditations. Ignatius received this vision with a more or less open and searching mind and laid the foundation for the spiritual life that led to his conversion and his firm determination to follow the Lord. If we stop to consider the object of the abundant lights of Manresa—without denying the absolutely exceptional character of these graces and the renewed understanding of the mysteries of the faith they evoke—we must admit that we find in them a deepening which continues along the line of the message encountered at Loyola. It makes little difference in which order the *Autobiography* lists the graces received in Manresa—whether in chronological order or in order of excellence. Two facts remain: Those graces center on the fundamental truths of the Christian life—God, Christ, and the created world in their ordinary and necessary relationship; secondly, these lights find their unity in the illumination on the banks of the Cardoner which embraces all the mysteries of the faith and harmonizes them.[93]

91 *Autobiog,* no. 9.
92 Ibid., no. 17.
93 Various authors have tried to clarify the content of this illumination of the Cardoner. According to Laínez, Ignatius "was especially helped, spiritually inspired, and enlightened in his soul by the Divine Majesty, in such a way that he began to see all things with other eyes" (*FN,* I, 80); "he received so much light from the Lord that in regard to almost all the mysteries of the faith he was enlightened and consoled by the Lord" (Ibid., 82). Polanco states that he "was all of a sudden the object of a special visit of the Divine Mercy in which he received marvelous illumination concerning divine things" (*FN,* I, 160), that he received "light on the mystery of the Most Holy Trinity and on the creation of the world, as well as on the other mysteries of the faith" (*FN,* II, 529), "on all things both human and divine" (*PolChron,* I, 20). With Nadal, there is question of a "great knowledge and intense emotion concerning the divine mysteries and the Church" (*FN.* I, 306-307); other statements of Nadal are to be found in *FN,* II, 406; from his *Dialogi pro Societate, FN,* 238). [The full text of Nadal's *Dialogi pro Soc.* is in *MonNad,* V, 524-774. Ed.] Among the commentators, Leturia writes: "It is clear that the central idea of the Foundation, the descent of creatures from God and their necessary ascent and reintegration into their final end, which is the same God, constitutes one of the liveliest experiences of the great illumination" ("Genesis de los Ejercicios de san Ignacio y su influjo en la fundación de la Compañía de Jesús," *AHSJ,* 10 [1941], 32). Calveras, for his part, closely follows Nadal's narrative, in "La Ilustración de Cardoner y el Instituto de la Compañía de Jesús según el Padre Nadal," *AHSJ,* 25 (1956), 27-54. We shall return later to the point of view of Cantin in the article we have

It is important to notice above all, however, that here too in this illumination, at the center of everything we again find Christ as the mediator of revelation. It is through him that Ignatius again reaches the extremes which the Incarnation reunites.

Whereas all the other visions or illuminations are single events which occur each at a moment which the account clearly states, that of Christ in his humanity is frequent and fills the whole scene of Ignatius' spiritual life. In addition to these particular graces, we know from the testimony of Nadal that Ignatius passed his time contemplating the life of Christ. We also know the statement of Polanco attributing Ignatius' instruction to Christ our Lord, an instruction such that it made him capable of teaching others, even without the subsequent study of Scripture and the Doctors; and this happened through the years between Manresa and Paris.[94] The Pilgrim himself attests to this: The vision of the Trinity occurred "one day as he knelt on the steps of the Monastery reciting the Hours of Our Lady."[95] As for creation, "on one occasion he was given an intellectual understanding . . . of how God created the world." On the subject of Christ in the Eucharist he says: "One day when he was hearing Mass in the church of the monastery he clearly saw how Jesus Christ our Lord was present in that most Holy Sacrament."[96] Finally, there is nothing more unique or with its circumstances better described than the illumination on the banks of the Cardoner: "One time he was going . . . to a church a little more than a mile from Manresa . . . called St. Paul's. . . . The road ran next to the river."[97]

On the contrary, as for what concerns the apparition of Christ in his humanity, we are told that "often and for a long time, while at prayer, he saw with interior eyes the humanity of Christ. . . . He saw this at Manresa many times. If he would say twenty or forty, he would not be so bold as to say it was a lie."[98] While speaking of these visions, even before treating the one on the banks of the Cardoner, and while referring to the Scriptures and the content of "these truths of the faith" upon which he had received so many

already quoted. With regard to Silos' article, he touches on the contents of the illumination only as a conclusion (pp. 39–42); his attention is directed more to the subjective aspect of the experience, in "Cardoner in the Life of Saint Ignatius of Loyola," (*AHSJ*, 33 [1964], 3–43). We too shall come back later to this subjective aspect.

94 See *PolChron*, I, 22–23.

95 *Autobiog*, no. 28.

96 Ibid., no. 29.

97 Ibid., no. 30.

98 Ibid., no. 29; see also Nadal, *Diálogi*, in *FN*, II, 239: "During this time Christ and the Virgin Mary appeared to him frequently."

lights, Ignatius concluded that "he would be resolved to die for them only because of what he had then seen."[99] The faith which Ignatius had in the light he received in Manresa will never diminish.[100]

We need not go further into detail about the extremely enlightening "lessons" of Manresa. It suffices that we keep in mind these principal elements of a theology of salvation and sanctification based on the vital relationship which Christ reestablishes between the whole of creation and its Creator and Lord. Let us also remember the fact that Ignatius penetrated intensely into this mystery, with the grace of God, and that he centered his whole life and work around it. We shall analyze the unquestionable testimony of this more fully.[101]

c. The Illuminations, on the Subjective Level: The Experience Aroused by the Message

An examination of the fruits produced by the retreat in Manresa greatly clarifies the experience Ignatius had during that time, and it also makes more precise the teaching which the Lord lavished upon him. We could not, in fact, deepen our understanding of this religious experience without referring constantly to the divine message that brought it about. We have seen that, in a first stage in Manresa, Ignatius reached an authentic spiritual poverty and a detachment from self which freed him from his too ambitious eagerness for sanctity. Through the humble supplication which he discovered when he had reached the point of despair,[102] he learned how to surrender himself to the impulses of grace which permitted him to link his commitment on the level of

---

99 *Autobiog,* no. 29.
100 Laínez used to say about Ignatius: "He is firm on anything about which he once forms a judgment either through divine light or through reasoning, as long as he remains convinced; and in other matters too he does not easily drop his opinion" (*FN,* I, 140–141).
101 We shall treat this subject in ch. 2 below. We have been aiming to throw some light on the content of the illuminations of the Cardoner, by pointing out the harmony which exists between the *meditations* of Loyola and the *events* of Manresa such as they have come down to us in the *Autobiography,* Already now, however, it is interesting to note that, antedating ourselves, others too have treated our topic, but by reasoning from an opposite direction, and have nevertheless arrived at almost the same result. Thus Cantin in "L' illumination," *ScE,* 7 (1955), 40 ff. analyzes the *eximia illustratio* by starting from the fruits it has produced: the transformation that took place in the soul and the life of Ignatius, and the dynamic conception which found expression through his works which were born from it, namely, the *Exercises,* the Society, and the *Constitutions.*
102 *Autobiog,* no. 23.

his own activity and his commitment to the infinitely more powerful action of God. The religious experience which followed that of his purification was an experience of intense faith. Ignatius opened himself up to the Truth which frees, the Truth which sanctifies,[103] and he received it without any restriction. The respectful reception of the divine mystery, as it presents itself, modifies the decisions of Loyola, by bringing them into harmony with the sole good pleasure of God. Evangelical poverty or humility of spirit and an enlightened understanding of the mysteries of the faith—these are the first two spiritual fruits at the origin of the happy transformations to which Manresa and the whole life of the saint testify.[104] By their authenticity these fruits of Manresa awaken a new attitude, deeply theological, manifesting the unity of the lived experience. In fact, the awareness of one's profound misery would be enough to make a person surrender to grace; but it ought also to be accompanied by a keen awareness of the loving presence of God. The attitude resulting from these complementary periods of purification and instruction consisted, for Ignatius, in a complete surrender, both active and passive, of himself. This will henceforth always be his way of acceding to the mystery of the divine encounter and of being faithful to it.

Through this, too, we can understand the insistence of the fifth and fifteenth Annotations of the *Exercises* which open an Ignatian retreat. The *Autobiography* also insists on the fact that the Pilgrim wanted, above everything else, to be faithful to this gift of self founded on an absolute faith in the divine Goodness and Omnipotence. Leaving Manresa for Barcelona Ignatius "wanted to go alone, for his whole purpose was to have God alone as his refuge." In his *Autobiography* he explains this rather surprising attitude at length.[105] On several occasions, from Barcelona to Jerusalem and on the return journey, Ignatius will again come back to this matter essential for him, this indispensable attitude of detachment and of absolute trust in God. The contrary attitude of desire, of possession of self, leads invariably to pride. Ignatius had experienced this in his attachment "to the vanities of the world": as well as in the too ambitious pursuit of his first ideal of sanctity.[106] What was definitively thrust upon him, in the light of the mystery of this

---

103 "The truth will make you free" (John 8:32); "Sanctify them in the truth" (John 17: 17).
104 Cantin, who in "L" illumination," *ScE,* 7 (1955), 40 ff., analyzes the transformations which took place in Ignatius' soul, groups them under the following headings: origin of a new ideal of holiness, progress in the art of discernment of spirits, a man of "discreet charity," very profound modesty, and humility.
105 *Autobiog,* no. 35.
106 Ibid., nos. 1, 13–35.

relationship with God which encompasses all of creation, was a strongly theological spirituality which his devotion to the Trinity will express and deepen until the end of his life.

Moreover, it is important to keep in mind that the theological orientation characteristic of Ignatius' later life found its dynamism in his enlightened awareness of Christ's role as mediator and savior. At the same time that the visions of our Lord were frequent and prolonged, the meditations on the Kingdom and the Two Standards were the center of his spiritual reflections in Manresa.[107] This means that Christ, who is at the heart of everything, continued to reveal himself as the Way leading to life. Christ showed himself as being not only at the center of the relationship which unites man to God as in the Kingdom, but also at the very heart of the conflict which sinful man ought to wage against the powers of darkness, a conflict in which Ignatius had experienced great anguish. Without the standard of Christ we can hope for no victory. It is by delivering man from evil that Christ introduces him into the glory of his Father. After Manresa all of Ignatius's life will crystallize around this dynamic truth. It will characterize his vision of Christianity and will direct the future conduct of the apostle.

By introducing him thus more consciously into the real "history of salvation," Christ reveals to Ignatius the place he himself ought to take in it. The call he received at this point was so decisive that for the rest of his life he will refer to the experience he had in Manresa.[108] That is perhaps the most authentic fruit of this "sanctification in the truth." Nadal writes: "At the same time the desire to help his neighbor was born in him."[109] The new manner of life he will adopt is in keeping with the significant expressions which we find henceforth in his writings: "to help souls, to bear fruit."[110] This life will also result

107 *FN*, I, 306–307.
108 Nadal recounts that very often when offering a solution to a problem that had been submitted to him Ignatius would reply: "I refer to Manresa" (*FN*, II, 6 and 406). Câmara made the same statement (*FN*, II, 609ff).
109 *FN*, 190. Nadal also recounts: "And at the time when Ignatius was doing penance and praying, God gave him the Exercises. Thus he himself, eager for the salvation of souls, later assembled them and gave them to others, moved, as can be piously believed, by this impulse from God to give these same Exercises to others" (*DirSpEx*, p. 174). Polanco, too, writes: "God had impressed this zeal for souls very profoundly in his heart" (*PolChron*, I, 25). See also R. Rouquette, "Le developpement de la spiritualiaté apostolique de saint Ignace de Loyola," (*Chr*, no. 2 [1954], 22–45).
110 See *Autobiog*, nos. 26, 29, 45, 50, 54, 57, 63, 70, 71, 85, 88, 98, 99. See also the Introduction of A. Thiry's French edition, *Le Récit du Pèlerin*, pp. 14, 72 (note 3), which gives references to the corresponding Scriptural texts. Ignatius will again use this expression shortly before his death, as his Letters of 1555 and 1556 testify (see *LettersIgn*, pp. 402 and 421).

under the guidance of the Holy Spirit, through his studies and his searching for companions burning with the same zeal, in the founding of a strictly apostolic religious institute with the ends he proposes for it.

From Loyola onward he found himself all on fire with the desire to serve God. But with Manresa, this service advances beyond his personal homage as the basis of his deeds. He opens himself to the history of salvation as it progresses in the Church, and he profits from the enlightening lesson of spiritual poverty and of self-renunciation which grace teaches him. He will not be able, without the help of God, to work either for his own sanctification or the salvation of others. This is the lesson of discretion, of discernment in love and in the gift of self to the service of the Lord: the measure which is set by the glory of God and the good of souls. Thus we see the Pilgrim renouncing the penitential exploits of the saints he had chosen as models. He states: "At Manresa, too, where he stayed almost a year, after God began to comfort him and he saw the fruit which he brought forth in treating souls, he gave up those extremes he had formerly observed, and he now cut his nails and his hair."[111] Even the pilgrimage to Jerusalem, which he kept in his plans, acquired a new apostolic thrust which gradually changed its perspective.[112] From now on Ignatius will exercise a spirit of discernment in his action and his fervor—that discernment which was brought to him by the humble opinion of himself which he acquired, and above all by his concern about God, his service, and the good of souls.[113]

As he departs from Manresa Ignatius takes with him the essentials of his *"Spiritual Exercises,"* the precious fruit of his experience of a year of soli-

---

111 *Autobiog,* no. 29. St. Ignatius had gone back to eating meat again, since there was no doubt concerning the origin of this "motion" which he felt (see *Autobiog,* no. 27).

112 Ibid., no. 45. Also *LettersIgn,* I, 63; Nadal, *Dialogi,* in *FN,* II, 242; D. Mollat, "Le Christ dans l'expérience de saint Ignace," *Chr,* no. 1 (1954), 29–30; English trans. in W. J. Young, trans., *Finding God in All Things* (Chicago, 1958), pp. 74–75.

113 Here we have analyzed the spiritual evolution of Ignatius through the diverse *subjective experiences* he underwent at Manresa, but in evident relationship with the content of the mysteries or truths which were entailed in his experiences. On the level of this *objective message,* we noted that the illumination beside the Cardoner is presented as a synthesis of things already known; we similarly think that on the subjective level this striking grace gathers together the several elements which already structured Ignatius' spiritual experience and gathered them into a more complete unity. In both cases, the objective and the subjective, the illumination, through the synthesis that has been achieved, allows a forward movement projecting Ignatius into the future. Still further, it remains as a point of reference for his spirit or tenor of thought; and the radiation from this spirit will be inexhaustible. Silos, whose article we quoted above,

tude, of struggles, and of great graces.[114] He had already used them in a germinal form with persons who came to consult him, and this with much fruit.[115] Indications of the important transformations which had taken place in his soul through his Exercises will follow him everywhere. With the experiences of the passing years his *Exercises* will be enriched, but they will remain substantially the same. They will guide the spirituality of the saint himself and his life in the concrete, and also all the apostolic endeavors of the future founder of a new institute.

3. Ignatius' Experience of God's Plan, and His Later Experience of Christian Salvation

There is a strange coincidence which makes clear the unity of the divine plan of salvation, St. Paul's "mystery of Christ": To meet Christ, who reveals the Father and his love, is to enter further into the divine plan for saving human beings through Christ, and also to turn ourselves toward men and women, our brothers and sisters; and to deepen our awareness of our vocation to the divine life is to embrace the work of salvation in its universality.[116]

places his research on the level of the subjective experience, where the elements, when grouped together, seem to be synthesized around a dynamic principle which for Ignatius is always a determining force. We feel that seems to be the point of his work, but it still needs to be completed by an analysis of the objective content of the illumination. Ignatius said that he "understood and knew many things." One ought not to overlook the determining influence which this content had on his subjective experience. Nadal's point of view, accepted by Calveras and clarified by Cantin's investigations, retains its full value, explaining a good part of the illumination by its relationship to the meditations on the Kingdom and the Two Standards. The relationship that exists between the objective and the subjective levels is an early trait in Ignatius' development. It is a characteristic of the dialectic or interacting reasoning processes in his own personal experience.

114 I. Iparraguirre, in *Obras completas*, pp. 179–187, gives a good treatment of what the content of the "first Exercises" could have been at the end of the stay at Manresa; he continues his thought on this point in his *Adnotationes initiales*, p. 78. Ignatius certainly continued to correct, polish, and enrich his *Exercises*, but without changing their substance. See also *PolChron*, III, 530 and *FN*, I, 319. Also H. Coathalem, *Ignatian Insights*, pp. 6–8.

115 The evidences are very explicit; see *FN*, II, 160–164, 526–527; *PolChron*, I, 25; *PolCompl*, I, 507; Câmara, *FN*, I, 70; I. Iparraguirre. *Práctica de los Ejercicios de San Ignacio de Loyola en vida de su autor (1522–1556)*, (Rome, 1946), pp. 1 and 282.

116 Certain expressions proper to St. Ignatius confirm this opinion. At Manresa God had revealed Himself to him as "the common Master and the God of all creation" (*Obras completas*, 1st ed., [1947], pp. 705–706); as "Lord of all the world" (Ibid., p. 622, *SpEx*, [145]); as Him "whose sovereign name must be praised and exalted by all creatures . . . created and ordered to so just and

Our approach, through prayer and correspondence with God's grace to his revealed plan, stimulates in ourselves a spiritual readjustment, which always leads to further progress and a more enlightened and more generous participation in the mission of Christ. This seems to us, as we conclude this section of our study on Ignatius, to be *the* experience of Christian salvation, an awareness that Christ's saving doctrine and graces are being applied day by day in our own case. It is an experience of a deepening of one's insertion of oneself into one's own place in the divine plan here and now as it unfolds in the history of salvation. The universe, drawn by the love of God who created it, is set on its course toward the Father, through the Son, in his Spirit. And the humble and privileged human creature, who by a divine vocation is called to unite himself or herself to Christ the Mediator and thus to form one Body with him, enters into this ascension of the universe in its return toward the Father. The meditation on the Kingdom, which is at the center of Ignatius' experience in Manresa, presents "Christ our Lord, the Eternal King, before whom is assembled the whole world. To all, his summons goes forth, and to each one in particular." The desire of Christ is explicit: to conquer the whole world and all his enemies and thus to enter into the glory of his Father.[117] Donatien Mollat concludes his article on "Christ in the Spiritual Experience of Ignatius" as follows:

> The spiritual experience of St. Ignatius is simply a becoming aware of the divine love present and working in the world through Jesus Christ and the Church, a collaboration with his work, a docility to his Spirit. This perception of the mystery of the love of God in Christ situates this experience at the center of the biblical revelation. The brief in which Pope Paul III in 1548 approved the *Exercises* recognized that "these *Exercises* were composed from a knowledge of Sacred Scripture and from a long experience of the spiritual life."[118] No doubt since he was especially a man of action, little given to speculation, for a long time little educated and then formed in a school of rather nominalistic scholasticism and exegesis, Ignatius did not have the intellectual tools which would enable him to exploit fully the intuitions of a St. Paul about the Body of Christ, his life in us, and the recapitulation of all things unto him. But to those simple notions which were in the mind of the old-soldier student, such as lordship,

worthy an end" (Ibid., pp. 664–665). Christ is the center of history and human beings find their place in history through their relationship to Him, "our eternal Lord" (Ibid., p. 651, *SpEx*, [71 and 98]). Quoted from D. Mollat, "Le Christ dans l'expérience spirituelle de saint Ignace," *Chr*, no. 1 (1954), 39–40; Young, *Finding God*, pp. 88–89.

117 *SpEx*, [95].
118 *SpEx*MHSJ, p. 216.

honor, service, grace was able to communicate such a charge, divine power, and vitality that through those ideas the glory of the eternal Lord radiated brilliantly anew.[119]

Ignatius always spoke with a certain veneration of Manresa, which he called "his primitive church."[120] This primitive church was one of *discovery* and of *fervor;* and his discovery and fervor were both deeply rooted in the death and resurrection of the Christ who saves us, and in the gift of his Spirit who transforms our powers of love and action. Ignatius, who has followed Christ in the mystery of his Passover, desires only to be faithful to the motions of his Spirit all the days of his life in homage of the Divine Majesty.

C. A Way of Interpreting Ignatius' Book, Spiritual Exercises

What we propose in this work is an interpretation of Ignatius' *Exercises* which is based on the capital fact which our first chapter has endeavored to establish: Through his attentive readings at Loyola and the great illuminations of Manresa, Ignatius encountered God as communicating his mystery or plan of salvation. He is the God of revelation whose unique Word, proclaimed in the silence of the soul and received by the heart which disposes itself for it with discernment, creates a new world, makes its foundations solid, and opens the way wide for a life of love. This experience which Ignatius lived and developed is expressed in his book of the *Exercises,* which has this manifest purpose: to foster in others a similar itinerary of purification and of appreciative attachment to the powerfully efficacious light of God's plan for salvation and spiritual growth. The relation of Ignatius' book to his experience in Manresa no longer needs to be further established, since masters have already given us their studies on "the genesis of the *Exercises.*" For our part, we hope we have shown that through the intermediary of Ignatius' experience at Loyola and Manresa, the relationship to the "mystery of God" is also fundamental. In their very genesis the *Exercises* draw their vitality from this encounter with God; and in the measure of their fidelity to the Ignatian experience they constitute an opening of oneself to the chief truths of this revelation, the graces of God, and the experiences which spring from all of these.

If the divine plan for our salvation and spiritual growth is the point from which the *Exercises* start in order to convert us profoundly, then our under-

---

119 D. Mollat, *Chr,* no. 1 (1954), 46–47; Young, *Finding God,* pp. 88–89.
120 ". . . which he was wont to extol and call his primitive church" (Laínez, *FN,* I, 140–141).

standing of this revelation disposes us for an interpretation of the *Exercises* which makes them a source for our admiration and grateful contemplation of this wonderful plan of our loving God. This begets an experience of deepening our Christian vocation, and of our inserting ourselves here and now into the place God offers us in the unfolding history of salvation.[121] Hence we are now adopting a way of interpretation which, above all, is based on the transcending guidance of the "mystery of God" or "mystery of Christ." We must never forget that Ignatius had this experience which was focused on God's salvific plan before he ever wrote the *Exercises*.

They are the fruit and the expression, more or less faltering, of this experience. It would be futile to try to give an adequate explanation of them without explicitly referring to this divinely revealed plan which they embody and express in their own way. First of all, they are a proclamation of God's word. Then they are accompanied by exercises based on prayer and direction which, through the communication of the revealed truths of the faith, dispose one for an enlightened and generous response. This subjective aspect by which one disposes oneself for docility and response is itself awakened and specified by the nature and the demands of the message which the *Exercises* present.

In other words, we must know how to distinguish—both in Ignatius' *Exercises* and in his spiritual experience—between the objective level (the divinely revealed saving message) and the subjective level (the experience evoked by the exercises).[122] To be set on wanting to justify the techniques

121   This claim that Ignatius' mentality was so profoundly biblical and theological might meet with this objection: "Ignatius was a man of his own era. Therefore he was a man whose studies and formation were scholastic and nominalistic." Such an objection, however, would be overlooking an important fact. What is essential—in the proper sense of that term—to the Ignatian *Exercises* was not in any way taken from the teachers and schools of that era, or drawn from the studies which Ignatius later pursued in Paris. We have sufficiently emphasized the perspective that was revealed to him at Loyola and Manresa to make us think that the *Exercises* (as far as their substance is concerned) have nothing in common with the spirit of the times. (The problem of language or expression, of course, is something else again.) St. Francis de Sales used to say that he found in the *Exercises* a "holy method, familiar to the ancient Christians, but since then almost completely left aside until the great servant of God, Ignatius of Loyola, gave it back to us" (*Oeuvres complètes*, [ed.Migne, 1861], III, 951), quoted in *SpEx*MHSJ, p. 25.

122   *SpEx*MHSJ, pp. 676, 678–684, gives the testimony of Doctors A. Cuesta and B. Torres concerning the "catholic and holy doctrine" which the *Exercises* present. On the subject of the "theological truths" contained in the little book, see I. Iparraguirre, *Adnotationes initiales*, p. 15. L. Bouyer states in his *Introduction to Spirituality* (New York, 1961) that "the study of the object toward

suggested by the book and the successive stages of the experience of purification and the commitment it entails solely from the psychological or philosophical point of view, or without continual reference to the revealed message and to the theological understanding we might have of it, would be to cut ourselves off from the only fully satisfying source of interpretation. The framework, the techniques, and all the steps of various kinds which make up the book of the *Exercises,* have as their only purpose the transmission, the revelation, and the realization of the salvific plan, the mystery of God in Christ. "The Exercises have that efficacy because they teach a method of preparing oneself to receive the word of God and his gospel," stated Ignatius' companion Nadal.[123]

In some periods of the past, interpreters strove to expound especially the riches of the Ignatian techniques and the spiritual and psychological evolution of the retreatant which was stimulated by the various stages of the Exercises. They directly took up the doctrinal aspect properly so called—that of the message proposed to the retreatant—only at and in those points where the letter of the text made it more explicit, such as the First Principle and Foundation, the Kingdom, the Incarnation, the Two Standards, or the Contemplation for Love.[124]

Our intention is to proceed in the opposite direction, precisely because of this transcendent importance of God's plan of salvation. This is the genuine doctrinal topic and content of the *Exercises.* Because of Ignatius's experi-

which the psychology of the religious person is orientated and centered . . . is of capital importance here" (p. 18). We think that this principle can very well be applied to Ignatius' *Exercises.* Without this transcendental relationship the *Exercises* would not be any longer existent. "Faith [which is an act, an experience] is inseparable from its content" (R. Guardini, *Vie de foi,* p. 24). There are other ways of expressing the same distinction: d'Ouince speaks of an "objective pedagogy" and a "subjective pedagogy" (*Chr,* no. 13 [1957], p. 92); and Fiorito distinguishes between the "thematic, normative, and practical documents" in the *Exercises* (*CyF,* 20 [1964], 96ff.). Let us add that a doctor of the Sorbonne, a contemporary of the saint, M. Mazurier, stated that he had "never met a man who expressed theology with so much sovereignty and majesty" (*FN,* I, 181; II, 198-199 with fn. 35). Finally, the most surprising statement of all comes from the lips of Ignatius himself on the subject of Manresa: "I saw, I perceived within myself, and I penetrated all the mysteries of the Christian faith" (Vidi, inquit, sensi et intellexi omnia fidei Christianae mysteria) (*FN,* II, 123). [On Ignatius' knowledge of theology, see C. de Dalmases, *Ignatius of Loyola, Founder of the Jesuits: His Life and Work* (St. Louis, 1985), pp. 122- 124. Ed.].

123   Nadal, "Commentarii de Instituto S. I.," in *MonNad,* V, 788.
124   See, for example, the article of Philip J. Donnelly, "The Dogmatic Foundations of the Spiritual Exercises," *WL,* 83 (1954), 131-157.

ence of this divine plan of salvation—which experience the *Exercises* communicate—we turn our attention directly to the theological understanding of this mystery of God, as better understood through the centuries-old reflection of the Church and propounded now in books on biblical theology. Our aim is to throw light upon the *content* which the *Exercises* expressly present, and upon its relation to the *experience* which they aim to awaken in the soul of the attentive exercitant.

Such will be our procedure: Not to start from the text of the *Exercises* in order to find points of contact with the revealed message, but to start from the supremacy of God's plan itself for the salvation and spiritual growth of women and men. Our method will be to explain more deeply how the *Exercises* present a pedagogical method guiding a retreatant to an experience of God as He is communicating His plan of salvation through Christ—that "mystery of Christ" about which St. Paul shows such enthusiasm in his letter to the Ephesians. Thus the *Exercises* enable us to understand better, too, our opportunity to insert ourselves into our own place in the ongoing history of salvation, and to verify in our own case the continual adaptation of that insertion which Ignatius' *Exercises* propose. They are a judicious guide for our reflection, since they stimulate our knowledge of the revealed message and at the same time encourage a definitely more enlightened and more generous Christian commitment.

To sum up: Our study makes a distinction between the objective content and the subjective aspect in the making of the Exercises. The objective content is God's revealed message of salvation as found in the Scriptures and proposed to the exercitant. Thus the call which he or she perceives corresponds with the very data of God's revelation. The subjective aspect is everything in the Exercises which concerns the exercitant: his or her efforts to become docile so as to facilitate correspondence with God's enlightenment and graces, and to allow for a more conscious, intelligent, enlightened, and free adherence to His saving plan. This is in accordance with the manner which His revelation itself proposes, since the subjective techniques are especially awakened and specified by the nature and demands of the message. The response, in its turn, will be realized according to the same data of revelation, where the personal and unique character of the exercitant is always highly respected. In other words, the attitude which the *Exercises* aim to foster and develop, with the grace of God, is properly that same attitude which the revealed mystery of salvation calls forth.

The starting point of our procedure is the study of the objective content, the subject matter of biblical theology in order to come to the subjective aspect particular to the *Exercises*. We hope to give a more spiritual and thoroughly unified interpretation of them which will help us to understand better the life-giving practice of Christianity which the *Exercises* aim to stimulate and guide.

Chapter 2

THE SERVICE OF THE DIVINE MAJESTY

A. *The Necessity of Preparing Oneself for the Exercises*

1. *The Preeminence of God's Plan of Salvation*

The studies which have been made on the genesis of the *Exercises* have sufficiently shown the relation that exists between them and Ignatius' spiritual experience at Loyola and Manresa. For our own part, we have been trying to see (1) how his conversion serves as a typical example of one who is in the process of experiencing Christian salvation; and (2), how Ignatius' insight into this experience is an insertion, more conscious and generous, of himself into the history of God's unfolding plan for the redemption of mankind. When this background is made the light in which the Exercises are studied, they are readily seen in their relationship to one's personal experience of the plan of salvation which God has revealed. The guidance drawn from his divine plan for spiritual growth is given the place of supreme importance.

For the good progress of one making the Exercises, however, a serious problem seems to be raised by their point of departure. In the First Week Ignatius seems to launch us right off into an experience of our sinful condition. That is a vital experience which cannot be merely relegated to the realm of ideas, or considered as a simple "preparation for a good confession."[1] Besides, an experience of this kind cannot be evoked by willing it. The Bible and Christian practice, as the example of the saints illustrates, teach us that such an experience is always the result of a real encounter with God, and with his guiding and saving plan which reveals to us our own poverty along with his divine magnificence. "Depart from me, O Lord, for I am a sinful

---

1 St. Ignatius preferred that, if possible, the retreatant should make his confession "before starting the Foundation" (see his Dictated Directory in *SpEx*MHSJ, p. 790). The "general confession" normally comes at the end of the ,First Week and should not interfere with the pace proper to this week. We shall return to this point.

man."[2] There is a real similarity between this cry of Peter, uttered when he was struck by the majesty of the Lord, and that of the Chosen People when they became aware of their culpability each time that God, in the course of history, made his presence felt. It was also the cry of the prophets who were called by God, like Isaiah who, crushed by the vision of the divine glory, avowed that his lips were impure.[3] One cannot all of a sudden decide to enter into an experience of such dimension. The most one can do is to prepare and dispose oneself for it with respect for a considerable time, since it is above all the fruit of grace. More than human considerations on the misery of human existence are needed if the *Miserere* of the First Week is to burst forth from the depths of the heart and purify the soul. We must receive the light which shines in the darkness. The experience of the First Week presupposes an encounter with God which both precedes and accompanies it. Here we come back to that guiding function of God's plan for us. It affirms the necessity and the gratuity of the divine initiative, especially when it pertains to the realm of salvation.

We have seen that the case of Ignatius illustrates this priority of the divine initiative which awakens and in some way directs our human spiritual experience. At Loyola and Manresa Ignatius encountered the message of God under one form or other. In both instances this experience revealed to him the need for purification; and this led him to a commitment that came closer and closer to what God desired for him.[4]

2. The Dispositions Necessary for the Experience of the Exercises

All the requisites necessary for one to enter into an experience of Christian salvation were what inspired St. Ignatius to determine, not only the matter and the procedure of his First Week of the *Exercises,* but also the preparation of the exercitant for them. They guided him especially in the choice of retreatants and enlightened him on the dispositions he expected of them. He asked particularly that the Exercises be proposed only to those

---

2 Luke 5:8.
3 Isa. 6:4. On this subject read J. Guillet, *Jésus Christ hier et aujourd'hui,* (Paris, 1963), pp. 35–51; English trans. by J. Duggan, *Christ Yesterday and Today: Introduction to Biblical Spirituality,* (Chicago, 1965), pp. 26–41; P. Michalon, "La foi selon l'Ancien Testament," *NRTh,* 75 (1953), 587–600.
4 The contemplation of the life of Christ has in itself a purifying value, according to Ludolph the Carthusian. He states this fact when he quotes Heb. 12:29: "For our God to whom he adheres 'is a consuming fire,' working a purification of sins." He also quotes John 1:5 and Num. 21:9. See *Vita Christi,* I, Prooemium, no. 3.

persons who were animated with a great desire for perfection *(muy deseosas de perfección)*.[5] The fifth Annotation suggests to the retreatant this generous attitude of self-offering as the desirable starting point for these steps in spiritual deepening. "It will be very profitable for the one who is to go through the Exercises to enter upon them with magnanimity and generosity toward his Creator and Lord, and to offer him his entire will and liberty, that his Divine Majesty may dispose of him and all he possesses according to his most holy will."[6] If the retreatant is not ready for this attitude, if he or she does not sincerely aspire to it, that retreatant cannot undertake the Exercises in their entirety. Preparatory exercises ought to be given first. Moreover, for the thirty-day retreat Ignatius demands "intellectual capacities" which make one open to God's mystery or saving plan and receptive to his divine light. These qualifications definitely correspond to a certain maturity and freedom of the person. The *Exercises* are addressed to persons who "are free to decide for themselves" and who are not blinded by any "disordered attachment," so that they can truly "resign themselves thoroughly into God's hands."[7]

Ignacio Iparraguirre, who reconstructed the history of "the practice of the Exercises during the life of their author,"[8] gives us some interesting details on Ignatius' manner of preparing persons for the Exercises. On this topic the evolution which the saint underwent is especially significant. In the beginning at Manresa, Barcelona, and Alcalá, Ignatius gave the Exercises to all pious persons of good will, especially women. These were Exercises which, while not being "intensive," were nonetheless "extensive." They lasted about a month and included many instructions in the form of spiritual conversations. Ignatius, filled with God's action in him and its marvelous fruits, desired only one thing: to share the benefits of the Lord with others.

He had some successes, as he said, but also some failures. That is why he modified his method of presentation in Paris when he undertook to communicate the same spiritual message to students, professors, doctors, and even the rector of the university. The Exercises became truly "intensive" and were based on complete seclusion, continual prayer, and personal direction throughout. They began to include a preparatory stage which consisted in

---

5 *EppIgn*, I, XII, 677.
6 *SpEx*, [5].
7 See *SpEx*, [18–19]; *LettersIgn*, pp. 95, 247–248; *SpEx*MHSJ, Dictated Directory, p. 786. It would be of interest to consult the article of L. Beirnaert, "Discernement et psychisme," *Chr*, no. 4 (1954), 50–61.
8 I. Iparraguirre, *Práctica de los Ejercicios (1522–1556)*, ch. I, especially pp. 1–13, which we are using here, and of which a résumé in English is found in *Ign*, (1956), 209–211: "St. Ignatius as Retreat Master," by F. Sopeña.

that work which the extensive Exercises had already accomplished with the women of Alcalá. Ignatius had understood that in the future it would be necessary to prepare his retreatant for a long time if the Exercises properly so called of thirty days were to bear the lasting fruits he hoped for.

There is one point that emerges in a particular way which indicates the extraordinary importance St. Ignatius attached to this preparation for the Exercises. He did not allow anyone to make the Exercises in their entirety if he or she did not have the necessary dispositions, and he used some of the same Exercises in an embryonic form, as a means of preparation for the later work.[9]

Regarding this preparatory work carried on by means of these same Exercises, Iparraguirre writes:

Note that the fruit obtained by this preparatory work is substantially the same as that which the women of Alcalá obtained, that is, peace of soul and strength to lead a fervent life.[10]

The example of Favre, whom Ignatius himself prepared for the Exercises, very well illustrates the method he followed. In 1529 Pierre Favre had a great desire to make the Exercises. Ignatius, who knew him well, was satisfied to give him some preparatory exercises in order to stabilize certain indispensable dispositions in him, especially that he might have peace of soul and might mature. Favre was to be admitted to the Exercises in their entirety only in the beginning of the year 1534, four years later, in the months that preceded his ordination to the priesthood and his vows at Montmartre.[11]

3. The First Principle and Foundation

It was also in Paris, as he was intensifying the stage of preparation for the Exercises, that Ignatius revised his First Principle and Foundation.[12] The way in which he used it is rather well known. It went through a significant

9 I. Iparraguirre, *Práctica de los Ejercicios (1522–1556)*, p. 6.
10 Ibid., p. 7.
11 On this subject read P. Favre,. *Memorial,* trans. de Certeau, (Paris, 1959), pp. 112–115 (also pp. 136, 251); I. Iparraguirre, *Práctica de los Ejercicios (1522–1556)*, pp. 6–7; L. Beirnaert, art. cit., *Chr*, no. 4 (1954), 56; *MonFabri*, pp. 84, 85, 89, 107, 165, 174.
12 It seems that the Principle and Foundation, which we shall henceforth designate in this study by the sole word Foundation, was composed at Alcalá. But the studies of Leturia, Iparraguirre, and E. Hernández have gradually established Paris as the location of its first appearance. There is a good reésumé of this question in H. Coathalem, *Ignatian Insights,* p. 61, [where Coathalem states that the substance of the Foundation came from Manresa, but the literary expression of it from Paris. Ed.].

evolution. In the beginning its use was very simple. Having prepared his candidate for the Exercises for a long time ahead, Ignatius could put into practice what he himself taught about the Foundation, namely, that it should be explained *(declarar)* at the same time as the method of the examens. Then, "in the afternoon of the first day" he should begin the exercises on sin.[13]

The text of the Foundation thus played a double role. First, it recalled briefly to the retreatant a vision of the whole to which, no doubt, the preparatory stage had initiated him, since Ignatius was anxious that the retreatant should have the desire for the Exercises and for the experience they offer. The Letters and the Directories will insist on this psychological necessity. The Foundation, however, as a vision of the whole, had another end which went beyond the simple recall or actuation of a desired ideal. Within the restricted framework of the realities evoked, it aimed to focus attention on the retreatant's place in God's plan of creation and salvation. Such a vision of the ideal, sketched in broad lines, posed right at the starting point the difficulty in responding to God with fidelity. This exercise thus serves as the preparation for and entrance and enticement into the subsequent exercises. The Ignatian Directory dictated to Father Vitoria expresses this clear purpose of the Foundation as follows:

> Then the Foundation is given to him and explained in such a way that he will be able to find what he desires. It would be well to state it in this manner: "In order that you may perceive how difficult it is to use with indifference the means which God has placed at our disposal to attain the end for which he created us; and in order that, understanding it, you may place yourself entirely into his hands— Here is the Foundation in which you will find what we desire."[14]

Before long, however, Ignatius seemingly perceived that because preparation was lacking—due no doubt to the growing number of retreatants—the Foundation had to be more than an occasion of recall. There was need for it to become a time intended for the retreatant to familiarize himself or herself with the ideal which implants the requisite dispositions. Otherwise, he became fully aware, there would be a return to the formula used at Alcalá, in which the Exercises, based only on good will, were limited to being only "preparatory exercises." That is why, in the same dictated Directory, he suggests as a means of perfecting the preparation of the retreatant to "keep

---

13 *SpEx*MHSJ, Ignatian Directory, pp. 782, 791–792. See also I. Iparraguirre, *Práctica de los Ejercicios (1522–1556)*, p. 181. The nineteenth annotation of the *Exercises* contains a remark that is closely related to this use of the Foundation.
14 *SpEx*MHSJ, p. 792.

him on the consideration of the Foundation, and on the particular and general examens, for three or four days or even more, so that he may grow more mature."[15]

Thus the Foundation, which had started out as a simple "statement," came to be divided "into points" and transformed into a text for meditation. Our Ignatian Directory states clearly the three parts of the text which express the main ideas: the end of man, the means, the difficulty. It ends with the following statement: "From this will arise the felt necessity of placing oneself in a state of equilibrium."[16] The first companions soon adopted this manner of proceeding in their presentation of the Foundation, some using three points, others four.[17]

There is a final testimony confirming what we have said on Ignatian practice regarding the preparation for the Exercises by means of the Foundation. It is the response given by the *Annotata Neapolitana* at the time of the elaboration of the Directory of 1591. This Directory, which was submitted to the Society for its approbation, divided the Foundation into three parts so that it might be given the time necessary to produce its fruit: Ignatian indifference.[18]

The Neapolitan examiners then presented the obvious objection which they expected: To meditate on the Foundation for two or three days seemed to go against the practice recommended by the words "to explain" *(declarar)*.[19] The Commission for the Directory of 1591 formulated the following response which emphasizes the necessity for the preparation; and for this it appealed to the authority of St. Ignatius.

> The reply is: Above all, we ought to understand this well. To attain the goal of the Exercises, a thoroughly complete and many-sided penetration of the Foundation is of capital importance. For this reason Father Ignatius customarily devoted two days to the consideration of it. Hence, it is highly useful to distinguish several brief points in the Foundation as a whole and to give them separately to the exercitant.[20]

15 Ibid., p. 791
16 Ibid., p. 792
17 Canisius divided the text into three points: "*Why* man was created, *what* the uses of creatures are, *how* he should conduct himself in using them" (*SpEx*MHSJ, p. 986; *DirSpEx* [1955], p. 134). Polanco proposed four points: creation and the end of man, the end of creatures, the use of creatures, indifference (*SpEx*MHSJ, pp. 829–830). Several authors adopted this division, e.g., González Dávila (ibid, p. 910), *Directorium Granatense* (ibid., p. 952).
18 Ibid., pp. 1036–1037.
19 Ibid., p. 1096.
20 Ibid., p. 1107.

From this examination of the question we should retain the principles of the Ignatian practice that emerge regarding the preparation for the Exercises. If we have the occasion to direct someone in the ways of the spiritual life, like Ignatius we should prepare the person for a long time for the experience of the Exercises in their entirety. The preparation which St. Ignatius himself used remains rather typical: to become aware, in the light of the divine saving plan, of the reform that must take place in every life, and to dispose oneself, with the help of God's grace, to grow in the desire to be faithful. The saint considered this desire to be indispensable. It is in this way that the Foundation will fulfill the role for which it was originally conceived. At the time when the retreatant enters into the Exercises it will simply reanimate, in all its purity, the ideal which places one back again into the heart of the issue.

However, if this long remote preparation has not been given before the date of entry into the retreat (a case which often occurs), the Foundation will have to fulfill the second role which Ignatius and the first companions attributed to it. It will itself become that time of preparation which opens the mind and stimulates generosity. This will come before posing the question of our difficulty in being faithful which draws us into the exercises of the First Week. One will not consider this stage, more or less long according to need, as being strictly part of the Exercises; and this will allow one full liberty in its presentation in the manner of proceeding. To assure this preparation and the fruits that follow from it, a director will have recourse to whatever helps toward the end to be attained, and really to open the horizon of the exercitant by imparting a certain maturity and spiritual knowledge.

The Foundation will be, first of all, the occasion of initiating the exercitant into an inspiring perspective, a vision of the whole—one which includes the chief elements of the Christian faith, though not in detail. During this time which preceded the Exercises, Ignatius strove to open the mind and the heart of the future retreatant, and to dispose him or her as much as possible to "surrender himself to his Creator and Lord" (fifth Annotation). It would be naive to think that during this period Ignatius took care to avoid speaking of Christ, of the Church, of a lively faith, of the love which engenders service, or of the other essential mysteries or truths of Christianity which were at the very center of his Christian vision of the world—those marvelous truths whose unity he had grasped at Manresa and particularly beside the Cardoner.

The Foundation, we repeat, is no longer the occasion of a brief recall that aims solely at placing us in our position before God. Rather, it has now become that time of preparation which is absolutely necessary, one which introduces the person into such a vision as will awaken in him the desire to have the experience proposed by the making of the Exercises. It will also foster the required dispositions (fifth Annotation). This vision of the whole is, in our opinion, precisely what Ignatius gained during his encounter with God through the meditations at Loyola and the mystical graces at Manresa. It was the global outlook which his life of union with God and of apostolic service continued to enrich. This vision, as we shall see, presents to the exercitant the principal revealed truths of our Christian faith, organically structured in such a way that each retreatant readily sees the important and place which human beings, endowed with intellect and free will, occupy in God's plan of creation, salvation, and spiritual growth. Each retreatant, too, can readily understand the role which he or she personally has the opportunity to play in God's scheme of things. Hence it is highly desirable, or even necessary, to initiate the Ignatian retreatant into this vision of the whole. Then the text of the Foundation, in its conciseness and with the purity of its key ideas, will truly pose the question which opens on the problem of the First Week. In a word, it is only at the end of a period of preparation—remote or immediate—that the text of the Foundation takes on its full meaning. Furthermore, it is in the light of this vision, which is the framework of the whole thought of Ignatius, that a person will be able to understand and respect the function of the Foundation and to work through it so as to make it an effective entrance into the exercises of the First Week.

B. Ignatius' Conception of God, the Universe, and the Human Person

1. The Sources from Which We Learn It

We are here speaking of the Ignatian experience and vision. The experience takes us back to the events of Loyola and Manresa which we have already considered. The Ignatian vision, which springs from this experience, goes beyond it. It contains that concept of Christian existence which Ignatius acquired and developed. It encompasses the great truths and problems about God, creation, mankind, Christ, human activities, and the like. This is the vision or world view that we must find and use for the authentic interpretation of the truths put forth in the *Exercises*. To do this we should normally have recourse to the various sources in which this vision was expressed: Ignatius' *Autobiography,* which recounts many of his experiences from Loyola in 1521 to Rome in 1555; the *Exercises* themselves; his Letters, which capture on-the-spot applications in daily practice of his characteristic ways of seeing and judging; the *Constitutions* where we find, now formulated into principles, the dynamism of the saint's apostolic activity; finally, his *Spiritual Diary,* the evidence for an intimate part of his interior life. To these we should add the multiple and varied sources collected in the Monumenta Historica Societatis Iesu, especially the writings of the first companions about his life and work. These are the indirect sources to be drawn from if one wishes to reconstitute the vision of the whole into which the future retreatant must be initiated during the period of preparation about which we have spoken.

We feel, however, that if one has some knowledge of these sources and forms of expression of the Ignatian world view, the major parts of the *Exercises* themselves would be enough to reconstitute this life-giving framework which brings the Christian ideal into prominence and helps to open up the mind and heart to the dimensions of the global vision into which Ignatius desires to introduce his retreatant. The major elements or exercises which we propose as the basis of our description of the Ignatian universe are the Foundation and the Contemplation to Attain Love in their relation to each other, with the Kingdom and the Two Standards as the point of convergence. Other important elements will also be brought to light, such as the sense of evil, the purpose of the election, and the indispensable contemplation of the mysteries or events of the life of Christ, especially the Paschal Mystery to which Ignatius will dedicate two Weeks out of the four.[21]

2. His World View

In his small book on St. Ignatius and the historical development of his spirituality, Hugo Rahner writes:

> Beyond the very sober words of the *Exercises,* and beyond the measured sentences of the *Constitutions,* there exists in truth a whole world view, the world enclosed in Ignatius' heart, the world full of brightness and warmth which he constructs with the help of some illuminations he received during his mystical encounter with God. We want to penetrate into this world in order to try to form some idea of the forces that enabled our saint to exercise his tremendous achievements.[22]

21 The close relationship existing between the Foundation and the Contemplation to Attain Love has often been stressed, and that right from the beginning: see the Codex Regina of the *Exercises* between 1534 and 1538 and the Anonymous Directory B2 (*SpEx*MHSJ, pp. 796–897). It has also been adopted by commentators such as Leturia, H. Rahner, I. Iparraguirre, G. Fessard, J. Levie. The same holds true of the central place occupied by the Kingdom and the Two Standards in the experiences and meditations of Manresa (see J. Nadal, 0. Manare, J. Calveras, I. Iparraguirre, and others).

22 H. Rahner, *The Spirituality of St. Ignatius,* (Westminster, 1953) p. xi. [The remarks, made on p. x above, about the conflicting opinions on the use of nonexclusive language and of the "resumptive" personal pronouns in the third

This "world enclosed in Ignatius' heart" is what we call his world view, his global vision, his expansive outlook on God, the universe, and on the human person. It is a comprehensive "weltanschauung." True, this vision enlightens us greatly about the dynamism and the orientation of the concrete life of the saint. We shall first formulate this world view concisely here in four statements, and then develop them in detail through sections a, b, c, and d on the pages below. That will put us in position to return to the Foundation, and to conclude this chapter by taking up a problem which the Foundation poses. This problem will, in its turn, point out the necessity for spiritual exercises and then, above all, determine their interpretation and procedure.

In Ignatius' conception of God, the universe, and human persons, several key ideas are prominent.

First, God, Creator and Lord, Father, Son, and Holy Spirit, is he who, both triune and one, in a gesture of an ever-present love, creates, gives life and gifts of every kind. For Ignatius, God is a continual act of love offered to the creature and calling for the hearts of women and men.

Second, as a result of God's creating love and his desire to share his happiness, the universe is called from nothingness and set in motion toward his glorification. This movement consists in its actualizing unceasingly that initial movement which made it spring from nothingness and which also gratuitously calls it to play a role, beyond that of its merely natural existence, in the final glorifying or praising of God by all the saved human beings at the end of time. It fulfills that role by mirroring forth God's goodness to the men and women who through it come to know, love, serve, and praise or glorify him because of it. The world in its totality, attracted by God, is in its movement working out a continual response of ascent to his attracting love.

Third, human beings are placed, by a special vocation, at the center of this economy or divine arrangement, with Christ and in the Church, as indispensable cooperators in the work of creation, redemption, and glorification of God. Ignatius' awareness of this responsibility, tremendous and profoundly exalting, is what led him to commit himself to a loving service characterized by a total self-giving united to a humble "discretion," that is, discernment. It is service which embraces the world;

person ("he or she," "he/she") when they refer to an antecedent of common gender (such as person, who, etc.) are particularly applicable to the present chapter, especially in the sections dealing with *l'homme*, "man" in its generic sense. Ed.]

which seeks, not to reject the world, but to lead it to its spiritual destiny, that of its being a means to the praising or glorifying of God by women and men. This is the unique fulfillment of the purpose for which the world was created.

Fourth, there is, however, the problem of evil. Human beings, being free creatures, can also commit themselves to collaborate with the Adversary, "the enemy of human nature," in order to impede the movement of the universe in its progress toward God. For personal sin, which hinders the salvation of man, is opposed both to the good of the whole of creation and to the glorifying of God.

In conclusion, Ignatius perceives that the destiny of the divine work rests on the weak shoulders of each man and woman. Each one is unceasingly under an obligation to order his life with regard to all created things in the light of God's plan and of the many manifestations of his divine will. We now proceed to study each of these four assertions in detail.

a. His Conception of God

Ignatian spirituality is strongly trinitarian and Christocentric. The unity of the mystery of God is certainly not thereby obscured. However, there is a paradox here which is not resolved solely on the level of the idea of God. The manifest dualism of these two thrusts brings about, in fact, a division in the concrete life of Ignatius. Its Christocentric aspect is manifested more clearly in his works of communication or of a more objective character, such as his Letters, the *Exercises,* and the *Constitutions*—and also in the apostolic work which the *Constitutions* regulate: the nature and structure Society of Jesus born from the Kingdom and the Two Standards and dedicated to the service of Christ and the Church).[23] On the contrary, the works of a more subjective, confidential nature, such as the *Spiritual Diary* of 1544 and the *Autobiography* insofar as it mentions the graces connected with his intimate spiritual life, testify more lucidly to an interior life which, to go back to the word of

---

23 In the course of these last years several studies have deepened this Christological character of the *Exercises.* See, e.g., D. Mollat, "Le Christ dans l'expérience spirituelle de saint Ignace," *Chr,* no. 1 (1954), 23–47; H. Rahner, "La vision de saint Ignace à la chapelle de La Storta," *Chr,* no. 1 (1954), 48–65; Young, *Finding God,* pp. 77–89; G. Rambaldi, "Christus heri et hodie—temas cristológicos en el pensamiento ignaciano," *Mnr,* 28 (1956), 105–120; J. Solano, "Jesuscristo en la primera semana de los Ejercicios," *MiCo,* 26 (1956), 165–176; M. A. Fiorito, "Cristocentrismo del 'Principio y Fundamento' de San Ignacio, *CyF,* 17 (1961), 3–42; H. Rahner, "The Christology of the Spiritual Exercises," in *Ignatius the Theologian,* trans. Barry, (New York, 1965), pp. 53–135.

Nadal, was spent in an almost continual presence of the Trinity.[24] It has been said that the Ignatian mystique is profoundly trinitarian, such as is found in the lives of few other saints,[25] and that it is, in addition, a mystique for service in Christ.[26] To find the center of unity of Ignatian spirituality, beyond these two frequently mentioned emphases, will enlighten us as to Ignatius' understanding of the structure and the dynamic character of the Christian life and its relation to God.

We have seen that, over and above the religious ideas he had already acquired from his education, Ignatius made a very marked rediscovery of God. Through the authentic Christ of revelation he was placed in presence of the Divine Majesty which transformed his life. For him Christ is the entrance into God, that majestic and adorable God who created and saved the whole world and who now came to bestow on Ignatius all the gifts that his life can enumerate: especially this encounter which drew him, first of all, from a life which was being lost in vanity (Loyola), and then from despair in which the spirit of Satan was already beginning to triumph (Manresa). It is important to understand that for Ignatius Christ, who leads us to the Father, and who transmits the divine life, is much more than a dogma on mediation to which faith adheres. He is the reality who delivered Ignatius from evil and committed him to the way of service. Christ is God and, in a sense, all the Trinity, who leans towards us in a continual act of love, who creates, sustains, delivers, and involves. It is through Christ that God comes to Ignatius, and it is in Christ that he lives God's life.[27]

---

24 Nadal heard this from Ignatius himself (see H. Rahner, "La vision de saint Ignace à la chapelle de La Storta," *Chr*, no. 1 (1954). Even if this direct witness comes to us especially from the *Spiritual Diary*, and thus begins in early 1544, it was not the privilege of only the later years of Ignatius' life. Although this mysticism deepened with time, it nevertheless had its roots in the far distant soil of the experiences of Loyola and Manresa (see ch. 1 above). G. Fessard rightly affirms this "unfailing continuity . . . between the mystic at Manresa building the structure of his *Exercises* and the later superior general favored with the highest visions of the Trinity" (*La dialectique des Exercices spirituels de saint Ignace de Loyola* (Paris, 1956), p. 185.

25 See G. Fessard, ibid., p. 181.

26 The chief study on Ignatius' mysticism, which brings out its principal characteristics, is that of Joseph de Guibert, in *The Jesuits: Their Spiritual Doctrine and Practice* (French original, Rome, 1953; English trans. by W. J. Young [Chicago, 1964]). See also his article "Mystique ignatienne. A propos du 'Journal spirituel' de S.Ignace de Loyola," *RAM*, 19 (1938), 3–22, 113–140.

27 "God our Creator and Lord, . . . as Creator looked with an infinite love upon his creature, and although infinite, made himself finite and willing to die for him," *LettersIgn*, p. 56. This concrete mediation which puts us in relation with the Trinity is very well expressed in the *Spiritual Diary;* see also the commen-

In this context we understand that at the time when Ignatius really encountered Christ (whose name Jesus signifies "Savior"), Christ in turn imparted to him a consciousness of his unique and universal mission—the one stimulated by Ignatius' experience of the illuminations of Manresa. Why did Ignatius' heart suddenly open up to a desire for service which evolved from desire for exploits bringing personal honor to concern to help the neighbor? At the center of the meditations at Manresa is found the contemplation of the Kingdom, which forms the axis around which the *Exercises* will revolve.[28] It was while contemplating "Christ our Lord, the Eternal King, before whom is assembled the whole world, and at the same time each one in particular" whom he creates and calls "to enter into the glory of his Father,"[29] that Ignatius' heart was opened to the apostolic ideal centered on the service of the Divine Majesty and the glory of God through the universal reign of Christ.

Thus, from the beginning of the saint's journey, Christ assumed the full place that is his, but he is a Christ who is the active presence of God entirely propitious to man and introducing him into divine intimacy. One person can help another to find Christ, or help him or her to seek intercessors. But Christ alone can reveal and really bring about the life-giving encounter with the Divine Majesty. Ignatius will always be extremely respectful of this point of encounter where the Creator unites himself to his creature, "communicates himself to the devout soul, inflaming it with his love and praise."[30] He will call to the attention of the director who is proposing the Exercises and directing the retreatant, that he should not disturb this divine order, so that, in his own words, "the Creator may deal directly with the creature and the creature directly with his Creator and Lord."[31] During Ignatius' life his *Spiritual Diary* will receive the confidences of his soul in intimate union with the divine Persons. The rest of his work will manifest his loving attention to make known to others the way which leads to God and proclaims his glory.

Hence no one will find confusion in the manner in which Ignatius speaks always of the Divine Majesty, the Creator and Lord, the Eternal Lord,

tary of D. Mollat, in *Chr,* no. 1 (1954), pp. 44–45; English in Young, *Finding God* ,pp. 87–88. Also on this subject see I. Iparraguirre, *Espíritu de san Ignacio de Loyola* (Bilbao, 1958), esp. ch. 3, "Jesu Cristo," esp. pp. 36–40.

28 On this subject see Manare, *Exhortationes,* p. 344, and in *FN,* I, 307, fn. 1; see also Nadal ibid., 306–307.

29 *SpEx,* [95].

30 Ibid., [15].

31 Ibid.

whether he is referring to the Trinity, the Father, the Son, or the Spirit.[32] In no way did these divine names separate in his mind the unity of the Trinity and his relation to each of the divine Persons. Though there is distinction, there is concretely no distance between Christ and God, between Christ and the Father, between Christ and his Spirit. When he encountered Christ in truth, Ignatius found himself in the presence of the God of Majesty, Father, Son, and Spirit. When he speaks of Christ, he is referring us to the same God

---

32 In varying cases, Ignatius attributes the title of "Eternal Lord" (SpEx. [63, 95]) not only in general to God, but also specifically to the Father or to the Son. He attributes the title "Divine Majesty" to God, but equally to the Son (*LettersIgn,* p. 44) and to the Spirit (ibid., pp. 181–182). Further, he writes of Christ also as "our Creator, Redeemer, and Lord" (*LettersIgn,* p. 29); or in speaking of the Eucharist, he indicates the profit "which the soul gains in the reception of her Creator and Lord" (*LettersIgn,* p. 85). In his practice and attributions in the *Exercises,* Ignatius makes precise use of the divine name only when he applies it explicitly to one or another divine Person because of reasons made clear by the context. On the contrary, when he can abstain from this precision, he is inclined to designate God by making reference to the divinity alone, to the Divine Majesty, and to the titles of Creator and Lord, which in his mind bring in the unity of the Persons and the harmony of their action toward the creature. The proof is this: When Ignatius is treating matters pertaining to the end and the procedures toward it, as he does about the requirements of the *Exercises* (Annotations 1–20), and about the necessity of examining oneself in the light of divine Truth (*SpEx,* [25–43]), and about the graces to be asked for throughout the Exercises, he does everything he can to put the retreatant in the presence of the God of Majesty who for him is necessarily Father, Son, and Holy Spirit, Creator and Lord. In the *Exercises* he will make precise use of the term "Father" only some fifteen times, especially on the occasions of the final colloquy or during reflections on the relationship of the Father to the Son. The same holds true for the Holy Spirit, whom he will mention only seven times. (We shall see the reason for this silence when we treat of the Second Week.) On the contrary, Christ, whose place ought to be emphasized often in those meditations where his earthly life and his re-deeming mission are concerned, will be named in each case as the context will require. The designation itself (under varying names, such as Christ, Jesus Christ, Christ our Lord, Jesus, the Son, the Word Incarnate) is found more than 150 times. Despite that, the other divine names common to the three Persons (God, the Lord, the Creator and Lord, the Divine Majesty) appear around 175 times in the *Exercises.* We have made a similar calculation for the Letters and the *Constitutions,* where we find the same consistency on the part of Ignatius. In six important letters from 1524 to 1536, the name of the Father appears 5 times, that of Christ some 12 times, and that of the Lord, of the Divine Majesty, about 105 times. In the *Constitutions,* according to the *Index de l'Examen Général et des Constitutions* published by Christus in 1962, we find the following figures: God the Father, 8 times; the Holy Spirit, 10 times; Christ, about 100 times; but God and the Divine Majesty, 255 times. Only the *Spiritual Diary* presents some peculiarities, because it analyzes the motions in Ignatius' soul in his relationship to each of the three Persons.

of Majesty, of whom the Word is the incarnate expression, drawn near to us in space and time. We recall that already at Manresa Ignatius had perceived this kind of Paradox in his prayer. He said that he then had "a great devotion to the Most Holy Trinity, and that each day he addressed a prayer to the three Persons individually." Then again he would spontaneously address another prayer to the entire Trinity. "He began to wonder how he could say four prayers to the Trinity." The problem posed itself only on the level of ideas. In practice there was no difficulty. He felt his prayer was sufficiently ordered, no doubt because it was linked to a center of unity which he could not explain. He continued in this fashion without further concern and stated that this thought "like something of little importance scarcely bothered him."[33]

On the level of ideas, the solution to Ignatius' seeming dichotomy between Christ and the Trinity is found in the unquestionable unity of the mystery of God. On the level of his lived experience, from the start and throughout his life, the answer to the problem lies in Christ who, in one and the same movement, reveals—that is gives—the Father and reunites the human race to God. Besides, it is only in Christ, the God-Man, that women and men are really able to recognize the unity of the divine mystery. Christ, the Word incarnate, tells us the most intimate secret of the Father; for he is the thought of the Father expressed for man. To come to this divine secret is already eternal life: "This is eternal life, that they know thee the only true God, and Jesus Christ whom thou hast sent."[34]

b. His Outlook on the Created Universe

A characteristic of the divine pedagogy seems to be this: To educate the human person's heart, and thus to form him or her into a likeness to Himself, through the very fact that God communicates Himself to this person, according to the manner in which He chooses to reach him. In fact, God rarely reveals himself by giving to the person a concept or description of what He is in Himself. Rather, He does so in function of the person to whom He speaks—through deeds which concern his or her destiny and that of the universe. The constant use of the divine name "Creator and Lord" which Ignatius applies to God (to the Father or the Son, and indirectly on several occasions to the Spirit), testifies to the unity of his vision of God. It also shows that he has discovered an outlook on the world and life by starting from that light which comes "from above." God manifested himself to him, through Christ, as one always acting in favor of human beings, whom he calls

33 *Autobiog,* p. 37.
34 John 17: 3.

with the whole universe to "enter into His glory." At the same time that the heart of Ignatius was opening itself up to the whole world, he was learning to respect the source of the grandeur of this world: its origin in God and the purpose for which God created it. That end is to mirror forth God's perfections to women and men, that they might praise Him for them and be happy by doing it. Henceforth it is "in the light of the Creator" as he says, and "with a love which comes from above," that he will look on all reality as animated by the divine dynamism of creation which sets it on its course toward God. It is "in the light of the Creator" that he will look on the world, interpret it, love it, use it.[35]

In the light of this experience of God as Creator, the ever active principle or source and the satisfying ultimate end of the whole of creation, two truths will impress themselves upon Ignatius' mind and dominate his very positive attitude toward the world. One concerns the subsistence of all created things in God from whom they draw their beauty; the other explains their orientation and the precious dynamism flowing from it. As a result of this outlook, for Ignatius the divine glory shines forth as something enshrined in even the tiniest atom of the created world.

Whereas God Himself speaks of "the people whom I formed for myself that they might declare my praise,"[36] and whereas the Apostle repeats "From him and through him and unto him are all things,"[37] men and women make themselves restless and anxious by starting from creatures. "If the world did not speak so much about You, my anxiety would not be what it is,"[38] and, "everything raises a question."[39] We have the power to rise from things visible to those invisible, even to God Himself who through them manifests "His eternal power and deity."[40] If creation can thus lead us to God, it is because it is, in its own way, the language and revelation of God. It bears the mark of

---

35 "May our Lord give us the light of his holy discretion, that we may know how to make use of creatures in the light of the Creator," *LettersIgn*, p. 421. "The love that moves and causes one to choose must descend from above, that is, from the love of God," *SpEx*, [184; also 338]. "In His light we judge objects with the same criterion with which God views them," I. Iparraguirre, *Líneas directivas de los Ejercicios ignacianos*, p. 35; trans. Chianese, *A Key to the Study of the Spiritual Exercises (1955)*, pp. 49–51.

36 Isa. 43:21.

37 Rom. 11:36.

38 P. Claudel, La messe là-bas, ed. NRF, p. 16. [See also Augustine, *Confessions*, I,1,1: "You have made us for Yourself, and our heart is restless until it finds its rest in You." Ed.]

39 P. Claudel, Le soulier de satin, ed. NRF, p. 330.

40 Rom. 1:20; Wis. 13:1.

God. Ignatius writes, "The same divine Spirit is present in all,"[41] and "All the good which is sought in creatures is present with greater perfection in Him who created them."[42] Hence "we must attribute all of the good that we see in creatures"[43] directly to God. Hugo Rahner links this sense of the subsistence of the whole created world in God, in Ignatius' vision, to his mystical experience, once more emphasizing the transcendence of God who awakens and directs the Ignatian experience and vision:

> His union with the Triune God, "Creator and Lord," was not just a time of quiet surrendering to the mysteries of contemplation. It was a "discovery of God in all things," or more exactly a contemplation of all things as starting from the Trinity. Ignatius contemplates "all created things" in this mysterious unity, the secret of which was graciously given him by God. Already at Manresa he contemplated "how God had created the world," how all creation had issued from this trinitarian life, from the eternal light. The vision on the banks of the Cardoner, which Ignatius could not fully describe, was a contemplation of a unique order, which remained forever fixed in his memory, "of all things in God and God in all things."[44]

Through these steps we perceive again an idea fundamental for Ignatius, namely, that "all the other creatures on the face of the earth," from the fact that they are part of God's design, constitute that way which enables us by means of these creatures to attain our own end: to praise and serve God. In the measure in which one will know how to discern in each creature its natural aptitude to proclaim the glory of God, and in the measure in which his purified heart will pay attention to this aptitude, he or she will insert himself into the universal order of creation, an order sacred and divine. At the end of his *Constitutions* Ignatius formulates this wish: He hopes that his spiritual sons will make themselves cooperators in the work of God "according to the arrangement of the sovereign providence of God our Lord. For he desires to be glorified both through the natural means which he gives as Creator and through the supernatural means which he gives as the author of grace."[45] In the life of Ignatius, the foundation of this attitude comes as a fruit of his genuine encounter with God: respect for, and love of, all creatures because they are in God. The Psalmist sings, "The heavens are telling the glory of God. . . . There is no speech, nor are there words; their voice is not

41 *LettersIgn*, p. 22.
42 *LettersIgn*, p. 309; see also *EppIgn*, V, p. 488.
43 *LettersIgn*, p. 18.
44 H. Rahner, art. cit., *Chr*, no. 1 (1954), 61–62.
45 *Cons*, [814].

heard; yet their voice goes out through all the earth, and their words to the end of the world."[46]

By his creative act God imprinted in all of creation a mark which proclaims, according to its degree, the name of God as "Creator and Lord." This same act which calls it into existence gives to the created world also a movement and an orientation. "For he commanded and they were created."[47] Caught up in its divine source, this act illumines the movement it initiates: Everything it touches it sets into motion, on its course toward the glorification of God.

In Manresa when Ignatius received the graces enumerated in his *Autobiography,* he enjoyed this experience of the God who communicated Himself to him in His creative activity.[48] In his case also "this experience of our continual springing forth" from God was transformed into "an experience of being loved."[49]

> God, by the same movement by which he gives being to the creature, leads the creature back to himself. Thus the creative "let there be" signifies "come" ("No one can come to me unless the Father . . . draws him" (John 6:44). In man there is an ontological and spiritual dependence with regard to God, but it is a dynamic dependence in which God, "deeper within me than my innermost depths" (*intimior intimo meo* [Augustine, *Confessions,* VIII, 6, 11]) draws man to himself. According to the fifteenth Annotation, God is the one who "communicates himself to the soul, inflaming it with his love and praise." By one and the same act God creates us and attracts us.[50]

This reasoning which sees everything as starting from God could not let human beings remain in isolation in regard to their relationship to God. Thus Ignatius perceived all of creation, and himself within it, as being drawn into this movement of "the Light of the world" who creates and attracts. As a consequence, this "economy" or plan of the creative act influenced Ignatius'

46 Ps. 18:2,4–5.
47 Ps. 148:5.
48 *Autobiog,* no. 29.
49 J. Corbon, *L'expérience chrétienne dans la Bible,* coll. Cahiers de la Pierre-qui-vive (Paris, 1963), p. 36.
50 Extract from the notes of a course on the *Exercises* given by J. Lewis, (Immaculée-Conception, Montréal, 1961). [For the tradition of dogmatic theology on God's purpose in creating, see,e.g., P. J. Donnelly, "St. Thomas and the Ultimate Purpose of Creation," *Theological Studies,* 2 (1941), 53–83; "The Doctrine of the Vatican Council on the End of Creation," ibid, 4 (1943), 3–33; J. Pohle, *God, the Author of Nature and the Supernatural* (St. Louis, 1934), pp. 80–90; L. Ott, *Fundamentals of Catholic Dogma* (Rockford, Il., 1974), pp. 81–82. Ed.]

outlook on the created world. Things not only subsist in God and draw their goodness from his goodness, but they are set in motion on their course toward him—all of creation longs "to enter into the glory of God." For the moment Ignatius did not trouble himself to understand the modes of this return to God, on the different levels of being, such as spiritualization, or divinization. He took the problem from a higher level, from the divine purpose, from God who loves his creation and who calls it back to himself. For God, who drew everything out of nothingness through love, could not have done this and then have what he loves perish; only the free creature, the human person, would be able to withdraw himself from this divine attracting of the whole created world. The Scriptural prayer says to God: "Thou lovest all things that exist, and hast loathing for none of the things thou hast made; for thou wouldst not have made anything if thou hadst hated it." He is the Lord, lover of life, whose "immortal spirit is in all things."[51] That is why "all creation waits with eager longing for the revealing of the sons of God," for the manifestation of the children of God through whom, as intermediary creatures ordained to God, the rest of creation will attain its end.[52]

St Ignatius has insisted much on this consideration, not only of the original grandeur of the created world, but also of its ordination to God, a positive ordination which he considers as starting from God who creates in order to attract to himself. He will say, "May His holy name be praised and exalted in all and by all creatures, which are created and ordained to an end that is so just and proper."[53] It was in view of this divine glory that "all creatures were created and ordered by His eternal wisdom."[54] As a consequence, "not merely among men, but not even among the angels, is there a nobler work than glorifying the Creator and bringing His creatures to Him as far as their capacities permit."[55] The person who makes himself or herself conscious of

---

51 Wis 12:1; see the whole context, 11:21–12:2.
52 Rom 8:19. In its note k on this verse, the *Jerusalem Bible* (ed. 1966, p. 281) makes the following comment on this passage of St. Paul: "The material world, created for man, shares his destiny. It was cursed for man's sin, Gen. 3:17, and is therefore now deformed: impotent and decadent, vv. 19–22. But like man's body, destined to be glorified, it too is to be redeemed, vv. 21, 23; it will share the glorious liberty of the children of God, v. 21. For the Greek philosopher matter was evil and the spirit must be delivered from it; Christianity regards matter as itself enslaved and to be set free. In other texts also salvation is extended to creatures (especially angels) other than man, see Col. 1:20; Eph. 1:10; 2 Peter 3:13; Apoc. 21:1–5."
53 *LettersIgn* p. 83.
54 Ibid., p. 131.
55 Ibid., pp. 122–123.

the love of God thus manifested, will have to devote himself, in concretely and in a spirit of fidelity, to "our Lord, in whose service, praise, and glory life and all things else should be ordered."[56] The work of salvation, of which Ignatius is speaking, like the end of man, truly takes in "all the other things on the face of the earth" as made for the glory of God.

c. *His Concept of the Human Person and His or Her Vocation*

i. *In Ignatius' Own Experience*

The Ignatian vision of the world, as it has been described thus far, flows from his becoming aware that the whole universe is in movement toward God. Without knowing it, the world proclaims its Lord and evolves toward a fuller participation in the divine glory. Thus it is a mirror revealing God's power and splendor to us, who by means of it can come to know God better, and praise and love him better, and be self-fulfilled or happy by doing this. This outlook on the world touches also the personal life of Ignatius and places it within this universal movement. The substantial changes which his experience of the mystery of God introduces into his life amply testify to this. The human creature, a conscious and free creature, ought to assume the responsibility for this return of the world to the Father.

Some directors and writers, by neglecting the amplitude which in Ignatius takes in his outlook both on God and all his creation, rather ordinarily give to the text of the Foundation of the *Exercises* an interpretation which is too literal. In this way they limit the ideas contained in it to the following:

> The human person is created for God, for His glorification;
>   and everything else ought to be used to lead him or her to God.
> Therefore, *I* am destined for this end, and everything else ought to help *me*
>   toward it, for the glorification of God and the salvation of my soul.

Ignatius himself drew from the Foundation a different interpretation which he lived out in practice. It proceeds, too, in a different direction (at least in part, for obviously it in no way excludes the seeking of one's personal salvation which God desires). We now present that interpretation, which is more open and more in conformity with Ignatius' spirit or tenor of thought. For it receives its authority from (1) the saint's whole life in the concrete, (2) the spirit and even the letter of his *Constitutions of the Society of Jesus,* and

---

56   Ibid., p. 216.

(3) the internal logic of the *Exercises* themselves. This interpretation runs as follows:

> The human being is created for God, for His glorification; and everything else ought to be considered as a means to lead him or her to God.
>
> Therefore I shall use all the rest of creation as means to lead *humankind* to God, that is, to the praising and glorification of Him which is the salvation of any person man and the well-being of all creation.

The whole difference lies in this: When Ignatius says, *"the human being"* is created for God," he does not intend the conclusion to be first of all or exclusively that *"I"* am created for God, but "the human being," that is, *"all* human beings"—the whole human race of which I am a member—are "created for God." Ignatius' founding of the Society of Jesus will be an exemplification of this understanding of the Foundation, and of his living it out in practice. In other words, Ignatius will be making, in the spirit of the Kingdom (*Exercises,* [96]), a use as enlightened as possible of the human and "natural means" and also of the "supernatural means" (*Constitutions,* [814]), in order to lead mankind, in the concrete, to its end, which is God. It is interesting to note that the first "Formula of the Institute," which was approved by Popes Paul III in 1540 and Julius III in 1550, before the definitive redaction of the *Constitutions,* did not make even an allusion to personal salvation in formulating the end explicitly pursued by the new Society. Whoever wanted to join this Society was to seek to work for the good of souls through the various means proposed by its Institute.[57]

ii. *In His View of the Dynamism of the Created World*

If we come back to the luminous source which informed Ignatius' spiritual understanding—his experience of God's mystery or saving plan as our chief source of guidance—we understand that everything is measured by that supreme end which is also at the origin of the human race: the glory and

---

57 The Formula of the Institute of 1540 reads: "Whoever desires to serve as a soldier of God beneath the banner of the cross in our Society . . . should keep what follows in mind. He is a member of a Society founded chiefly for this purpose: to strive especially for the progress of souls in Christian life and doctrine." The official text of Ignatius' *Constitutions* (1558) will state: "The end of the is Society is to devote itself with God's grace not only to the salvation and perfection of the members' own souls, but also with that same grace to labor strenuously in giving aid toward the salvation and perfection of their fellowmen" (*Examen,* [3]; see also *Cons,* [156, 163, 204, 258, 307, 603, 813]). The praise or glorification of God, Ignatius' supreme end to which he ultimately subordinates all other things, is mentioned 259 times in his *Constitutions* alone.

majesty of God. The last grace of the *Exercises,* for which the retreatant asks in the Contemplation to Attain Love, takes up again this sublime end to which are ordained all intermediary ends, the use of natural and supernatural means, as well as the very work of the salvation of others and of personal salvation: "that . . . I may in all things love and serve the Divine Majesty."[58]

There is a text of Ignatius which expressly testifies to the fact that in his mind the use of human means (such as intellectual work) and of supernatural means (such as progress in charity) was really oriented to this universal end beyond the concern for one's own salvation: to lead the world back to God in the perspective of a cooperation with the divine work. The text in question is in the letter of May, 1547, "to the Fathers and Brothers of Coimbra," in which Ignatius states to the scholastics who were studying:

> And I wish that you should preserve this union and lasting love, not only among yourselves, but that you extend it to all, and endeavor to enkindle in your souls the lively desire for the salvation of your neighbor, gauging the value of each soul from the price our Lord paid of His life's blood. This you do on the one hand *by acquiring learning* and on the other *by increasing fraternal charity,* making yourselves *perfect instruments of God's grace and co-laborers* in the *sublime work* of leading *God's creatures back to Him* as their *supreme end.*[59]

For Ignatius, the vocation of men and women in the divine plan is found clearly defined by the purpose God has in mind for the whole of creation. On the one hand, creation is offered to them as a way or means to attain their end; on the other, they transforms themselves into a way or means, willed by God, by which all of creation evolves until through them it reaches and praises God in the whole Christ. The Creator thus gives them the means of praising Him: and this praise is achieved by means of their freely accepting their responsibility to insert themselves into this same movement of creation on its return to God. All this is done in order that through the hearts of men and women the whole of creation may sing of the praise or glory of God.

It was when he was converted at Manresa that Ignatius became aware of this economy or arrangement of solidarity which is an image of the unity of the divine plan, St. Paul's "mystery of God" (Col. 2:2); and henceforth,

---

58 *SpEx,* [23 and 233]. The end of the text of the Foundation concerns a particular person, the retreatant, the personal "I." That is in perfect harmony with the larger vision we are suggesting, the vision of the salvation of mankind. That is the Ignatian style as we shall see in the Kingdom where the task that is proposed in the text is explicitly universal, while the end aims at the very personal work of purification.

59 *LettersIgn,* p. 128; the italics are ours.

setting out from God, he will turn toward creation to contemplate the traces of God within it. In a return of love for this divine countenance which he found offered to him in the created world (his sense of God's immanence), he will devote his entire self to the task of saving the world and of leading it to God. On this subject mention has been made of a mystique of "the acceptance of the world."[60]

According to the study of Adolph Haas, which Maurice Giuliani quotes, "the Ignatian mystique," as it is expressed in the *Spiritual Diary,* is perfected "in a humble love, turned toward the earth, and given with reverence and service."[61] Ignatius wrote to Diego Miró: " . . . if all we looked for in our vocation was to walk safely, and if to get away from danger we had to sacrifice the good of souls, we should not be living and associating with our neighbors. But according to our vocation we do associate with all; rather, as St. Paul says of himself (1 Cor. 9:22), we should make ourselves all things to all men to gain all to Christ."[62] Similarly he wrote to a bishop: "While we should not give up tasks which we have received and are fulfilling for God's honor, it is possible that the greatness of love which overwhelms the soul should find relief even in things that are earthly and base, but loves them all for God our Lord and insofar as they are directed to his glory and service."[63]

It is in the light of his "divine" sense or outlook on creation that we must interpret Ignatius' insistence on the use of human means, "employed not that we may put our confidence in them, but that we may cooperate with divine grace, according to the arrangement of the sovereign providence of God our Lord."[64] This practice which seeks the glory of God is measured by "the love of God in all things." Ignatius asks, as a grace, for continual growth in this love: "May it please our Lord for his infinite and supreme goodness to increase these desires of yours to love him above all things, so that you will place not only a part but the whole of your love and desire in the same Lord, and in all creatures for His sake."[65]

---

60 See *Ign,* (1956,) 139–141, "Abreast of the World," condensed by F. Jonckheere from the article of B. Schneider, "Der Weltliche Heilige Ignatius von Loyola und die Fürsten seiner Zeit," *GuL,* 27 (1954), 35–58.
61 M. Giuliani, in *S. Ignace: Journal Spirituel, traduit et commentée* (Paris, 1959), Introduction, p. 33. Dostoevski expresses a similar mysticism *The Brothers Karamazov.* When Aliocha, after the vision of the wedding feast at Cana, kisses the earth and promises it eternal love and leaves on the advice of the starets Zozime "to live in the world" (Bk. 7, ch. 4).
62 *LettersIgn,* p. 284.
63 Ibid., p. 131.
64 *Cons,* [814]. See also *LettersIgn,* pp. 191–194, 401–402.
65 *LettersIgn,* p. 50.

In the mind and language of Ignatius, this vocation which is proper to man implies some characteristics which make its meaning more explicit. First, this mission is directed toward the world, which was created as a means to lead us to God. Yet by a curious inversion of perspective, Ignatius rarely defines it in direct function of the world, but always by starting from God: He calls it willing "service of the Divine Majesty." Second, it is in Christ—the whole Christ which includes his Mystical Body, the Church—that Ignatius locates this signal service of God through creation. Third, the measure of "discreet charity" always goes hand in hand with the authentic service of God accomplished through any created reality. An examination of these three characteristic notes will take us back to that source which gives its truth and its depth to Ignatius' vision, that is, the transcendence of the divine plan of creation and redemption.

A First Characteristic: Service of the Divine Majesty

Ignatius designates the role which mankind has acquired in the work of creation and of redemption by the phrase "service of the Divine Majesty." "To serve" summarizes his whole thought on the meaning of human existence, and at the same time it reveals its grandeur. For to serve is to accept that task which completes the divine work entrusted to women and men for their own fulfillment. To serve is to collaborate with God in order to accomplish his glorious work. By respecting this orientation of creatures, by helping other persons to save themselves, they take an active part in the plan and the very work of God, who draws from this arrangement greater praise or glory to Himself, with proportionately greater happiness for themselves through eternity. God made everything for this purpose; everything is called to enter into the divine glory. In this sense, a person's fullest collaboration with regard to creatures as they are being drawn by God to Himself results in an "ever greater glory of God."[66] This collaboration is a humble service and a continuous homage rendered to the Divine Majesty. We should notice that by our looking at the problem of service and by our starting with the grandeur of man's destiny in God's plan, and in function of the universe in its movement toward its fulfillment in God, the human person is not threatened with depreciation in any way. He or she will never be more completely fulfilled in the movement of his created being than by taking his place in this

---

66 This is the meaning of the motto which directed Ignatius' life and which he left to the Society: for the greater glory of God *(ad majorem Dei gloriam)*. [The phrase is also his criterion for the making of decisions. See W. Ong, " 'A.M.D.G.': Dedication or Directive?," *Review for Religious*, 11 (1952), 257–264. Ed.]

divine economy or arrangement which reveals to him the real meaning of his existence. Having come from God, the person is, by his or her nature, set in motion toward God. To integrate oneself, by grace, in this movement of all creation is to exist more fully. And to serve the Divine Majesty is, in this perspective, to offer oneself freely to this ascension which Christian salvation entails.

However, if we are to be correct and complete, we must add that Ignatius perceived this view of the service of God in a dynamic context, that of the lover who gives himself and seeks to be loved for the good of the one beloved. That is why Ignatius' attitude will ripen into a sort of obsession for serving God. To refuse this service, to take it lightly, or to separate any part of one's life from it, is not only to neglect a tremendous responsibility or to hamper the work of the salvation of souls; but even far more, it is to be ungrateful, and thereby to fail to respond fully to the Love who has given himself without measure. Ignatius writes: "How he, the Creator, has become man, and has passed from eternal life to death here in time, and death for our sins."[67] If, from now on in his life, Ignatius reaches out to everything, commits himself to everything, makes use of everything, the reason is, we might say, that everything should return to God. There is still more: The love of God becomes involved in everything. The interest of his Divine Majesty is playing a part everywhere, since everything exists for God.[68]

---

67 *SpEx*, [53]. See also below on the subject of evil conceived as ingratitude.
68 This discovery of the service of God is truly characteristic of Ignatius' conversion. Following the illuminations which brought about this discovery, he transformed his life into a quest for the service of God in all things. He then set out on a long road which, from the pilgrimage to the Holy Land and his studies in Spain and Paris, led him after twenty years of faithful searching to this form of service which God was asking of him as founder of a new religious institute. Thus the idea of the service of God cuts across all his writings just as it animates all his works. For examples, see *Autobiog.*, nos. 11, 14, 21, 27, 36, 60, 82, 99, and also Thiry's Introduction to *Le Récit du Pèlerin*, p. 19). In the *Exercises* it is mentioned almost forty times (see St. Ignace: *Exercices spirituels: Traduits et annotés* par F. Courel (Paris, 1960), p. 223 s.v. *Service* and *Servir*; SpExMHS-Jte, Index, p. 732; *LettersIgn*, pp 73, 184, on "the greater glory of God" outside a context of decision-making; esp. too, see *SpEx*, [9, 15, 16, 20, 46, 97, 155, 157, 169, 233, 263, 370]. His Letters are similarly filled with statements about this same topic; see, e.g., three letters of 1532 and 1536, respectively to Martín García de Oñaz, Isabel Roser, and Jaime Cazador (*EppIgn*, I, 77, 83, 93; *LettersIgn*, pp. 5, 9, 12), where the expression appears 13, 11, and 12 times. The *Examen* and the *Constitutions* are also revealing in this respect: In them everything is dictated and measured by the service of the glory of God, from the end and general orientation of the Order (see *LettersIgn*, p. 188) to the points of detail concerning the admission of candidates, the experiences of the novices, the vows, the curriculum of studies, dismissals, the choice of superiors and of minis-

A Second Characteristic: "In Christ."

"We are helpers of God." The task of any person (which is willed by God, determined by him, and consists in the service of the Divine Majesty in everything), is accomplished "in Christ,"—in Christ "our Creator, Redeemer, and Lord." This is a further characteristic of the vision of Christian existence in the Ignatian universe as viewed in the light of God's plan of salvation. Our aim here is not to prove that Ignatius really affirmed the necessity of going through Christ. The entire Christocentric aspect of his work, and especially of the *Exercises,* is sufficient evidence for that. What is important here is that we understand how this fact becomes a part of Ignatius' own experience, gives it its depth, and reveals the religious and psychological dynamism of the service of God as he explicitly envisages it.

At the beginning of Ignatius' spiritual life, let us remember, he found deliverance in Christ, while he was experiencing the marvel of Christ's mediation. At that same time Christ introduced him to the intimacy of the divine trinitarian life. He is the Christ of Majesty, the eternal Lord whom Ignatius encountered at Loyola and Manresa, and through whom he underwent an experience of discovery, a discovery which placed him in the presence of the true God who is always present to human beings and to the whole of creation, to keep them in existence and to share his glory with them. This knowledge of the divine power, grandeur, and goodness which in the Word Incarnate have come so near to mankind, arouses in the soul that is open, the deepest sentiments of adoration and gratitude.

This dialectical interaction of understanding, adoration, and gratitude, within the economy of grace which delivers and divinizes, engenders the desire for service, a desire which "comes from above,"[69] and which disposes one for the most perfect form of charity, of love lived out: service of the Divine Majesty through the whole of creation made to issue in praise of God.

tries, and the like. See the *Index de l'Examen Général et des Constitutions* (Paris: Christus, 1962). Other references on the same subject are: R. Cantin, "Le troisième degré d'humilité *et la gloire de Dieu selon saint Ignace de Loyola," ScE,* 8 (1956), especially pp. 256–262; *DeGuiJes,* pp. 55–59, 176–181; H. Rahner, *Chr,* no. 1 (1954), 40–41; Coathalem, *Ignatian Insights,* pp. 22–23; and *LettersIgn,* pp. 73, 112–113, 184, 190–194, 268; [see also Ganss in *ConsS-JComm,* pp. 3, 4, 7–11; in *Jesuit Religious Life Today* (St. Louis, 1977), pp. 17–20. Ed.]

69 "These desires, which come from the Lord and Creator of us all rather than from any natural cause. . . ," *LettersIgn,* p. 43. "And yet you see and you understand that these desires of serving Christ our Lord are not your own, but come to you from our Lord," ibid., p. 20. Ignatius will have the retreatant ask for these spiritual desires, which he considers to be a criterion for discernment, as a fruit of the Holy Spirit (see *LettersIgn,* pp. 50, 100, 154, 232, 236–237, 282.

This is the movement which the Contemplation to Attain Love recalls at the end of the Exercises when the retreatant, purified through contact with the saving plan of Christ, can comprehend interiorly the extent and the depth of the divine gift which calls for a return of love and service. Ask, Ignatius specifies, for "an intimate knowledge of the many blessings received, so that filled with gratitude for all, I may in all things love and serve the Divine Majesty." "The liberality of God," writes Dumeige, "invites the generosity of man, and man then draws all things along with himself in an upward movement to present them to the untiring goodness of the Creator. God is infinitely generous, inexhaustibly liberal in his love for man; and man in his turn ought to work for God's praise, truth, and glory."[70]

From the time of his experience of God's closeness at Loyola, while he "was spending some time in writing and praying," Ignatius tells us that "his greatest consolation flowed from his gazing at the sky and the stars, which he did frequently and for long periods of time because it was then that he felt an extraordinary desire to serve our Lord"[71] This contemplation not only intensified his sense of the Divine Majesty that he had encountered in Christ, but it also aroused an interior movement of return to God which is primarily reverence, adoration, and gratitude, but which also seeks to express itself in a gift of self, in loving service of the Lord.

Ignatius' initial desire, which was nourished by his contemplation of God and his work of creation and redemption, and which urged him to give himself,[72] never failed him. It is expressed, first of all, as the call addressed to him by the eternal Lord in the Kingdom, inviting him to associate himself with him and labor with him *(mecum)* for the salvation of the world. And later, after the graces of Vivarola[73] will have deepened the community aspect of his life, his desire and his insistent prayer will find their realization strongly expressed in his vision at La Storta in November 1537, in which God the Father appeared to him, "placed him with his Son," and said to his Son, "I desire you to take this man as your servant." The foundation of the Society of Jesus, coming at the end of this movement toward service of God in Christ, manifested it in a new way, a way entirely communitarian and ecclesial. Hugo Rahner concludes: "This indissoluble link of all service of

---

70 *SpEx,* [233]; *Lettres,* p. 16.
71 *Autobiog,* no. 11.
72 "For the love of Christ controls us" (2 Cor. 5:14).
73 H. Rahner, *Chr,* no. 1 (1954), 57.

Christ with the visible head of the Church will henceforth be the distinctive mark of all the graces which Ignatius will receive."[74]

A Third Characteristic: "In the Measure of Discreet Charity"

If the service of the Lord became a sort of obsession with Ignatius, if it engendered an abiding drive toward achieving it in all things, it was never transformed into an ideal for human action which got lost in the temporal order and which was assured by its visible and immediate results there.[75] Its source is the vision of God; its measuring rod remains the divine purpose or will. Ignatius posed the famous problem of a greater perfection and of the imitation of Christ, considered, not in themselves, but in relation to the greater glory of God.[76] For him, the perfection of our life, as disciples of Christ, is not measured by our way of seeing things, no matter how objective it may be, nor is the perfection of our service measured by its chances of success; rather, everything is measured by starting from God's viewpoint— from his universal plan, and from his will in particular cases. For his part man commits himself to God without reserve and is unceasingly attentive,

74   Ibidem. See also J. Solano, "Fundamentos Neotestamentarios y Dogmáticos de la Espiritualidad Ignaciana," *Mnr,* 28 (1956), 123-134.

75   "When he undertook something, most frequently he seemed not to count on any human means, but to rely only on divine providence; but in carrying it out and bringing it to completion, he tried all means to achieve success. Yet here too he used cautious care to place the hope of accomplishing it, not in the human means (which are used as instruments to achieve it), but in God, the true author of all that is good; so that, however a matter might turn out, he was always in a spirit of joy and peace" (Ribadeneira, *Vita Ignatii Loyolae* (1572), Book 5, ch. 11, in *FN*, IV, 882). [The same thought, differently worded by Ribadeneira, is found in *FN*. III, 631, no. 14, and *FN*, IV, 846; and similar thought from Ignatius' own writings appears in *Cons*, [813-814]. *FN*, IV, 846, fn. 27 gives a paradoxical phrasing of Hevenesi in 1705: "So trust in God as if all the success of affairs depended on yourself, and nothing on God. Nevertheless, so work in them as if you were to accomplish nothing in them, and God everything." Neither of these formulations, precisely so worded, is found in Ignatius' own writings, and either can be interpreted in a way consonant with sound theology. Both of them have been formulated more simply and regarded as Ignatian maxims, (1) Ribadeneira's as "Pray as if everything depended on God, and work as if everything depended on you," and (2) Hevenesi's as "Pray as if everything depended on you, and work as if everything depended on God." Since the 1950s there have been extensive and subtle discussions of these two formulae. See *FN*, III. 631, fn. 14: *DeGuiJes*, p. 148, fn. 55; and *Studies in the Spirituality of Jesuits*, X (1978), 320; also fn. 70 of ch. 3 below. Ed.]

76   Cantin studied this problem very carefully in "Le troisième degré," *ScE,* 8 (1956), 237-266.

under the guidance of the Spirit, to know the desires of the divine good pleasure. Such a person will ask: What will be more pleasing to God, and consequently more conducive in the long run to my spiritual growth and happiness? For the amount or extent of the service which she or he will give "without counting the cost" comes to him "from above," from the ways of God which are not always our ways.[77]

In the Foundation, the use or rejection of something "insofar as" *(tantum . . . quantum)* it helps or hinders, according to the interpretation we have proposed for this text, is presented as a measuring rod which does not depend solely or exclusively on the nature of created things, (since all things are good in themselves), but on the general and particular will of God.[78] It directly touches on the problem of discreet charity *(caritas discreta),* of this "more" *(magis)* or "greater" *(major)* in a love which in no way does away with discretion. It directly touches also on a "discernment" which is measured or guided by starting from God and the action of his Spirit in a human person.[79] Ignatius ended almost all of his letters by asking, for himself and his correspondent, "the grace to understand God's will so as to accomplish it entirely." This petition, through the many varied forms it takes, is always related to the divine plan of salvation. To understand God's present will in order to accomplish it is to insert one's own life and action into that plan, in the measure proposed by God. This demands from one a continual self-purification, for the purpose of ordering oneself to God in such a way that one can act "without coming to a decision through any disordered attachment." For there does exist, in our lives, evil under its many forms and appearances.

d. Ignatius' View on the Problem of Evil

The preceding reflections give rise to a few conclusions on the problem of evil, to which we shall limit ourselves here. For we shall devote a whole

---

77 In this case Ignatius' measuring rod, "from above" *(de arriba),* is often concretized and comes to us through the intermediary of superiors, laws, and the hierarchical Church. However, no fixed limit can be imposed upon it; and this requires that official interpreters should have a flexibility which is always attentive to the movements of the Spirit. On this subject read the study of J. Lewis, *Le gouvernement spirituel selon saint Ignace de Loyola* (Paris, 1961).

78 "Insofar as" *(tantum . . . quantum): SpEx,* [23; see also 16, 98, 146, 147, 155, 168). See G. Fessard, *La dialectique,* pp. 305ff., and 0. Cullmann, *Christ et le temps* (1957), p. 152.

79 See H. Carrier, "La 'caritas discreta' et les Exercices spirituels," *ScE,* 8 (1956), 171-203.

chapter to the problem of evil later, when we treat the exercises of the First Week.

What we have said about Ignatius' vision of the created world and the mission of man as conceived in the supreme guiding light of God's plan of salvation and spiritual growth gives greater precision also to Ignatius' outlook on evil. Indeed, this dynamic vision of the relationship that exists between the world and God, in a context of continual exchange inspired by love, emphasizes the meaning and the import of sin. That is, sin is a disorder that man has introduced into his life and into the universe, and simultaneously an infidelity to God's indefatigable love. It is a disorder, that is, a deformation of the original and real world order, an order related to the loving God who gives himself and draws all things to himself. In this context sin is a horror which man experiences great difficulty in recognizing fully. Sin is an act that is against the nature of creation as well as against the Love who raises and draws created being to himself. The movement of finality inscribed in the created nature of the universe is indeed disturbed and scoffed at by man who had been created to order it according to the image and likeness of God. Consequently, what had been destined for the glorification of God and for salvation properly speaking, became "subjected to futility"[80] and doomed to everlasting death. So the sin which started out to be a simple refusal to accept the natural order of things is transformed into a rejection of the Divine Love, whose only purpose in creating was love. Sin, in the Ignatian universe, is an upside-down world. The world, conceived in so positive a fashion in God's plan, and restored to its original rectitude by the saving efforts of Christ, experiences an upheaval that uproots and transforms it into an instrument of evil that strikes against the glorification of God.

Thus, for Ignatius, evil is found primarily in the heart of the human being. Indeed sin, when considered in its origin and reverberation, is defined from the human point of view as a disordered use of creation, a use deviating from the initial creative order. The human free will, meant to portray the trace of God and to proclaim his glory, now profanes its own sacred character and devotes itself to serving another purpose which is its own satisfaction and, indirectly, the building up of the kingdom of Satan.[81]

Furthermore, to think about the presence of evil in the world is, for Ignatius, also to call to mind the work of an agent who is very active, one

---

80 Rom. 8:20.
81 See the meditation on the Two Standards where sin, like the good, is envisaged under an aspect which is at the same time personal, particular, and universal (*SpEx*, [136–147].

whom man must confront time and time again. Ignatius calls Satan "the enemy of human nature."[82] Satan is the one who exploits a person in his or her use of creation and pushes him in the direction to which his weakness is already inclining him. If "beauty seduces the flesh to gain passage to the soul,"[83] a person may readily come between creation and its God; and creation which should find in human beings a road to God, comes up against a wall of selfishness that upsets the destinies of human beings and the universe. Sin makes them a captive of itself and draws all creation into its prison. In the *Exercises* even the sin of the angels is characterized by this opting for self which opposes the creature to its Creator: "recalling that they were created in the state of grace, they did not want to make use of the freedom God gave them to reverence and obey their Creator and Lord, and so falling into pride, they were changed from grace to hatred of God, and cast out of heaven into hell."[84] Human persons too follow a similar path in the world of sin.

This understanding of evil is drawn from the positive concept Ignatius had of created existence and its basic orientation. Seen in the context of the spiritual formation of the saint which impressed on him the fact that God created the harmonious relation existing between Himself, man, and the world, evil is necessarily situated, in his vision, on this theological or religious level which is both individual and cosmic. Only this more open horizon can explain the "cry of wonder accompanied by surging emotion" of the Ignatian meditation on "personal sin," where the extent of the pardon that has been granted is measured by the extent of man's sin against God and the whole of creation:

> Fifth Point: This is a cry of wonder accompanied by surging emotion as I pass in review all creatures. How is it that they have permitted me to live, and have sustained me in life! Why have the angels, though they are the sword of God's justice, tolerated me, guarded me, and prayed for me? Why have the saints interceded for me and asked favors for me! And the heavens, sun, moon, stars and the elements: the fruits, birds, fishes and the animals—why have they all been at my service! How is it that the earth did not open to swallow me up, and create new hells in which I should be tormented forever![85]

---

82 *SpEx,* [7, 8, 10, 12, 135, 136, 217, 274]; see also the Rules for the discernment of spirits, [313–336], and the Notes concerning Scruples, [345–350]; and *LettersIgn,* pp. 18,19, 51, 56, 57, 184.
83 Simone Weil, *La pesanteur et la grâce* (Paris, 1950), p. 170.
84 *SpEx,* [50].
85 Ibid., [60].

Only a keen sense of sin viewed as an offense and infidelity against God and the whole of creation can give birth to such sentiments of guilt, love, and admiration—where perhaps a touch of mystical graces can be seen.[86]

3. Conclusion: The Necessity of Ordering One's Life

a. In Ignatius' Global Vision

The characteristic mark of Ignatius' global vision is primarily the amplitude which it draws from its starting point and the very personalized precision of its term. It takes its start from God's purpose and his very gaze on all creation, and it culminates in the heart of man—precisely this present person in the concrete. This path corresponds exactly with the path that Ignatius' own life followed. In the light of the divine mystery or plan of salvation, he discovered the meaning of his own personal situation and ordered his life in function of the divine work in the universe. Generally, in his mind, the universal order throws light on the particular, and this allows the particular to be integrated perfectly, with accuracy and truth, into the universe which it joins in its movement of return. The universe comes from God, who manifests himself to man and who continually places him in a particular place and time as part of his overall plan; and man opens his heart to the dimensions which the divine plan reveals to him and which grace allows him to attain.[87]

---

86 *SpEx*, [60]. A similar expression is found in a work of Dostoevski, in which a young man, before dying, discovers his "guilt" toward the whole of creation: "His room faced the garden, planted with old trees; the buds had blossomed, the birds had come and were singing under the window; he looked at them with great pleasure and began to ask pardon of them: 'Oh birds of the good God, joyful birds, forgive me for I have also sinned against you.' None of us could understand him, and he wept with joy: 'Yes, the glory of God surrounded me: the birds, the trees, the prairies, the skies; I alone lived in shame, dishonoring creation, I perceived neither their beauty nor their glory.' " (*The Brothers Karamazov*, Bk. 6, ch. 2).

87 It is perhaps at this level that we should seek the common denominator which ought to exist in the more or less variable methods of conducting exercises and retreats. The end to be attained in all of them is to foster in the exercitant this encounter with the universal and the divine. The encounter throws light on his or her personal destiny, serves as the measure of his or her actions, and effectively brings about the readjustment that this meeting with the Truth imposes on him or her. The "Truth frees and sanctifies" only on condition that he or she truly meets and welcomes it—or better, Him. But the ways in which God communicates Himself are certainly multiple. Some of them count directly on the revealed message, or on the liturgical actuation of the Christian mystery or plan of salvation, or on the community experience which reveals God through the authentic

But what really characterizes this vision is its existential realism. Not only does it take hold of a particular concrete person, in the very situation in which he finds himself, to involve him in the working out of his own destiny; but it also reveals to him the tragic side of his destiny. It shows him the profound rift that exists in his being, a rift that without God's grace would render his position forever untenable. This division is caused by the encounter or opposition of the extremes he experiences within himself: his grandeur expressed by his position in and his responsibility for creation, and his profound misery, resulting from the evil within him which delivers him up to the grip of the created world and to the inexhaustible wiles of Satan. True peace which will overcome this conflict will be the fruit of grace which ordinarily comes with a certain spiritual maturity. However, it will be a peace that must be won daily. "Watch and pray."

Looked at in this way, man is always in trouble and in need of God. With God's help he must continually strive for order in his life, so that he may respond to man and God, stay in the state of grace, and accomplish the complex work of his human and divine destiny. Ignatius is the enemy of false peace which blinds, of calmness parading as "common sense," which too often masks a lazy refusal to offer the Lord one's "good will," to which alone God responds. He accepts "the divine risk" in his life without compromise. Having started on such a high level, continually referring to the greater praise and glory of God, Ignatius all of a sudden seems to lose himself in a maze of details concerning the ordering of one's life. Only in this light can the "Ignatian paradoxes"[88] be understood: They indicate a very exact grasp of reality rather than a more or less fanciful taste for minutiae. For in this regime of details—Ignatius loyally practiced what he preached—he remained sovereignly free, capable of rising to the heights, and constantly desirous of being

meeting with men and women. The Ignatian method of the *Exercises,* for its part, sets forth a clarifying understanding of the revealed message, aims to make all the person's faculties ready to grasp that message, and attributes a capital and characteristic importance to prayer (under its many, varied, and flexible forms) that in it the "Creator and Lord in person" may "communicate Himself to the devout soul in quest of the divine will, that He inflame it with love of Himself, and dispose it for the way in which it could better serve God in the future" (*SpEx,* [15]).

88 "As is always the case with Ignatius, the spiritual inspiration penetrates into the material details of his life," states Dumeige in his Introduction to *Lettres,* p. 247. See also Fessard, *La dialectique,* pp. 96–100, who discusses the problem by considering the differing opinions of Bremond and Cavallera, and proposes his own interpretation.

faithful to the Holy Spirit.[89] His incredible respect for small practices, far from imprisoning him and blocking his response to graces, even mystical graces, finds him always ready to offer himself to the Lord who alone completes in us the work of grace and salvation.

b. In the Principle and Foundation of the Exercises

The necessity of ordering one's life in all things is the reason, to a great extent, for the logical march of thought adopted in the Ignatian *Exercises*.[90] It envisages practically all the areas of life in which a person can be the victim of an attachment which he fosters for his self-interest and which gives rise to "disordered affections." Ignatius uses this term to express the source of evil that exists in the heart of man, who alone is the source responsible for the disorder introduced into the universe in its movement toward God. Ignatius intended the Foundation of the Exercises to be a starting point to introduce the retreatant to the problem. We have seen that the preparation for the Exercises ought to awaken the retreatant to a spiritual ideal that will fill him with a sincere desire to respond to God's will in all things (fifth Annotation).

89 Among other well-known letters of Ignatius is the famous one he sent to Juan Nuñez in Ethiopia. It is a long letter—the text is almost nine pages in the *LettersIgn*—filled with very detailed advice on the most varied subjects. Ignatius concludes this letter with these simple words: "Everything set down here will serve as directive; the patriarch should not feel obligated to act in conformity with it, but rather with what a discreet charity, considering existing circumstances, and the unction of the Holy Spirit, who must direct him in everything, will dictate" (*LettersIgn*, p. 390).

90 The necessity of ordering one's life is expressed in many ways in the *Exercises*. It affects the general structure of their sequence, as we shall see in the following chapter. It touches especially on those numerous areas of one's life where the affective life of man demands constant attention in order not to go astray. See, for example, the Annotations, Additions, Rules with regard to Eating, for the Distribution of Alms, for Thinking with the Church, for Discernment of Spirits, and for Scruples. For the vocabulary itself, we refer to the following sections where there is question of putting order into the different areas of our lives (*SpEx*, [1, 16, 20, 21, 40, 46, 63, 157, 169, 172, 214, 240, 316, 342]. Finally, according to Ignatius, we should know how to order our lives in the choosing of what is good, as we see in the Rules for the Discernment of Spirits of the Second Week; see also letters to Francis Borgia on the subjects of abstinence and corporal penance (*LettersIgn*, pp. 179-180). Thus the task of ordering one's life progresses from the level of strict moral necessity (opposition to evil) to that of the "more" or "greater" *(magis)* and of discretion in charity in view of the greater glory of God.

This ideal, which the Foundation recalls in broad lines, aims directly at pointing out just how difficult it is for a person to be faithful.[91]

In his "Dictated Directory," Ignatius suggests three points for the presentation of the Foundation: the end, the means, and the difficulty. The end and the means point out human beings' location in God's plan of creation, and the vocation which they acquire from the fact that they are placed at the center of "all created things on the face of the earth." To speak of the end and the means is to recall the meaning of the universe and of created existence. But to emphasize the "difficulty" draws attention to the human person's interior division between misery and grandeur. This consideration helps the retreatant to move from the ideal situation of the human person to his present situation in the concrete. And when one becomes aware of this difficulty, one has already started on the way toward a humble recognition of one's need for God, which Christ, the Word of God and the Savior of humankind, has come to satisfy beyond all expectation.

In regard to this topic, we ordinarily speak of "indifference," the term which the text of the Foundation uses. The problem of indifference is precisely the problem of the difficulty we have been discussing. The Ignatian Directory states: "In order that you may perceive how difficult it is to use with indifference the means that God our Lord has placed at our disposal to enable us to attain the end for which he created us, and in order that, understanding it, you may place yourselves completely into his hands, here is the Foundation in which we find what we desire."[92]

This attitude of Ignatian indifference is not simply self-renunciation. It is a preference, beyond all natural and interior attachments, for the divine order of creation which embraces all things in a movement of love and service. It is our opting for God, in all things, without giving in to the sensitive likes or dislikes which spring from our nature.[93]

---

91 See I. Iparraguirre, *A Key to the Study,* pp. 49–51, where he quotes different points of view, emphasizing the synthetic or the problematic aspect of the Foundation: Böminghaus, Ceccotti, Gagliardi, Segarra, Vilariño.

92 *SpEx*MHSJ, p. 792.

93 "As a result, the reason he wants or retains anything will be solely the service, honor, and glory of the Divine Majesty" (Annotation 16, in *SpEx,* [16]; see also *LettersIgn,* pp. 131, 182, 217). It is important to note that indifference is explained only through a reference to a higher motivation which rises above natural affection without necessarily suppressing it. This motivation orders natural affection to something higher which, in turn and on its own level, exercises a new attraction. We shall return to this matter in ch. 6, when we treat of the kinds of humility. See R. Cantin, "L'indifférence dans le Principe et Fondement des Exercices spirituels," *ScE,* 3 (1950), 114–145, and K. Rahner, *RAM,* 35 (1959),

Moreover, this constant rising above ourselves, which is required in the many daily choices we must make, and in the many ways of using creatures, demands a purification that is motivated above all by a stronger attachment to God, to his work, and to Christ, who is at the center of it all. An exact presentation of this outlook on human beings and their lives, which places the Foundation in the light of God's saving plan, necessarily leads to an awareness of our ceaseless need to bring order into our lives. We accomplish this by using all the natural means at our disposal, and by doing that with a view to surrendering ourselves more freely to the work of grace in us. At the end of his reflections on how to present the Foundation, Ignatius says: "From this there will be born the need to place oneself in a state of equilibrium."[94]

---

esp. pp. 148–149; English on pp. 125–127 of his "Ignatian Spirituality and Devotion to the Sacred Heart" in his *Christian in the Market Place* (New York, 1966).

94 *SpEx*MHSJ, p. 792). We have sufficiently presented the spirit which should animate the presentation of the Foundation as an immediate preparation for the Exercises. We have also determined its content in relation to the Ignatian world view into which the experience of the Exercises is inserted. Finally, we have indicated the finality of this text and of its correct use. For further details on the practice of the Foundation, consult H. Rahner, "Notes on the Spiritual Exercises" (*WL,* 85 (1956), 281–336, esp. 308–311; I.Iparraguirre, *Líneas directivas,* English, *A Key to the Study;* Coathalem, *Ignatian Insights,* and M.A. Fiorito, "Cristocentrismo," *CyF,* 17 (1961), 3–42, esp. 34–38, on the pedagogical, theological, and spiritual function of the Foundation.

Chapter 3

_____

THE EXERCISES OF ST. IGNATIUS: THEIR OBJECTIVE AND
PROCEDURE

The preceding chapter was directed toward reconstructing the dynamic
framework in which Ignatius' thought evolved and in which, as a result, the
Exercises are placed and interpreted. We now desire to bring out their message and purpose. We shall also indicate in summary manner what characterizes the pursuit of their objective. We shall speak of the "integral" Exercises.
This expression does not necessarily refer to the matter of time, that is, to the
"thirty-day retreat." In fact, the making of the Exercises does not derive its
value principally from the framework in which they are given, nor from the
precision of details and their technical apparatus. Their authenticity is measured, instead, by the quality of the spiritual experience which they foster, by
their helping the retreatants to prepare themselves for the salutary encounter
with God, in Christ.

This experience necessarily includes stages progressing from purification to a more conscious and generous Christian commitment. In our meaning, the "integral" Exercises are those which take in these complementary
stages. Learning from Ignatius, we shall then know how to deal with the time
to be spent and with the aid to be expected from the modest human means
which, in some way, direct the retreatant's efforts to make himself or herself
open and available to God. Thus we avoid starting from these external conditions in our effort to understand, define, and appreciate the authenticity of the
Ignatian Exercises. By doing that, we would risk missing what is essential.
How many there are who have scrupulously respected their structure and the
instructions given—perhaps for thirty days—without really having undergone
the salutary transforming experience of the Exercises! What we shall say,
then, does not specifically refer to a retreat of thirty, twenty, ten, or seven
days. We shall speak of an objective to be attained, and of a procedure to be
followed, which take account of the length of time but aim especially at the
acquisition of certain spiritual fruits. It is for this that the retreatant must

dispose himself or herself if he really wishes to surrender himself to God.[1]

A. The Objective of the Exercises

1. The Different Tendencies of Interpretation

About the purpose of the *Exercises,* as many commentators have expressed it, we find a diversity of opinions which are not always easy to untangle. The terms used intersect, contradict, and complement one another. The strangest thing about them is that they often supplement one another just when they seem to be in mutual opposition. Sometimes, too, we find the sharpest differences within the same categories—for example, an election? or perfection? We have reviewed the thought of some twenty of these commentators on this point and have gathered together the principal expressions which link and cover almost all the opinions expressed.[2] In these various opinions, the *Exercises* have as their end man's purification in view of a greater service of the Lord; or they allow one to order one's life in imitation of Christ; or they aim at a liberation of the soul in order to submit it to the action of grace, or to the divine embrace, or to discover the will of God, or to fulfill the divine will; or, finally, they seek union with God. However, several authors prefer to emphasize the sequence of the intermediate ends, which eventually stress one or another of these ends: to find the divine will, to accomplish this will, to be united to God, to serve him.

Frequently enough today, these opinions are classified under two schools of thought, according to whether the idea of election predominates or the idea

1. On fidelity to the Exercises, see J. Lewis, *Conduite d'une retraite ignatienne* (Montréal, 1963) p. 31.
2 These are the authors we have consulted on the "purpose of the Exercises": J. Brucker (*DTC*, t. 27, c. 726), Calveras, *Mnr.* (1925), and *Que Fruto se ha de sacar de los Ejercicios Espirituales de San Ignacio?* (1951); English, *The Harvest Field of the Spiritual Exercises,* trans. J. H. Gense (Bombay, 1949); Coathalem, *Ignatian Insights* (1961); de Coninck, *NRTh* (1948); Debauche, *NRTh* (1948); Dirks, *NRTh* (1948); Fessard, *La dialectique des Exercices spirituels* (1956); Fiorito, *CyF* (1963 and 1964); Giuliani, Chr, no. 10 (1956); Gómez Nogales, *Mnr,* (1952); Hernández, *La elección en los Ejercicios de San Ignacio* (1956); Iparraguirre, *Líneas directivas* (1950), trans. *A Key to the Study; Dirección de una tanda* (1962); Lewis, *Conduite* (1963); d'Ouince, *Chr,* no. 13 (1957); L. Peeters, *Vers l'union divine par les Exercices de saint Ignace* (1924); Richter, *Martin Luther and Ignatius of Loyola* (1954); Roig Gironella, *Teoría de los Ejercicios Espirituales de San Ignacio* (1952); Suárez, *De Religione. S.I.,* L. IX), and finally the opinion of other authors, collected from those who quoted them: Fathers Casanovas, Goodier, de Grandmaison, de Guibert, Hummelauer, Iglesias, Orlandis, de la Palma, Schilgen.

of union (the "school of election," electionists and "the school of perfection," unionists). In general—and more than one would think—these two schools complement each other.[3] Nevertheless, within these same schools some rather serious differences attract our attention. In our opinion, the differences are less serious among those who hold "perfection" as the end of the *Exercises*. The original position of Louis Peeters is well known. He presents the *Exercises* as a school of prayer and a way to the unitive life.[4] However, in his position we find points of agreement with those who subscribe to a more obviously contrary trend, that of the election. In fact, the life of union and contemplation described by Peeters is of the Ignatian type in which the "mystique of service" predominates. In speaking of "ordering one's life" according to the spirit of Ignatius, Peeters writes: "To order a Christian life is not just harmoniously to develop one's personality; it is to put it in its proper place in the universal plan; it is to render it suitable to fulfill with all its resources, in communion with the social life of the Church, the mission assigned it by Providence." In this sense, he sees the Exercises "as intended to form perfect apostles by forming perfect contemplatives."[5] In our opinion, that is indeed the end of the Exercises; but we readily add that to reach this end by following the route traced out by book of the *Exercises*, we must give to the election the importance conferred on it by the Ignatian dialectic or reasoning process.

The other commentators of this same school, who orientate the *Exercises* in view of the perfection to be acquired, in general relate this perfection to the search for, and the accomplishment of, the divine will in our lives, in such a way that their view utilizes the election in the same sense as do many of the electionists.

Among the commentators who stress the election, we find a much more serious difference of opinion. It concerns the object of the election. This object indirectly transforms the end of the Exercises into a way either of

3 This complementary aspect of the two opinions is underlined by Coathalem, *Ignatian Insights*, p. 44.

4 See Louis Peeters, *Vers l'union divine*, 1924, and "Cual es el fin principal de los Ejercicios?" *Mnr*, 2 (1926), 306–321. In *Mnr*, 24 (1952), 33–52, "Cristocentrismo en la teología de los Ejercicios," S. Gómez Nogález discusses the position of Peeters and de Grandmaison which we shall meet further on. There is a résumóf Peeters' doctrine in English in *Ign*, 1956, pp. 177–181. Iprraguirre does not include Peeters' theory (the Exercises as a "school of prayer") among those who present the Exercises as a means of ordering one's life in view of perfection; thus he distinguishes three groups of opinions, (*Obras completas*, [1963], p. 202, fn. 21).

5 L. Peeters, *Ver l'union divine*, p. 90.

"finding one's vocation" or of "reforming one's life." Léonce de Grandmaison is the one who in 1920 posed this problem more directly, by "demonstrating" that the *Exercises* are intrinsically ordered to the choice of a state of life. In his opinion, the directive "to Amend and Reform One's Life and State" (*SpEx*, [189]) was only an appendix to the method of making an election. Gaston Fessard, as we shall see later on, analyzes this opinion and shows that what De Grandmaison considers to be merely an appendix is a natural, spontaneous, and indispensable continuation of the dialectic of the *Exercises,* especially of the election. This fact transforms and enlarges the end of the *Exercises* from within the "electionist" point of view. Miguel A. Fiorito follows Fessard on this point and their opinions agree with those of Hernández and Iparraguirre, for whom "the choice of a state of life" and "the reform of one's life" have always been two of many possible elections.[6]

De Grandmaison considered that the *Exercises* were originally conceived in view of the choice of a state of life. His reflections on the psychological origin of the *Exercises* regarding the election conclude that the material in *SpEx* [189] represents, in treating of the reform of life, "clearly an afterthought, an appendix, not the primary intention and general tenor of the *Exercises.*" His view is: "To make use of the Exercises to amend one's life in a vocation that has already been chosen, to convert people, and the like, . . . does not contradict the intentions of the author, but goes beyond the original hypothesis of the work."[7]

Fessard is quite right in wondering whether Ignatius, when he offered "his book for papal approbation, would have agreed to omit this paragraph" ([189]) as something considered to be an appendix or secondary application. That would have reduced the *Exercises* to a simple means of choosing one's vocation, and it would have restricted them to a very small group of retreatants. "This would have made it impossible to understand the success of the book in history and the rapid spread of the spirituality to which it gave birth."[8] Fessard then demonstrates that the application of the election to the reform of life ([189]) is a natural continuation of the primary meaning of the election. It is a dialectic which, according to him, moves from the particular to the universal in a movement which springs from within. "Such precise

---

6 "The election of a state of life and the reform of one's life are nothing more than two cases in the application of the general purpose of the exercises" (I. Iparraguirre, *Dirección de una tanda de los Ejercicios* (Bilbao, 1962), p. 48).
7 See L. de Grandmaison, "L'interpretation des Exercices," *RScR,* 11 (1920), 398–408.
8 G. Fessard, *La dialectique,* p. 93.

details," he writes (drawing from [189 and 338–344]), "clearly prove that for Ignatius the *Exercises,* and in particular their methods of election, have an absolutely universal scope. The value should not be restricted only to the decision that embraces the whole of one's life, or even only to this less important decision regarding a plan for reformation of life. . . . Any decision in life, no matter how small, falls within their scope."[9] And responding explicitly to De Grandmaison, he affirms: "This paragraph is a secondary application in the sense that it is a logical consequence of the primary intention of a work whose essential fruitfulness it marks. So much so, that to cut it off would not mean removing an "appendix," but rather would be literally to emasculate it."[10]

We willingly accept Fessard's conclusions. We find, however, that they are not sufficiently based on the historical origin of the Ignatian method of election, on Ignatius' thought as he expressed it in many places, and on his practice where his manner of acting is worth as much as any interpretations of his words. Therefore we feel obliged to supplement Fessard's views. He accepts, too uncritically, the hypothesis that the *Exercises* were primarily conceived for the choice of a state of life. "Indeed," he writes, "to help one choose his state of life was the reason why Ignatius composed the *Exercises.* . . . But it would be expedient to show also by a theory of freedom that all of our acts are governed by the principles of the *Exercises* as much as is the choice of a state of life. We would also have to explain that these principles are capable of being applied to all the states, and that they normally lead to the highest perfection."[11]

In our own opinion, the *Exercises,* in Ignatius' later practice and in their final formulation, were being directed more and more toward the election as a choice of a state of life, and this because of definite historical circumstances. However, we see this as a point of arrival rather than an original structure. On the contrary, in their origin and in their fundamental structure, they go far beyond this particular point of view, and they are oriented intrinsically, from their beginning, toward a deepening understanding of the Christian vocation; that is, in other terms and in the language of our day, toward Christian life and an interior renewal which are concrete and realistic, whether one's state of life has been already decided upon or is still to be chosen. This is demonstrated not only by the internal logic of the *Exercises,*

9 Ibid., p. 89.
10 Ibid., p. 93.
11 Ibid., p. 5. Another statement in the same vein, p. 88: "Elaborated at first to guide one in the choice of a state of life."

which we shall study later on, but also by the history of the early practice of Ignatius and his companions.

2. *The Historical Point of View*

When Ignatius made the Exercises at Manresa as the first exercitant, he was not trying to decide his vocation. The success of the Exercises he made was measured by his complete conversion to God, by his commitment to live with fidelity in the following of Christ. In no way did this consist in his choosing between the world and the priesthood or the religious life. The priesthood will not be his until fifteen years later in 1537, and he will raise the question of religious life only in 1539. But immediately after the transforming experience of the Exercises, he undertook, at Manresa, Barcelona, and Alcalá, "to help souls" to enter upon this same spiritual movement which transforms one's interior life. We know that he reached out to everyone of good will.[12] In Paris, the method became more precise and the *Exercises* were enlarged, but the objective and the substance of the message remained the same.[13]

During this time, some of his future companions experimented with the Exercises under the watchful eye of Ignatius. But Favre did not make them until 1534, shortly before his priestly ordination and the vows of Montmartre. This was long after he had decided to join Ignatius' group and had already decided on the future course of his life. Furthermore, Xavier made the Exercises in September of 1534, a month after he had pronounced the vows of Montmartre. This shows that he had already determined the orientation of his life. It is clear enough that, right from the beginning, Ignatius in the Exercises he directed was aiming at *a profound transformation of the soul and a more faithful commitment to the Lord,* for His service and glory.

However, experience taught him that the Exercises, if made seriously, gained for him companions eager to share his ideal of a poor and apostolic life. He used the Exercises to recruit his first companions. But that never prevented him from continuing to give the Exercises to every category of

12 Basing himself on the data of the process of Alcalá, and on the opinions gathered by Polanco, Iparraguirre shows that this teaching of Ignatius in no way aims at "extraordinary transformations" to be introduced into one's life, but at the accomplishment, "with a more Christian awareness," of the obligations of one's life. This, furthermore, entails "a very great transformation" in one's personal life and "significant progress in the spiritual life" (see *Práctica de los Ejercicios (1522–1556)*, pp. 4–5).

13 On the subject of the essentials or the "substance" of the Exercises, dating from Manresa, see *FN*, I, 82 (Laínez), 163 (Polanco), and Nadal (MonNad, IV, 826).

persons from whom he could hope for "great spiritual fruit." Indeed at Paris at this same period he gave them to several professors, doctors in theology, the rector of the University, a religious—all of them persons who needed to put order and depth into their lives more than "to find their vocation" in life. Likewise at Rome, we see Ignatius giving the Exercises to, among others, the physician Iñigo Lopez, Cardinal Contarini, several eminent ecclesiastics, Doctor Ortiz (who retired to Montecassino), and also, it seems, to some ladies of the house of St. Martha.[14] Even though Pierre Favre had used the Exercises to recruit for the Society such worthy subjects as Jay, Broët, and Codure, he continued to give them, as Ignatius was doing, for an evident end of "interior renewal." Thus he gave them to a vicar general of Espira, Cardinal Truchsess, two chaplains of the court of Spain, a Carmelite, and in 1534 to the Carthusians of Cologne who, according to their prior Gerard Hammont,[15] reaped great fruit from them. Broët also had a similar experience when he gave the Exercises to several priests, two canons, a Carmelite, as well as to Alessandro Cervini and his wife Girolama Bellarmino in their lordly estate, "giving them rules for the reform of their lives in accord with their state."[16]

Finally, we have the example of Nadal and Laínez. Nadal gave the Exercises at Messina to the bishop, his vicar general, and his two chaplains; Laínez gave them at Brescia to a large number of priests. Many other examples could be given, all of them drawn from Iparraguirre's history of the practice of the Exercises during Ignatius' lifetime. These examples testify to the original openness of access to these Exercises, which were always given to people of every sort who were faced with a variety of problems. Among these problems, the choice of a state of life is one type to which the procedures of the Exercises are eminently applicable. But we should not let ourselves become prisoners to this one type alone.[17]

---

14 I. Iparraguirre, *Práctica de los Ejercicios (1522-1556)*, pp. 286, 290.
15 J. Nonell, *Analyse des Exercices spirituels de saint Ignace de Loyola* (1924), pp. 106-107.
16 X. M. Le Bachelet, "Bellarmin et les Exercices spirituels de saint Ignace," *CBE*, 37-38 (1912), p. 10.
17 All the examples we have quoted took place between the years 1523 and 1556. They were collected by Iparraguirre, who in his valuable *Práctica de los Ejercicios (1522-1556)*, Appendix III, pp. 267-296, gives a list of 1,293 instances of retreatants or groups of retreatants to whom the Exercises were given during those years. The variety of conditions of these retreatants leaves no doubt concerning the use made of the Exercises right from the beginning. If they have often been given to young people, and have attracted numerous vocations to the Jesuits—245 out of the 1,293 references were related to persons who entered the

To this evidence of historical facts is added that from writings which express the spirit that animated the practice. The first Companions, with Ignatius as their leader, felt no need to change the original structure of the *Exercises* in order to open it up to other useful ends. They themselves made them within a framework far wider—their concern to deepen their spiritual lives and their generous response to live in Christ. This was the context that shaped their own practice in giving the Exercises. The term customary in that era was "interior renewal" *(renovación interior)*. This renewal, we think, coincides with what we saw as a spiritual way to a more conscious and more generous Christian commitment. Ignatius' work for souls at Manresa has already been described along that line: "He then began to give himself fruitfully to the service of his neighbor by proposing a plan and a method of purifying the soul from its sins through contrition and confession, and of making progress by means of the meditations on the mysteries of Christ's life, by a method of *making a good election* concerning a state of life and *any other problem*, and finally by anything likely to *inflame the heart* with divine love."[18] In a letter written in Ignatius' name, Polanco describes this very succinctly: "Your Reverence knows that there is one outstanding means among those which of their nature are wont to be a help to men interiorly. I mean the Exercises."[19]

There is another text, entitled by the editors of the Monumenta Historica Societatis Iesu "Defense of the Exercises by an Unknown Jesuit Author." Written toward the end of the sixteenth century, it insists on this important orientation of the *Exercises* as intended by Ignatius: "Our Father Ignatius, by wonderful skill, disposed even worldly souls for interior reform by beginning with the Kingdom of Christ." And he makes that more precise along this line: In the light of the contemplation of Christ, the retreatants, whoever they may be, ought to arrive at an election that will incarnate this "interior reform" in function of the imitation of Christ in their daily lives; "and with an immense desire, to arrive at what is more perfect and more generous, they should meditate on his life, each one according to his ability doing what will be better and more conformed to the life of Christ, whether it be the choice of a state of life or a commitment to the highest works for the greater glory of God."[20]

Society)—the fact is that they were more often directed to other groups where there was no question of vocation.

18 Polanco, De vita P. Ignatii et de Societatis initiis, in *FN*, II, 527; the italics are ours.

19 *LettersIgn*, p. 434.

20 *SpEx*MHSJ, pp. 694–695.

In this spirit and as far as the substance of the message is concerned, the *Exercises* are addressed to all kinds of people. This long "apology for the *Exercises*" from which we have just quoted returns to this point on several occasions. The same thing is found in certain Directories which could be believed to have been reacting against an inevitable movement or practice which was reserving the Exercises too exclusively to possible candidates for the priestly or religious life. González Dávila wrote, in about 1573: "We have the testimony of men from many ranks and states, ecclesiastics, religious, and lay persons, who, with the help of the Exercises, accomplished a marvelous reformation and change of life."[21] More directly still, and without any possible equivocation, the Directories of 1591 and 1599 repudiated the opinion that would thus restrict the Exercises. "We should do all we can to eradicate the opinion which leads some to think that the Exercises are beneficial only for religious or those who want to become religious. Since all have need of God's grace, not only religious, but lay persons also, because of the dangers amid which they constantly live, ought to seek those aids which will be most effective in disposing them to receive that grace."[22]

3. The Statement in the Exercises

Finally, in spite of first appearances, the text of the *Exercises* itself supports our opinion.[23] It is true that in this the method of election is developed in terms of the problem of vocation—perhaps because practice revealed the need of making the application of the method to this topic more precise, or perhaps because the problem of vocation best illustrated the principles to be applied to "every good election." Thus, in our opinion, the movement goes from the general or universal to the particular, and we are looking here more at the application of the method to the particular and important problem of the choice of a state of life, rather than at a generalization of it when it is treating about the reformation of life. By means of an explanation of the choice of a state of life, we believe ourselves able to see signs of the application we have just been discussing.

As a first example, let us examine *SpEx,* [135], the "Introduction to the Consideration of Different States of Life." After a few reflections on the need of asking God "in what kind of life or in what state His Divine Majesty

21 Ibid., p. 905.
22 *SpEx*MHSJ, p. 1012, and the parallel text of the Directory of 1599, ch. 1, no. 6, on p. 1120.
23 The preceding arguments could suffice to determine the primary end of the *Exercises*. However, we are aiming to reply to certain difficulties raised by the very text of the *Exercises*.

wishes to make use of us," Ignatius indicates the path to be taken, through contemplation of the mysteries of Christ and reflection on the "intentions or strategies respectively of our Lord and of Satan. Now, this path envisages an end that goes beyond the search for a state of life. What emerges at last as the objective of this "Introduction" is, in Ignatius' words, "how we ought to prepare ourselves to arrive *at perfection in whatever* state or way of life God our Lord may grant us to choose." The vocation itself, in reality, is not an end, but a means adjusted to each person, the place where one realizes one's end, that end which Ignatius had placed so prominently at the head of the *Exercises* ([23]): "to praise, reverence, and serve God our Lord." Whether one's vocation has already been decided or remains to be discovered, the path outlined by Ignatius for the Exercises, the path within the truth of Christ as opposed to the lies of Satan ([135]), remains the same for all. It tends to "dispose" us to be receptive of that perfection which Ignatius sees as something dynamic, something at the service of God's glory and achieved through creation ([170-174]). He then develops his method and applies it directly to the problem of vocation ([169-188]). Now, it is evident here that he is stating principles which go beyond the sole problem of vocation, for he found it necessary immediately to draw his reader's attention to the problem of vocation. Indeed, he speaks ([171]) of an irrevocable choice because of its object (thus marriage, the priesthood), and of a revocable choice (for example, the disposition of "temporal goods"). He also speaks ([170]) of things that must be "indifferent or good" in themselves, and in some way are lawful within the Church. Furthermore, no matter what is to be decided, the authentic and only orientation that must be kept in mind remains the same as it was stated in the "first point" of the preceding "Introduction" ([169]): "In every good choice, as far as depends on us, our intention must be simple. I must consider only the end for which I am created, that is, for the praise of God our Lord and for the salvation of my soul."

When speaking ([178]) of the "First Way of Making a Good and Correct Choice of a Way of Life" in the "third time" of tranquillity, from the very first point, Ignatius mentions "anything . . . that may be the object of a choice subject to change." Hence, he is not talking here of a state of life, but of something that could be changed within it. Then, once more, to the problem he is treating he joins the end to be sought in all things (second point, [179]): the praise of God and the salvation of one's soul. Clearly therefore, throughout the particularism of the method and object to be chosen, the work is always brought back to the unique task, the true end of the Exercises: to order one's life in function of this end which is both personal and vast in Ignatius' mind, our own salvation and the divine glory which embraces all of creation. All this, in our opinion, confirms the fact that Ignatius starts from general, universal principles and then immediately applies them to the particular case of vocation as one of special importance. Even in this case, we see his care to put the problem back in a context that goes beyond it, by his constant repetition of the theme of man's unique and supreme end.[24]

To conclude, let us look at the passage most important ([189]) in this question: "To Amend and Reform One's Own Life and State." Here we find a small contradiction in the terms which Ignatius used, which shows the two meanings that the word "election" had taken on in his mind. After he has written detailed, precise directions about the method of making an election about the choice of a state of life (both here in the *Exercises* and also in the Directories called "Ignatian"[25]), he makes here ([189]) a distinction between the Exercises in the case of those who have an election to make about a state of life and of others who do not.[26] His section [189], therefore, calls attention to those who have no reason to make an election *in this sense* of choice of a state. However, Ignatius does not expect the retreatant to continue the Exercises as if nothing remained to be done. On the contrary, he says that for such persons "in place of a choice, it will be very profitable . . . to propose a way for each to reform his manner of living in his state of life." This, we recall, is the way that Favre and Xavier made the Exercises, since both had already made their choice of their future. For such persons, this work of reform should take place within the perspective of submitting oneself—one's whole creaturehood, in Ignatius' concept—to God, with the purpose of ordering all

24 Polanco writes that in the *Exercises* Ignatius proposed "a method of making a good election bout a state of life and about any other matters" (*PolChron*, I, 21, cited in *SpEx*MHSJ, p. 30). Concerning the matter about which the election is made ([170–174]), see the study of Eusebio Hernández, which emphasizes the flexibility of Ignatius' method and its being ordered to a higher end, or even the supreme one (instead of tying the election to one choice, that of a state of life). See *La Elección en los Ejercicios de San Ignacio* (Comillas, 1956), pp. 12–15.

25 This practical insistence of Ignatius leads us to believe that, in conversations with the other fathers, the problems of vocations must have often come up—not only because they were connected with the problem of recruitment facing the young Society, but also because they arose spontaneously among those who were not committed to a state of life, and were proposing difficulties during the Exercises. Ignatius was often consulted. We know that the "Ignatian Directories," of which only one is an autograph, are the fruit of these conversations and of the directives given by Ignatius. At Rome he closely followed those who gave the Exercises. "Our Father," writes Polanco in 1554, "wants each one to write him weekly about what he is doing concerning the Exercises" (letter from Polanco to P. Leerno, February 3, 1554, in *EppIgn*, VI, 281).

26 Several times Ignatius makes an allusion to the election in this sense: see *Letters*, pp. 247–248; *Memoriale* of Cámara, no. 254, in *FN*, I, 676.

of it truly to "the glory and praise of God." That ordering of everything in the retreatant's life, therefore, is something which must be done in every state of life, and it is the real task which ought to be proposed to the exercitant. It is, moreover, something beyond the problem of choosing a state of life.

This work was already alluded to in the introduction "to the states of life" ([169]) and in the directives preceding the election ([175-187]), where practically every numbered section recalls this objective by referring to the end of man as a creature. In order to show that Ignatius is here linking the end of the *Exercises* (as expressed in the Foundation) and the first function of the election, let us note that this link is clearly brought out later on in the same section [189]: "If one is really to attain this end" [of ordering to God, of amendment and reformation], "he ought to consider much and ruminate, *by means of* the exercises *and ways of making an election as explained above*" ([178-188]), "how large a household he should maintain," and so on. This is tantamount to Ignatius' stating: In the case of those who do not have an election to make, because they have no need of an election of a state of life in order to seek the perfection proper to their end ([135,169-188]), place them directly into awareness of this end and of any changes which they ought to bring into their lives to achieve the perfection proper to that end, *by means of the election,* to arrive at the perfection proper to this end ([135, 189]).[27] From this consideration centered on the purpose of our being as creatures ([189]), Ignatius descends to concrete details of daily living which have to be adjusted within this dynamic perspective which is his, and in which there is continually, in fact, matter for a revocable election. Here he speaks of life style, of one's way of governing, of the duty of setting a good example for those for whom one is responsible, of the administration of one's

27 It is not exact, then, to speak of a retreat in which one proposes either an election to be made or a reformation of life (election or devotion). The two (election or reform) are made strictly by means of the election (as is every spiritual decision for Ignatius). Let us add this remark that has often been borne out by the experience of giving the Exercises to young people: When spiritual preparation in general is lacking, it seems rather rare that a young person is ready to make the Exercises as a procedure in which the primary, immediate, and direct purpose is the choosing of a state of life. Such a procedure could easily jeopardize the genuine experience of the Exercises. The problem of vocation would absorb too much energy, divert the attention from that which the choice itself presupposes, and which is precisely what the Exercises, through an interior renewal, are helping to obtain: first of all, to become rightly ordered, in the full sense of that term or, in other words, to be in equilibrium before God and in regard to the direction which one's life will take. It is only after the completion of the Exercises, made in this sense, that many retreatants are ready to envisage, in true interior liberty, the problem of their vocation.

goods, and the like; and he ends by turning his attention back to the universal, to the divine Truth who enlightens and situates each person: "Let him desire and seek nothing except the greater praise and glory of God our Lord as the aim of all he does. For everyone must keep in mind that in all that concerns the spiritual life his progress will be in proportion to his surrender of self-love and of his own will and interests" ([189]). This very Ignatian framework fits in perfectly, from every point of view, with the general structure of the *Exercises,* and it is valid for every election, whether it is focused on "the choice of a state of life" or "an interior renewal."[28]

4. Conclusion

What is the end of the Exercises? If we start from the text of the *Exercises,* we should express it in function of that task which they recall in all their various ways—through their doctrinal message, their practical directives, and their various Rules: to order one's life toward achieving its end, which is God. The election at the center of the *Exercises* will be the discovery, as "coming from above," of the point around which we ought to accomplish this ordering, which is always moving forward, always a task of the present, and never completed.

But if we wish to be very faithful to the Ignatian meaning of the words he used to express this intention throughout the text of the *Exercises,* we must refer them to the realities which they express by starting from this vision of the world and of life which Ignatius drew from his own experience of the divine mystery or plan—the experience which gave birth to the *Exercises.* To bring order into one's life, then, means to become aware, in the light of the divine truth, of one's creaturehood with all that it implies, and consequently to insert oneself into the magnificent plan of the Creator and Redeemer, into the history of salvation. Now, for Ignatius, this history is also the history of the fall which affects us intimately; and our entering into the divine plan immediately places us face to face with the evil which man introduced into the world through his sin. This bringing of right order into one's life entails a precise point as its objective, here the opposition offered to the Adversary— in one's own life; but this is done in order to make a full, positive response to

---

28 This is, furthermore, the same reasoning process which Ignatius will apply to all particular choices. Fessard shows the possibility of such choices when he speaks of a macro-decision and a micro-decision (see *La dialectique,* pp. 88–89). On this subject read, too, the commentary of M. A. Fiorito in *CyF,* 19 (1963), 414, note 19. For examples of choices in diverse orders, but inspired by the same spirit of spiritual election, see *LettersIgn,* pp. 84–85, 257–258, 274–278, 353–354, 401–402, 410–411, 416–417.

the call and the work of God, Creator and Redeemer. The Exercises will help one to find one's place in God's plan by offering to him or her the divine message and by bringing him to ask for grace—in order that, aided by God's light and grace, delivered from evil by Christ, and incorporated into Him in the Church, he may truly dedicate himself for the accomplishment of His divine mission, which is the return and entrance of all creation into the glory of the Father. Or, as Jacques Lewis writes more briefly, "to make the Exercises is to contemplate the history of salvation, while discovering within it God's will for oneself; or rather, it is to contemplate this mystery for the purpose of discovering within it God's will for oneself."[29] This is the sense in which we present the Exercises as "an experience of the salvation which God has revealed."

B. The Procedure

When the Exercises are viewed as aiming at so lofty an objective—to confront within a few days of intensive retreat the universal and the particular, to contemplate the divine plan of salvation in all its amplitude, the retreatant's present and personal insertion of himself or herself into that plan while struggling against the action of Satan—the book of the *Exercises* proposes a procedure which is necessarily delicate and complex. If we desire to gain the fruit which these Exercises promise, we must appreciate their profound unity and the meaning of their demands. The Exercises "are a place to be both feared and desired," writes François Courel, "where God makes himself known and where man, freed by the grace of Christ, learns how to adhere, through a choice increasingly lucid and free, to the action of the Holy Spirit in him."[30] Here we shall emphasize the principal elements of this procedure, to make them evident before we treat the irreversible movement of the Exercises. What remains will be explained more precisely as we proceed. Our reflections will center on the most characteristic points, as follows: (1) the

29 J. Lewis, Conduite d'une retraite ignatienne, p. 7. This purpose is similarly treated by d'Ouince, *Chr,* no. 13 (1957), 92, and by Coathalem, *Ignatian Insights,* p. 10. When Fessard explains the method of the *Exercises,* through his description he reaches a definition of the end of the Exercises which restores all their breadth. "They are," he writes, "a method which teaches the retreatant to assimilate the truths he already knows, but whose relationship to his concrete daily life he has not yet grasped. Only in proportion as the unity between theory and practice is thus realized does it appear, especially at the end, that the result of the method is not only practical—the change in one's life, its Christian right-ordering—but also theoretical: The meaning of religious truths is revealed to freedom in view of its historic commitment." See *La dialectique,* pp. 9–10.
30 *Exercices spirituels,* trans. Courel, Introduction, p. 8.

dialectical interactions of the universal and the particular, and of the work on both the objective and the subjective levels; (2) the roles of the intellect and the will; (3) human effort and grace.

1. *The Interaction between the Universal and the Particular, and between the Work on the Two Levels, Objective and Subjective*

The dialectical interaction of the Exercises has multidimensional aspects. It comprises a logic or mental process which continually juxtaposes opposing forces. It is best explained *by the complex horizon where the human and supernatural act of Christian faith* is lived out. The complexity of this dialectic comes from the fact that the Exercises are the place where the divine and the human meet in a search for harmony between them. But they meet in areas where they are most likely to become locked in struggle. In God's plan, the one who wishes to save his life, loses it. To give the Exercises well to a retreatant, we need to know more than general and applied psychology; we need also to know the mental activities evoked by God's revealed message which includes the history of the fall and the experience of salvation, and still further, to be initiated into the discernment of spirits which accompanies the accomplishment of salvation in the case of the destiny of this particular retreatant. We constantly go from one level to the other, from the objective to the subjective, from the universal to the particular. We do this in practice by knowing that all these aspects form one unity, and without ever considering them as independent one from another. Further, we do not disassociate or extract them from their unique meeting place, the heart of this particular person who is trying to open himself or herself to Divine Truth.[31] There are, however, flexible but well-determined directives which enlighten and guide this interrelationship. They clarify the kind of collaboration which the retreat director employs when he or she is either proposing the message of salvation or directing the retreatant.

The experience proffered by the Exercises is, like that of Ignatius, an experience that is both personal and universal, because it is profoundly true

---

31 "There is a place for the Christian experience, and that place is to be found in the depths of the soul—in the heart, or the spirit—where God calls, forgives, and gives life, and where each man replies in secret, and is converted each day by choosing God. This means that the Christian experience is one of absolute inwardness. It takes place in man's hidden depths; it involves his entire spiritual freedom; it only exists in this freedom; everything that can—and must—produce it outside, only has value as a reflection and an expression, a relation to this spiritual source in the spirit" (J. Mouroux, *The Christian Experience,* trans. G. Lamb [New York, 1954]), p. 118.

and accomplished in the Truth. Being personal, it touches the real person in the concrete situation in which he or she lives. But further, since it is initiated and literally informed by the power of the divine message presented in its universality, it is transformed into an experience of cosmic dimensions which give this retreatant his or her place and commitment within the divine plan. Being personal, it not only discerns the present defective situation, but it also clarifies the very concrete adjustment which it proposes to the exercitant for his election, under the action of the Holy Spirit; and being universal, it directly links the readjustment of this situation to the final supreme end which embraces the whole of creation in God. When this experience is surveyed from God's point of view, the retreatant, not only as a human being but also as a unique person living here and now, is seen as one in a universe which extends far beyond him or her and draws him onward, and in which he finds a place that is always new and that no one else will ever occupy. Thus, there is a double movement—not a chronological movement, but one so living that it results in a reciprocal benefit: the universal enlightens the personal, and the particular, touching on what is most personal, is seen against a background which includes God's total, expansive truth. In a word, the universal augments the personal by plunging it more deeply into the universal.[32] This continual movement of descent and ascent corresponds to the profoundest movement within our being as creatures. For there is question, beyond the time of the Exercises, of a descent which began with God's unceasing creative act and of an ascent started by His first putting creation into movement toward himself. This is the innate movement which the experience of the Exercises takes hold of in a privileged moment, and which it makes explicit on the level of man's spiritual faculties, his mind and will, where the divine light stimulates and directs a more conscious and generous commitment of the faithful retreatant toward his destiny.

---

32 On the subject of this alternation of movements between the universal and the particular, Iparraguirre speaks of *circumvectio*. In his *Adnotationes initiales,* pp. 22–23, he writes: "From soteriological facts [Ignatius] passes through theological principles to the problems of the exercitant. From these he again directs his thought up to Christ and God, from whom he again descends to the world and men. As a result, there is a certain circular motion which is continuous and complete, and it moves always in the field, not of personal development, but of transcendental realities." He also states: [Ignatius] "considers a thing first in itself and in others. Thus, for example in the meditations on sin or on a vocation from God, he considers its objective nature. After he has considered these carefully, he comes at length to the mind of the exercitant and ponders the "motions" which arise in his or her soul. In this way egocentrism and subjectivism are avoided, and all things are judged in accordance with true love."

We have become aware of these dialectic interactions first of all from Ignatius' own experience at Loyola and Manresa (chapter 1 above) and from his vision of God, the created universe, and man's place in it (chapter 2). We recall how his discovery of God's mystery or plan of salvation through Christ shaped his experience of conversion, while his clear outlook on the meaning of man and of creation in the divine plan strengthened his commitment and then nourished his action and his prayer through the rest of his life. During the Exercises, the same dialectic ought to animate the spiritual experience of the retreatant from their beginning to their end, from the Principle and Foundation viewed as a preparatory stage to the Contemplation to Attain Love, which allows the retreatant to relish their fruit. This dialectic is based on the two extremities of this vivid and present meeting which the Exercises foster: God, always the same, infinite, transcendent, and the retreatant touched, through the grace of Christ, in the very depths of his or her personal self. Finally, this dialectical interaction clearly outlines the work that must be done for this end on the interconnected levels of the objective message of God and the subjective Experience of the retreatant.

The relationship that exists between the two levels, the objective and the subjective, is at once simple and disconcerting. Simple, if we consider it in the conclusion it dictates: to present the divine message, not merely as it is in itself, but as God himself puts it into effect—that is, in function of the human person and of the experience which the hearing of God's efficacious word engenders. But if we wish to explain the imperative character of this result, the relationship between the objective and the subjective becomes complicated. For, as we saw in Ignatius' case, if there is a subordination of the subjective spiritual experience to the quality and the demands of the objective divine message, there are also from the same message several fundamental concomitants which can be explained in terms of human nature and psychology, and which God respects. So whether we start from a better knowledge of man or from a better understanding of the message, can we then conclude that we will reach the same result? Without dropping the other end of the chain, in the Exercises we evidently must give a primordial importance to the preeminence of the divine message. The Exercises are not primarily a course in gymnastics, even expert spiritual gymnastics. They are a confrontation with God, with his liberating and sanctifying truth. God's plan for salvation and spiritual growth throws infinitely more light on human psychology than our knowledge of human psychology casts upon the divine message. Although psychology finds in the ways of God, on some points, a remarkable agreement with its own conclusions, nevertheless, it could never of itself reach views of man as lofty as God's revelation does.[33] It is in the light of this divine revelation that man must learn to know himself and to live. God is man's end and this creates a dynamic attraction or tension toward an infinite term. But God is also the exemplary and efficient cause of this same vast movement which he offers to man. The entire mystery of man and of his existence receives immense illumination from the light and the truth of God, who speaks to man through Christ and in his Church. "On the human level," writes Jean Corbon, "this is the divine therapy we see at work: to propose the Light: and if man welcomes it, his outlook of faith becomes a view of truth and of humility, and he begins to be free."[34]

It was by starting from God, in the Christ who revealed him, that Ignatius came to know himself truly, not only as regards sin and the extent of the disorder from it which he found in himself, but also to know the grandeur that launched him forever upon the following of the Lord, a following which is tied in with the whole of creation. The truth of God generates the truth of human beings. The Exercises ought above all—and we shall return to this point when treating the role of the intellect—to open the human mind to God's plan or mystery, to enlighten this concrete retreatant with a light that "comes from above," so that by this light, he or she may fit himself into God's order, may choose, may commit himself. Thus, we come back to our first conclusion: The Exercises ought to present the divine message with intelligence, depth, and simplicity—never merely as it is in itself, that is to say, just for the presentation itself, but in function of this or that person who is hearing the word of God, and in the manner of the God who reveals himself by means of the events in sacred history.

Speaking on the objective level of the *Exercises,* we are for the moment content to make this affirmation: From the Foundation to the Contemplation to Attain Love, one finds in them the chief elements of God's saving plan, all

---

33 Let us think, for example, of abandonment of self ("mourning work") symbolized by the opening of oneself to another, the passage from the stage of taking to that of offering, the simple but authentic maturation of the personality which unmasks at all levels the infantilisms we carry around with us. On this subject read F. Künkel, *La psychothérapie du caractère* (Lyon-Paris, 1952), and books like those of René Hubert, *La croissance mentale* (Paris, 1949) ch. IV., section VI, "l'effacement de l'affectivité égocentrique et la germination des sentiments supérieurs," and ch. VII, "la phase de maturation"; of G. Cruchon, *Initiation à la psycgologie dynamique* (Mame, 1963), ch. II, III, and IV; and of A. Roldán, *Introducción a la ascética differencial* (2nd ed., Madrid, 1962), ch. III (pp. 135–255).

34 J. Corbon. L'expérience chrétienne dans la Bible, p. 103.

brought into a unified synthesis which is dynamic and completely adjusted to the history of this concrete person to whom they are now addressed. R. d'Ouince writes of the *Exercises* that they are "an objective pedagogy, resulting from the choice and the sequence of the themes proposed for meditation; by retracing the steps of the work of redemption, they help the retreatant to place his present commitment into the history and plan of salvation."[35]

The subjective stages are made clear in the text by the very sequence of the unfolding history of salvation, in which man finds himself exposed to Satan's stratagems, but also delivered from evil by Christ and associated with the universal work of redemption. These stages are: the encounter with the true God, the God of revelation, the purification which flows from this saving encounter, and the Christian commitment which is conscious, realistic, and generous. These stages correspond to the major divisions of the *Exercises:* the preparation (or the Foundation), then the First Week on the one hand, and on the other the Second, Third, and Fourth Weeks taken as a unit. But they should be continually renewed within each particular stage. There should be a placing of oneself in the divine presence, self-humiliation in the truth of one's being and the awareness of one's needs and the gift of self to the divine action which leads to effective and universal love in Christ as Savior (the experience of Christian salvation).

The relationship between the objective and the subjective levels in the Exercises is brought into action according to the following procedure, briefly described: The Foundation and the Contemplation to Attain Love present the essential elements of the Ignatian vision, the awareness of the world in movement toward God, the return to the Father, "the entrance into his glory" (*SpEx,* [95]). But two units come between the Foundation and the Contemplation for Love, between the ideal and its realization in the heart of the retreatant who is placed into the order of the divine plan. These two units are the unit of evil (First Week) as a present obstacle to the divine plan, inasmuch as creation can find itself turned aside from its goal and stopped in its movement toward God; and the unit of the return taken on in Christ, the unique way to salvation (the Kingdom). In this new economy the human being, now called to unite himself or herself to Christ by a free choice (Second Week), passes from death to life (Third and Fourth Weeks) and once again becomes capable of a love that expresses itself in the service of the Divine Majesty by using all of creation as it moves toward its goal, the glorification of God.

---

35 R. d'Ouince, "La formation de la librté par les Exercices," *Chr,* no. 13 (1957), p. 92.

The one who gives the Exercises ought to be vividly aware of the continual relationship that exists between the two levels, where the experience of the Exercises takes place, so as to respect the interaction between the universal and the particular which directs this movement, sustains it, and gives it its force. This awareness is what will make the director absorb the dynamism truly proper to the transcendence of the divine plan of salvation, while neglecting no human resources in order to help the retreatant dispose himself or herself concretely for the reception of divine grace.[36]

2. The Roles of the Intellect and the Will

What we have said of the origin, nature, and purpose of the *Exercises,* and what we have been considering about their dialectic interactions, allow us to suspect the importance of the intellect and the will in the spiritual experience being proposed. We are not speaking only of the objective importance of these faculties in every human activity, whether because of their nature or because of the relationship that unites their operations. Here the traditional data of philosophy and theology need to be integrated into the perspective of the *Exercises,* where they lose this impersonal character of objective analysis and, while remaining faithful to themselves, take on a particular and functional aspect which the dynamism of the Exercises assigns to them. The intellect and the will are the proper field of the human and the divine activities. Looked at from the side of the human activity, the procedure of the Exercises could be summarized in three words: to understand, to choose, and to act (or "serve"). To understand is the starting point we should appreciate at its full value, if we do not want to fall, by defect, into a vague sentimentalism, or, by excess, into abstraction and sterile intellectualism.

Intellect: the Work of Reflection and Petition for Light

"The spirit of the Society," writes Nadal, "is a clarity that grips us and leads us on. It was in this way that someone [probably Nadal himself] felt that Ignatius was led on."[37] Too often we forget that which best characterizes

---

36 A text from the Epistle to the Hebrews (12:1-2) sums up very well this movement of purification and commitment in Christ: "Therefore, since we are surrounded by so great a cloud of witnesses, let us also lay aside every weight, and sin which clings so closely, and let us run with perseverance the race that is set before us, looking to Jesus the pioneer and perfecter of our faith, who for the joy that was set before him endured the cross, despising the shame, and is seated at the right hand of the throne of God."

37 *Orationis observationes,* [85], in *MonNad,* VI, 55; see also *Dialogi (1562-1565),* in *MonNad,* V, 723-725; Nadal, *Journal spirituel,* (trans. Laval),no. 50.

the Ignatian experience and marks the method of the *Exercises:* an experience of light which purifies one and draws one on. Ignatius' readings at Loyola and especially the graces of Manresa were, above all, food for his spiritual understanding, light for "his intellect." We recall that the imaginative support for his insights into the mysteries of the faith was always reduced to a minimum: for the Trinity, "three keys of a musical instrument"; for creation, "a white object from which came rays of light"; for the Eucharist, "white rays coming from above"; for the humanity of Christ, "like a white body, neither very big nor very small, but he did not see the members distinctly"; likewise for Our Lady, "in a similar form, without distinguishing parts."[38] Furthermore, the light he received was always intense for his spirit: "His understanding began to be lifted up," "it was given to him to see in his understanding," "he saw with interior eyes," "the eyes of his understanding began to be opened," "he understood and knew many things," "he experienced a great clarity in his understanding," "this was so great an enlightenment that everything seemed new to him."[39]

Now these graces of light are always the beginning of other graces, of a different order, which Ignatius generally calls spiritual sentiments or spiritual relish. We should notice especially that these spiritual emotions—which are also graces—follow an experience of light, brought into relationship with this perception of the truth and of the divine plan of salvation. They express, therefore, an interior work of renewal leading to a deepening of faith until it becomes a "living faith," committed and transforming, in an effective love and a will to serve. When speaking of the lights received during his vision of the Trinity that had practically no imaginative element whatsoever, Ignatius said: "this brought on so many tears and so much sobbing that he could not control himself. . . . He could not hold back his tears until dinner time; after eating he could not stop talking about the Most Holy Trinity . . . with great joy and consolation."[40] The vision of creation was also a cause of "great spiritual joy."[41] Finally, the numerous apparitions of Christ in his humanity brought him to this conclusion, important also for us: "These visions strengthened him and always gave him such strength in his faith that he often thought to himself: If there were no Scriptures to teach us these matters of faith, he would be ready to die for them, only because of what he had seen then."[42] The case, therefore, is the same as that of Scripture, which also gives

38 *Autobiog*, nos. 28–29.
39 Ibid., nos. 28–30.
40 Ibid., no. 28.
41 Ibid., no. 29.
42 Ibid.

birth to an experience of knowledge and growth in Christ, as St. Paul tells the Colossians:[43]

> And so, from the day we heard of it, we have not ceased to pray for you, asking that you may be filled with the knowledge of his will in all spiritual wisdom and understanding, to lead a life worthy of the Lord, fully pleasing to him, bearing fruit in every good work and increasing in the knowledge of God. May you be strengthened with all power, according to his glorious might, for all endurance and patience with joy, giving thanks to the Father, who has qualified us to share in the inheritance of the saints *in light* (italics ours).

When Ignatius desires "to help souls" by means of the Exercises, he draws his inspiration from the particular graces of Manresa on two complementary levels. From these favors he draws the interpretation of the plan of salvation through Christ, that interpretation which guides the choice and the organization of his topics, and which also finds expression in the meditations that are typically Ignatian. He also elaborates his method by which the soul, by means of its natural powers or faculties, strives to become open to the mystery proposed, so as to welcome it fully and submit to its transforming action. This experience generated a methodology by which he stimulated anew the same experience in his advisees or retreatants. Already to the women of Alcalá Ignatius' "instructions" had presented the "articles of the faith" *(los articulos de la fe)* and explained the faculties of the soul *(las potencias del alma)*.[44] In the written *Exercises* the orientation of this activity seems to be intensified. It is addressed to the exercitant who seeks to understand and is searching for light in view of a more complete spiritual fruit corresponding to his choice and his commitment. It is also aimed at the activity of the director which it subordinates to the spiritual experience of the retreatant, both in presenting the meditations and in directing the soul.

Later on we shall see that, at one and the same time, the Exercises depend completely on the personal effort of the retreatant and completely on the action of grace. In Ignatius' perspective, God's grace is in its beginning a spiritual understanding which enlightens the recipient and then leads him to a more generous commitment in peace and joy. That is why Ignatius, in the Annotations, tells us he is proposing exercises which call for acts of the intellect *(SpEx,* [2, 3]), and consequently require certain intellectual capacities on the part of the retreatant ([18, 19]). During the Exercises, the retrea-

---

43 Col. 1:9–12. italics ours.
44 Iparraguirre, *Práctica de los Ejercicios (1522–1556),* p. 3, which quotes MHSJ, *Scripta de S. Ignacio,* I, 609.

tant should strive to know and understand the divine saving plan so as to relish it. But he or she should especially ask for the light that comes from above. And this "intermediary" grace of light will lead to those spiritual fruits proper to each stage of the Exercises: grief, shame, repentance, gratitude, commitment, service, and the like.[45] This principle of correspondence between the activity of the intellect and the grace to be petitioned is applied to each one of the Exercises which Ignatius is going to propose. Or to be more exact, the personal activity of search and of reflection is *always* necessary; the grace to be asked for often specifies this need for light, for illumination; it goes directly to the fruit which should flow from it and which brings about the desired interior transformation. Thus, whether it concerns meditations properly so called, contemplations, repetitions, applications of the senses, or other forms of prayer, the activity of the exercitant starts from a seeking of light by means of intellectual effort. What Ignatius says of each of these forms of prayer, when he is describing their technique, holds also for the continual application that the retreatant will make of them throughout the Exercises. Let us verify this statement in Ignatius' text.

The method of meditation properly so called is explained in *SpEx* [45–54], on "the three sins." But precisely when Ignatius is talking about the meditation itself, in each of the three classical points, he refers explicitly to the work of the intellect: "in applying the understanding by reasoning upon this sin"; "so, too, the understanding is to be used"; "use the understanding to consider. . . ." ([50, 51, 52]).[46] When Ignatius takes up the points for contemplations, on three occasions he will describe them more extensively: those for the Incarnation, the Nativity, and the Contemplation to Attain Love. There also, in the precise points which make up the body of the prayer, he will call for this work of the intellect. Thus, in the points on the Incarnation, the term "to reflect" is used three times ([106, 107, 108]); for the Nativity, to "reflect on oneself" is found three times ([114, 115, 116]); and in the Contemplation for Love, where there are four points, four times does Ignatius ask one to "reflect on oneself" ([234, 235, 236, 237]). When he speaks of repetition for the first time, he specifies: "I have called it a summary because the intellect, without any digression, diligently thinks over and recalls the matter" ([64]); and on the subject of the application of the senses,

---

45 On the gratuity of these spiritual fruits see *LettersIgn,* p. 181.

46 It is interesting to note that here there is question of concrete facts (the history of the fall). Ignatius really wants the retreatant to reflect on them. Other Ignatian meditations also start from facts and demand the same intellectual activity (see, e.g., *SpEx,* [141–142, 144–146, 164]).

which seems at first sight to be an entirely different type of prayer, the text says twice, "reflecting on oneself" ([123. 124]). Finally a glance at the Three Methods of Prayer reveals the following expressions: "to consider and to think over" ([241]); "to the examination and consideration" ([242]); "meditating on this word as long as he finds various meanings" (252]); "if he finds in one or two words abundant matter for thought" ([254]); "the attention is chiefly directed to the meaning of the word" ([258]).

In Ignatius we find an insistence which is absolutely sure: God has revealed Himself to him as a Light that dissipates the darkness; he desires that the retreatant, through prayer—even of contemplation and of the application of the senses—should offer his or her entire understanding to the divine power. The retreatant's work is totally directed to welcoming this light, which conditions the desired interior renewal. Ignatius writes: "We should have recourse to the true and sovereign Wisdom to ask for greater light and to obtain that clearness of vision which will order everything to his greater service and praise."[47] As a consequence of this subordination of activity to grace, the *Exercises* will often formulate the "grace to be sought" in the language of knowledge, of better understanding of God's plan of salvation for the purpose of living better:[48] "to ask the grace to know my sins" ([43]); "that I may have a deep knowledge of my sins, . . . the disorder of my actions"; "that I may have a knowledge of the world" ([63]); "asking for a perfect understanding of the commandments" ([240]); "to understand the faults committed" ([245]); "to ask for a better knowledge of the deceits of the rebel chief . . . and a knowledge of the true life" ([139]); "to ask for an intimate knowledge of our Lord" ([104]); "to know better the eternal Word Incarnate" ([130]); "an intimate knowledge of the many blessings received" ([233]).

These are the principal factors that make up the interior procedures of the retreatant during the Exercises: the work carried out on the level of understanding and of reflection, together with the petition for grace to enlighten the understanding. These two elements—manifestly in proportion to the measure in which the action of God and that of the exercitant are linked—help first of all to purify the retreatant's spirit, to reject the darkness to which Satan constantly draws him or her by inclining him towards the goods of this world and personal satisfaction. "For every one who does evil hates the light, and does not come to the light, lest his deeds should be exposed. But he who

47 *LettersIgn,* pp. 29-30.
48 On this subject read the interesting article by L. Teixidor: "Sentido teológico de las peticiones que señala S. Ignacio en los Ejercicios," *Mnr,* 5 (1929), 101-123.

does what is true comes to the light, that it may be clearly seen that his deeds have been wrought in God."[49] Thus, the one who does the truth by welcoming the light is at the same time delivered from evil and discovers the way to become fully committed. According to Ignatius himself, the Second Week of the Exercises corresponds to the illuminative way ([10]), in which the positive aspect of the spiritual experience is intensified, and in which also the light received orients one toward progress in attachment to Christ and devotion in his service.[50] As Ignatius wrote to one correspondent, "May God give you great light and fervent charity to serve him holily."[51]

Finally, this Second Week culminates in the most explicit act of man's free will, that is, the election. In it the exercitant bases all his activity on an experience of knowledge: discernment of the choice to be made, through signs which reveal, on the one hand, God's general will (his plan of salvation), and on the other hand, his particular will about choices of the present moment. This problem of knowledge extends far beyond the Third Time of Election ([177]), in which references to the activity of the understanding are more clearly expressed: "I should use the understanding to weigh the matter with care and fidelity" ([180]); "This will be to weigh the matter" ([181]); "After I have gone over and pondered in this way every aspect of the matter" ([182]). The other Times for election ([175, 176]) have recourse directly to the discernment of spirits, and furthermore are rather an experience in "interior knowledge" which makes use of everything that went before in the Exercises as an opening to the divine light, which envelope each destiny and which the Lord wishes to communicate to us. Ask and you will receive.[52]

49 John 3:20–21. See the analogy of this text with Rule 13 for the discernment of spirits for the First Week, where Satan, under the guise of a "false lover," wishes to keep the soul in isolation and secrecy, inviting it to flee self-revelation (*SpEx*, [326]). See the practical commentary on John by R. Guardini, *La figura di Gesù Cristo nel Nuovo Testamento* (Brescia, 1959), pp. 24–25.
50 *SpEx*MHSJ on p. 885 quotes the early *Directorium anonymum BI*, which in its section treating the Divisions of the Exercises states about the Second Week: "After the errors arising from the intellect and the sins have been banished, the remaining work is first of all that of illumining the intellect, that is, that it may know God and the things of God, namely, one's own self and the vanity and low worth of human things; for the will does not tend toward embracing something unknown. Here we have the aforementioned second division, called the illuminative section. The communication of it is begun in the Second Week."
51 *EppIgn*, II, 606.
52 On this subject read the very elaborate article of Karl Rahner on "The Ignatian Logic of Existential Knowledge: Some Theological Problems in the Rules for Making an Election in the Spiritual Exercises," in K. Rahner, *The Dynamic Element in the Church* (New York, 1964), [of which an English digest by H. Weidman is in *Ignatius . . . .: His Personality and Spiritual Heritage*, ed. F. Wulf

The Will: The Work of Disposing Oneself and of Spiritual Relish

We have insisted on the importance of the intellect in the Exercises for two reasons. First, because in accordance with our study of their spiritual origin, the Exercises appear from their beginning as an experience of light which communicates, in addition to the necessary but limited activity of the retreatant, an interior spiritual understanding of God's plan for salvation and spiritual growth.[53] Second, because only in this perspective can we understand well the eminent and subtle role of the will during the Exercises. Like the understanding, the will too operates on two levels; for if we ignore the openness of the will to find, through the mediation of the intellect, God's invitation and plan for spiritual growth, we reduce the will to its efforts on only the natural level, and we expose it to a sterile voluntarism which is often pharisaical. On the contrary, whereas on the natural level a generous effort is required to assure constancy and fidelity and to sustain the renunciations without which one cannot make oneself truly open to the divine promptings, nevertheless on the level of the divine action the will is corresponding to an interior motion which is aroused by the powerful graces of light which push it to a meeting with the divine will, in order to embrace it in a supernatural, effective love. The *Exercises* state precisely that "we make use of the acts of the will in manifesting our love" (Third Annotation). The election highlights this double activity, more exterior and more spiritual, of the retreatant. But all the Exercises are based on this same movement: the understanding, "enlightened by divine grace," carries the will along in its movement toward God and makes it "taste interiorly the things of God."[54] In these conditions the transformation of the soul is effected under the action of grace which acts at the levels both of the intellect and of the will, by deepening the natural

---

(St. Louis, 1977), pp. 280–289. Ed.] Read also the reflections of M.A. Fiorito in *CyF,* 20 (1964), 335–346. See also J. Aleu, "La epistemoloía sobrenatural en los Ejercicios de S. Ignacio," *Revista de Espiritualidad,* 23 (Madrid, 1964), 424–441, in which the author deepens the theological and existential meaning of the Ignatian "sentir," and presents it as "an interior perception of a motion from God." [See also J. Toner, *A Commentary on St. Ignatius' Rules for the Discernment of Spirits* (St. Louis, 1982), pp. 292–313. Ed.]

53 On three occasions, and on points of capital importance, Ignatius has the retreatant ask for the grace of "an interior knowledge": of his sins, of the Lord, and of the blessings received (*SpEx,* [63, 104, 233]).

54 The early *Directorium Breve* states (*SpEx*MHSJ, p. 976), states: "To attain the end of the Exercises, it is necessary that through them the will may be enkindled with a desire for the virtue recognized by the intellect, in order that the will thus inflamed with desire may work efficaciously and consciously until it obtains that virtue, or surely, help and grace from God for attaining it."

activity that is demanded and by giving it a salutary and sanctifying value, which man, left to his own powers, could never attain. For Ignatius, "to will consists undoubtedly in making an effort, but an effort which receives its impulse from God in the depths of the soul and which is pursued under the divine impulse. Dispose of me according to your will: the whole of spirituality consists in my considering with relish that God is directing my whole self, and in my surrendering myself to his activity. That is love and divine familiarity."[55]

According to Nadal, during the Exercises Ignatius expected from meditation "fruit in the intellect and especially in the will."[56] His prayer of offering, "Take, O Lord, and receive all my liberty," is not the result of a strenuous effort but of a movement of love in the will. It was far more by building upon this interior experience of love, rather than by having recourse to some psychological notions on the "powers" of the soul, that Ignatius arrived at this dialectical procedure of the Exercises on the level of the human faculties. He expresses this again more explicitly when he is giving direction for the reflective activity of the exercitant, teaching him about the "powers of the soul"; but he is spontaneously faithful to it when, in formulating the petitions for grace, he always makes their finality precise: to know my sins, yes, but in order "to rid myself of them" ([43]); to have an interior knowledge of my sins, of the disorder of my actions and of the world, but "so that filled with horror of them, I may amend my life and put it in order" ([63]); to have an interior knowledge of our Lord, but "that I may love him more and follow him more closely" ([104 and 130]); to ask for a knowledge of the deceits of the rebel chief, "to guard myself against them," and a knowledge of the true life in order to imitate Him ([139]); to ask for an intimate knowledge of the many blessings received, "that filled with gratitude for them, I may in all things love and serve the Divine Majesty" ([233]). And at the end of almost all his letters, Ignatius asks for the grace to perceive the divine will, in order to accomplish it more completely.

In our opinion, Nadal focuses on the center of these motions, on the levels of the intellect and the will, of the natural and the supernatural activities, when he writes: "It is in the heart that we find the beginning of every grace and of every spiritual understanding."[57] In the *Exercises* Ignatius alludes to this deep center where the activities of God and man are united, when he wishes that the soul, through its efforts to collaborate with the

55 J. Lewis, *Notes de cours.* p. 5.
56 Nadal, *Journal spirituel* (trans. Laval), no. 190; also no. 254.
57 Ibid., no. 203. See also fn. 31 above.

abundant grace of God and placed in the presence of God, "may have an interior understanding and relish of the truth" ([2]), and that "without any eagerness to go on till I have been satisfied" ([76]).

The Role of the Director

From what we have said, we can draw certain conclusions about directing the Exercises. It seems clear enough that this characteristic activity of the intellect, completely oriented toward the spiritual fruit that moves and engages the will and the whole person, conditions the work of the director both in proposing the meditations and in giving spiritual direction. We shall speak of this direction again in the following paragraph, when we shall consider more in detail the problem of human effort and of grace in the Exercises. For the moment, therefore, we limit ourselves to the task of presenting the gospel message, "of giving the points of meditation." We summarize, schematically, the work of the exercitant in order to illustrate that of the director. As we have seen, the experience of the Exercises is accomplished on four levels of activity: intellect and will, human activity (nature) and divine activity (grace).

When the director is proposing the meditations—and once again there is not question here of spiritual direction—he or she is at work on the first of these four levels. He is addressing himself to the intellect in order to open it up to the salvific plan and action of God. It is a work of great importance. It starts man on his journey to the true God,[58] toward the divine Light which alone will transform him, by delivering him from evil and engaging him fully. Two errors, then, must be avoided: a neglect of this opening of the intellect which offers the whole soul to the divine power, and a desire to arouse from without, by strong emotions, these "spiritual sentiments" which should be the fruit of grace, products of God's action in the soul. Consequently, the role of the director must be modest, sober, and respectful: to open ways. To this end it will be a precise, intelligent work, drawing its inspiration as much as possible from a spiritual, living understanding of the divine plans and actions. We have some interesting testimonies on this subject, which reveal the specific thought of St. Ignatius. There is, first of all, the Second Annotation, which indicates that the director's work should be ordered exclusively to the personal reflective activity of the retreatant, an activity which disposes him or her to relish spiritually, by the mediation, as the Annotation states, "of the grace of God enlightening his mind." This

---

58 "A knowledge that does not bring us closer to God is worthless. But if it makes us approach Him badly, that is, as an imaginary God, that is worse." S. Weil, *La pesanteur et la grâce*, p. 64

clearly indicates the most usual, but not the only, causal sequence of events in the Exercises. The director clearly exposes the truth, in a way which encourages the retreatant to reflect on it and disposes him for light. This light is the source of spiritual sentiments apt to bring about an interior renewal. In Ignatius' letters there are some allusions which, although they do not always have the Exercises as such in mind, directly concern the presentation of the gospel message, the instruction of the faithful. To Teresa Rejadell, who complained that the abundance of counsels she had received left her, because of their vagueness, confused, Ignatius replied: "I agree with you that, when one is indefinite, one does not understand, and helps less."[59] On this subject the Directory of De Fabiis wisely states that we must not be content with a meager knowledge, and with the mere reading of the text of Scripture, especially for what concerns the explanation of the mysteries; he calls also for study of them by those who give the Exercises.[60] Ignatius likewise speaks of "an understanding of Holy Scripture" (*SpEx,* [363]). In a letter to the fathers sent to Trent, in 1546, he writes: "Thus try to enkindle in souls a love of their Creator and Lord, explaining the meaning of the passage read."[61] To the fathers sent to Germany in 1549, he writes: "They will propose a solid doctrine, without multiplying scholastic terms (which are generally detested), especially if they are difficult to understand. Their lessons will be clear and nourished with learning; sustained, but without verbosity and presented with a certain elegance."[62]

Finally, the best example of this presentation of doctrine along with an opening of the person to God's plans can be taken from Ignatius' practice. In his writings there is an outline of catechesis which gives us the framework within which he explained Christian doctrine. This framework, which for the simple explanation of the commandments really amounts to an explanation of the history of salvation, certainly holds true even more for the explanation of the fundamental themes of the *Exercises:* the history of sin and the experience of salvation in Christ. In this document, entitled "On Christian Doctrine," Ignatius gives an explanation of the commandments, a teaching which is, by its very nature, moral. He then remarks that, sometime before, we should speak of "the history" which establishes a link between divine revela-

---

59 *LettersIgn,* p. 24; see also, *SpEx*MHSJ, pp. 691–692.
60 Ibid, p. 947. In the autograph Directory Ignatius, using similar terms, advises the director not to read the text of the *Exercises* in the presence of the retreatant, but to possess, as something well studied in advance, what he is about to treat.
61 *LettersIgn.* p. 95.
62 *EppIgn,* XII, 242; also in *Lettres de saint Ignace,* trans Dumeige (Paris, 1959), pp. 202–203.

tion and the problem of the Law. In a brief paragraph (certainly subject to development in the presentation), he narrates this history which extends from creation to the promulgation of the decalogue. His narrative contains the following elements: the creation of Adam and Eve, the promise of salvation, the propagation of the human race amid hope and sin, the history of Abraham and that of the "chosen people," the offenses of Pharaoh and the plagues of Egypt, the passage through the Red Sea, the preparations of the people in the desert, and the promulgation of the Law. "God our Creator," he states, "disposing the chosen people in the desert, led them to prepare and wash themselves in all purity and reverence for life."[63] Twice in the course of this brief narrative of our beginnings, Ignatius finds a way of speaking explicitly of Christ, "Son of God, Creator and Lord," when he is speaking of the creation of man and at the moment of the promise of salvation. These traits coincide very well with the Ignatian world view which we studied above in chapter 2.

To terminate, we have a perfect example of this evangelical cathechesis in the episode of the appearance of Christ to the disciples at Emmaus. On the way, the Lord roused their hearts so "slow to believe all that the prophets have spoken," and he interpreted to them "in all the scriptures the things concerning himself," and the disciples avowed that their hearts "burned within" them while he "opened to them the scriptures." Having thus welcomed the Word of life, they themselves received the broken bread from the risen Lord and were filled with joy.[64]

3. Human Effort and Grace

In treating of the problem posed by "human effort and grace," we shall not examine it from a strictly objective point of view; that belongs to the domain of theology.[65] Rather, we shall look at the aspect which this problem takes on in Ignatian spirituality. In fact, we have already touched upon this subject when we established the principles that govern this important relationship between nature and grace in the case of one making the Exercises. What now remains for us to do in practice is to verify and appraise the logic and the realism of its application.

When we spoke of the movement of the Exercises, based on the relationship between the universal and the particular, a relationship which intensifies

---

63 *EppIgn*, XII, 668, in II, Appendix sexta, no. 10, *Doctrina christiana*, pp. 666–673.

64 Luke 24:25–32.

65 See C. Baumgartner, "La place de l'effort dans la vie spirituelle," *Chr,* no. 22 (1959), pp. 196–210.

the particular by plunging it into the universal, we have already situated our dialectical movements of the Exercises on the conjoined levels of nature and grace. The relationship described as progressing through the Exercises corresponds to a maturing of faith when the constant divine call takes hold of this person with his or her individuality, and when he or she, enlightened and purified, gives himself or herself to God, to the infinity of His unfathomable self.

When we distinguished the objective and subjective levels, the message and the experience, we found the same problem on the level of the ways and means of communication which establish and maintain the vital dialogue between the person and God, and which direct his or her growth, in the Exercises as well as in the Christian experience. These considerations led us to specify the place which this spiritual dialectic reserves positively for the person's intellect and will, for his "understanding" and his "willing." As obediential powers of communion with the divine transcendence, the intellect and will are the place of convergence for the lines of force of the Christian experience, the place where the human and the divine, the eternal and the transitory meet in an atmosphere of great mutual respect; where the infinite plan is lived out in a human heart—small, concrete, here and now. At that time we made a distinction between nature and grace, personal effort and continual petition for grace with a view to "interior knowledge" and "spiritual relish" which bring about a deep transformation. We also affirmed this paradox, namely, that "the Exercises simultaneously count wholly on personal effort and wholly on the action of grace." The problem that our exposé brings to light is situated in a perspective that is clearly existential. For us it is the last word on the interactional procedures of the Exercises. We do not pretend to exhaust it, for this word opens on to the mystery of the action of God; and man must be content with modest approaches, happy if it is given to him to feel some comforting warmth. He is like the blind man whose fireplace, although invisible to his eyes, nevertheless is always radiant, and draws him infallibly.

The Importance of Personal Human Effort

Ignatius attaches enormous importance to the natural effort which consists in using the means given by God in view of man's end. This use manifests a person's sincere desire ("id quod volo") to respond effectively to the divine calls which spring from creation, redemption, faith, and love. Furthermore, Ignatius puts all his confidence in God, the author of every gift, of every grace, and the indispensable aid of every free human response. "The more God acts in a man, the more is the man free."[66] Let us try now to make the meaning of our first statement just above more precise. Ignatius calls for all the personal effort which the retreatant can furnish; yet in reality he counts only on God's grace, the source of every ordered activity and of all goodness in creatures.[67] How can we explain this paradox, to which Ignatius will hold throughout his life? More than common sense, even supernatural, is needed to maintain this position with such constancy and lucidity. Following the dazzling experience of Manresa, Ignatius acquired an extreme awareness of his position as an "unprofitable servant," from whom nevertheless the Lord solicits entire, humble, and ingenious service.[68] At the origin of this principle of action, we find Ignatius' intense contemplation and his outlook on creation which restores to every action its ontological significance: God, Creator and Lord, offers to man a universe to explore, but he remains its Author, the constantly flowing, acting, and vivifying Source, in such a way that nothing comes unless ultimately from him.[69] Once again Ignatius' attitude is dictated by man's place before God rather than by psychological tenets which would suffice to justify the "judicious use of the retreatant's faculties" in the Exercises, but which could in no way account for the entire subordination of man's activity to that of God, on this level where the accepted necessity of the human takes nothing away from the absolute of the divine.[70] "But he who has placed," writes Ignatius, "the foundation of all his hopes in God and who carefully makes use in His service of the gifts which He bestows, interior and exterior, spiritual and material, in the thought that His infinite power will do all that it wills, with or without these means, and who thinks that such solicitude pleases Him when it is properly turned into love of

66   This phrase, which one of our philosophy professors loved to repeat, expresses very well the economy of the plan of salvation, in which the gratuitous emancipation of man reveals, at the same time, his true dignity.

67   *LettersIgn,* pp. 18, 309.

68   Do we not see this here?—that Ignatius is asking God to give him "His love and a relish for His service in preference to anything else" (*EppIgn,* IV, 565); also, that he is declaring in the *Exercises,* [370] that "though the zealous service of God our Lord out of pure love should be esteemed above all else, we ought also to praise highly the fear of the Divine Majesty."

69   We might say that Ignatius "experienced" interiorly and mystically this reality of Scripture: "In him we live and move and have our being (Acts 17:28).

70   In the statement of this principle we recognize the equivalent of the much-discussed Ignatian maxim as reported by Hevenesi [in 1706], to which Fessard fortunately does justice in his *Dialectique,* pp. 305–363. [On the varying formulations of Ribadeneira and Hevenesi, see also fn. 75 in ch. 2, above. Ed.]

Him—this is not to bend the knee to Baal but to God, in recognition of His authorship, *not only of grace but of nature too.*"[71]

The one who gives the Exercises has constant recourse to "human means" and proposes them for use by his retreatant. If he or she does this without placing himself inside Ignatius' ordered vision of God, he easily derogates from the *Exercises* and runs the risk of deforming the spiritual perceptiveness of his retreatant. The human means proposed in the *Exercises* are many and detailed. They ought to be the expression in the concrete of a sustained interior movement toward God, and the manifestation of a sincere, faithful, and ordered desire to give oneself. Consequently, one should always be flexible in their application. The prescriptions recommending them should never be observed for themselves alone. The important thing is to maintain, under all circumstances, the dynamic principle which gives them life and justifies them, this principle which always reminds us of our dependence on God according to the interpretation which Ignatius gives to those prescriptions: My faith in God, the author of grace and of nature, ought to express itself in my faithful, human, and intelligent activity, because my faith is founded absolutely on the divine power. To escape the paradoxical balance of this economy or arrangement willed by God is to give oneself over to human perfectionism which leads to spiritual pharisaism, or to abandon oneself to fainthearted effort, deceptively self-indulgent, which definitively wards off the burning touches of grace. To make the Exercises well is to dispose oneself with all one's heart to the gratuitous divine action; it is to take seriously "the risk involved in meeting God."

Prayer and Grace

Fortunately for us, Ignatius has centered his Exercises so clearly on prayer and contemplation that the Holy Spirit reserves for himself, even without our being aware of it, times normally propitious for his action. "Above all, pray that the windows of light may be open for you, for no one can see nor understand if God and his Christ do not grant him to understand."[72] So in order that the Exercises might be an experience of light and of spiritual relish coming from above, Ignatius made of them an experience of prayer. Conceived in prayer, they can be made only in prayer. From one day

---

71 *LettersIgn,* pp. 192–193 (italics ours). This letter was written by Polanco, who declared that he was "merely the pen," and asked that the whole letter be accepted "as coming . . . from our father, who has given the orders" (ibid., p. 190). See also *LettersIgn,* p. 401.
72 Justin, quoted by R. Aubert, *Le probléme de l'acte de foi* (1945), p. 18.

to the next, from one Week to the next, under all the forms they may take, they are nothing but prayer. In addition to emphasizing in several places the importance they give to prayer, they suggest no less than five or six ways of examining oneself and almost ten ways of praying. Several excellent studies have examined this point, prayer as the nerve and the life of the Ignatian Exercises.[73] In the context of the reflections that have led us to emphasize the presence and the importance of prayer in the Exercises, we would like to note what characterizes the Ignatian insistence on this subject. First, through continual prayer in which the times of the meditations are privileged heights, the whole activity of the retreatant is ordered to what is spiritual. The most material details[74] do not escape this orientation. They prepare and sustain the climate of prayer,[75] assure the detailed conditions of its success, and prolong its fruit. First of all, it is through the intermediary of prayer that human effort, in the Exercises, gives to God the worship of the entire person whom

73 Being unable to develop this subject, we shall simply give a few helpful references. For prayer and contemplation in the *Exercises*, see L. Peeters, *Vers l'union divine par les Exercices de S. Ignace;* J. Brucker, "Ignace de Loyola," *DTC,* t. 27, c. 726; J. Lewis, *Conduite d'une retraite,* pp. 7-8. On the examen, see I. Iparraguirre, *A Key to the Study,* pp. 57-58; L. Lallemant, *Doctrine spirituelle,* pp. 196-197, 228-229. For the composition of place, see L. de Coninck, "Adaptation ou retour aux origines," *NRTh,* 70 (1948), 925 ff; Fessard, La *dialectique,* pp. 134 ff; H. U. von Balthasar, *Prayer* (New York, 1957), pp. 103-114. On the review of the meditation, see M. Giuliani's presentation of the Ignatian practice in his Introduction to the *Journal spirituel,* p. 16. Concerning the application of the senses, see J. Maréchal, "Notes sur la Méthode d'application des sens dans les Exercices de S. Ignace," *CBE,* 61-62 (1920), 50-64; L. Torfs, "The Application of the Senses," *Ign,* 1956, pp. 137-139. See also nos. 19 and 20 of *Chr,* (1958); [A. Brou, *Ignatian Methods of Prayer (Milwaukee, 1949). Ed.].*

74 The numerous techniques or didactic means that are proposed especially in the Annotations, additions, and notes for each Week—all this makes up another topic which we cannot develop in detail here. What we have to say about them concerns practically only their finality and their significance in the divine economy of creation and of the orientation of every person to God. The psychological aspect has often been studied by others; it takes into account more the meaning, on the human side, of this finality and this significance. On the subject of the "judicious use of the faculties of the retreatant," see J. Nonell, *Analyse des Exercices spirituels,* pp. 115-119; on the subject of the "exploitation of resources and of natural tendencies," see Fessard, *La dialectique,* pp. 8, 15, 35 (note), 37, 96-100, 202-203; and on "the activation of the whole man," L. de Coninck, art. cit., *NRTh,* 70 (1948), pp. 922 ff.

75 "Before making a vow, prepare yourself; and do not be like a man who tempts the Lord," Sir 18:23. Giuliani's Introduction to Ignatius' *Journal spirituel* (p. 18; see also pp. 84-85) shows us concretely what Ignatius meant by "the preparation for entering into prayer.

it disposes for and opens up to the gift of grace. It is in this way that fidelity to the ways of God is guaranteed, through the movement of our being toward its end. Second, to attain so noble an end, Ignatius recognizes the need of a prayer that is "ordered," directed to a specific goal,[76] and to this end he proposes an intelligent prayer which he elevates as much as possible to the level of spiritual awareness. He accomplishes this by specifying in terms of the activity and the graces to be asked for, the roles of the intellect and the will. However, he subordinates these roles to the spiritual fruit being sought, and he clearly recommends that one should feel free to linger in order "to taste interiorly the things of God" when this blessing is granted to the soul.[77] It is also in view of this end that Ignatius multiplies meditations, that he varies their forms, and especially that he recommends the repetition in which the "intellect, without any digression, thinks over and recalls the matter contemplated in the previous exercises."[78] Finally, let us note that it is through prayer, itself guided and ordered in the light of the revealed message, that one experiences a deeper understanding and a relish of the plan of salvation through Christ, a deepening facilitated by the internal structure of the *Exercises.* There the intellect can clearly discern the logic of the divine pedagogy, but if the intellect does not give way, in prayer, to the spiritual relishing which transforms interiorly, the soul will not make any progress in this way of purification and commitment, of death and resurrection.

c. The Role of the Director

In the making of the Exercises the delicate problem of nature and grace is partially resolved by the dynamic orientation which God's plan of salvation imparts to the spiritual experience, and by the primacy of prayer which integrates the full activity of the retreatant, including the "judicious use of his natural faculties," into this progression. We now take up the role which the director should take on within these perspectives.

As we have already pointed out, the director is the one who proposes the message, who opens up the retreatant's understanding of God's plan and indicates the way the retreatant should follow in the search for light; but he is also the one who discreetly and fraternally accompanies the retreatant for the whole length of this intense, delicate, and difficult journey.

As an instrument to accomplish this task, Ignatius gives the director the directives for the discernment of spirits or spiritual "motions" which are

76 *SpEx,* [46, 75, 76, 254]; and, indirectly, [5, 20, 234]; see also *Cons,* [277].
77 Ibid., [2, 76, 254].
78 Ibid., [64]; also [62, 118].

caused in the soul ([313–336]). In them he clearly indicates the nature of the director's collaboration.[79] But to guard himself against getting lost in this immediate task in which the spirit of analysis is predominant, the director should have clearly in view the full significance of the experience which is proper to the Exercises, in order to subordinate his particular measures clearly into this overall experience. For it is in this same radiation of light from God's salvific plan, which illumines and directs the process of the Exercises, that the director will find the real significance of his humble but indispensable work. God, Creator and Lord, places the retreatant in motion toward Himself, by means of what is human and natural in creation. And when Ignatius gives the Exercises, he devotes himself to the service and praise of God in the retreatant, his brother or sister, to whom he is giving humble service. This same divine center ought to be the pivot—within the discreet charity which it inspires—of the activities of the director and the exercitant. From this divine center comes the unity of all the initiatives on the diverse levels of the Exercises.

This spontaneously fostered relationship to the divine transcendence in no way interferes with those principles which assure, in a human manner, a healthy and effective "spiritual direction"; rather, it allows these principles to become rooted in his center of unity which gives them their continual supernatural orientation. We must not forget that the Exercises take hold of the psychological and spiritual development of the retreatant at a special time in his or her experience. The psychological and theological laws of "pastoral dialogue" will find a special application in the use of the discernment of spirits which gives a special quality to the experience of the Exercises. But this work itself will always remain subordinate to what is essential, to authentic union with God, in which the real drama of the Exercises, and of the Christian experience, takes place in the most inviolable intimacy. Ignatius recalls that the director "should permit the Creator to deal directly with the creature, and the creature directly with his Creator and Lord."[80] If the direc-

---

79 Ibid., [17, 6–14, 313–336]. On the role of the director, several interesting studies will complete the restricted point of view which limits us here; e.g., J. Nonell, *Analyse des Exercices,* 122–123; J. Lewis, *Conduite,* pp. 19–26; Iparraguirre, *A Key to the Study* (passim), and *Dirección de una tanda,* pp. 20–49; *How to Give a Retreat,* pp. 23–58; L. Lallemant, *The Spiritual Doctrine* (1946), pp. 77–78; J. Jacquet, "Le rôle de l'Instructeur de la retraite," *Chr,* no. 10 (1956), pp. 208–224.

80 *SpEx,* [15]. In his course notes on spiritual direction, L. Mendizábal studies the essential character of the "direction of the Spirit in the economy of the New Testament." He develops this point especially by starting from the exegesis of

tor has not thoroughly grasped the import or structure of the Exercises, and has not completely understood the complex way in which they develop and in which the supernatural accomplishes the entire work of salvation, but counts instead entirely on the ready availability and the constant flexibility of the natural, he will very easily let his activity be diverted from this single goal. Either he will presumptuously take into his own hands the spiritual development of the retreatant and the influence of divine grace, the one and only effective force in this development, and thus make of it a purely human and psychological gymnastic; or he will abandon the retreatant to the accidents of his route, without using discernment, thus causing him or her to waste his precious energies which he ought to be organizing in order to submit them to God.[81] An exact knowledge of his role will protect the director from these errors and assure his humble cooperation which God desires to take into account to accomplish His own marvels.[82]

Whether we look at it from the point of view of the retreatant or of the director, to follow Ignatius and to be faithful to his spirit is not an easy thing. The extremes which come together in him and are accepted by him with so much respect are often disconcerting to us, for our manners of acting and judging are characteristically less tolerant of one or the other extremity. Ignatius destroys neither one, but accepts each extreme with human warmth. He draws his love for everything from the very heart of God, for him the real source of all life, even natural life, which he meets, touches, and contemplates. Thus trusting in God alone, but filled with the gifts which he receives from Him, he is always gravitating toward that praising of God which is so attractive to him. Jean Daniélou rightly thinks that the characteristic mark of Ignatius' work is a "certain classic style resulting from genius as well as from holiness, that balance between discipline and adventure of which Apollinaris spoke, and which seems to bring a unity into that powerful inspiration

Heb. 9:6–14. See his *Dirección Espiritual: Teoría y práctica* (Madrid: Biblioteca de autores Christianos, 1978) this topic forms a chapter, pp. 5–32, as "The Place of Human Direction in the Spiritual Economy of the New Testament." Ed.]

81 The "director ought to conduct himself as a helper of divine grace," Directory of Cordeses, quoted by I. Iparraguirre, *Dirección de una tanda*, p. 28.

82 There is an interesting article on a parallel subject, starting from the same divine center, God's plan of salvation through Christ. It brings to light the principles that should guide anyone who wishes to help another spiritually: J. P. Ramseyer, "Principes christologiques de la cure d'âme," *Verbum Caro*, 14 (54, '60), 136–152. See also A. Godin, *La relation humaine dans le dialogue pastoral*, (Paris, 1963); R. Hostie, *L'entretien pastoral*, (Paris, 1963); K. Rahner, Mission et Grâce, II, "Serviteurs du peuple de Dieu," Mame, 1963; R. Barbin, *Pédagogie religieuse et relations humaines*, (Paris, 1966).

possessed by a saint as well as by an artist. When this inspiration falters and when method becomes more important than genius, there is degeneration into a false classicism. . . . The rules then function within a vacuum. They become mechanical and burdensome, a mere book of recipes. One who has not mastered them will do best to drop them. Classicism has no place for mediocrity; it always demands greatness."[83]

> "Not to be limited by the immeasurable,
> and yet to keep oneself concerned with the tiniest,
> is something divine."

Such was the epitaph intended for Ignatius' tomb, according to the *Imago Primi Saeculi*. On this subject Daniélou writes: "The 'immeasurable' is the divine inspiration which leads one into the abyss of the wonderful works of God; the 'tiniest' is fidelity in little things, attention to detail, the examen, the election. 'Nothing should be neglected.' Yes, there is a meticulousness, and this meticulousness is attention to what is least. But to be attentive to little things when one is engaged in important matters, there is the divine."[84] There is only one way to understand Ignatius well, and that is to go through the gospel, through God's whole plan for salvation and spiritual development which informed his entire life.

83   J. Daniélou, "Le message ignatien et notre temps," *Et*, 290 (1956), p. 10.
84   Ibid., p. 11.

CONCLUSION TO PART 1

GOD'S PART IN A PERSON'S GROWTH

In this Part I of our book, we have tried to sketch the chief elements and the interacting forces which are found within the Ignatian method—those factors through which with God's grace it stimulates that experience which is truly characteristic of itself. We then singled out the fundamental principles which enable us to base an interpretation of the *Exercises* on factors which are oriented toward a unified and consistent Christian experience. Still another step remains to be taken now if we wish to follow Ignatius completely. This step dominates these different dialectical considerations and interacting forces previously mentioned, and it also facilitates our own necessary passage from theory to practice. For Ignatius, as we should clearly recognize, theory does not in any way stifle practice, especially when this practice springs with fidelity from theory which has become life-giving and inspiring. Here we have the reason why it is difficult to be faithful to Ignatius' spirit. For his spirit is a dynamism which draws us on towards attracting goals. This interior dynamism, although nowhere fully explained, is also what alone explains the nature of a willing and flexible application of his principles, rules, and methods, to which it then imparts the true reason for their existence.

The question which arises for us is to know how Ignatius, who was more or less aware of the problem, was able to be faithful to this unifying center which animated all his procedures, without ever losing himself in the multitude of details which accompanied them. To find the way which leads us to this vital center is to apply to the problem of "theory and practice" the same solution which Ignatius himself employed, without his being able to formulate its secret for us in so many words. Furthermore, for us just as for Ignatius before us, to find this way will bring back into one coordinated unity the many elements which our analysis has so far distinguished—on the levels of the universal and the particular, of the objective and the subjective, and above all, of the preeminent guiding and inspirational functions of God's plan for salvation and spiritual growth, coupled with our experience of his accomplishing it within ourselves. All these factors work together in producing the spiritual experience of the exercitant, by means of the interrelated activities of the intellect and of the will, of nature and of grace, of the director and of the retreatant.

The Dynamism of Desire

The superiority of Manresa over Loyola, of the mystical and ineffable prolongation of that first encounter with the Lord of Majesty, is to be sought along the line of an unlimited opening of the mind to God's universal plan for the salvation of women and men through their continual growth in Christ. In this ordered vision of all things, seen now from the viewpoint of the Creator, an exercitant finds himself or herself suddenly animated and caught up in his whole being, by a movement which projects him, along with along with all other creatures, toward God, in and through His Christ. For the Word took on himself the original thrust of Creation; and human beings, by becoming divinized through the Incarnation of the Word made flesh, contemplate the radiant and eternal transfiguration of their own destiny. From this point on, they finds themselves enroute, through grace and in their nature now both human and divine, toward this unexpected fullness of God. They, with their human condition and its weight of universal misery, not only emerge from darkness, but are invited into the full bright light which draws them on toward God. Their approach, which depends on the gratuitous and bountiful action of grace, incorporates the very substance of the miseries inherent in the human condition: painful wounds which are so heavy a burden in this world but which will also be brought within the experience of the glory of the resurrection. They, in union with the Only Beloved Son of the Father, lead the whole world, which is the object of the love and praise of the Father, along their laborious path of human self-development and self-fulfillment. They call it to transcend itself and enter, through them and with them, into the divine glory.

For anyone, to grasp this movement of being ceaselessly invited to grow as a person journeying toward the divine presence through an ever closer union with the whole of creation—that is to submit it to the vivifying action of the Holy Spirit groaning within us. Moreover, to maintain oneself there through the graced good will of a total gift of self—this was the difficult life Ignatius led and the secret he continues to transmit to us through the medium of the *Exercises*.

But will we know how to understand it, under the often awkward language he uses to express it? Will we learn how to extract the precious metal from his heavy and dense ore? Or will we let what is essential escape us? Karl Rahner wrote in 1959 wrote that the originality of this spirituality "will be fully understood" only "in the future." This spirituality "is not typical of our time; it is not characteristic of the modern era which is nearing its end. It is, rather, a sign of the approaching future. It is an open question whether his sons and disciples of the past will be the authentic representatives of this spirit in the future."[1]

To state it simply, it is in the unexplored theme of *spiritual desire* that we have found, now drawn together, all the elements which we have been studying, and also the dynamism or synthesizing force which organizes them toward spiritual growth. In Ignatius' life and work, a spiritual desire, born of God, faithfully accepted, and submitted to the discretion of charity, (and expressed also in the *Exercises*), drew Ignatius in an irresistible movement which channelled and harmonized the multiple data we have just been studying. Consequently in Ignatius' view of the case of every soul, the presence of this spiritual desire is a divine grace which means an opening to the light. Its permanence and discreet growth simply follow the profound tension of the soul in its movement toward God and are, moreover, an expression of this movement of the person whose self-fulfillment is being directed more and more by grace. A human being is completely a being of desire. This natural and metaphysical fact is perhaps the one which Ignatius understood best— among the many factors within the movement imparted by grace to regenerated being. Let us take a closer look at this fact in the life of the saint, that we may better understand its expression in the spiritual movement proposed by the *Exercises*.

In the Experience of the Saint

In Ignatius' own soul, the true point of departure on his spiritual journey, which started at Loyola and was never interrupted, was the appearance of new

---

1 K. Rahner, "Spiritualité ignatienne et dévotion au Sacré-Coeur," *RAM*, 35 (1959), 151, of which an English trans., "Ignatian Spirituality and Devotion to the Sacred Heart," is on p. 126 of ch. 7 in K. Rahner, *Christian in the Market Place* (New York, 1966), pp. 119–146; see also ch. 6, "The Theological Meaning of Devotion to the Sacred Heart, pp. 105–118; [for more references, see below in fn. 118 of ch. 5]. On the same theme, read the reflections of H. Bremond, who considered the *Exercises* as not really having survived St. Ignatius; see also the discussion of Fessard on this subject, starting from Bremond's ideas in *La dialectique*, pp. 90–91. Besides, we have a statement of Ignatius himself, recounted in the *Memoriale* of Câmara, April, 1555. The statement seems to reveal some disappointment of the saint, even though it bears on certain precise features of the Exercises, [such as spending three days without eating or drinking]; they had, he feared, already lost something of their original rigor and vigor (*Memoriale*, no. 305, in *FN*, I, 704.

and intense desires for the service of God. They came to him in his reading the life of Christ, accompanied by prayer for long periods, in his contemplating the examples of the saints, and in his gazing at the star-filled heavens. At first it was a modest desire which disturbed his selfishness and his thirst for worldly pleasures and little by little made him feel the need to reform his life;[2] and this ultimately led to a commitment to follow Christ in his search for the divine will. When he left Loyola, he took with him a heart "inflamed with the love of God"; he was filled with a great "desire to imitate the saints" and a "resolve to serve Our Lord," and his soul was "animated with a great desire to serve in any way that God might ask of him."[3]

But as we have seen, this initial desire, although efficacious, was scarred by the residue of that human ambition which used to motivate the knight in him, and which would be the object of the healing experience of Manresa. Now it was precisely the permanence of this desire—a gift of God to which Ignatius was faithful—that enabled him to cling, despite an exhausting struggle, to the ideal he had found. Had it not been for the fact that this desire was strengthened and nourished by the rich and substantial spiritual reading at Loyola, the encouragement of the pious people he met, and the careful reading of the Passion and the long prayer periods at Manresa, he would easily have foundered before the pressures of common sense and the powerful traps of Satan. But "his resolve to go forward in the service of the Lord,"[4] a grace flowing from his first conversion, supported him and enabled him to overcome that most subtle temptation which tries to make us forego a good which is greater and decisive for our divine destiny. The trials of Manresa seem to have whittled down Ignatius' desire and cleansed it of its initial grandiose ambitions; in fact, it is purified of self-love, strengthened and greatly ennobled, and thus ready for anything that the work of salvation might ask. "At the same time," writes Nadal, "there was born in him a desire to help his neighbor."[5]

When Ignatius leaves Manresa, he takes with him this same desire, but it is now a desire which is matured and solidly rooted in God's plan of creation, salvation, spiritual growth, and ultimate beatitude—all the elements which make up St. Paul's "mystery of Christ." It is a desire that is limited only by discreet charity. From now on it is desire to seek refuge in God alone; to live

2 *Autobiog,* nos. 8, 9, 10.
3 Ibid., nos. 9, 11, 13, 14. [See also E. Kinerk, "Eliciting Great Desires: Their Place in the Spirituality of the Society of Jesus," *Studies in the Spirituality of Jesuits,* XVI, 5 (Nov., 1984), 1–29. Ed.]
4 Ibid., no. 21.
5 *FN,* II, 190. For other texts of Nadal and Polanco, see above, ch. 1, note 107.

by the virtues of faith, hope, and charity; and to consecrate his life to the good of souls.[6] This desire—this intention, *intendere*—will be the guiding light of all his actions. Engendered in him, once and for all, it is as firm as the ordered movement of his being which expresses it; so firm that nothing short of his total separation from God can interrupt it. In 1522 Ignatius writes: "I would ask Him even to take away my life rather than to grieve Him in anything or grow slack in His service and praise."[7]

If we look very closely at this intimate movement of the soul, the fruit of grace, we see in it all the components of the spiritual experience we studied above. Through his whole being as a creature, this man has been set into motion toward his end; the graces of light and energy come to order this movement and give it an inclination which is one of a new, inexhaustible love. The action of the Holy Spirit in us is not violent; it follows the bent of our being and orients it to the true Life, through the natural path of desire which it opens into infinite capacities.[8] For Ignatius, this spiritual desire which will animate him in everything is a gift from God. Even in those matters which are not attractive to our sensitive nature, it gently moves the soul towards its end, an end which, through grace, suddenly takes on all the splendors of the divine glory. Love engenders and nourishes this desire, while the desire itself seeks the perfection of love in the praise and service of God. Through these simple words of desire, will, and spiritual relish, as we shall see, Ignatius understands and expresses the whole natural thrust of a human being who has been invaded by grace, to project himself or herself ever forward in order that, "inflamed with the love of God," he may be capable of accomplishing everything God may ask of him:

> For souls that are inflamed with a desire for His greater service, praise, and glory, by whetting each other's appetites, are always roused and helped by an unfailing solace and spiritual progress. As the object is infinite and the potency finite, there will always be room for improvement.[9]

6 *Autobiog*, no. 35.

7 *LettersIgn*, p. 7.

8 B. Lonergan analyzes the theory of St. Thomas on this subject, together with the evolution which he observes as taking place, beginning in the *Sentences,* continuing in the *De Veritate,* and finally in the *Summa.* St. Thomas' teaching on the gifts of the Holy Spirit is well presented in Ia-IIae, q. 68, a. 3. Lonergan concludes by saying: "Similarly habits are of two kinds: the virtues perfect the individual who possesses them, but the gifts of the Holy Ghost make connatural to the creature the external guidance and aid of the Spirit of truth and love." Lonergan, "St. Thomas' Thought on Gratia Operans," *TS*, 3 (1942), esp. 70–72.

9 *LettersIgn*, p. 69.

The first thing to remember, then, is this: For Ignatius, spiritual desire is a divine gift; and it has God as its ultimate object, since it is a movement of the soul toward this end which grace reveals as being completely desirable. In the famous letter of 1536 to Teresa Rejadell, which is considered as a "commentary on the period at Manresa," Ignatius writes:

> If you look closely, you understand that these desires of serving Christ our Lord are not your own, but come to you from our Lord. If you were to say that our Lord gives you great desires of serving Him, you would be giving praise to the same Lord because you are making known His gift, and you glory in Him, not in yourself, because you do not attribute that grace to yourself.[10]

He reminds other correspondents too that their desires for an ever greater perfection and a more perfect service depend on God. He writes of "the desires and holy aims that come from" the Holy Spirit, and of "your sincerity of purpose and the desire which God gives you for his greater service."[11] This is what will guide Ignatius in the help he gives his correspondents in order that they may "employ the good inspirations and desires given by God."[12] In the same way he invokes the Holy Spirit for one correspondent: "That having granted you the desire to help in this matter, he may grant you his copious grace to accomplish this task."[13]

In his own case too Ignatius recognizes his dependence on God in regard to the interior movement he feels, that he may submit its orientation willingly to Him. To his townsfolk of Azpeitia he writes: "His Divine Majesty well knows how much and how often he has given me the sincere wish and earnest desire to be of some spiritual service, even though it be slight, and to do what kindness I can in the Divine Goodness to all the men and women of my native land. . . . These desires, which come from the Lord and Creator of us all rather than from any natural cause, led me five years ago from Paris to your city. . . . Let me repeat that there is no desisting in my earlier desires that you continue to enjoy in this life peace and quiet of heart in the true peace of our Lord, not in the peace of the world."[14] When he was elected general of the Society, these same desires became part of the special vocation which Providence gave him. In 1547 he writes of them to his brethren at Gandía: "And I feel a loving desire in keeping with this obligation, a desire

10   Ibid., p. 20.
11   Ibid., pp. 409 and 418.
12   Ibid., p. 353. See also pp. 69, 407–408, 363.
13   Letter to Bishop Weber, Dec. 9, 1550, *EppIgn,* III, 250–252; for a French version, see *Lettres,* trans. Dumeige, p. 226.
14   *LettersIgn,* p. 43

which God our Lord bestows upon me, to see it [the good of the Society] increase. This leads me to consider by what means we can advance the interests of the Society and its members, to God's honor and glory."[15] In asking for help from some important person or in offering the services of the Society, this desire to serve God is what guides him surely. In soliciting help from the Archbishop of Toledo, he states that it is in view "of better accomplishing the desires, given us by the Author of every good, to serve God and to help the neighbor."[16] Likewise it is "this great desire in our Lord," or "the intense desire to be useful in the Lord," that impels him to offer his services in the hope of bearing fruit for the glory of God.[17] Such is the logic which animates Ignatius, within the framework of a charity which orders all his energies to God, "since," he writes, "the soul that truly desires to serve its Creator and Lord seeks every possible means that will help it"; again this "desire always to be of service" to others he strives "to keep . . . as holy charity demands."[18]

Now, as the soul grows in the love of God, so its very desire grows likewise and is focused more directly on the very heart of God's saving plan, Christ on the cross, whose suffering it longs to share. On the subject of the soul which he describes as "enlightened and illumined," Ignatius writes: "Its whole desire is to desire nothing other than Christ and him crucified."[19] Along this line, when he is trying to explain himself to the king of Portugal in 1545, he holds this discourse, of which we find a direct echo in the *Constitutions:* "You will understand that, the more we desire to succeed, apart from offense on the part of our neighbor, in clothing ourselves with the uniform of Christ our Lord, which is woven out of insult, false witness, and every other kind of injustice, the more we shall advance in spirit and earn those spiritual riches with which, if we are leading spiritual lives, our souls desire to be adorned."[20] When speaking of this increase in spiritual desire, as we shall see

15 Ibid., p. 140. The *Constitutions* will require of the general the same attitude of "holy desire" toward the good of the Society, for the glory of God (*Cons,* [790]); they expect the same of every superior (ibid., [424]).
16 From the letter to Juan Martínez Guyeño [Siliceus], Archbishop of Toledo, June 1, 1552 (*EppIgn,* IV, 264; see translation in *Lettres,* p. 264).
17 *LettersIgn,* pp. 85 and 69.
18 Ibid., p. 50, and letter to Bernardino Taro, May 17,1556 (*EppIgn,* III, 250–251; *Lettres,* p. 495). See the text of Nadal on the origin of the desire that pushed Ignatius to write down the *Exercises,* in order to be helpful to his neighbor (cited above in ch 1, fn. 107).
19 Ibid., p. 69.
20 Ibid., p. 81; see also p. 331: "As to the dispositions which Your Ladyship desires as a preparation for the cross, God will arrange it in His own time—I mean at the moment when patience will be necessary for you." In this sense of

in the *Exercises* on the subject of the third kind of humility, Ignatius will have only to recall its existence as the object of humble prayer and divine grace: "If one desires to attain this third kind of humility, it will help very much to use the three colloquies at the close of the meditation on the Three Classes of Men mentioned above. He should beg our Lord to deign to choose him for this third kind of humility, which is higher and better, that he may the more imitate and serve him, provided equal or greater praise and service be given to the Divine Majesty."[21]

In the Making of the Spiritual Exercises

The *Spiritual Exercises* are, from the beginning to the end of their sequence, a resumption of this spiritual journey of Ignatius. They will express anew this dynamic concept of a person in an intense effort both natural and supernatural toward a God who is reached and served, through Christ, in the created world immediately present. Consequently this phenomenon of spiritual desire—spontaneous, sincere, gratuitous, and always increasing—is what will principally guide Ignatius in achieving his plans which structure the *Exercises*. In them he develops their component parts with the ease of one who has understood everything, and for whom everything is simple and resolved through the total opening of self in loving response to divine grace. We now take up again the chief stages in these *Exercises*, to apply briefly to them this consideration to which Ignatius' experience inspires us, and which Part II of our book will treat in greater detail.

Ignatius based his hope for lasting spiritual fruit on the presence in the retreatant of an initial desire, firmly determined, which is already the fruit of divine grace, a call or attraction from God, and which involves both God and man by engaging them to start out on the road of an irreversible spiritual development. Indeed, this is what he detects in many of his correspondents; and it attracts his attention and causes him to answer their letters. For he sees in this desire the foundation of an assured spiritual fruit.

To Agnes Pascual he writes, June, 1536:

I thought I should write to because of the great desire I know you have of serving our Lord.[22]

the third kind of humility Ignatius wrote that he very much desired to be taken again, reprimanded, corrected, and humiliated, and furthermore he hoped to find this disposition among those who desired to enter the Society (*Exam*, [101-102]; *Cons*, [292]).

21 *SpEx*, [168].
22 *LettersIgn*, p. 3.

To Teresa Rejadell, June, 1536:

Your letter . . . brought with it much joy in our Lord, whom you are serving and whom you desire to serve even more earnestly, and to whom we must attribute all the good that we see in creatures.[23]

To his sister Magdalena de Loyola, May, 1541:

I received your letter a few days ago. It gave me much satisfaction in the Lord to see therein your good desires and holy affections for God's greater glory.[24]

To Manuel Santos, bishop of Targa, May, 1547:

I have had much comfort and consolation in our Lord from your lordship's letter. 1 find in it a proof, not only of the kindly remembrance of your lordship but also of the great charity which animates you to desire both our spiritual advancement and the glory of God in us.[25]

To the members of the Society in Portugal:

It gives me great consolation, my dear brothers in our Lord Jesus Christ, when I learn of the lively and earnest desires for perfection in his divine service and glory which he gives you, who by his mercy has called you to this Society.[26]

To Nicholas Gaudano, in November, 1553:

It gives me great edification to see the desire you have of being of help to souls in Germany.[27]

To Juan Pérez, in December, 1555:

I was greatly consoled in Christ our Lord to see that his Holy Spirit, and the desires and holy aims that come from him, shine through your letter.[28]

23 Ibid., p. 18.
24 Ibid., p. 50.
25 Ibid., p. 131; see also pp. 153–154, a letter sent to T. Rejadell during the same year. It contained a similar piece of advice.
26 *LettersIgn*, p. 287, March 1553, on the subject of obedience.
27 Ibid., p. 311, and p. 409 (Dec. 1555).
28 Ibid., p. 409.

When we spoke of the stage of "preparation" for the Exercises, we saw how Ignatius insisted that they be given only to persons of great desire *(muy deseosas de perfección).*[29] This is the thought behind the twentieth Annotation: "To one who is freer, and desirous of making as much progress as possible, all the Spiritual Exercises should be given." When this is the case, the Annotation continues, the retreatant will adopt all the dispositions necessary to respond fully to the divine advances, in order "to seek diligently what the soul so much desires." That is the reason why we insisted, while treating the preparatory stage, on the necessity of awakening the retreatant to an ideal which will really make him or her desire the experience of the Exercises and of an encounter with the Lord, and help him to enter into this experience with confidence and without reserve. If the initial attitude of the soul ought to correspond as much as possible to the description given of it in the fifth Annotation, then we understand that, for Ignatius, the entrance into an experience of such quality ought not to be made in ignorance or without a firmly determined will—a will directed by a clear conscience and nourished by a great desire for God. On the occasion of some fathers leaving for an important and delicate mission in 1549, Ignatius wrote: "Your first and greatest asset will be a distrust of self together with a great and magnanimous trust in God. *Join to this an ardent desire, enkindled and sustained by obedience and charity, to attain the end proposed.'*[30]

The Ignatian expression, "what I desire" *(id quod volo)* occurs repeatedly in petitions throughout the *Exercises.* On condition that it is the spontaneous expression of a desire, of a movement of the soul, this *id quod volo* will assure the permanence of this initial and exceedingly important attitude throughout the whole duration of the Exercises. It will also make sure that the evolution of this desire will take place in accordance with the orientation which the *Exercises* propose, through reflection on the glorious end of man, on Christ as the unique way of reaching that end, and on the many ways one has of worshiping one's Creator. The genuine dynamism of the *Exercises* is that of this desire which gives rise to prayerful search, and which divine grace comes to purify and to open, the desire to open up to all the lights revealed through God's salvific plan.

29 *EppIgn,* XII, 677.
30 *LettersIgn,* p. 212 (italics are ours). On this disposition in the Exercises, see [5 and 350]. Remember that Ignatius gave the Foundation by committing us to a search for "what we desire." There are other texts which express Ignatius' explicit attention to basic dispositions, based on the desire for progress, perfection, and service of God (see *LettersIgn,* pp. 50, 124–125, 131 (twice), 245, 281, 298–299.

The Exercises, then, ought to open on a note of desire, which is normally formulated in the prayer of petition. Right from the start,[31] Ignatius often repeats the expression "what I desire" *(id quod volo),* in order to bring out that attitude of desire which is to be maintained to the very end: "To ask God our Lord for what I want and desire." He will use this same verb to have the retreatant beg, in the colloquies and at the moment when he humbly offers himself to be received, to be "placed with Christ."[32] If we carefully attend to this dynamism of desire in the Exercises, we shall see that the sum total of efforts and activities of the retreatant which accompanies it is not the result of an exterior and voluntaristic imperative. Instead, the desire itself in what brings these activities into existence. They are the retreatant's effort to respond to a need he feels in the depths of his being. And the more serious is his desire, the more careful will he be to neglect none of those humble means which will sustain and direct his search for God. Ignatius explicitly points out, on several occasions, that everything he proposes by way of annotations, additions, notes, even penances, is directed only to this end: "to find what he desires."[33] This setting of oneself into availability is an attitude of sound logic which that ardent initial desire arouses and sustains.

Moreover, the object of this desire is of capital importance It greatly conditions the spiritual journey of the retreatant at its highest point. It even affects the evolution of his or her desire itself. We have written enough about the preeminent importance of the goal which allures this desire, God and his plan of salvation, spiritual growth, and beatitude,[34] and we need not insist on it further here. We shall simply point out that the growth of this desire, under the influence of God's revelation and the authentic reception of its object or content, follows very closely the route of Ignatius' own experience from Loyola to Manresa. It is the route of a desire that progressively mounts, through purification, toward full indifference, and then the radical choice in favor of the crucified Christ; of Christ as the Savior. Indifference, then, is not the extinction of desire;[35] it is desire in its purified form, allowing it to rise to a higher level where ardor and discreet charity are paramount. This means that the soul is increasingly enlightened, "illumined," to borrow Ignatius' phrase, and becomes more and more aware of the only motivation that

31 *SpEx,* [48], the second prelude of the first exercise, no. 48.
32 Ibid., [98, 168, 199].
33 Ibid., [20, 73, 87, 89, 133, with an explicit mention of desire.
34 See the whole of ch. 1 above, and in ch. 2, section 2,c on Ignatius' Concept of the Human Person and His or Her Vocation.
35 The text on indifference ([23]) ends with these words: "Our one desire and choice should be what is more conducive to the end for which we are created."

counts, a motivation corresponding to the deepest movement of the created being, a movement which engages his or her whole life in all its aspects: the end of man made more concrete, achievable, and present—in Christ, the Church, and all of creation. The deepening of this supreme end, coupled with the motivation it supplies, makes the retreatant aware that everything comes from God, is measured by Him, and that a person's whole task should be to submit himself or herself to the Holy Spirit, in regard to all the designs of the Father and the Son in the present work of salvation.[36]

After the retreatant has been purified through the experience of divine mercy in the First Week, he or she will want to express the sincere desire that Ignatius felt at Loyola, a desire that is felt by every person who "turns himself" toward the One whom he has offended: "What ought I to do for Christ." Here there is question of a spiritual desire which entails taking a necessary and inevitable position—like Ignatius going from Loyola to Manresa—and which needs the light of the following Weeks and the discernment which accompanies their completion. Ignatius will show us how to order the impetuosity of this desire "in the school of God"; yet it must exist in us, as the fruit of a spiritual experience which has shown us the meaning of sin and its action in our lives, and has revealed the greatness of God's mercy toward us. That is why the Autograph Directory insists twice that the retreatant should not begin the exercises of the Second Week if he or she does not manifest "much fervor and a great desire to continue."[37]

As was the case at the beginning of the Exercises, their continuation should be a response to an interior need. Only then will the retreatant, through the strength of his desire, submit to the dialectical procedures of the *Exercises,* a dialogue of revelation, of the action and demands of grace in relation to the human totality of this particular person in this particular situa-

---

36 It is important to understand the meaning of "discreet charity" within this movement of a desire which is a tension toward God and against which the will places no restrictions. The divine will alone will measure its accomplishment, and that in its own way. But independently of the divine measure added to the efficacy of the desire, the gift of self implied in this sincere desire is already accepted by God, becomes meritorious, and bears its fruit. Ignatius knew this, when he recommended "good desires" in view of helping others: "The neighbor is aided by desires before God our Lord (*Cons,* [638]). Again in the letter to the Fathers and Brothers of Coimbra he asks them to work for the glory of God "by fervent desires" (*LettersIgn,* p. 122). He further affirms the "design" of God "to recompense . . . good desires . . . in his eternal beatitude" (ibid., p. 318).

37 *SpEx*MHSJ, p. 780. The *Directorium Breve* also emphasizes this necessity of desire at the beginning and throughout the Exercises (Ibid., p. 976; see also fn. 52 in ch. 3 above).

tion. Hence, as the retreatant is purifying his or her desire through the meditations which prepare him for the election (the Two Standards, the Three Classes of Men, the Three Kinds of Humility), a purification which mounts, even in regard to the good, toward a total and positive indifference; as he pursues more single-heartedly the glory of God, this motivation absorbs all the tendencies of his being,[38] so too does he grow simultaneously in a greater desire to know, love, and serve the Lord, our Way and our Life.[39] Thus all the movements of his or her being are used, in various and complementary ways, to lead him to his unique end: God and his service, in the Christ who is our Salvation. The very experience of becoming like Christ, in his Passover mystery which becomes our passover, results in a unique and immense desire which is born of contemplation and is an image of the desire that animates God Himself in his love for his creatures. "I will ponder with great affection how much God our Lord has done for me, and how much He has given me of what He possesses, and finally, how much, as far as He can, the same Lord desires to give Himself to me according to His divine decrees."[40]. Similarly, "I have no doubt concerning that Sovereign Goodness, who is so eager to share his blessings, or of that everlasting love which makes him more eager to bestow perfection on us than we are to receive it."[41]

The one who has understood that such is the meaning of life, and that his whole being is made to espouse its dynamic forward thrust, can no longer desire anything except, under the movement of the Spirit, "to love and serve the Divine Majesty." But conscious of his or her poverty and of the absolute dependence of his being as a creature, he humbly continues to ask the Lord to increase this interior desire,[42] and in that way expresses his fidelity to the grace of his vocation, that is, to the grace of its origin and its purpose—a response to the call of the Father in the Son: "No one can come to me unless the Father who sent me draws him."[43]

---

38 Texts of the *Exercises* in which there is question of this love which comes from above, and of this higher motivation which elevates the movement of the soul in its natural aptitude for desire, are: [16, 23, 151, 155, 166, 167, 168, 177, 185, 339]. These texts throw some light on the meaning of spiritual desire according to St. Ignatius, and also on its dynamic function in the Exercises. We shall return to this topic more at length in Part II below.

39 The same role of desire, on another level, is suggested in *SpEx*, [104, 130, 146, 169].

40 *SpEx*, [234].

41 *LettersIgn*, p. 121.

42 "We should desire these gifts, in whole or in part, and these spiritual graces, in the measure in which they can help us for the greater glory of God" (*LettersIgn*, p. 181, in a letter to Francis Borgia, September 20, 1548).

43 John 6:44.

Such seems to us to be the guiding thread which permits Ignatius to open up his own mind and heart in order to start soul on his or her spiritual journey, to accompany him faithfully, attentively, with graces of discernment, on a route along which the only things that count are unceasing dependence on God and total submission to the action of his Spirit in us. This is the spirit, the tenor of thought which keeps a steady and respectful eye on all the realities involved—namely, the reality of God, his Word, and his Truth, and the reality of the personal and unique soul of the retreatant who is seeking God. This too is the spirit or attitude in which we wish to propose the following interpretation of the *Exercises* of St. Ignatius. We wish, beyond their letter, to find their spirit.

PART II

OUR EXPERIENCE OF GOD
AS ACCOMPLISHING WITHIN US
HIS PLAN FOR SALVATION AND SPIRITUAL GROWTH,

This, then, is what I pray: . . .
May God . . . enable you to grow firm in . . .your inner self
so that Christ may live in your hearts through faith,
and then, planted in love and built on love, . . .
you will have the strength to grasp
the breadth and the length, the height and the depth;
so that, knowing the love of Christ, which is beyond all knowledge,
you may be filled with the utter fullness of God.
(Ephesians 3:14–19)

For the message of the cross is complete absurdity
to those who are headed for ruin,
but *to us who are experiencing salvation*
it is the power of God.
(1 Corinthians. 1:18–19, in *The
Liturgy of the Hours*, II, page 1956).

Chapter 4

THE FIRST WEEK:
THE STARTING POINT FOR THE EXPERIENCE OF SALVATION
"The Mystery of Christ"

A. The Structural Thrust of the First Week

1. The Initial State of the Soul

In the preceding chapters, we have already adequately treated of the import and context of the Foundation as a preparatory stage for the Exercises. We should note especially the very positive character of this first consideration. Although it emphasizes the difficulty which one always experiences in keeping oneself in proper balance in order to remain faithful to the ideal shown to him or her by the Foundation, it also makes one turn toward God in order to ask with confidence for God's help. Besides, our very awareness of this difficulty makes us see it as flowing from our relationship with God. In the Directory which we already quoted, St. Ignatius well states that "The retreatant, perceiving this difficulty, will be led to place himself entirely in the hands of God our Lord."[1] Whether one takes a long or short time to prepare oneself for the retreat, the consideration of the Foundation should aim at a twofold result concerning our relationship with God: a lively consciousness of being in debt to him, and an intense desire of fidelity as our generous response to all his requests from us. If we recall the state of Ignatius' soul at Manresa, we shall better understand the import of these assertions.[2] To obtain this grace, in addition to begging for it, the retreatant will need to dispose himself or herself through reflection on the ideal of life

---

1 *SpEx*MHSJ, p. 792.
2 Ignatius' perception, in the depths of his being, of this debt to God, coupled with his desire of fidelity in responding to the divine will, is what led him to the self-humiliation and salutary spiritual poverty which brought him to God. Furthermore, this whole period of difficult struggle was sustained by the dynamism of this faithful desire which stimulated the penitent to serve the Divine Majesty. At Manresa Ignatius was, in the full sense of the term, "a man of good will"; that is why he did not allow the transforming encounter with God to miscarry.

which emerges from Ignatius' vision of created existence, a vision which attracts one to generosity, gives rise to a desire to be faithful, and reveals to man his great need of grace.

2. *The State of the Question: The Bible and the First Week*

The two great themes of the First Week are sin and Christ. On the objective level, the message proposed is the history of the fall from the state of grace, original justice. On the subjective level of personal experience, the retreatant's deepening of the sense of sin is achieved in the atmosphere of the presence of Christ on the cross, God's mercy toward the sinner. We should be careful here not to form our attitude on these two realities—Christ and sin— by setting out from the letter of the text of the *Exercises* and considering its relation to the categories known from theology which are more or less speculative and academic. That is, in the present situation there is no need to analyze the text in the light of a priori norms, by asking, for example, if sin is considered in a moral or religious sense, or if we are in the presence of the Christ of history, or of the Christ of faith, or of the glorified Lord *(Kyrios)*. Here Ignatius, in contrast to such work of the classroom, desires us to seek our sense of sin and of Christ within the framework of his global vision as it was presented in chapter 2 above.

For Ignatius, the question is one of facts which have a significance already acquired, once and forever. Jesus Christ is forever the Christ of Majesty, the "eternal Word Incarnate" ([130]).[3] Whether Ignatius considers him on the cross, in the crib, or speaking in the temple, Christ is never dissociated from the fullness of his being which keeps him attached to the Father, to the Trinity, and also intimately connected with the cause of mankind which he makes his own. Even when Ignatius is speaking of the historical Christ, he cannot refrain from contemplating him as forever glorious, the "eternal Lord of all things." Throughout the *Exercises* from one end to the other, the Christ presented to us is always the same; the varying situations merely point out the different aspects of his self-revelation.

The same is true for sin. We have already seen, when treating of evil in chapter 2, that Ignatius defines sin by starting from his vision of God, of man, and of all creation. He will always view sin as a profound disorder introduced by man into the plan of God who orders all things to His own

---

3 On the use of parentheses () and square brackets [] with references to the Spiritual Exercises throughout this book, see fn. 3 in ch. 1 above. For other similar editorial treatments, see the Editorial Note on the Term "Spiritual Exercises," in the REFERENCE MATTER below.

praise or glory; and as a consequence, sin is a frightful ingratitude on the part of the creature toward his or her all-loving Creator. Evil exists first of all in the heart of man, who, for his own satisfaction, through a "disordered affection" turns creation aside from its advance to God. If Ignatius saw sin only as a "transgression," the purpose of the First Week would be a good confession and a return to the state of grace. For Ignatius, however, as we shall see, sin is something which goes far beyond this horizon.

These concepts of Christ and of sin, drawn from Ignatius' experience of God's whole plan for saving men and women with all its implications, are profoundly biblical.[4] Consequently, the Bible will be our great help in presenting them for the retreatant to ponder. In fact, to the same extent that we shall know how to find these realities and their correct interpretations in Scripture shall we also be able to fathom better the data which Ignatius offers. However, his order of exposition in the *Exercises*, which follows its own particular logic, ought to be carefully respected. This is what characterizes Ignatius' way of presenting the gospel message, and it is not separated from the fruit being sought. It is quite possible to speak of sin even in a very biblical sense and to meditate on it with fruit, and still miss something of the *Exercises*; but it is not possible to give the genuine Exercises of Ignatius and speak of sin otherwise than in the sense in which the Bible reveals it to us.

3. The Objective and Procedure of This First Stage

"From that time, Jesus began to preach, saying, 'Repent, for the Kingdom of heaven is at hand,' " words which John the Baptist had already used. God's call is a call to conversion.[5] The First Week aims at our becoming aware of our condition as sinners and this, when well ordered, becomes the

---

4 We cannot develop this point now; but several indications lead us already to this conclusion. We shall come back to this problem below, in the paragraphs on the topic of sin. However, we now suggest the following principal references: A. Lefevre, "Péché et pénitence dans la Bible," *MD*, no. 55 (1958), 7–22, and S. Lyonnet, "le péché," *SDB*, VII, col. 481–567 (This latter contains a development of the following ideas: "sin, in the heart of man" and "sin, slavery to Satan".) See also Lyonnet, s.v. "Sin," in *DBTh*, pp. 551–557. For the problem of the glorious Christ in the *Exercises*, we shall speak of it again when we treat the principles of exegetical interpretation which flow from the Ignatian logic (ch. 6); there we shall see how Ignatius has the same point of view as the apostles, for whom the risen Christ could never disappear from their lives. He is the one who directed their understanding in their reflective reviewing of the life of Christ, that is, of his words and deeds. On this subject see J. Guillet, trans. Duggan, *Jesus Christ Yesterday and Today: Introduction to Biblical Spirituality* (Chicago, 1965), pp. 5–7.

5 Matt. 4:17; cf. 3:2; see also J. Mouroux, *The Christian Experience*, p. 93.

point at which one gets a first grip on the genuine experience of Christian salvation. In scriptural terms it forms an experience of repentance and conversion.[6] How does Ignatius attain this end?

As we have already pointed out, he is not primarily concerned with an examination of conscience and confession. He will present "personal sin" only after the consideration of the universal history of sin. And even then the retreatant will not ponder his personal sins with a view toward a proximate confession.[7] The methods for examination of conscience found at the beginning of the book of the *Exercises* aim at preparation for the retreat rather than for a confession. Ignacio Iparraguirre considers them as a concrete way of introducing the exercitant to a prayer that engages him or her at the present moment, with all that he or she is. If the Foundation puts the person in position to profit from the retreat, the examens too as a form of prayer contribute their part to this preparation. Ignatius insisted that the retreatant who is not sufficiently prepared should be made "to continue in the consideration of the Foundation, in the particular and general examens, and other such exercises, . . . for three or four days, more or less, until he matures."[8]

To obtain this end of repentance and conversion in the First Week, Ignatius presents five exercises, but without indicating the length of time for each. This is a contrast to the other Weeks where he specifies the approximate number of days to be spent on each stage.[9] The first two exercises give the history of sin from its beginnings to the exercitant's own time ([45-61]); then follow two repetitions which treat the same matter in view of spiritual fruit more and more profound ([62-64]).

At the end of this consideration thus prolonged, there is "the meditation on hell" ([67-71]), which ends with a gaze on Christ, the center of the

---

6 These are two complementary but distinct moments or aspects, which the New Testament expresses by the words *metanoiein* and *epistrephein*. We shall return to this subject in the following paragraphs. See also J. Dupont, "Repentir et conversion d'après les Actes des Apôtres," *ScE,* 12 (1960), 137-173; also R. d'Ouince, "La formation de la liberté par les Exercices," *Chr,* no. 13 (1957), p. 95; [and Paul V. Robb, "Conversion as a Human Experience," *Studies in the Spirituality of Jesuits,* 14, 3 (May, 1982), esp. pp. 5-8 on first and second conversion, with the references in fnn. 6 and 7. Ed.]

7 *SpEx*MHSJ, p. 784, where we are told that confession is made only after the five exercises of the First Week have been completed. See also *Exercices,* trans. Courel, p. 48, note 1.

8 *SpEx*MHSJ, p. 791. This Directory notes that it is useful to give the particular examen during the Exercises by applying it to the matter of the retreat (p. 793).

9 "With regard to the exercises of the First Week, our Father is not of the opinion that they should be given together, and he himself never gave them in that way, but one at a time until all five were completed," (ibid., p. 782).

universe and its salvation ([71]). Hell and the cross—these are the two extremes to which the action of sin leads. Thus, on the objective level of the message proposed, Ignatius embraces the whole history of sin in those chief stages in which its theological significance is most enlightening. He describes it as a movement or antithesis which is completely opposed to that of service and of love, and which ends in the death of God-become-also-a-man.[10]

On the subjective level of the experience, through the consideration of the universal, which here is the world of evil, the Exercises augment the retreatant's personal awareness of himself as a sinner and his inevitable relationship to this universal. For, even if this consideration focuses more and more on our own personal and interior state, nevertheless we are invited to situate ourselves as creatures within this world of sin which appears to us as essentially rebellion against the movement which the divine love had inspired. It is in the light of this universal framework that we deepen our awareness of our sinful condition; otherwise our sins are reduced to minimal transgressions whose gravity is measured by the immediate harm done to our neighbor. However, as a balance to this experience aroused by our confrontation with the mystery of evil surrounding us, the *Exercises* unceasingly propose for our consideration the mystery of mercy which God, in his eternal love, offers to unfaithful man. The meditations of the First Week should always be made at the foot of the cross and before God. Here the cross is not only God's response to man's sin in general, but the source of my own personal salvation here and now.

The experience of the First Week, as we see, is achieved by starting with a consideration of the history of sin which evolves around Christ, our salvation. The activity or effort supposed by this consideration involves the one who proposes the meditations and the retreatant, who is asked by Ignatius to "use the memory in considering the subject" ([50, 51, 52]). This activity, however, should deepen tremendously in prayer where it gives way to the action of grace. Mental prayer aims at "spiritual fruits" which were prepared for by "an enlightening of the mind." We shall return to this point later on in this chapter; here we are merely indicating the direction in which the spiritual experience of the First Week develops, in accordance with the "graces asked for."

In the first two exercises the retreatant asks for shame, confusion, intense sorrow, and even tears because of the ingratitude inherent in his sins

10 We shall see later on that we can add other exercises to these five; but we shall specify more precisely under what conditions this can be done if we are to respect Ignatius' concept of the movement of the First Week.

([48, 55]). The repetitions bring depth to this spiritual fruit, for when they speak of "interior knowledge" of the "disorder of my actions" and of the "knowledge of the world," they specify that these fruits are directed toward "personal reform, ordering of self," effective detachment from "worldly and vain things" ([63]). There is question, then, of an awareness which is slowly deepened by "repetitions," and which more surely disposes one for a transformation that is interior and open to a commitment of self which is effective and generous. Such are the fruits of repentance and conversion of which Scripture speaks, and which the grace of Scripture, the efficacious word of God, arouses from within and leads to maturity according to man's correspondence with grace. The subjective experience of the retreatant, like that of Ignatius earlier, must be aroused and directed primarily by divine revelation, that plan of salvation which in the First Week takes hold of the person who has come to grips with all the evil of the universe. That perspective places him or her in an attitude of supplication before the only One who can deliver him from evil. "Shower, O heavens, from above, and let the skies rain down righteousness; let the earth open, that salvation may sprout forth, and let it cause righteousness to spring up also; I the Lord have created it."[11]

We shall now examine the two aspects of this experience of the First Week: (1) our becoming aware of our condition as sinners, (2) which becomes the beginning of our experience of salvation. We shall try to deepen our understanding of these complementary stages by examining the means proposed through the *Exercises* for their realization. These means are personal activity (the consideration) which draws one's attention to the objective message, and grace (petition and spiritual fruit) which both directs and expresses the intimate experience of the retreatant and also, to a certain degree, allows its analysis.

B. Our Becoming Aware of Our Condition as Sinners

1. Our Place in the History of Evil

The first exercise emphasizes our making ourselves aware of the world of evil in which we already have a place. But the meaning of this place is given greater depth especially in the Second Exercise. The repetitions fuse these two subjects in order that we may gain a more complete and interior knowledge of the mystery of evil. Finally, Ignatius proposes a meditation on hell to turn our thought to the future.

11   Isa. 45:8.

First, then, the world in sin. It is not Ignatius' intention to present doctrinal developments on sin during the Exercises. His method is to put one in the presence of a concrete dynamic reality, as Scripture reveals it. This method also demands that one "reflect" on this revealed history and "apply one's understanding" to it. We should know how to draw from the facts we contemplate a spiritual theological significance which helps us grasp its import, and which opens the intellect to the light that God communicates through signs and events. God does not speak only to report facts, but to instruct and educate man's heart through these facts. At this point, on the level of the message proposed, it is important to examine the link which binds together all the scenes that are contemplated, those proposed by the book of the *Exercises* and those we might fittingly add to them. To isolate these facts, and to consider them as independent units, would be too great a dispersion of our efforts. Ignatius is not trying to save time by considering the history of sin all at once (in the First Exercise) and then coming back afterwards to one or another episode. In this sense, it is important, not to multiply the scenes, but to prolong our reflection on those chosen. In each one of them we consider the same unique reality of the sin whose mystery we wish to explore more fully.

Sin is iniquity, disorder, ingratitude and slavery to Satan. Here Ignatius integrates all these biblical ways of expressing what is evil into one dynamic consideration of the history of sin. It is a history which concerns not only the past, which is not completely ended, but which also marks the present and truly affects man's destiny. It is the history of a burning reality filling time and space, in which even the redeemed man of the New Covenant has, against his will, a part. It is in the context of a full, present, and serious reality that Ignatius proposes his first meditation on sin. He enjoins us to gaze steadily on this continuing history which starts with the rebellion of the angels and continues until it reaches our own transgressions, and to seek to understand its significance by referring not only to its bitter consequences but also to its denial of the love of God—that God who, from love and a desire to share his own happiness with us, created us for his own praise and the happiness his creatures would have by means of their praising him. Ignatius insists on the retreatant's making himself or herself present to this history of evil as it floods through the world, so as to enlighten his own situation. Man sees himself as a participant in this immense and free movement which goes back to the first fall and continues to snatch the creature from his supernatural destiny, to submit him or her to the empire of Satan, in revolt against divine love. Indeed, at each point of this meditation—as well as in the prelude which specifies the grace to be asked for—the retreatant should relate the scene being contemplated to himself or herself: How many times have I merited a similar chastisement for my numerous faults?

a. The First Exercise: The Universal History of Sin

The first meditation of the *Exercises* is quite short ([50–53]), and thus covers matter that is rightly undefined. St. Ignatius constructs his history of sin around three events to give direction to our reflection. There is the sin of the angels, which draws attention to their insubordination as creatures, and then to its radical consequence, hell. Next comes the sin of Adam, whose significance he also determines, above all as the beginning of all the chief evils and disloyalties of the human race. Finally, these defections lead to the particular sin of some person who is damned; and this points toward some person of the twentieth century, here and now a sinner, who in his own case makes himself a résumé of the whole history of sin, along with its tragic consequences.

The sin of the angels[12] draws our attention to what essentially constitutes sin: to refuse, to the extent that one is free to do so, the creative act and the divine call it implies. The angels expressed their refusal by rejecting the end for which God had created them. Ignatius writes: "They did not want to make use of the freedom God gave them to reverence and obey their Creator and Lord, and so falling into pride, were changed from grace to hatred of God, and cast out of heaven into hell" ([50]). This movement of sin (based on the very nature of created being, but in the case of the angels deprived of other contingent circumstances such as concupiscence of the flesh), throws much light on our own sin against God. Their sin is, in a way, sin "in its pure state," a free creature refusing to submit to its God. That is why the punishment is so clear and final: existence in hell forever separated from divine love. Here Ignatius emphasizes the horror of sin in itself, a sentiment which he has the retreatant ask for as a grace. But he relates this to the exercitant[13] whose numerous sins, despite a lesser responsibility, are of the same nature and give rise, through the comparison that has been made, to interior feelings of shame and confusion. Such are the fruits (horror, shame, confusion) which this meditation seeks for the retreatant through the activity of his intellect, a growing awareness of this situation, and prayer from the heart.

Original sin, that of Adam, allows the retreatant to explore this horizon of sin to an even greater degree, inasmuch as the meditation treats not only of

---

12 2 Peter 2:4; Jud. 1:6.

13 The *Imitation of Christ* (a Kempis), on a different note, proposes the same relationship, in Bk. III, ch. 14.

the creature as such, but of man himself—man who was created in circumstances which are more familiar to us, and given a mission to work his way
toward a glorious destiny which the Foundation has already explained and
made attractive. Here the Bible is more explicit and clarifying. Through
every form of sin whose significance it mentions, it shows us its infinite
consequences. In a dozen lines Ignatius repeats these pages of Genesis whose
message we must interpret. His résumé presents the two principal dimensions
of the history we are meditating: that of sin itself, as a fact, and its consequences for our first parents and the entire human race. They ate of the
forbidden fruit and as a consequence lost original justice and endured a long
period of penance. For their descendants there ensued that corruption which
puts so many of them on the way to hell ([151]).[14]

The narrative in Genesis (chapters 1 and 2) shows us man created in the
image and likeness of God, with a view to dialogue and communion with
God—this repose of the seventh day on which God comes, at the time of the
breeze, to converse with man. But the complete revelation of the divine
message in both the Old and the New Testament gives us a deeper sense of
this communion with God and teaches us, especially through the theme of
God dwelling with us and in us, the richest meaning on earth of this communion which is a sharing in the divine life, a divinization of man. Man, however, must wait until God, through the test of time, grants him this fullness of
divine life in eternity.[15]

Since man is open to the infinite, he would like to skip the stage of time,
that of becoming, and through his own abilities grasp what God alone can

14 For brief developments, in the sense we have indicated, and more or less speculative according to the cases, see the following:

(A) On the objective reality of man's sin: J. A. Hardon, *All my Liberty:
Theology of the Spiritual Exercises* (1959), pp. 14–17; R. Bellemare, *Le sens de
la créature dans la doctrine de Bérulle* (1959), pp. 49–51; G. Fessard, *La dialectique*, pp. 45–50; M. Oraison, *Amour ou Contrainte? Quelques aspects psycho-
logiques de l'éducation religieuse* (Paris, 1956), pp. 37–38, 108–109; J. M.
Yurrita, "La Reconciliaión como experiencia religiosa," *RyF*, 164 (1961), 50ff;
C. Bodard, *La Bible, expression d'une expérience religieuse chez saint Bernard*
(Rome, 1954), p. 38; St. Augustine, *De Trinitate*, XV, XXIV; Hermas, *Le Pasteur*, Similitude X, 112: 4; H. U. von Balthasar, *Heart of the World*, (San Francisco, 1979), pp. 19–21 and ch. 8, Jailhouse and Cocoon, pp. 133–144.

(B) On the subject of the universal consequences of the sin of man: A.
Frank-Duquesne, *Cosmos et Gloire* (Vrin, 1947), pp. 75–76, 88–89 (biblical
aspects); S. Weil, *La pesanteur et la grâce*, p. 174; Pius XII, Christmas Message, 1949, for the opening of the Holy Year 1950, quoted by Lombardi in *Pie
XII, pour un Monde Meilleur*, II, pp. 148–149.

15 On this subject read the excellent development of H. U. von Balthasar, *A Theology of History* (German ed. 1950, English trans., New York, 1963), pp. 30–33,

work in him. "You will be like God" (Gen. 3:5). Thus, instead of trusting the word of God, man, greedy and proud, prefers his own food to that which he ought to expect from heaven. And cutting himself off from the only source that can bring him to God, he imprisons himself in his finitude, doomed by nature to death and dust. Furthermore, man was commanded by God to rule over all creation; but in his fall he draws this creation with him, and "subjects it to futility" (Rom. 8:20). The garden of Eden is transformed into a desert and the earth produces nothing but thorns and thistles. In the words of the prophet: "I looked on the earth, and lo, it was waste and void; and to the heavens, and they had no light. I looked on the mountains, and lo, they were quaking, and all the hills moved to and fro. I looked, . . . and all the birds of the air had fled. I looked, and lo, the fruitful land was a desert."[16] The revolt of the angels had created hell; that of man had created the kingdom of this world; and the two are ruled by Satan, the prince of darkness and the father of lies.[17]

In meditating on the sin of a person who has been condemned to hell for all eternity, we look into the heart of a woman or man who bears not only the weight of his sin but also its terrible consequences. Ignatius shows us that this history can be summed up in one person and produce its fruit of death with just as much violence, and in a way that is just as irremediable. Here he looks at the fact as accomplished, before envisaging it as something possible of coming to pass in the life of the exercitant (Second Exercise). And he insists that this particular case is not unique: "Consider also countless others who have been lost for fewer sins than I have committed" ([52]).

There is no need to imagine this or that person as one so condemned, or to consider various hypotheses about his or her case. What we should do is to apply all the previous reflections to this particular case, and then see the whole history of sin as coming to a head in it, even today, in this one person who willingly commits serious sin. Through this action this person acquiesces in his solidarity with the world of evil. He freely chooses it by refusing

---

16 Jer. 4:23–26.
17 Numerous biblical narratives and particular themes (such as "brothers at enmity" or "Canaan, paradise lost") can nourish this meditation on the consequence of evil for man, the human race, and the whole of creation: Cain and Abel, the Deluge, Babel, Israel's slavery in Egypt, its wandering in the desert, the idolatry which followed the installation of the kingdom, the schism, and the captivity. There are also the parables lived and recounted by the prophets, especially Hosea, Amos, Isaiah, Jeremiah, and Ezechiel (e.g., chs. 16 and 20). Let us not forget that through the history of Israel, it is the whole of humanity that has fallen away and has been taken back by God.

to submit to God, like the angels; and like Adam, by choosing to be Satan's subject, working with him to destroy the harmony of the universe. At the term of this association in which the sinner is caught by temporal death, he finds himself damned. He has made his choice, for eternity. It is thus that the person as sinner, no matter through what transgression, "commits sin" and "is of the devil."[18] In other words, he "participates in Satan's opposition to the kingdom of Christ and thus excludes himself from that kingdom."[19] Insubordination of a created being,[20] slavery to Satan, positive disorder introduced into the divine plan which orders all things to God, ingratitude toward the God whose creative love is rejected:[21] This is what sin is, one sin alone. Its whole history lives again in the heart of this person, and its dialectical process which inexorably brings about his destruction and damnation. "Frightful nudity of a man stripped of his God."[22]

At the end of this path of destruction and of death which has continued down to our day, the retreatant who has been spared, places himself again at the foot of the cross, on which he sees the most frightful accomplishment of this mass of sin.[23] It is as if the history of the human race were to lead through time to Calvary where God meets man in the depths of his sin. "Imagine Christ our Lord present before you upon the cross, and begin to speak with him, asking how it is that though He is the Creator, He has stooped to become man, and to pass from eternal life to death here in time, that thus He might die for our sins" ([53]). "Now when they heard this, they were cut to the heart, and said to Peter and the rest of the Apostles, 'Brethren, what shall we do?' "[24]

---

18 1 John 3:4, 8.
19 See I. de la Potterie, *Adnotationes in exegesim Primae Epistolae S. Joannis*, p. 73. For a more complete development, read De la Potterie's article "Le péché c'est l'iniquité (1 John 3:4)," *NRTh*, 78 (1956), 785–797, and S. Lyonnet, "Sin," in *DBTh*, pp. 551–557.
20 "Gravity and malice of sin against our Creator and Lord," according to the Ignatian vocabulary ([52]); see also Rom. 9:20–24; Job, ch. 38.
21 Again, Ignatius' words, "against the Infinite Goodness" ([52]); see also Hosea, ch. 11.
22 Sister Geneviève Gallois, *La vie du Petit saint Placide*, (Paris, 1954), p. 61. It is in this sense of an ontological destitution that the Fathers of the Church have often interpreted the text of Genesis according to which man, after sinning, "saw his nakedness."
23 "The mirror for sinners is Christ crucified; for in Him appear my sins in his sufferings and death" (Nadal, *Journal spirituel* (trans. Laval), no. 59. See also Y. de Montcheuil, *Leçons sur le Christ* (1949), p. 14.
24 Acts 2:37.

b. The Second Exercise: Personal Sin

The following exercise, on Personal Sin ([55–61]), could lead one to believe that Ignatius has departed from the history of sin as the focus of his presentation. For the retreatant, this departure does take place if the meditation on "personal sin" becomes focused on an examination of conscience, a kind of conclusion and moral application of the preceding exercise, and if it is used, more or less consciously, to prepare the retreatant for confession.[25]

However, this meditation finds its true significance in its relationship to the preceding exercise. As the lot of the condemned sinner seemed to immobilize the history of sin by showing its term forever fixed in hell, this history is taken up again and given a new reality in the history of the retreatant. It moves away from consideration of the universal, something outside the retreatant, but it comes back again in the case of the retreatant's own life with the same dynamism it had in the universal, by developing insubordination, iniquity and slavery, disorder and ingratitude. I see the same history of sin as repeated throughout my own life. Furthermore, I see the history of my life as something unfolding within this tragic history of human sin. In this meditation I see myself caught up from the beginning in this movement where God and Satan confront each other. In my personal struggle, the diversity and the opposition of the spirits that pull me toward the evil I hate and away from the good I desire, are only the continuation inside my own heart of the immense evil that would like to destroy creation. The history which I ought to be considering is a history still moving forward, that of my own existence subjected to the power of sin; and this malevolent power attacks the whole fabric of my life to accomplish in it the same work of perversion and infinite ingratitude ([57–59]) which we have already considered on the universal level, and whose consequences go beyond the particular level of my existence to rejoin this universal history of humanity to which I am committed by my privileged condition as a creature of God ([60]).[26]

---

25 "More or less consciously": For there are some directors who note explicitly that this is not the purpose of this meditation. But they present the topic in so static a manner that it is cut off from its function in the overall movement of the thought of the First Week, and inevitably leads the retreatant into such an examination of conscience as we have described.

26 We do not think we are exaggerating our picture of sin according to the spirit of Ignatius and of biblical theology. This outlook on sin goes far beyond the juridical point of view. Ignatius himself gave elsewhere his distinctions between mortal and venial sin, and their possible limits, in order to enlighten one's moral judgment ([32–42]). But in the present meditation he returns to the language of the mystics, where the sinner sees himself profoundly caught within the mystery of evil; and only God's grace can snatch him from it.

Later on we shall see that this perception of our intimate collusion with the evil in our lives, when considered "in the presence of God" and within the vision of his whole plan of salvation, gives us a much greater understanding of the divine mercy which each stage of the history of sin already brought to our attention. This abyss between the perversity of evil and God's infinite mercy forces from Ignatius' lips "a cry of wonder accompanied by surging emotion," as he states in the meditation ([60]). The colloquy this time can be only a colloquy on mercy, expressing the retreatant's profoundest gratitude ([61]). So these meditations—or better, this one meditation on the unique history of sin which incorporates my own history into itself, as will be done by the repetitions which fuse the two topics—will culminate exclusively in love of God. This love springs continually, in human experience, from the "intimate knowledge of the many blessings received, that filled with gratitude for all, I may in all things love and serve the Divine Majesty" ([233]). The first of God's gifts, which man can taste interiorly, is that of pardon and salvation, that is, of having been loved while still a sinner.[27]

c. The Repetitions: A Return to the Source of the Evil

The repetitions of the first and second exercises are intended to deepen our grasp of the matters we have already meditated. That is shown not only by the nature and purpose of the repetitions as indicated by Ignatius ([64]), but still more by the grace to be asked for, which is specified in the preludes and the suggested colloquies. In general, the colloquy develops affections contrary to those that should be uprooted. In these affections the intellect gives way entirely to the interior and enlightened movement of prayer. Still further, on three or four occasions during the Exercises, Ignatius recommends the triple colloquy. He does this always at a moment in the Exercises when the movement should come to a summit which is decisive in the pursuit of the spiritual experience. The movement is transformed, so that it becomes a more earnest petition to obtain from God the fruit desired.[28] In this present case the repetitions are especially effective, through the triple colloquy, for snatching the soul from the movement of sin and uprooting all the attachments to sin that still remain in it. This grace is clearly expressed by Ignatius when he specifies what is to be asked for in the triple colloquy—which should be taken up again in each repetition ([63, 64]). Beyond repentance and

---

27 Rom. 5:8; I John 4:10, 19.
28 Passages in the *Exercises* where the triple colloquy is proposed: the repetitions on sin, ([63, 64]); the Two Standards and the Three Classes of Men, ([147, 156]); the Three Kinds of Humility, ([168]).

grief for one's faults, the ideal to be attained is an interior knowledge of their source: in myself, the disorder of my activity; outside of myself, the evil of the world. In emphasizing self-knowledge and knowledge of the world of the adversary, Satan, these graces bring me to a more correct vision of the evil in my life, viewed precisely as an obstacle to the divine work in which I wish to collaborate. They also directly prepare the way for me to make a sound and realistic election which will place me with Jesus, to struggle for God and against Satan. Ignatius wants my repentance, under the influence of grace and my correspondence to that grace, to move toward a sincere conversion, in order that I may be in the truth.[29] The first of his three petitions ([63]) thus takes up again the fruit of the preceding exercises: a deep knowledge of my sins and a feeling of abhorrence for them. The second and third petitions ask for that deepening we have already mentioned in view of an effective reform of my life: "An understanding of the disorder of my actions, that filled with horror of them, I may amend my life and put it in order"; then "A knowledge of the world, that filled with horror, I may put away from me all that is worldly and vain" ([63]).

In his book of the *Exercises,* Ignatius included only these three, plus that on hell to end the Week. Since the exercises of the First Week can easily take from five to ten days to complete, he must surely have expected his retreatant to give long and careful rumination to these compressed but highly organized exercises. Indeed, in his own way, he summarily presents the whole history of sin, both universal and particular; and he asks us to spend much time in prayer meditating on it, until the work of purification is accomplished in the quiet of the retreat and in the intimate encounter between "the Creator and his creature."

Afterwards, however, and already during his lifetime, exercises on death and judgment were added, and there is no sign that he objected. This matter is closely connected with that of sin. In using it, however, there is a danger of departing from the historical and existential movement, that history of sin by which Ignatius, in his book, binds the meditations of the First Week into a carefully structured sequence. If we consider death and judgment as entities in themselves with only a remote reference to our sinful condition, we run the risk of detouring the Exercises into an examination of conscience. The Exercises fulfill this function only by the confrontation they foster between our personal history and the history of the world of evil, still moving forward

29   See M. Alcalá, "Los Ejercicios de San Ignacio como memorial soteriologico," *Mnr,* 32 (1960), 349.

and involving ourselves. That is why, if we introduce another subject, it is important to do it with full knowledge of what we are doing and with great respect for the dynamic which is essentially characteristic of the Exercises as structured by Ignatius himself.[30]

d. The Last Exercise: A Realistic Perspective on the Future

The final exercise of the First Week is the meditation on hell ([65-71]), for which Ignatius does not prescribe a repetition. This meditation is certainly a delicate topic and difficult to handle. Let us recall a few details which can give some direction to our interpretation. The preceding meditations have constantly alluded to it as the extreme consequence of sin ([48, 50, 51, 52, 60]); the retreatant is always saved from it by the divine mercy (ibidem). Finally, all these considerations were made in an historical and existential perspective. But if for some, angels and men, the history of sin has already been pronounced forever and is irremediable, for me it still remains open and moving forward. Ignatius asks me to push it to the limit, into my own future, and then suppose that if on some day I should "forget the love of the eternal Lord" and be unfaithful, I ought to see myself as necessarily moving in the direction of the eternal death and hell fire which is the end result of this history of sin in which I see myself already so actively involved.

Ignatius wants me to take a good look, without any dilution, at the reality of the history of sin in general and of my own sins, and see where they will inevitably lead me if the love of God should ever disappear from my heart. In other words, this movement of sin which I have perceived in my own self during the preceding meditations, and which I have begged to regard with horror—Ignatius now wants me, in humble prayer in God's presence, to gaze on this movement, as something unchained and abandoned to its own

---

30 For help on how to meditate on death and judgment in the First Week, one might consult I. Iparraguirre, *Líneas directivas,* p. 41, [English: *A Key to the Study,* pp. 60-61]; and W. de Broucker, "La première semaine des Exercices," *Chr,* no. 21 (1959), 22-39. Certain Scriptural texts, if carefully interpreted, can also orient these meditations into the dynamic perspective of the *Exercises:* thus in the Prophets, Dan. 12:1-4; Joel 4:1-2, 12-18; Mal. 3:13-21; in the Epistles, 2 Peter 2:4-10; 3:3-18, Gal. 6:7-8; 1 Thess. 5:1-10, Heb. 4:2-16; in the Book of Revelation, 6:12-17; 14:6-15; 20:11-15; 22:10-15. Concerning biblical meditations which may be inserted in the same framework to prolong the action of the First Week by renewing it, see *Directorium Granatense,* in *SpEx*MHSJ, p. 955, where it is suggested, e.g., that one meditate on how God, because of sin, destroyed the world through the flood, how he forgave David the sins of adultery and homicide (2 Kings 12), and finally what he made his Son endure for the sins of the world (continuation of the colloquy of *SpEx,* [53].

terrible momentum, to plunge itself into the depth of that eternity in which the Evil One desires me to be. It is a great grace, which the saints obtained, to have a keen awareness of hell. It crowns our awareness of the existence of evil and makes us sensitive to its terrible reality.[31] This meditation, if well inserted into the movement of the Exercises, needs practically no commentary. We approach it humbly and are filled with thanksgiving and love for the loving Savior, the salvation of the universe who desires its good. It is he whom the colloquy places at the center of history and of time, a companion in this history which is always moving forward ([71]).

2. The Ambivalence of This Interior Experience

As we have stated, the First Week considers the problem of evil and hell straightforwardly. St. Ignatius, however, does not fall into the trap of any moral pessimism when he meditates on these realities in all their harshness. On the contrary, the movement of the *Exercises,* if clearly understood, specifically ends on the note of love for God and the gift of self to him. Such was the history of Ignatius' own life whose orientation, drawn from the painful experience of his sinful condition, is in no way equivocal. Instead, it was clear and simple: to love and serve the Divine Majesty in all things. These two characteristics of the experience of the First Week—the consideration of sin which in no way spares our sensitivity, and its absolutely positive orientation—make its treatment difficult. For every attenuation of the divine message is trying to avoid these two extremes. To lessen the gravity of sin out of consideration for our human feelings merely removes from the experience of our sinful condition its thrust toward love. In the *Exercises,* the First Week lays the foundation for a deepening of the experience of Christian salvation. To weaken it produces an experience which is, perhaps, profitable from several points of view, but which has lost that radical spiritual character of

---

31 See Ignatius, *Journal spirituel,* trans. Giuliani, p. 92; also p. 109, on "respect out of fear" when "respect out of love" is lacking, and *LettersIgn,* p. 356); see also St. Teresa, in *The Collected Works of St. Teresa of Avila,* trans. Kavanaugh-Rodriguez (Washington, 1976-1985), "The Book of Her Life," chs. 32, 37, pp. 213-220, 251-256. This is similar to Marie de l'Incarnation's experience of a soul plunged into sin (see Dom Jamet, *Le témoignage de Marie de l'Incarnation*), pp. 13-16. We also have the testimony of St. John of the Cross quoted by J. de Guibert (*RAM,* 1925) and W. de Broucker (*Chr,* no.21, 1959). Further texts on hell: The *Imitation,* Bk. I, ch. 24; Dostoevsky, *The Brothers Karamazov,* Book 6; R. de Pury, *Ton Dieu règne* (1946), pp. 98-100. Among the commentators: Fessard, *La dialectique,* pp. 50-52, 134; J. Rovira, "La meditacón del infierno en los Ejercicios Espirituales de San Ignacio y la Sagrada Escritura," *Mnr* 3 (1927), 211-216; H. Coathalem, *Ignatian Insights,* pp. 114-115.

the authentic Christian experience in which the gospel demands are not in the least betrayed. In order that the Exercises may bring one to this conscious and generous acceptance of the gospel message, with its disturbing paradoxes, the starting point must not be weakened by any facile deviation on either the objective or the subjective levels.

a. On the Objective and Doctrinal Level

The first danger of a deviation consists in staying too long on the objective level, the level of logical and intellectual considerations which[32] one extends into examination of all the ramifications as completely as possible. The multiplicity of opinions can be harmful to the subjective experience of grasping an awareness of the malice of sin. Thus one level is emphasized at the expense of the other.[33] When this occurs, the purpose of the message ceases to be that of fostering the experience, but had become the bettering of the quality of the presentation of the message, which has itself now been aimed at improving the instruction of the retreatant. The Exercises should never be transformed into a doctrinal treatise or pure preaching. They ought to be a subjective experience which is aroused, enlightened, and directed by the objective data of the gospel message, which participates in the power of God's revealed word.

The director of the Exercises is especially threatened by this danger. He or she runs the risk of distracting from what is essential by enlarging the consideration of the universal, or by turning this consideration away from its true objective, which is to enlighten the retreatant and to foster the spiritual experience desired.

But the retreatant too is exposed to this same danger. Without the director's realizing what is happening, the exercitant could confine his or her activity to the level of ideas. Making the Exercises is not an occasion for intellectual research even on the subject of the Exercises themselves (by turning the retreat into a study of them). The retreatant can even stay in this trap with only dim awareness of the fact, where the intellect is feeding on matter without directing it sufficiently toward commitment—somewhat like the diver who hesitates to plunge into the water and, to allay his fears, ad-

---

32 The knowledge gained in making the Exercises is more intensive than extensive. On the difference between knowledge as "conoscimiento formal" and knowledge as "experiencia cognoscitiva superior," see J. Aleu, "La epistemología sobrenatural en los Ejercicios de S. Ignacio," *Revista de Espiritualidad,* 23 (1964), 429ff.

33 The *Directorium Granatense* recalls this subordination of levels; see *SpEx*MHSJ, p. 958.

mires the beauty of the surrounding countryside. Once the intellect has been enlightened, it ought generously to give way to the prayer of the heart. That is why Ignatius grows fearful ([6, 89]): If nothing happens, question the retreatant, learn what he is doing, the way he prays; use the rules for discernment.

Now, to find the right measure in the communication on the objective level (the role of the director), and to harmonize the activity on both the objective and subjective levels (the role both of the director and of the retreatant), it is highly important to observe that the consideration of evil in the First Week differs from that in the Second Week. If this is neglected, we have the blind leading the blind. The director discourses at length about evil and sin, without taking proper account of the fruit which is being sought; and the success or failure of the enterprise depends ultimately on haphazard circumstances.

However, there are various ways of presenting this difference between the considerations of evil respectively in the First and Second Weeks. The principal criterion should be the purpose of these meditations, which we can know by examining the petitions of the triple colloquy in the First Week, and the role of the meditation on the Two Standards in the Second Week. By this procedure we soon see that the exercises treating of evil are of quite different orders: The first set aims more at a well-ordered affective experience, while the second greatly intensifies the retreatant's knowledge as a preparation for the later experience of the election. Indeed, as we have seen, during the First Week the exercitant considers the universal history of sin in order to see his own history as a particular instance within it; in other words, as a force carrying him along within that same unfolding evolutionary process. The purpose of this knowledge was his or her becoming realistically aware of his own present insertion into this world of evil, and the thrust of its evolution, whose end result also becomes clear, with its opposite poles of hell and the cross. Thanks to this confrontation, the retreatant sees just where his compromise with evil is leading him. This awareness, then, aims at an effective horror of sin and the world of sin in order to separate us from evil and its roots in us. The experience is profoundly affective and reaches to every level of one's being.

In the Second Week, the retreatant once again examines the situation created by sin, but no longer for the purpose of fostering this subjective experience that snatches him from the horror of evil which is now recognized as disorder and ingratitude. Rather, it will be a time of calm, reflective search, even if in this activity the universal still leads to the application to the particular. The intellect examines "the deceits of the rebel chief" in order to resist them with God's help. We shall see that this exercise seeks to enlighten and purify the understanding in order to orient the person toward a more conscious and realistic commitment. Thus the consideration of evil on the objective level of the Second Week is for the most part separated from the affective experience of sin in the life of the retreatant. If the Second Week still considers the disordered affections which must be known and uprooted, it does so in quite a different perspective: Through the world of evil which surrounds him, the retreatant seeks concrete signs of God's will. If the director is going to harmonize properly the activities of the objective and subjective levels, especially on points that are common to both Weeks, he must understand the general thrust of the Exercises and know what he ought to expect from each stage in particular. Otherwise he runs the risk of falling prey to a second danger which is much more serious than the first.

b. On the Subjective Level of the Retreatant's Experience

This second danger consists in confining the exercitant's subjective experience to the psychological and moral level. This not only renders the experience less efficacious but, in the case of the Exercises, it can falsify the religious conscience and its relationship to God. Here we touch on the heart of the problem of the subjective experience in the First Week. The warning we have just given on the danger of intellectualism—both for the director and the retreatant—forestalls a certain deadening of the experience of the Exercises. This experience is necessarily subjective and affective. It integrates all the person's powers, as his relationship to God normally does. Because it is affective in this way and engages all the levels of his being, the experience of the First Week requires a great deal of discernment. Ignatius realized this, and for that reason, in several Annotations and Additions, he added fourteen rules "for understanding to some extent the different motions produced in the soul" ([313–327]). He did not do this to stir up in the exercitant, on the occasion of the problem of evil and the awareness of his own sins, just any kind of experience, such as sensible pity, a psychological depression not clearly oriented, resentment and false guilt, scruples, or the like.[34] A few important factors—among many others—protect the experience of the First Week against these deviations and assure the conditions necessary for its positive spiritual authenticity.

---

34 "The sense of sin is not absent, but it is deformed in the bad conscience, collective or individual," states P. Antoine, in "Sens chrétien du péché," *Chr,* no. 21 (1959), 47. He devotes a paragraph to these various deviations and to the false sense of piety which they presuppose.

First of all, our taking cognizance of our sinful condition is a spiritual and affective experience which must be dominated by the action of grace. Any other experience of the same subject, which turns us away from this divine control, is not the experience proper to the Exercises. We must hold tenaciously to this subordination of human activity to that of grace, as described by Ignatius in the fifteenth Annotation. To this end, the perspective of the message presented is of prime importance. Sin is not limited to a transgression which threatens to imprison a man in himself, but as understood now, it even tears him loose from his deep seated egoism. For in this case of a new outlook, the reality of his sin leads him to a historical and existential—and not merely theoretical—awareness of his relationship to God, to the whole of creation, and to the world of evil. Furthermore, this perspective enlightened by God's saving plan and its constructive thrust toward right order reveals to man the concrete meaning of the love which he has opposed. God's love for man is His act of continuing creation, and all creation is scarred by man's offense against God.[35] In the First Week, sin is a mystery of iniquity which allows man to experience divine mercy. Finally, this awareness, enlightened from above and realized under the action of grace, is concretized in the dialectical interactions of the Exercises, and this facilitates our efforts at collaboration and fidelity. It is by means of those spiritual fruits which are asked for over and over again and prepared for, to the extent possible, by the activity of the intellect opening itself to the light, that this affective spiritual movement is produced through which grace works an interior transformation. To conform ourselves to the logical progression of the Exercises, as we have described it above by expounding the meaning of the five exercises, is to assure our humble collaboration in practice, and to forestall the numerous obstacles which the soul so easily puts in the path of grace.

In this interpretation of Ignatius' views and of what they call for, we shall not find an answer to all our problems. Despite our care not to use some exterior means to arouse those affections which should be the fruit of grace,[36]

---

35 "In religious repentance, what causes the sinner the greatest affliction is that he has offended against not only a Law but also a Love; he has despised not only a Legislator, but also a Father. Nevertheless, what afflicts him at this point is also what encourages and reassures him: He is not asking a pardon from an inflexible Law, but from the infinite mercy of a God who has revealed himself as Love" (B. Häring, *La Loi du Christ,* [1955], I, p. 564).

36 Ignatius has the retreatant ask for the graces of shame, confusion, and tears. In [74] and [78] he suggests certain interior attitudes capable of maintaining these spiritual sentiments or at least disposing one for them. On the subject of tears as a gift of God, see *LettersIgn,* p. 312.

but to give intelligent submission to the divine action in the soul, the affective reactions of the retreatant do not lose their complexity. What Jean Mouroux says about the question of affectivity in this matter concerns the Christian experience which runs throughout the spiritual life; and it has even greater application to the time of intensified experience during the Exercises. "The fact that affectivity," he writes, "plays such an enormous part in the Christian life, arises mainly from man's structure: The spiritual life is essentially a matter of self-giving and the consecration of one's freedom to God. But affectivity prepares the way for it, then goes hand in hand with, and then crowns the movement of liberty; unless, conversely, it successively blocks it, paralyzes it, and dries it up."[37] Similarly, the desire to commit oneself to the Lord does not of itself clarify the psychological situations of the retreatant, to which should be added his or her "experience of the spirits" in their multiple nuances. That is why Ignatius, in addition to this spiritual dialectic so completely ordered toward God, has left us a final instrument of great value, his rules for discerning "the spiritual motions of the soul." In accompanying the retreatant on his spiritual journey, the director will make frequent use of these impulses, urges, repugnances, and the like, in order to help the retreatant discern, amid the disconcerting totality of all these interventions, those which come from God and his Holy Spirit, and to submit to them knowingly and generously.[38]

C. The Point of Contact with the Experience of Salvation

1. Spiritual Poverty and the Tension of Love

What we have stated thus far about the experience of the First Week may seem rather negative: our becoming aware of our sinful condition and of our insertion into the world of evil. However, in speaking of the ambivalence of this intimate experience, we pointed out the positive orientation which ought to be given to it. But it is not enough to avoid the possible deviations, especially those more easily discernible, in order to make this awareness of our

---

37 J. Mouroux, *The Christian Experience*, p. 269. He devotes two chapters to this problem of affectivity and of feeling ("sentir") in the Christian experience: ch. 9, pp. 234–272, and ch. 10, pp. 273–320.

38 On various occasions Ignatius insists that the director should be very careful in following what is happening to the retreatant: See *SpEx*, [7, 8, 9, 17]; *SpEx-MHSJ*, p. 779, *Directoria autographa;* also p. 783, *Directoria tradita.* We should remember that, for Ignatius, discernment of spirits is itself "a grace which grows within and is helped by one's own activity, esp. his prudence and learning" (*Lettres*, p. 188; *LettersIgn*, p. 197).

sinfulness attain its salutary purpose. We now wish to deepen the positive character of Ignatius' First Week: a new awareness of our condition as sinners; and this in turn has become a point of contact with the genuine experience of Christian salvation. In this way the last part of this study will keep our attention almost exclusively on the level of the spiritual fruits in which grace is especially active. This will enable us to analyze further the experience of the retreatant in the First Week as something truly spiritual. What we have already said pertained directly to the logical progression of the *Exercises;* what follows belongs to activities of grace. As always, in the Exercises there is a meeting and a fusion of these two activities into one; and this fusion is best explained by the theology of the relationship between nature and grace. Here we come back to the affirmation made in chapter 3 on the total and multidimensional dialectic of the *Exercises,* a process that has many interactions. Even though we cannot truly dominate each of these dialectical actions, nor explain all their nuances, it is nevertheless important to submit ourselves to them more consciously, in order to grasp the concrete harmony of these interacting movements in the Exercises which reciprocally influence one another and evolve in common interdependence, whether absolute or conditioned.

The awakening of awareness about which we have been speaking, such as Ignatius conceived it, is accomplished only within the truly spiritual experience which we shall now describe. It is in this sense that the action of grace should dominate the affective experience which accompanies the deepening of our perception of our sinfulness. If the fruits we seek—confusion, grief, tears—have grace as their origin, they correspond to an interior work of repentance as Scripture understands this word. This repentance leads to a real conversion in which the person surrenders to God. It was this divine interior pressure that Ignatius submitted to at Manresa, when he was delivered from that human spiritual ambition which had until then directed his striving for holiness. And when a person, rid of all self-seeking, truly abandons himself to God with all the freedom of his being, God will not refuse to work his marvels in him. However, more is needed than an act of the will saying, "Take O Lord and receive"; there must also be a maturation of the movement of one's being, purified and dynamically directed toward God. The experience of the First Week helps the retreatant to surrender himself or herself to this gospel purification which sets in motion a profound gift of self to God. The remainder of the Exercises, with God's grace, will lead the person to maturity, with an attention which exceeds all our expectations and which alone can arouse the authentic experience of God's plan of salvation and spiritual growth.

Hence, we now take up anew here our examination of this development in the First Week, in order to study it strictly from a spiritual point of view in which all the steps so far considered on their several levels will be integrated. For the purpose of our analysis we shall distinguish three stages. These stages are not chronological, but in reality spiritual, and should coincide, at least partially, in each moment of the experience. We shall simply note a more marked presence of one or other element as the experience develops.[39]

a. The First Stage: the Fundamental Attitude

As we have seen, the fundamental attitude flows from placing oneself in the presence of God, and of contemplating his present and universal plan of creation, sprung from his love. This brings us face to face with the problem of the difficulty we experience in being faithful, which changes into a sentiment of indebtedness to God and of our need of grace; and this in turn increases our desire for a greater fidelity. Ignatius insists that every meditation ought to return to this point of departure, ought to revivify the fundamental attitude which continually arouses a spontaneous movement toward God. "Blessed are those who hunger, for they shall be satisfied" (Matt. 5:6). That is why Ignatius asks that the preparatory prayer for a meditation ([46, 75]) should repeat, over and over again, the attitude of the preparatory stage of the Exercises: that of putting oneself in the presence of the true God, Creator and Lord, with an act of reverence and humility. This is not a matter of mouthing formulas or of posing "prefabricated" acts; rather, it is one of coming back, with an attentive mind and heart, to the fundamental interior attitude, and of maintaining oneself in it as much as we can with God's grace, which we beg for this purpose. God "is always present. But as his presence is essentially gratuitous, it is on our side that the question arises: Are we receptive of this gratuity or not? Are we on the path to meet him, or are we searching somewhere else? Have we truly found the area of our misery which coincides with the field of his mercy? . . . To descend to the depths of our misery is not passivity nor apathy, but rather our supreme activity. We are never so much ourselves as when we become 'capable' of God. To become capable of receiving him is to welcome his fullness with the whole of our being."[40] The fundamental attitude, which is open both to our misery and to

---

39 Already in the First Week, this phenomenon corresponds to the problem of the circularity of the Exercises treated in ch. 8 below, in connection with the Contemplation to Attain Love. The problem refers more to the whole of the experience which has been proposed, as Fessard has shown.

40 J. Corbon, *L'expérience chrétienne dans la Bible,* (Paris, 1963), pp. 133–134.

God, submerges us in the consideration of the sin in which we are concretely situated. We ought not to avoid this confrontation, painful as it may be, if we desire that humble purification which delivers us to the Lord.

b. The Second Stage: the Descent into the Mystery of Evil

If we consult the studies in biblical theology on the problem which concerns us, we shall see a remarkable convergence between Ignatius' views and those of the Bible—not only from the point of view of the matter proposed for meditation, the mystery of sin, but also with regard to the interpretation supposed by his presentation of the message and the fruits being sought. Ignatius' thought remains based on and focused on what is essential in God's whole revelation, right from the First Week on; and no secondary, minimizing interpretation turns him away from it. To verify this, we shall draw our matter here from the article on "Repentance-Conversion" in the reference work, *Dictionary of Biblical Theology* (edited by Léon-Dufour), and also from the study we have already quoted of Dom Dupont.[41]

In the Bible and in the *Exercises,* the one same route is pointed out to be followed. Furthermore, the attitude which the basic elements of the problem require is the one we have described as the "first stage" of the experience now being studied. "God calls human beings to enter into communion with himself. Now, there is question here of sinful people. They are sinners from birth (Ps. 51:7). Through the fall of their first parents, sin entered into the world (Rom. 5:12) and has continued to live in the depths of the human heart (7:20). They are sinners also because of personal falls, for each of them 'has been sold to the power of sin' (7:14) and has freely welcomed this yoke of sinful passion (7:5). A personal response to God's call must, therefore, begin with a conversion."[42]

But the biblical term "conversion" contains shades of meaning which show a development in religious thought according to the measure in which the understanding of God's message becomes interiorized. The Hebrew word *shaab,* which indicates rather an external action, "to return, to change direction, to go back," has been translated in the Septuagint by means of two words: *metanoein* and *epistrephein,* respectively "to repent" and "to be converted." In the Acts of the Apostles St. Luke distinguishes these two meanings when he says: "Repent therefore and turn again" . . . "to God."[43] "To

41 See J. Giblet, in *DBTh,* pp. 486–491; Dom J. Dupont, "Repentir et conversion d'après les Actes des Apôtres," *ScE,* 12 (1960), 137–173.
42 *DBTh,* p. 486.
43 Acts 3:19; also 26:20. On this topic see the important note by which Dom Dupont replies to those who do not accept the distinction he has proposed, on the

lead their hearers to turn to be converted," writes Dom Dupont, "the apostles had to awaken in them sentiments of repentance."[44] To the Jews Peter speaks of the Christ whom they had crucified; Paul awakens the Gentiles to the impiety of their idolatry.[45] In every case, there is question of becoming aware of one's sin in order to experience its horrors, and of turning oneself toward the One from whom pardon is expected.[46] "The sense of sin" says Dupont, "seems to constitute a point at which one catches hold of the message of salvation."[47] *Metanoia* is, therefore, an interior experience of repentance which in the course of time was substituted for the ancient penitential liturgies to which corresponded a "rather crude sense of sin."[48] "Jesus makes no allusion to the penitential liturgies. He even mistrusts their rites as being too showy (Matt. 6:1–18.). What counts is a conversion of heart which makes one become a little child (Matt. 1:3). Thereafter it is the continuous effort to 'seek the Kingdom of God and his justice' (Matt. 6:33), that is to say, to order one's life in accordance with the New Law."[49] To seek the Kingdom of God, to order one's life in accordance with the New Law, and to surrender oneself to the Lord—in all this is the true unfolding of the experience of conversion. For, to be converted is to return effectively to God, to the Lord, and to "become aware of the demands imposed by the divine person whose lordship one recognizes. This recognition cannot be purely theoretical; it entails a radical change in one's view of life; it calls for a transformation of one's conduct. To be converted, is . . . to place oneself on the path indicated by God which ought to lead one to him."[50]

The biblical experiences, then, are clearly based on our taking cognizance of our sinful condition, along with an interior sentiment of repentance

---

basis of the one sole Hebrew word being translated by two words in Greek ("Repentir et conversion," p. 140, note 8). In addition to being "sensitive to the nuances of the Greek words," as Dupont notes, would not Luke have made himself part (just as he does elsewhere) of this development of the New Testament, a movement which goes back to the prophets themselves, and which seeks to nuance the term in order to make it express a reality which is becoming more and more interiorized and spiritual? The verb *epistrephein*, which means "to turn oneself" or "to be converted," could have been sufficient to translate *shûb* in the sense of a "return"; but this return is based precisely on the reality of a completely interior *metanoia*, "change of heart."

44 Dom Dupont, "Repentir et conversion," p. 149.
45 Ibid., p. 152, about Acts 2:37–41 (Peter to the Jews); 14:16 (Paul at Lystra); 17:24–30 (to the Athenians); 26:18 (before King Agrippa).
46 Ibid., p. 148.
47 Ibid., p. 156.
48 *DBTh*, pp. 486–487.
49 Ibid., p. 489.
50 Dom Dupont, art. cit., p. 148.

and an effective return, the gift of self to God. It is to this, above all, that the Exercises dispose the retreatant, by means of a pondering of the chief divinely revealed truths. The Exercises do this by leading the exercitant to fathom in all possible depth the rich significance of these realities, by means of a dialectic or mental activity which is both historical and existential. Let us recall how the exercises of the First Week, constituting a tightly knit whole, enable the exercitant to see his own life caught up in the movement which is the history of sin. Let us recall especially that all this activity seeks, through the graces petitioned, to arouse those interior spiritual sentiments, fruits of the Spirit according to Ignatius, which deeply transform the retreatant and effectively turn him or her toward the Beloved: "A cry of admiration with an immense love." We might ask ourselves whether there exists a more radical and more nuanced formula uniting the proclamation of the divinely revealed message a person, with one's disposing oneself, in one's whole being and in a Gospel manner, to such openness that one may become fully submissive to God's efficacious words. Even the possible deviations themselves are largely foreseen. First are those deviations which an understanding of the dialectical interactions of the *Exercises* can present in the human transmission of the divine message. Then too there are some definite techniques for directing the activity of the retreatant in accordance with the spiritual principles which order him or her toward what is spiritual, while the directives for the discernment of the motions within the soul protect this experience against things which commonly ensnare it. We again recall Nadal's statement: "They [the Exercises] have their efficacy because they teach the exercitant a method of preparing himself or herself to receive the word of God and the gospel."[51]

The experience of the First Week of the Exercises is, therefore, through the grief aroused by the reality of sin, the purifying experience of the desert in which the sinner discovers his tremendous need for God, and experiences and increases his hunger for grace. Such is the meaning of the test which Israel underwent on entering the Promised Land: "Remember the way which the Lord your God has led you these forty years in the wilderness, that he might humble you, testing you to know what was in your heart, whether you would keep his commandments, or not. And he humbled you and let you hunger and fed you with manna, which you did not know, nor did your fathers know; that he might make you know that man does not live by bread

51 *MonNad,* V, "Commentarii de Instituto S.I.," p. 788.

alone, but that man lives by everything that proceeds out of the mouth of the Lord."[52]

This was also Ignatius' experience during the first four months of his sojourn at Manresa, a realization that he was totally incapable of achieving, by his own efforts alone, the salvation and sanctification which he ambitioned. Through this painful purification which he details in his *Autobiography,* he discovers the meaning of spiritual evangelical poverty. It is a total surrender of oneself, a "handing over" of oneself with no further attachment to anything, even to the good as something possessed for itself. This experience of destitution, undergone in the presence of Christ as Savior and through His saving grace, is transformed into a tension or surge of love which surrenders a person's goodwill completely into the hands of the Lord.

c. The Third Stage: The Presence of Christ the Savior

"He is our peace."[53] "This tragic discovery of myself as a sinner! The intensity of this thought would be unbearable if it were not accompanied simultaneously by the correlative discovery of myself as one saved. For St. Ignatius seeks the discovery of oneself as a sinner only to bring out with brilliance this further discovery of the God of Love."[54] This characterizes the whole movement of the First Week. In this sense, it is inseparable from what we have described just above as the "Second Stage." It is in the presence of Christ the Savior that the retreatant discovers, as coming from above, the real meaning of his sin, and the love of God which infinitely surpasses it. At the same time as he considers the horror of sin, he discovers the loving God who spares him, the sinner. It would be a mistake to think that the meditation plunges him into the mystery of sin and that the colloquy merely rescues him from it. From the prelude which determines the grace he is to ask for, and onward through each point of the meditation, the exercitant is invited to relate to himself the situations which he is considering. This is how he should do it. The enormity of the sin contemplated confounds me, not only by the horror it contains in itself, but especially through its relationship to the Being who is offended, and above all by the fact, now bought vividly to my attention, that I have been spared so many times. Thus the awareness of sin does not aim at

---

52 Deut. 8:2–3.
53 Ephes. 2:14.
54 L. Beirnaert, "Sens de Dieu et sens du péché," *RAM,* 26 (1950), 29. In the same sense, see P. Antoine, "Sens chrétien du péché," *Chr,* no. 21 (1959), pp. 51–52; F. Roustang, "Le Christ, ami des pécheurs," ibid., p. 6.

the annihilation of the sinner, but at the true discovery of God's love for him. The confusion which Ignatius tells the exercitant to petition achieves its full spiritual significance only if the evident relationship between the horror of the sin and the divine mercy is kept vividly in mind by the retreatant's meditation. In this sense, the experience of the First Week is something uniquely positive. Not only does it unfold in the presence of the Savior, but the abyss of sin is meditated upon only to allow us to sound the immense length and the breadth of the divine love for man.

One who gives the Exercises will with security orient this catching of awareness of our sinful condition toward the experience of God's mercy if he understands and respects the Ignatian perspective of the First Week. For this purpose, there is nothing better than the simple reading of Scripture, in which our awareness of sin is an awareness of having offended someone transcendent, a person worthy of adoration, God, or Jesus Christ.[55] This divine person, whose face is discovered through the pardon that extends to this moment of our life, and whose unfathomable death on the cross dominates all reality, protects us from that bad awareness which is negative and desiccating.[56] In the *Exercises,* the reference to God and to Christ is explicit and constant during the First Week. If the retreatant misses this reference and falls into negativism, it is not the fault of the *Exercises* themselves. Indeed, every meditation is made "in the presence of God," in the sense of the fundamental attitude, expressed in the preparatory prayer ([46, 75, 105]). The petition of the First Exercise immediately emphasizes this relationship to mercy: Confusion before the fact that I have been spared as often as sin has been dominant in my life ([48]). The consideration of the history of sin leads me back to this same realization ([50]). Finally, the colloquy directs my prayer to the Savior ([53]). The second exercise points also to this becoming aware of my sin which makes me grasp the magnitude of the love and of the pardon ([60]). The colloquy then spontaneously brings "mercy" to the forefront ([61]). And the repetitions lead, by definition, in the same direction. Finally, the meditation on hell, using the hypothesis that in my own history I have freely withdrawn myself from God's love, plunges me with still greater ardor into the heart of the Savior. Here the universal perspective of salvation is emphasized strongly and expresses the desire of leading everything back to God. Ignatius' last word, in this meditation on hell, which also brings the First Week to its close, is the following: "I shall also thank Him for this, that up to this very moment He has shown Himself so loving and merciful to me"

---

55   see Dom Dupont, "Repentir et conversion," pp. 148–149.
56   see P. Antoine, "Sens chrétien," p. 67.

([71]). "The Christian sense of sin," writes Pierre Antoine, "is inseparable from thanksgiving."[57]

2. *Law and Grace*

It goes without saying that this experience of the First Week is not the initiation of the retreatant to God's long-hidden plan of salvation and spiritual development; he or she already knows God and is united to Him. There is question now of deepening his condition as a Christian in view of a more mature commitment. But up to this point, in what sense has this deepening taken place? Now at the end of this first stage, we are in position to give a better response. God, whom the retreatant already knew, now makes himself known through the experience of our sinful condition. That is the way he chose from the beginning, in the Bible, to reveal himself to man. It is the way of the Law which is inseparable from the way of Christ; for Christ came to fulfill or perfect the Law.[58] "The Law came in," writes St. Paul, "to increase the trespass."[59] This, of course, does not mean that the Law makes man a sinner.[60] As we have seen, man is a sinner both "by birth and by personal guilt."[61] But the Law which has been promulgated, being both a divine and a human measure, becomes a mirror which enables man to become aware, through his transgressions, of his being in a condition of sin;[62] and through this awareness, which is more and more expounded in the Old Testament as being interior and delicate, man gains a better sense or vision of his relationship to God. There follows the vividly felt need of divine help—a need which God has desired to fill from all eternity, though he has had to wait so long for genuine petition for it from man. "Hitherto you have asked nothing in my

---

57 Ibid., p. 52.
58 This way corresponds always to our need for purification. To reject this way under the pretext that we are under the regime of grace is not only to contradict the Lord who does not abolish the Law, but it is to pretend that we are entirely submissive to grace (which would only make us substitute a new Pharisaism for the old Pharisaism of the Law). For the mystics themselves, the purgative way is never completed in this world. We shall return to this point when we speak in ch. 8 of the circularity of the *Exercises*, which is like those of the "the ways" or "stages" of the spiritual life.
59 Rom. 5:20.
60 The Apostle affirms, on the contrary, that the Law is holy and spiritual (Rom. 7:12, 14). "What then shall we say? That the law is sin? By no means! Yet, if it had not been for the law, I should not have known sin" (Rom. 7, 7). See the Jerusalem Bible, note a on Rom. 7:1-7.
61 *DBTh*, pp. 550, 486.
62 See S. Weil's development of this theme: Every sin shows me my essential imperfection, which is a salutary experience (*La pesanteur et la grâce*, p. 66).

name; ask and you will receive, that your joy may be full."[63] It is to some extent a revealing of this mystery that the story of Jonah gives us through its language of imagery, especially in the parable of the castor-oil plant by which Yahweh makes his prophet understand how much he desires repentance in the heart of man, in order that He may give the pardon which vivifies.[64] "And the Lord said, 'You pity the plant, for which you did not labor, nor did you make it grow, which came into being in a night, and perished in a night. And should not I pity Nineveh, that great city, in which there are more than a hundred and twenty thousand persons who do not know their right hand from their left, and also much cattle'."[65] The Law constitutes a mysterious revelation of God's justice which by its contact makes us conscious of our sinful state; but this revelation is always and necessarily accompanied by that of mercy—for God's justice is good and divine—and thus we find the way of our deliverance.

In the divine plan, then, the way of the Law is inseparable from what completes it, the way of God's revelation in his Christ. The revelation of the Law becomes, in the acceptance of faith, a revelation of grace, just as the awareness of God's justice helps us to measure the extent of his mercy. The "Law came in, to increase the trespass; but," Paul continues, "where sin increased, grace abounded all the more, so that, as sin reigned in death, grace also might reign through righteousness to eternal life through Jesus Christ Our Lord."[66] The retreatant, having used his knowledge of God as Creator and Lord—Father, Son, and Spirit—to measure the extent of his own infidelity, then finds himself faced with two inseparable realities in his own experience: our sin and Christ as Savior. It is the confrontation between these two extremes, taking place in man's heart, which reveals to him the true face of God. Christ reveals the Father; but through the Christ who dies on the cross for our sins, through the universal Christ in Ignatius' two principal colloquies ([53 and 71]), it is the heart of the Father, the merciful Father, that is revealed to us.[67]

---

63 John 16:24.
64 There is a similar statement in Ezech. 18:30–32.
65 Jonah 4:10–11.
66 Rom 5:20–21. On the problem of the passage from the order of the Law to the order of grace—the problem of a life of interior and sound faith—for the person who is tending toward spiritual maturation, see L. Mendizábal, *Annotationes de Directione Spirituali*, pp. 229–230.
67 See Lyonnet, s.v. "Sin," *DBTh*, pp. 550–557. See esp. p. 554, a presentation of the parable of the prodigal son in which the central role of the Father is highlighted. The author states that the parable would be better called "The Merciful Father."

The saving action of Christ, which allows us to become vividly aware of our sinful condition, points to a "merciful God" and unfolds for us the revelation of this face of God. "Be merciful even as your Father is merciful."[68] There we find the incarnation and the revelation which gives us the meaning of God's love for us. "And should I not pity Nineveh, that great city!" Because we are sinners and because we remain created "to praise and serve God," a divine Way has condescended reach down into the abyss into which we had fallen, in order to bring us back again to the height from which we had descended. And there truly we find the Way of salvation in Christ. The exercitant becomes aware of this Way, and he or she will desire in the future to commit himself or herself to the following of Christ, in order to go to the Father and to bring back to the divine Glory the world which was created for this purpose.[69]

68 Luke 6:36. Dom Dupont has shown how the attribute of mercy manifests, in divine revelation, the very being of God in his loving solicitude for man. During a conference given at the Biblical Institute in Rome on Oct. 28, 1963, he established the meaning of Luke's version: "as your Father is merciful" (6:23), by comparing it to Matthew's: "as your heavenly Father is perfect" (5:48). The point of departure of his study is the use of these words in the Bible and the writings of Qumran; his examination ends in the perspectives proper to each evangelist, perspectives that are known also by other means, but of which one here finds a typical illustration. This allows us to see that the term of a procedure, such as that of the First Week, in the light of mercy (see the colloquies of the *Exercises*), places us in the heart of revelation and of the Christian experience which is met there.

69 We think that the perspective of this conclusion to the First Week, on the following of Christ, gives us the reason for the opinion according to which the meditation on the Kingdom may be given before the day of relaxation; and then one is free to take it up again after this brief repose, in order to fathom it better before undertaking the second stage or Week of the Exercises (see Fessard, *La dialectique*, p. 59). Polanco's Directory states clearly that the meditation on the Kingdom may be proposed twice, "namely in the morning and in the afternoon; and for that day no other topics are proposed" (*SpEx*MHSJ, p. 810). See also *SpEx*, [99], and the *Directorium Granatense* (*SpEx*MHSJ, p. 960).

Chapter 5

THE SECOND WEEK:
THE CHRISTIAN SITUATION IN LIFE

A. Entry into the Second Stage

1. The Spirit of the "More" or "Greater" (the Magis)

On several occasions, as is well known, Ignatius recommended that the complete Exercises should be reserved only for those who are apt candidates for them. If we gather together what he has written on the subject,[1] we should conclude that the aptitude in question has to do with a certain maturity of the person, with the intellectual capacities which allow for a deepening of spiritual awareness, and finally with a great desire for perfection which allows one to expect a fruitful result.

These criteria for selection do not derogate in any way, in Ignatius' mind, from the obligation of every Christian to tend toward the spiritual development commonly called "perfection," in the active sense of perfecting oneself in accordance with Christ's command "You must be perfect, as your heavenly Father is perfect" (Matt. 5:48). But if there is a time for awakening one merely to this ideal of all Christians, it is an occasion different from that for which the complete Exercises were intended. They instead are a period for the exercitant to seek a deepening of this ideal of perfection which engages the totality of his or her Christian life.

> There is only one Christian experience: It is one in its principles, one in its objectives, one in its structure, and one in its standards. But there are degrees, ever stronger and stronger, of this experience, and of the awareness that goes with it. This is indeed a law of the Christian life, which goes from faith to faith and from light to light, until it reaches at last the light of eternity.[2]

1 This point is treated in one way or another in the following places: *SpEx*, [9, 18, 20]; *LettersIgn*, pp. 95, 247, 434. The Directories and the *Constitutions* also contain remarks on this subject. On this attitude of Ignatius, especially with regard to Annotation 18, read J. Clémence, "La méditation du Règne," *RAM*, 32 (1956), 158–159.
2 J. Mouroux, *The Christian Experience*, p. 362.

To the different stages of this one same religious experience correspond certain dispositions, which are related respectively to the spiritual understanding, the will to commit oneself, and the person's freedom before God. Ignatius often distinguishes between the Exercises of the First Week and the complete Exercises. The former remind us of the "preparatory exercises" of Alcalá; they orient a retreatant toward a better, more fervent, and more faithful life as he or she progresses in the Lord, through growing attachment to more frequent reception of the sacraments and constant personal prayer. The latter envisage an awakening of consciousness, far more vast, of the amplitude of the Christian vocation, along with a generous acceptance of the demands which it entails.

These Ignatian directives pertain above all to the selection of the retreatants before they enter upon the Exercises. However, there is one directive inserted in the very movement of the Exercises which is of capital importance for us. It is clear that the Exercises ought to respect the retreatant's own rhythm. For "it may happen," writes Ignatius, "that in the First Week some are slower in attaining what is sought, namely, contrition, sorrow, and tears for sin. Some, too, may be more diligent than others, and some more disturbed and tried by different spirits. It may be necessary, therefore, at times to shorten the Week, and at others to lengthen it" ([4]). Ignatius goes even farther, when he states in the Autograph Directory that sometimes it is expedient after the First Week, "to refrain from giving the exercises of the Second Week, at least for a month or two."[3] He states that this directive is directly linked with the state of fervor of the retreatant, namely, the fervor which is manifested in "a great desire to continue." The attention which Ignatius gives to desire in spiritual experience throws much light on the developing experience which he hoped would occur within the Exercises, and on the attitude required to proceed from the first to the second stage. This desire is the fruit of the First Week. The verse in the Gospel which best expresses this desire, which opens the way for the experience of a second stage that the retreatant now feels to be necessary, is that giving Peter's words: "Lord, to whom shall we go? You have the words of eternal life."[4] Let us explain.

As we have seen, at Loyola Ignatius' experience was crowned by a lively desire to serve God our Lord.[5] He considered this desire to be a precious

3 *SpEx*MHSJ, p. 780. Ignatius uses the expression twice: "a great desire to continue," an expression which G. Dávila took up in his Directory, and which is also attributed to Ignatius (see Ibid., p. 916).
4 John 6:68.
5 *Autobiog*, nos. 9, 11, 14.

grace,[6] and it was this desire which sustained him during the painful experiences of Manresa.[7] Without it he would hardly have been able to persevere to the very end of that trial. But every grace in the dynamic area of desire is threatened by the danger of ambivalence conferred on it by our sinful human condition. Desire in man, even spiritual desire, borders upon cupidity.[8] This ardent desire for service, which he attempted without discernment through his spiritual ambitions which were too human and not yet purified, led him into ways which almost destroyed him.[9] From this experience he learned more than one lesson, especially a principle of direction which discerns the action of the evil spirit: the temptation "under the appearance of good."[10] Satan seeks, with success, to draw evil from good—in a manner the reverse of God's.

From the very first meditation of the Exercises, on the horror of sin which culminates in the death of Christ on the cross, the retreatant asks himself: "What ought I to do for Christ?"—"Brethren, what shall we do?"[11] For several days now the meditations will deepen this initial sense of sin, while simultaneously through this prolonged prayer there will be a mounting urge of desire to give oneself to Christ the Savior. Since it is the fruit of interior experience, this desire, when viewed in the perspective of the First Week, is not simply logical or intellectual conviction flowing from carefully considered premises; rather, it is an interior fruit of grace and a motion of the soul. It orients the exercitant directly toward the second stage of the Exercises and strengthens his or her will to commit himself to the following of Christ. But this desire remains still fragile, and it is subject to all the interior motions of the soul which can corrupt the greatest of God's graces.[12] Our spiritual desires generate a precious dynamic thrust, and discernment should be the means of protecting them from the aberrations to which they are prone.[13]

---

6 Ibid., no.24 and a commentary of A. Thiry (French edition: *Le Récit du Pèlerin*), p. 52, note 2. On this subject see also our "Conclusion to Part I" on the dynamism of desire, above.

7 *Autobiog*, no. 21.

8 1 Tim. 6:10: "The love of money is the root of all evils."

9 *Autobiog*, nos. 14 and 20.

10 *SpEx*, [10, 14, 332]. Ignatius often returns to this danger for those who are seeking perfection. See *LettersIgn*, pp. 20–21, 23, 25, 51, 69, 127, 331.

11 *SpEx*, [53]; Acts 2:37.

12 See the rule for discernment of "consolation without preceding cause" (*SpEx*, [336]) and the magnificent commentary on it in *LettersIgn*, pp. 22–23.

13 One will find in this ambivalence, which is part of our very being, the source of those frequent disillusionments which accompany so many of our spiritual activities (retreats, recollections, and the like). In them the desire to be faithful

Here the Rules for the Discernment of Spirits for the Second Week are extremely useful.[14] But even they could not be sufficient, once the real experience of conversion has caught hold of one. Hence the Exercises which follow aim at an enlightened and deeper grasp of our Christian vocation; and the desire to be completely faithful to God will bind the retreatant ever more closely to this vocation and keep him or her on a solid and proven road.

Thus, through the maturing of this desire to follow Christ, the First Week normally issues into the possibility and even the necessity of pursuing the integral experience of the Exercises. There is no better means than the quality of the experience in this first stage for judging the aptitude of the retreatant to profit from the complete Exercises. The desire which arises in the penitent and purified soul can be at this point so determining that, with or without exercises, it will lead the retreatant to take committed positions which require light, discernment, nourishment, and graces of strengthening—all of which are objectives of the subsequent weeks. That is why the experience of the Second Week, much more than that of the First, will be an experience of discernment, through the light which comes from a better understanding of God's plan for Christian salvation. This will orient the soul toward its personal destiny with a powerful grace to form itself in the likeness of Christ. The aptitude for the complete Exercises, which is crystallized in the Ignatian "more" *(magis),* is to be understood in terms of this dynamic movement already begun through the experience of the First Week. There is question here not merely of an isolated and voluntary desire for perfection or service, but of a journey already undertaken which one finds oneself unable to drop, or even to halt along the way.[15]

---

increases with the need we feel for God. But in them the orientation is not sufficiently enlightened from above to allow us to attain the Truth that frees and sanctifies.

14 *SpEx,* [328–336], (directly for the second stage of the Exercises).

15 Hugo Rahner gives a very good description of the Ignatian "more" *(magis)* or "greater" *(major)* in his little brochure, *True Source of the Sodality Spirit* (St. Louis: The Queen's Work, 1956), pp. 2–6; see esp. p. 3. [Since this pamphlet is virtually unobtainable, we quote this key paragraph here. Ed.]:

"In the *Exercises,* 'more' means an ever closer identification with the crucified Christ, who by this means alone conquered the world. To promote the salvation of souls means to be gifted with an insight into the staggering truth that Christ has made the outcome of his salvific work and the destiny of His Church dependent upon man's cooperation. It means an interior realization that the success of God's work is also (though not entirely) measured by that joyful, selfless eagerness to serve, so characteristic of those who heed and understand the call of the King of the world; who discern in His summons the challenge to do more in the future. We may call this the theology of the comparative."

To this end, the next stage in the Exercises will have two objectives which clearly determine the conditions in which the experience will be pursued: to propose and to help. To propose: that is, the coming exercises ought to set forth, in all its clarity, the ideal of the privileged Christian life, the norm and cause of our "life for God" in Christ and his Church. It is a consideration of the Christian vocation, in theory and in fact: the presentation of its reality as an ongoing process, with the understanding one can get of it. But this first activity will be exercised to help the person to accept the amplitude of the human and Christian vocation, and to adapt himself or herself to the particular and present demands which it will bring to light.

The Exercises of the Second Week thus aim at changing and readjusting the exercitant's situation in life through the action of grace—that is to say, in the light of the ideal the retreatant is considering: the Christian mystery or plan of salvation in the whole Christ.[16] This divine plan serves as a pattern ("exemplary cause") and as a source of grace, with a view to its accomplishment in our lives, in and through Christ. At the end of this work of readjustment in which the human effort and the action of the Spirit are joined together, and which prolongs, deepens, and concretizes the experience of the first conversion, the Exercises will foster the authentic and efficacious experience of Christian salvation, of death and resurrection with Christ. This is an experience which should be reactivated ceaselessly in our personal lives, with the help of God's grace, for the good of the universe in its movement toward glorifying God. Continually we should insert ourselves into the present and living history of salvation, and not just once and for all with the false security of an anticipated eternity. "Watch and pray" (Matt. 26:41).

2. The Primacy of Contemplation

The retreatant who undertakes the second part of the Exercises is, therefore, desirous above all else to respond to the divine love manifested in Christ the Savior; but he knows that he cannot do this without God's abundant

[Rahner finds this theology exemplified in Phil. 3:12). Other interesting reflections by H. Rahner will be found in his *The Spirituality of St. Ignatius,* pp. 36–39. The "more" or "greater" is also Ignatius' chief norm for making decisions among two or more options; e.g., in *SpEx,* [23], and throughout his Constitutions, e.g., [622,a]. On this see W. Ong, " 'A,M.D.G.': Dedication or Directive?" *Review for Religious,* 11 (1952), 257–264. Ed.]

16 This is the objective of the whole of the Second Week; this mystery or salvific plan of God is here carried out in the very person of Christ, with all that his life brings forth for our life in union with him and his Church. See 1 Tim 3:14–16 and the Jerusalem Bible note on this text.

grace. For he knows his own extreme spiritual poverty and indigence. The authentic retreatant of the First Week has lost all pretension before God and others. Because of this experience his desire to love and serve is all the more lively and humble, more ordered and more open to the action of grace. That is why, instead of following his own lead and springing into action for this or that form of service or exploit, he or she will offer himself modestly and submissively to the transforming contemplation of Christ which Ignatius proposes. Humbly, willingly, with respect and attention, he places himself "in God's school." All grace comes from above, and any future offering of self, commitment, or even love itself will be dominated by the activity of the Spirit and accomplished under the divine motion with which grace itself enables him to cooperate.

It can happen that, if the director and the retreatant are insufficiently convinced of the absolute necessity of this enlightened submission to the slow action of grace, they may give way to a feeling of urgency and fall into the illusion of "practicality," an obsession to get the result. This danger is especially present when the Exercises are condensed into a few days. After the First Week has stirred up some well-determined generosity, the retreatant or director may feel impelled to press on to take with fervor the decisions which are seen ahead. The election, displaced and deformed, absorbs all the energies of the retreatant, and the time of the retreat is transformed into a struggle which makes him a prisoner of his own problems rather than one who is seeking to follow the divine action.

Ignatius too has a sense of the "practical." But his notion of practicality was reversed during the experience he underwent of God's mystery or plan of salvation and spiritual growth. For him, the "practical" became rooted in the invisible and the eternal, and was to be judged within the framework of the total vision, present and transcendent, of this divine mystery for saving and sanctifying mankind. The person is far from being practical if he or she does not know how, through a contemplative and divinely given ascent to God, to insert himself into this present dynamic movement of the world and of his own life, which has both its origin and its end in God's eternity. This immediate and unfathomable factor of a practical life, according to Ignatius' concept of it, will for him transform action into contemplation, that is, into a fruitful means to find God and a road to union with him. That factor is also what totally inspires him in regard to the road he will now propose to the retreatant.

Many directors have presented the contemplation on the Kingdom of Christ ([91–100]) as a repetition of the Foundation "realizable and realized" in Christ.[17] That is true, but on condition that we do not restrict this repetition to the level of logic. We are not dealing here with a development merely intellectual. The Kingdom is not the repetition of a spiritual theme now being made more explicit and amplified. True, the same reality is again taken up; for God's revealed plan, whether more or less elaborately explained, has not changed. What does change is completely on the side of the retreatant and his experience. Ignatius once again places his retreatant face to face with God and his unique plan for humankind. But the person of the First Week who has seen himself within this plan as one who is always in difficulty, will now see himself in the heart and love of Christ the Savior, who will deliver the retreatant from evil and draw him, along with the universe which has been restored, toward the glorification of the Father. The retreatant takes up again the same existential consideration, but his place in it has changed. Now instead of seeing himself as a sinner, he will see himself as one who is continually and actively being saved, loved, and led to God in the whole Christ. This is the reason why, having been purified and humbled, he will seek and find in the contemplation of this divine saving plan the response to his desire for love, and also the way of service which alone gives him his place in the whole of creation, and with God in Christ the Savior "who reconciles to himself all things, whether on earth or in heaven."[18]

The Second Week, from the Kingdom onward, will devote much time to contemplation with a view to being more practical, that is, to leading the exercitant to come to an "election" or decision under the influence of the Holy Spirit; or in other words, toward his or her working out a continual and realistic adjustment of his spiritual condition in accordance with God's own perspective, both eternal and present. The "graces to be asked for" will specify the meaning of this activity on the level both of the intellect and the will: knowledge and love—contemplation and election. "As soon as I awake," Ignatius suggests, "I should place before my mind the subject of the contemplation with the desire to know better the eternal Word Incarnate in order to serve and follow Him more closely" ([130]). The contemplation of the Kingdom, as the foundation of all the subsequent activity, will, from the very beginning, bring to light the two poles of the Ignatian dialectical interaction which distinguishes and subordinates the objective and the subjective, the universal and the particular. Here these poles are called "contemplation" and "offering." Contemplation of the universal throws all its light on the

17 Numerous commentators, after the first Directories (see *SpEx*MHSJ, pp. 694–695, 861, 917, 1046, 1148).
18 See Col. 1:20 and Ephes. 1:10.

particular vocation of the human being and arouses a generosity which renews and intensifies the response already given to the Lord. Nadal wrote:
"The grace which you received in your particular vocation should be seen as
being identical with the universal vocation of all men, that is, the grace of
Christ and the evangelical vocation. In it you will find charity in its greatest
extension, for this universal vocation is the very purpose of your particular
vocation; the latter is a part, the former is the whole; both graces, both
illuminations must be alive in us."[19] The *Exercises,* properly understood and
made, enable us to discover the unity of one's vocation. God's call is unique
and personal to each one of us, inviting us each one to be Christian, and that
in a particular place and manner, toward the harmony of the universe in its
movement toward the glorification of God.[20]

3. The Exercise on the Kingdom,
and Its Relation to God's Plan of Salvation

The previous thrust of the Exercises entices the retreatant to deepen, on
the levels of awareness and self-commitment, the sense of his or her Christian vocation as viewed within the background of God's plan for the salvation
and sanctification of humankind. We shall next present the meditation on the
Kingdom as a general view of this divine plan and also, consequently, as the
foundation for all the subsequent contemplations which reveal the unfolding
of that plan through Christ. However, before we study in detail Ignatius' own
text about the Kingdom ([91–98]), we ought to consider the significance of
this same divine plan in the whole of Ignatius' spirituality and in his Christian outlook on the world, both of them taken as a whole.

As we have said before, there is no doubt that Christ was at the center of
Ignatius' spiritual experience. He was there as the Christ of revelation who
manifests to sinful man the majesty of God in the mystery of his Mercy.
Ignatius' whole experience ended in this encounter with the divine mercy
which freed him from his aberrations and disposed him to give himself entirely, with Christ, to the Divine Majesty whom he desired "to love and serve
in all things." The *Exercises* give explicit evidence that the way to enter into

19 Nadal, Orationis observationes, folio 162, in *MonNad,* IV, 697; also *Journal
    spirituel,* trans. Laval, no. 96.
20 The fact that Ignatius refused to give up this ontological and theological unity of
    our "unique" movement toward God is, perhaps, the reason why he did not
    escape all ambiguity in the use of such terms as: perfection, election, vocation,
    call, "to this life or state," and the like. In the *Exercises* he did not sacrifice
    clarity, but in general he always tried to find the exact word, as the numerous
    corrections in his manuscript testify.

this life of service for the divine praise is, always and directly, that of union with Christ even to his glorious death. To this spiritual end the *Exercises* devote the last three Weeks, by means of the transforming contemplation of the mysteries or events of Christ's life, the election which effectively brings the retreatant to a self-commitment, and the experience of union with the paschal mystery of the Lord. Finally, the history of Ignatius' life also witnesses to the depth and the realism of this commitment in Christ, in the whole Christ, through his communitarian consecration to the service of the Church, and through the instrumentality of his vow of special obedience to the vicar of Christ. Ignatius' whole spiritual development points toward Christ as its center: the highest possible obedience to God in Christ as still living in his Church, for the universal salvation of souls and, consequently, for a greater glorification of God.

The present text of the Kingdom ([91–98]) is a résumé of this spirituality which is ordered to God in the whole Christ. This is indirectly proved by the story of Ignatius' own conversion. The meditation of the Kingdom was indeed at the center of his experiences at Manresa. The idea of the service of God had already been conceived at Loyola in his meditations on Ludolph's Life of Christ, which had inflamed his soul and had brought about his radical conversion. But at that time his idea of service was too much limited to a sincere and total offering of himself which was to be achieved by costly and difficult action such as a newly converted knight would spontaneously think of. After Manresa his idea of service will have been cleansed of every worldly and earthly connotation. "To serve" will become "to save" in union and collaboration with the Christ who comes "to help souls" to enter into union with the Father. As Damien Mollat writes, "with Manresa and the Kingdom, the horizon on which Christ stands out so prominently has been amplified; it extends as far as the infinity of the divine salvific plan. The glory surrounding it is no longer the glory of the military leader or the intellectual master; it is the glory of the eternal Lord of all things. His 'interior eyes'[21] have been opened; the great deeds of penance become subordinate to apostolic works."[22] The truth of the Kingdom, the truth of the divine plan of salvation and sanctification, now understood with all its radiant light—that is what has substantially modified the lifestyle which the Pilgrim had first adopted in his "desire to imitate the saints." In regard to this we do well to recall the testimonies already cited, especially that of Nadal, who

21 *Autobiog,* no. 29.
22 D. Mollat, "Le Christ dans l'expérience spirituelle de saint Ignace," *Chr,* no.1 (1954), 29; Young, *Finding God,* p. 74.

considered the Kingdom and the Two Standards as the source of the *Exercises* and a "tiny history" of the Society of Jesus.[23]

Authors earlier than ourselves have emphasized the relationship between the Kingdom as presented by Ignatius and the divine plan of Christian salvation. Nadal's commentaries on this topic are extremely rich. Maurice Giuliani, who gave us a translation of them in the first issue of *Christus,* rightly notes that "this commentary should be of lively interest to us because it gives to the Kingdom its true spiritual significance by situating it in the very heart of the whole theology of redemption. . . . The work of redemption is presented as a combat led by Christ against Satan and the powers of evil. These are the scriptural and traditional perspectives which modern theologians love to contemplate anew. The combat has already reached its end in Christ's resurrection. However, it is prolonged each day in the history of the Church, who is herself triumphant in the risen Christ but still suffering in each of her members, in whom Christ continues his passion."[24] This résumé gives us quite well Nadal's thought in his interpretation of the Kingdom. González Dávila has left us in his Directory a shorter commentary in the same vein. He writes:

> The first meditation [of the Second Week] is that on the Kingdom, the foundation of everything that is treated here. It is also a summary of the life and the works of the Lord, and of the mission which he received from his eternal Father. That work, of which Christ said, 'I have accomplished the work which you gave me to do', is the following: 'I have manifested your name to the men whom you gave me out of the world' (John 17:4,6). Moreover, Christ calls men and women to help him in this mission, each one according to his or her own degree; and from this comes, as we see, the diversity of degrees and of lives in the imitation of Christ.[25]

Among modern day writers we can recall the names of Mollat and Rahner, whom we have already quoted in their commentaries on the Kingdom, and

---

23 In his study on the Christology of the *Exercises* (*GuL,* 35 [1962]), 14–38, 115–140, [English in *Ignatius the Theologian,* pp. 53–92; 93–135], Hugo Rahner insists on the central place of the Kingdom, which he considers as the essence of the *Exercises;* the whole of the *Exercises* is built around this center and the plan of salvation it expresses. On this subject see the review written by Granero in *Mnr,* 35 (1963), 296; also H. Rahner, "Notes on the Spiritual Exercises," *WL,* 5 (1956), 298, 318–321.

24 See *Chr,* no. 1 (1954), 87.

25 *SpEx*MHSJ, p. 917.

also Iparraguirre, Clémence, Lewis, and Marín, who give the same interpretation.[26]

B. *Personal Salvation in the Whole Christ, His Mystical Body*

The contemplation of the Kingdom, which in a sense inaugurates a spiritual journey of light and commitment under the direction of the Holy Spirit, is extremely important.[27] It is essential to understand its ever actual character—something present, personal, and as urgent as "The love of God which overwhelms us"[28] and or urges us on. God's creative act continually keeps us in existence; it is, in God, a call which lasts eternally. Now the same divine word also continually invites us to a redeemed existence. Whether we are aware of it or not, whether we are close to God or far from him, we are always being called by God in Christ. Our response to the divine call ought not to aim at that definitive stability which God himself gave up for our sake through his plan of a new relationship with us—that by which we exist in time by being created, and are delivered from evil by being redeemed. His call and our response ought to be as prominent as possible in our spiritual consciousness, the domain of a living faith, in order that the call, along with the light and the plan of divine love which it reveals, may banish the hesitations in our response, even when we must go against the impulses of our nature; also, that the call may stimulate a complete generosity in our own love, now restored and ordered in the same Christ, the Word of life. The splendors of this mystery of Christ—that salvific plan of God as communicated and lived out in the whole Christ, Christ and his Church or Mystical Body—these splendors and they alone can establish us in perfect Ignatian indifference, and then go even farther and arouse that "supernatural desire" for what Ignatius will call "the third kind of humility" ([168]).

---

26 I. Iparraguirre , *Adnotationes initiales,* pp. 151–166; J. Clémence, "La méditation du Règne," *RAM,* 32 (1956), 145–176; J. Lewis, *Notes de cours,* pp. 31–36; F. Marin, "Aportaciones biblicas a la contemplación del Reino," *Mnr,* 35 (1963), 333–342.

27 The meaning of this new beginning, this new walking "in the light," is magnificently expressed in Paul's prayer in Ephes. 1:17–23: ". . . my prayers, that the God of our Lord Jesus Christ, the Father of glory, may give you a spirit of wisdom and of revelation in the knowledge of him, having the eyes of your hearts enlightened, that you may know what the hope is to which he has called you."

28 2 Cor. 5:14.

1. Ignatius' Parable: Making One's Historical Past Newly Real in the Present

Before Ignatius takes up, by means of the address of the eternal King ([95]), this presentation of the divine plan for Christian salvation (which is essentially a call or invitation from the Lord), he proposes a parable for our consideration. This is the only time he gives an introduction of this kind. Conscious of the importance of this moment, he wishes to deepen the retreatant's "fundamental attitude," which is always required, and to prolong his placing himself into an attitude of readiness and availability to understand better what it means "not to be deaf to His call, but prompt and diligent to accomplish His most holy will" ([91]). This is the grace begged, in the second prelude, for this exercise.

a. The Diverse Interpretations on the Objective and Subjective Levels

The aim of the parable in the first part of the meditation on the Kingdom ([92–94]) is to aid the retreatant to contemplate the life of the eternal King ([91]). Many directors, applying the Ignatian directive of proportional use *(tantum . . . quantum)*, and finding that some retreatants gain little profit in meditating this parable as it is presented in the book of the *Exercises*, either transform it completely or simply omit it.

But commentators, on their side, have loyally tried to determine the benefit to be drawn from it. In the various interpretations which have been proposed, we can note two levels on which the history of a temporal king gives aid for contemplating the Kingdom of Christ: the level of the objective reality to be contemplated (the call of the King), and the level of the effective commitment which both the parable and the plan of salvation in Christ envisage (the retreatant's offering of self).

In regard to the call of the king, we admit that the parable cannot clarify the revealed mystery. At most—and this without showing clearly the reasons for the delay it causes—it predisposes the exercitant to the wide expanse of the message about to come, and it gives him or her an intimation about a corollary from that message: the existence of a grand mission for which our generous help is required in ideal circumstances.[29] The value which the com-

---

29 "Argumentation from the lesser to the greater," states Iparraguirre in *A Key to the Study,* p. 69. "It reveals the intention of Christ in the mysteries of His life and death," writes J. B. Moyersoen, in "Notes for the Spiritual Exercises," *Ign,* (1956), p. 76.

mentators see in this message, therefore, is on the subjective level of experience, as a response to the call contained in the address of the eternal King. According to J. B. Moyersoen this parable, by its contrast with reality, disposes the soul for a more "prompt and diligent" response ([91]).[30]

According to Iparraguirre, the parable helps to remove the obstacles which block the retreatant's good will and delay his gift of self, his "sense of personal uselessness" and his "habitual lethargy." It enables the retreatant also to see the problem in others first—a technique dear to the heart of Ignatius. Finally, it makes the retreatant more aware of the grandeur of the person who is calling and of the call itself, and of how absurd it would be to refuse such an invitation.[31] Jacques Lewis considers the parable as "useful because it embodies our ideal of Christ, and thus enables us to verify our dispositions."[32] Finally, J. Clémence analyzes at length the purification of our sensitivity through this consideration which progresses from the level of nature to the level of faith in Christ. In this way Ignatius wishes to subject our human generosity to grace by enlightening and sublimating it.[33]

Starting from these diverse opinions, we would like here, in the context which interests us, to express the role of the Ignatian parable with greater precision. Like most of the commentators, we attend especially to the subjective experience. For if, on the level of the object contemplated, we go from the parable of the temporal king to the reality of the eternal King, somewhat like moving out of the shade into the sunlight, how can the shade help one understand the sunlight, except by emphasizing the contrast between the two? However, for that it is already necessary to have turned our attention away from the shade and to have begun to contemplate the sunlight. But in the text the parable is considered in itself and before the contemplation of the revealed mystery; hence it is in itself that it ought to be a help. We think it will truly be a help only to the extent that it will dispose the retreatant for the other consideration, which is the hearing of the call. In this sense the subjective experience which it stimulates, rather than the objective light which it throws on the problem, will exercise its influence. This is what happens if we respect the position of this contemplation in the concrete dynamic of the Exercises.

---

30 J. B. Moyersoen, ibid.
31 I. Iparraguirre, *Adnotationes initiales,* p. 54.
32 J. Lewis, *Notes de cours,* p. 32.
33 J. Clémence, "La Méditation du Règne," *RAM,* 32 (1956), 148–149, 156.

b. The Dynamism of Desire and Its Goal in the Second Week

We connect the influence of this parable, in the case of the retreatant, with the dynamism of the desire which is so necessary at the time when he or she enters the Second Week. We should remember the principle stated at the beginning of this chapter, namely, that according to the directive of Ignatius, the pursuit of the experience of the Exercises depends on the spiritual desire of the exercitant. Precisely because of its occurrence at this point, we think that the meditation on the Kingdom, and even more the parable leading up to it, should be viewed in their place within the movement of the *Exercises* as a whole, and not as something having its value independently from this large context. We would like to highlight this relationship between the Kingdom and the dynamic movement of the Exercises. It throws considerable light on our interpretation of the meditation on the Kingdom itself.

We might say briefly that the parable makes us, with our simple and immense human aspirations and with the capacities for responsiveness and generosity which they arouse in us, pause for a moment before we consider the divine realities which will fulfill them indefinitely farther.

Ignatius' experience functioned thus in his own case. For him the parable concretized the intimate movement of his whole past which then entered into the full light of Christ. If this pause within the meditation itself has a significance which the author of the *Exercises* maintains and desires to respect, we can rightly ask ourselves, not only what this pause means, but also why Ignatius, who so reverently respects the divine transcendence, took the roundabout road of a strictly human consideration. Is this procedure simply a maneuver intended to bring our powers of generosity into play? Is there truly need for this, here at this moment in the Exercises, after the experience of the First Week which normally grows into a "surge of love" toward the Lord? It is much more conformed to Ignatius' spirit to propose the discernment of charity to those who are apt for the ideal of the "more," now when their generosity is already becoming operative. His own experience in this matter had taught him much. Furthermore, this meditation is certainly addressed, through the insights gained from contemplating the divine plan for salvation and sanctification, to the exercitant's will or desire. It aims to lead him or her to hear and accept a divine call continually being addressed to us: "Behold, I stand at the door and knock," says the Lord in the Apocalypse; "if any one hears my voice and opens the door, I will come in to him and eat with him, and he with me."[34] There is no rightly ordered human prudence

34 Apoc. 3:20.

which will now consent to set its arbitrary limits to the generosity entailed in the response to such a call, a divine call. Is it possible to give oneself too much to God? The discernment which regulates the generosity ought not to impose its own limits. At one and the same time Ignatius seems compelled to confront these two realities which seem to be opposed to each other: to foster the ardor of generosity to which the retreatant will not dare ever to set the limit himself, yet also to propose to him or her the discretion of charity which is the fruit of the Holy Spirit. How will this parable of the temporal king, which engages the human level of our desires and willingness to self-commitment, help to establish this necessary balance between discernment and generosity? Why is it preferable, perhaps necessary, to arrive at this point by making use of a consideration which starts from the human level rather than from the divine plan itself?

Let us return to the thought of Ignatius, which is so existential. That is, since the time of the illuminations at Manresa, he has taken up and comprehended everything within the context of a continual movement by which all creation, through the call of God, sprang from the abyss of nothingness and was committed to an unceasing ascent back toward God as its end. For Ignatius, even the parable ought not to be separated from this unique, vivid, and prolonged movement, in which any human person, attracted by God, is elevated from the human, through human means and along with the human means, all the way back to God. Ignatius views nothing as being outside this universal and divine movement. He judges even his past life of sin in this light; and, also and even more so, the generous impulses in this past which sometimes sought fulfillment in an illusory good proceeding from evil. Consequently we would say, in our terms, that the parable should be made a part of anyone's personal history of salvation as it is rising toward the universal. Just as there is a personal history of our sins which lasts throughout our lifetime, so too is there such a history of our desires, our generosities, our obscure and unconscious reaching out to God. In Ignatius' case, this parable, constructed around the life of a knight, concretizes, rather than symbolizes, the long journey of his life of which he was more or less consciously aware. It was a life full of desires and generosities which finally led him to follow the same road taken personally and lovingly by the eternal Lord. Man, because he too is a creature, is always moving positively toward God, though often he is unaware of it; and because he has been redeemed, his ascent to God is called to a transfiguration in the eternal Christ. This is the passage from the disturbing dreams at Loyola to the brilliant light of the graces at Manresa. The meditation of the Kingdom, which passes from the parable to the contemplation, from the shade into the sunlight, joins these two positive poles of the human and the divine at a point where the action of grace respects a certain continuity which one finds in the depths of one's being as one journeys toward God. Ignatius had entertained all the dreams of gift and commitment, of service and labor, of victory and glory. The parable represents a high point in this journey. It is "the dream altogether spontaneous but also long matured"[35] which the parable here imaginatively recreates. It is the discreet parable of an entire life, but especially of that moment of exceptional generosity, the vibrant moment of Loyola which slowly turns toward the full light. Now Ignatius magnified this dream of the past for the sake of those who perhaps might have a dream greater than his own, in order that nothing might be taken away from that which an upright and generous human heart could desire. For Christ brings to him or her more, infinitely more!

Toward a Balance between Generosity and Discernment

Why, then, the parable, this more or less symbolic creation sprung from human desires—especially in the case of Ignatius? As several have stated: It is a means to help us become aware of our inexhaustible capacities for generosity and devotion. This is true especially in regard to the dynamism which strengthens these capacities; and they are what sustains our lives in our search for fulfillment, sometimes even through the illusory goods which emerge from something evil. That is why it is so important for us to become aware of this concrete, historical, existential dynamism which leads us to surrender ourselves more fully to God, in our own here and now.

But now another question arises. If we thus stir up desire which is related to idealized situations, is there not danger of arousing a false enthusiasm which would sap the vitality from the discretion of charity? Or conversely, why should we descend to a level strictly human and hypothetical, namely the retreatant's awakening his or her consciousness of these natural resources of generosity, at a time when this retreatant has already, at the end of the First Week, turned effectively to the love of the Lord? This is the last problem to be solved in order to bring together the two extremes, generosity and discernment. To harmonize these extremes is the aim of our interpretation of the function of the parable—indeed, to harmonize them in the concrete circumstances in which the exercitant now is. Briefly, we want now to explain that which hitherto we have merely described.

Let us remark, first of all, that the parable as it is conceived, does not in any way provoke the desire; rather, it helps the retreatant to become con-

---

35 R. de Ravinel, "L'appel du Christ," *RAM*, 29 (1953), 330.

scious of the human dynamism which strengthens his or her desires, as we have shown. Now, as the retreatant enters the Second Week, he definitely has a great spiritual desire for Christ, a desire that is either new or interiorly renewed. He finds himself in a time of his life when generosity is very active, and he is invited here to integrate into this desire the whole thrust of his being and of his life—just as Ignatius, turning toward the light, offered the whole of his life. In this sense there is a sublimation of our world of human desires into that desire which is predominant at this period in the Exercises; and which will be called upon, through the contemplations about to come, to add its own full weight to the dynamism of our own desires which is already existent in our lives. On the other hand and with a gaze backward, to increase the spiritual desire already in existence is not the function of the parable; rather, the parable should add its own weight to that desire, by uniting it to the exercitant's whole being in all its depth, and by impeding him from gradually slipping back into the more superficial level of human sensitivity. This sensitivity is something incarnate in or on the margin of all our life in our concrete circumstances. Life teaches us that every religious experience, even a deep experience such as that of the First Week, stirs up a longing for God, and that this longing is in danger of waning rather soon if it is not continually reattached to its points of reference in the source which first aroused it; or, as in the present case, if it is not deepened by being integrated into the whole ongoing life of the retreatant.

Thus it is that, on the one hand, the discernment necessary for a generosity which is total and well ordered is fostered by the parable. It does this by integrating into this precious spiritual desire everything that is human, both past and present, which one carries with its full weight within oneself, and which the parable suddenly mobilizes. As J. Clémence states, there is question here of a purification of the human sensitivity which will be more completely committed through the generosity aroused by the call of the Kingdom. But the important thing is that this purification be attached to precisely the present situation, when the retreatant is emerging from the First Week and when the desire for attachment to Christ is uppermost in his mind. As we have seen, this purification is accomplished by an integration of this desire into the total movement of one's being and life, a movement always in search of the divine life. On the other hand, this desire, fruit of the spirit, elevates the whole world of the spiritual desires which the parable evokes, and it carries them along with itself toward this higher and divine realization. The parable is that of one's own past. That is, it takes in the retreatant's own personal history, seen as the culmination of the contingent factors in his or her past which produced it. And the retreatant's own self along with his or her history in its most vital dimension—this is what should be offered to God in its totality and inserted into the grand history of salvation. The parable will bring this about with a growing awareness, step by step as the experience grows, and without any limit to the retreatant's generosity except that measured out by the grace given him or her by the wisdom and goodness of God. "Give me your love and your grace: this is enough for me" ([234]).

The Literary Structure of the Parable

This balance between discernment and generosity is a better explanation, we believe, for the disappearance of the parallel which some have tried in vain to maintain between the two parts of Ignatius' meditation. The parable helps the contemplation of the Kingdom by disposing the retreatant to hear God's call. Indeed, this contemplation is centered on a call and then develops around the response to be given to this call. The help to be given, then, bears on this central point of disposing the retreatant, in the sense of the second prelude ([91]), to hear this call and to be prompt and diligent in responding to it. The parable does this in a way which in fact constitutes a necessary initial phase. During this time, the retreatant gathers together all his generous human resources, in order to integrate them into this spiritual desire. This desire, in turn, will henceforth give direction to his movement toward God, in its ongoing history and in accordance with the factors received from its past.

Consequently, the similarity between the two parts in Ignatius' meditation could exist only on the level of the addresses conveying the two calls ([93] and [95]). When one moves forward to consider the problem of the response ([95–98]), one finds a different object, and there is no longer a possibility of a parity between the two parts. The first aims at a specific *preparation,* to listen with all of one's being; the second aims at the *progressive growth* in the giving of self in the response to the call. Hence if we accept this interpretation of the parable, that it is a "preparation for hearing the divine call" so as "to be prompt and diligent in answering it," we understand better that in the contemplation of the Kingdom there are three stages in the response to be given: the one suggested by the parable ([94]) and the other two found in the second and third points of the contemplation ([96–98]), in which we see a real development which should be respected. There is not a question of three possible responses proportioned to the retreatant's degree of generosity. The first point is of immediate interest to us and can be summed up as follows. To the call of the parable corresponds this freely chosen integration of the total movement of the exercitant's whole self into his or her present spiritual desire. In this privileged time of his history understood as an ascent toward God, his whole past—not only that of his sins purified in the First Week, but also that of his desires, deepest aspirations, and powers of acceptance—flows into this humble attitude of self-offering. Thus is opened up the possibility of the retreatant's personal history becoming a part of the universal history of salvation. This is the first step to be taken. It introduces the exercitant existentially into the full light of God's plan of salvation. Here the image of the "ignoble knight" who refuses "the invitation of such a king" finds a correct resonance. "How justly he would deserve to be condemned by the whole world," Ignatius comments ([94]).

The second part of the meditation, as we shall see, will not have to come back to this hypothesis of a refusal. The retreatant who is passing from the first to the second part of this same exercise is exercising the attitude required to undertake the second stage of the Exercises. He or she has already responded to this first call and has offered himself together with all the dynamism of his being to the attentive hearing of the divine call. He is ready to pass on to the first point of the second part ([95]), which immediately presents the discourse of the King, a summary presentation of God's plan for salvation and sanctification in the whole Christ.

b. Adaptation, Interpretation

One last question needs our attention. Does the parable, still expressed in Ignatius' terminology, remain apt today for attaining the objective which we attribute to it?[36] Evidently, the language and the symbol (to the extent that there is a symbol) can be modernized. But we do not see a necessity for such a change. What really counts is to explain it, to open up its significance. Then it remains for each exercitant, through this "illumination" of the movement of all creatures—which is universal—to discern his own way to the whole truth which is being offered to him, a truth which commits, liberates, and sanctifies. It remains for each one, as was the case with Ignatius, to follow the parable of his or her own past until it merges into this precise moment when he more clearly perceives his own particular call from the Word of God.

---

36 In his "Notes on the Spiritual Exercises," *WL*, 83 (1956), 321, Hugo Rahner emphasizes the universal and perennially relevant character of the title "king." Following Jung, he considers it to be an "archetype" of the human soul. L. Pouillier, for his part, provides us with a biblical study of this title as applied to Christ. He refers especially to the following texts: Ps 2:6; 28:10; 43:5; 73:12; Dan. 7:14, 27; Luke 1:32; Matt. 2:2; John 18:37. See L. Pouillier, "Allégorie du Règne," *CBE*, 61–62 (1920), 9–14.

2. The Connection with God's Plan for Salvation and Spiritual Growth

By means of the parable everything up to this point has been done to help the retreatant into a state of readiness to listen to the divine call from Christ. But as we stated at the beginning of this chapter, the intention of this meditation, as indeed of the entire Second Week, is to propose God's plan of salvation and sanctification, and to help the retreatant to accept it in truth. This mystery of Christian salvation is essentially an invitation from the Lord. It comes to this particular person and invites him or her to give himself freely to Christ the Savior, through whom the world achieves its end in God. To propose this mystery or plan is not merely to repeat its formulation verbatim; rather, it is to expound its themes by opening them up to the intellect for contemplation. Through the prayer that will follow, the call will be perceived as more intimate to the person, and the person will dispose himself to respond with a renewed and deepened spiritual awareness, and with a generosity better rooted in reality.

Before we view the expression, both simple and correct, of this plan of salvation as Ignatius presents it to the retreatant for meditation ([95]), we shall give some theological reflections on this mystery of salvation by starting with a biblical description. Our purpose here is to explain the content of this salvific mystery which the director ought to propose to the retreatant. We should remember that Ignatius offered his book of the *Exercises* as a guide for the director, a plan to be followed and a schema to be developed, soberly but intelligently. "He who seldom defines," Ignatius used to say, "understands little and helps even less."[37] His way of giving the Exercises, far from resembling the reading or repetition of a text,[38] easily became transformed into "spiritual conversation" on the topic in question. Thus we shall consider here how the mystery or salvific plan is, on the part of Christ who calls, "a priestly and sacrificial mission," and for us who are called, "a Christian participation" in that saving mission. Then we shall turn back to Ignatius' text and find there the synthesis of those principal elements which constitute the spiritual nourishment which the Kingdom meditation offers.

a. The Call: A Priestly and Sacrificial Mission

The Biblical Characteristics of the Work of Salvation

Addressing himself one day to the "mountains of Israel," devastated and delivered over to the pillage of the "foreigner," the enemy, God said: "For

---

37 *LettersIgn,* p. 24.
38 "The director should not bring the *Exercises* and read them to the retreatant,

behold, I am for you, and I will turn to you, and you shall be tilled and sown; and I will multiply men upon you, the whole house of Israel, all of it; the cities shall be inhabited and the waste places rebuilt; and I will multiply upon you man and beast; and they shall increase and be fruitful; and I will cause you to be inhabited as in your former times, and will do more good to you than ever before. Then you will know that I am the Lord."[39] Our salvation is the work of God. For centuries, through the specific events of the history of Israel, God made us understand that He alone "can draw us from the land of slavery," and "lead us back to the land of our forefathers," and transform anew the desert into a garden, Gan-Eden. "Thus says the Lord God: On the day that I cleanse you from all your iniquities, I will cause the cities to be inhabited, and the waste places shall be rebuilt. And the land that was desolate shall be tilled, instead of being the desolation that it was in the sight of all who passed by. And they will say, 'This land that was desolate has become like the garden of Eden; and the waste and desolate and ruined cities are now inhabited and fortified.' "[40]

The gratuitous work of salvation consists in the restoration of the "paradise lost" which leads us back to the beginning and to the source of life. It embraces the people of God, as a whole, and it also touches each of its members. It is God who thus remakes "the unity of his people," a unity destroyed by sin, and who transforms the "hearts of stone into hearts of flesh," putting into each one "his spirit" which vivifies.

The word of the Lord came to me: "Son of man, when the house of Israel dwelt in their own land, they defiled it by their ways and their doings; their conduct before me was like the uncleanness of a woman in her impurity. So I poured out my wrath upon them for the blood which they had shed in the land, for the idols with which they had defiled it. I scattered them among the nations, and they were dispersed through the countries; in accordance with their conduct and their deeds I judged them. But when they came to the nations, wherever they came they profaned my holy name, in that men said of them, 'These are the people of the Lord, and yet they had to go out of his land.' But I had concern for my holy name, which the house of Israel caused to be profaned among the nations to which they came.

"Therefore say to the house of Israel, Thus says the Lord God: It is not for your sake, O house of Israel, that I am about to act, but for the sake of my holy name, which you have profaned among the nations to which you came. And I

but he should beforehand study well the matter which he is about to treat," states the Autograph Directory (*SpEx*MHSJ, p. 780).

39 Ezek. 36:9-11.
40 Ibid., 36:33-35.

will vindicate the holiness of my great name, which has been profaned among them; and the nations will know that I am the Lord, says the Lord God, when through you I vindicate my holiness before their eyes. For I will take you from the nations, and gather you from the countries, and bring you into your own land. I will sprinkle clean water upon you, and you shall be clean from all your uncleannesses, and from all your idols I will cleanse you. A new heart I will give you, and a new spirit I will put within you; and I will take out of your flesh the heart of stone and give you a heart of flesh. And I will put my spirit within you, and cause you to walk in my statutes and be careful to observe my ordinances. You shall dwell in the land which I gave to your fathers; and you shall be my people, and I will be your God."[41]

This long prophecy of Ezekiel ends with these words:

"Then the nations that are left round about you shall know that I, the Lord, have rebuilt the ruined places, and replanted that which was desolate; I, the Lord, have spoken, and I will do it."[42]

However, over the centuries between the promise and its fulfillment, Scripture tells us: "In many and various ways God spoke of old to our fathers by the prophets; but in these last days, he has spoken to us by a Son, whom he appointed the heir of all things, through whom also he created the world."[43] God who expresses and reveals himself in his Word, who created us by his Word, has chosen to redeem us by the incarnation of his Word.[44] In the Son of God, become one of us, we receive the heritage of life reserved by the God of the Promise to his people for the "glory of his holy name." In him we find our own sacred place at the heart of the creation which is destined to glorify God, and there we enter into a new existence as sons of God in the eternal Son of the Father:

I mean that the heir, as long as he is a child, is no better than a slave, though he is the owner of all the estate; but he is under guardians and trustees until the date set by the father. So with us; when we were children, we were slaves to the elemental spirits of the universe. But when the time has fully come, God sent forth his Son, born of woman, born under the law, to redeem those who were under the law, so that we might receive adoption as sons. And because you are sons, God has sent the Spirit of his Son into our hearts, crying, "Abba! Father!" So through God you are no longer a slave but a son, and if a son then an heir.[45]

41 Ibid., 36:16–28.
42 Ibid., 36:36.
43 Heb. 1:1–2.
44 John 3:16–18.
45 Gal. 4:1–7.

Such is the revelation of the economy or plan of this mystery of salvation. We need to understand it better, that we may surrender ourselves more completely to the infinite power of the Son who accomplishes in us, in the name of God, the gratuitous work of salvation.[46] "For all the promises of God find their Yes in him. That is why we utter the Amen through him, to the glory of God."[47]

Nevertheless, in its realization, this plan "in Christ" is a rock of scandal to any a human spirit, "a stumbling block to the Jews and folly to the Gentiles."[48] For the Word of God, already emptied in the Incarnation, "humbled himself and became obedient unto death, even death on a cross."[49] Why was it necessary that the "Son of Man," who comes glorious in the clouds of heaven, be also the "Servant of Yahweh" who bears the sins of his people? Peter's reaction to the Lord's words at the time of the first prophecy of the Passion was human enough, but Jesus warned him that his thought sprang from a human viewpoint, not God's: "You are not judging by God's standards, but of man's."[50] Of the pilgrims of Emmaus he asked: "Was it not necessary that the Christ should suffer these things and thus enter into his glory?"[51] And the epistle to the Hebrews will echo, ". . . because of the suffering of death, so that by the grace of God he might taste death for every one."[52]

From the promise to its realization, as we see, the plan of salvation integrates within itself data as varied as human infidelity, the gratuity of the gift of God, the incarnation of the divine Word, suffering, and life. To these data we must apply our understanding so as to receive the light which this sanctifying plan casts upon our own vocation in the whole Christ.

The Metaphysical Conditions of the Work of Salvation

Two extremes have imposed their conditions on the work of our salvation: the very nature of salvation which is divinization, a communion with God, and the state of slavery to which sin has reduced us. Sin and divinization! The history of our salvation is an effort to reconcile these extremes which only the judgment of eternity will render forever irreconcilable: our condition as children of God and our condition as sinners. The history of

46   Heb. 1:3.
47   2 Cor. 1:20.
48   1 Cor. 1:23.
49   Phil. 2:7–8.
50   Mark 8:33.
51   Luke 24:26.
52   Heb. 2:9.

salvation—of that of all humanity and each one of us—follows a path which goes from the infinite to the infinite; from the infinite ingratitude of sin to the infinite gratitude for the divine life offered to man. It is Christ, the incarnate Word, who comes to reunite in himself and to reconcile these two extremes which are lost in the reaches of infinity. God alone could do this, and in the most unlikely way when it is considered from our human point of view: the death of God in the person of Christ.

Our salvation is "communion with God," divinization. Hence in regard to its origin, it is absolutely impossible for man to accomplish this. Man is metaphysically incapable of giving to himself what belongs to God alone, divine life. Open to the infinity of God, because he is made in his likeness, man, while disposing himself for this gift of God, can only wait for it. On the contrary, when he tries to procure by his own efforts alone that which can come only from God, he sins. "You will be like gods." Such was the first sin. Such was the sin of the Pharisees who sought justice, salvation, by their own works. Thus, by its very nature, salvation is entirely gratuitous and is dependent on a divine power of reunion, on a transmission of divine life, the priestly power. Priesthood is a "divine omnipotence" of reconciliation operating gratuitously in favor of man. "Every one who thirsts, come to the waters; and he who has no money, come, buy and eat! Come, buy wine and milk without money and without price."[53]

But salvation, although free and divine in its origin, requires for its realization man's collaboration, his free and concrete acceptance. While snatching a soul from the world of sin and uniting it to the divine life, salvation causes an upheaval in the depths of its being. This journey is made, on a path which goes from the infinite to the infinite, during the course of one simple human life! Because it is a going beyond oneself, an opening of one's human and sinful condition to the divine condition, salvation is necessarily and ontologically a tearing away from oneself, from one's closed world, a going out of one's self, an "exodus," a "passage" and ecstasy in the Greek sense of that word, in order to communicate with Him who is totally Other. "Go from your country . . . to the land that I will show you."[54] "Go, sell what you possess . . . and come, follow me."[55] The work of our salvation is priestly and also necessarily sacrificial.[56]

---

53 Isai. 55:1.
54 Gen. 12:1.
55 See Matt. 19:21 and Luke 18:22.
56 On the sacrificial character of our sanctification which is "a passage to God," see F. Bourassa, "Verum Sacrificium," *ScE,* 3 (1950), 150ff.

The Salvific Mission of Christ

The task of salvation, in the extreme conditions in which it was proposed, was undertaken by the Word of God through his Incarnation. The saving mission of the Son will be sacerdotal in nature: In Jesus we find incarnate the divine power of reuniting man with God, the divine work of reconciliation. "All authority in heaven and on earth has been given to me."[57] Offered as food for eternal life, Christ acquires the power to share his life with us. By joining men and women to himself, he communicates to them his filial existence through which these same men and women become the object of the predilection and pleasure of the Father. "Therefore, if anyone is in Christ, he is a new creation; the old has passed away, behold the new has come. All this is from God, who through Christ reconciled us to himself and gave us the ministry of reconciliation; that is, in Christ God was reconciling the world to himself, not counting their trespasses against them, and entrusting to us the message of reconciliation."[58] Later on in contemplating the "mysteries of the life of Christ" we shall see how this power of mediation acts for our justification, through the perfect homage of obedience which the Son renders to the Father in this world.

The mission of Christ will also necessarily be sacrificial. Having truly become one of us, Christ espouses our human condition in all its frailty so as to restore it from within, inasmuch as he is a creature submitted, in a sense, to the same laws of sanctification.[59] Scripture affirms:

> For it was fitting that he, for whom all things exist, in bringing many sons to glory, should make the pioneer of their salvation perfect through suffering. For he who sanctifies and those who are sanctified have all one origin. . . . Therefore he had to be made like his brethren in every respect, so that he might become a merciful and faithful high priest in the service of God, to make expiation for the sins of the people.[60]

Thus through Christ the condition of humankind is snatched from the lot proper to it ("You will return to the soil, as you were taken from it"[61]) and shares in the divine life. "For our sake he made him to be sin who knew no

---

57   Matt. 28:18 and 11:27; also John 3:25; 10:28–29; 13:3; 17:2–3. On reconciliation in Christ, see 2 Cor. 5:18–21.

58   2 Cor. 5:17–19.

59   On the extent of the reality expressed by the word *sarx* as applied to Christ, read the reflections of Karl Rahner, *Theological Investigations,* I, 196–197. On the sanctification of Christ in the "passible and mobile part of his being," see F. Bourassa, "Verum sacrificium," pp. 169ff.

60   Heb. 2:10–11, 17.

61   Gen. 2:19.

sin, so that in him we might become the righteousness of God."[62] In treating of the "sufferings of Christ" we shall contemplate more deeply this aspect of the mystery of our salvation: Christ having become obedient for us unto death.

What is the consequence for Christ himself of this mystery of salvation in the conditions in which he accomplished it in our place? "I will give you as a light to the nations, that my salvation may reach to the end of the earth."[63] The mission Christ completed in time won for him "the nations as a heritage."[64] He is the universal mediator and, consequently, the first-born of a new race to the glory of the Father. Already in God's plan, according to St. Paul, "He is the image of the invisible God, the first-born of all creation: for in him all things were created in heaven and on earth, visible and invisible, . . . all things were created through him and for him. He is before all things, and in him all things hold together. . . ." And after the fall which left its mark on all creation, it is also in him that creation is taken up again and the promised salvation is realized. That is why "He is the head of the body, the church; he is the beginning, the first-born from the dead. . . . For in him all the fullness of God was pleased to dwell, and through him to reconcile to himself all things, whether on earth or in heaven, making peace by the blood of his cross."[65] In virtue of this, Christ draws along with himself the whole of creation which was originally ordained to glorification of God. He takes up again the work of the first man—and of every person in him—to give him again his full significance, of an existence to be lived for him, and through him unto the Father. "For if many died through one man's trespass, much more have the grace of God and the free gift in the grace of that one man Jesus Christ abounded for many."[66] In Christ, our life, which was separated from its original attachment to the whole of creation in its movement toward God, once more finds its place in the universal rhythm, now unified and divine. It passes from this world to the Father.

---

62 2 Cor. 5:21.
63 Isa. 49:6, and the entire second song of the servant of Yahweh (ch. 49).
64 Ps. 2:8.
65 Col. 1:15–20.
66 Rom. 5:15. On the virtue of salvation in Christ, extended to the whole of creation, read K. Rahner, *Mission et Grâce*, II, p. 56, and *Ecrits théologiques*, 1, p. 136. On the subject of predestination and the salvation which embraces both the whole of humanity and each person in particular, see L. Bouyer, *The Seat of Wisdom*, trans. Littledale (New York, 1962), pp. 107–109; 0. Cullmann, *Christ et le temps*, p. 156; H. U. von Balthasar, *Prayer*, pp. 69–70; pp. 89–90; A. Gelin, *La prière des psaumes* (1961), p. 11.

Such is the plan of salvation and spiritual growth in Christ to which we must say our "Amen" to the glory of God!

b. The Response: Christian Participation

A Free Acceptance and Commitment

When we say "Amen" to the mystery of salvation accomplished in Christ, or to the great divine promises fulfilled in Jesus, exactly what do we mean? The whole path has been traveled by him who took upon himself the task of reconciling those two apparently irreconcilable extremes, namely God and the sinful humanity found in ourselves. But sinful man freely renounces the prison whose gates have been opened for him, he renounces the slavery whose chains have been broken; and this now liberated man freely enters into the divine life. Such are the frailty and the grandeur of the divine gift. "If you knew the gift of God, and who it is that is saying to you, ''Give me a drink,' you would have asked him and he would have given you living water."[67] Most often, in the language of Scripture, "Amen" is a word which commits. By it someone testifies his agreement with someone else (1 Kings 1:36); or someone accepts a mission (Jeremiah 11:5); or one assumes the responsibility for an oath and the divine judgment which will follow it (Numbers 5:22).[68] Our "Amen" will be the conscious acceptance of one who accepts and surrenders himself wholeheartedly to the divine plan in all its fullness. "And leaving all things they followed him." Let us examine more closely the meaning of this response demanded of man in the light of God's salvific plan which we have considered. Let us analyze its nature by examining the implications which this mystery reveals of man's taking a part in the salvific mission of Christ.

The Sharing of a Life

God knew us and created us in his eternal Word. He loves and saves us in that same Word of life who exhausts the knowledge and love of the Father. In the Son the Father has placed all his pleasure. We shall always be known, loved, and saved in proportion to our becoming like to and incorporated into the Son, into the Church, Christ's Mystical Body, to form with him this unique and privileged object of the love of the Father. Hence, the first fruit of the welcome we give to the "gift of God" is that which specifies the very work of salvation: configuration to Christ, a sharing in the divine life of the

---

67   John 4:10.
68   C. Thomas, *DBTh*, p. 13, s.v. "Amen."

Son, a divinization according to the manner of a filial existence which, however, takes account of our natural being, finite and mortal. Salvation is truly a meeting and reconciliation of these extremes (the natural and mortal existence of man and the eternal existence of God), and through them, the meeting and reconciliation of sinful man with God. It is through faith in the baptism we have received and through the sacramental life that we adhere to the saving work of Christ, to his divine and filial life which he shares with us, through his Spirit, in the Father.[69]

The Sharing of a Mission

"Therefore, holy brethren, who share in a heavenly call, consider Jesus, the apostle and high priest of our confession."[70] Our real vocation is to be in Christ. "For we shall remain co-heirs with Christ"[71] Can we share the life of Christ so intimately without at the same time communicating in that which is essential to that life: namely, that it is a life which saves? "You shall call his name Jesus, for he will save his people from their sins."[72] The life of the Word incarnate is strictly linked to the saving mission it is to accomplish: a mission that is, as we have seen, necessarily sacerdotal and sacrificial. Likewise, by his intimate union with Christ, the baptized Christian participates in the priestly power which unites the world to God. The Christian is by nature a savior of the world. Whether he realizes it or not, his sharing in the priesthood of Christ extends in space and time the divine work of reconciliation, the work of bringing back the whole of humanity to the Father.[73] St. Paul affirms that "All this is from God, who through Christ reconciled us to himself and gave us the ministry of reconciliation."[74] Hence it will be, above all, only by following the example of Christ, and under the same conditions of "denying himself" and "carrying his cross"[75] that the Christian can realize with Christ the work of salvation which is by its nature sacrificial, and which

---

69 On this aspect of salvation, filiation and divine life, see John 14:6–24; 6:44; 1 John 3:1–2; Rom 8:14–17; also the reflections of A. Liégé, in *Initiation théologique*, III, p. 472.

70 Heb. 3:1.

71 Heb. 3:14.

72 Matt. 1:21.

73 "The Christian is the one by whom and in whom Christ is now Redeemer, here on earth," G. Salet, "La part de l'homme dans l'accroissement du plan divin," *NRTh*, 78 (1956), 241. See also the beautiful development of the Epistle to Diognetus (ch. 6, vv. 1 ff.) on the following theme: "What the soul is to the body, the Christian is to the world."

74 2 Cor. 5:18.

75 Matt. 16:24.

demands that he be unceasingly reborn to a new existence through death and resurrection in Christ. "Looking to Jesus, the pioneer and perfecter of our faith, who for the joy that was set before him endured the cross, despising the shame, and is seated at the right hand of the throne of God."[76] "As the Father has sent me, even so I send you"[77]—in the same way, for the same mission, and under the same conditions created by our sinful condition. "A servant is not greater than his master."[78]

Hence, every gift—especially the gift of self—acquires a redemptive value before God through one's union with, and participation in, the gift which Christ makes of himself to the Father, more than through one's following the example of Christ. Because of his infinite grandeur and his divine transcendence, only God can truly give something to God. The one who knows this is the Christian who, having received everything from the Father and united himself to the divine sacrifice of Christ, repeats the words of the Psalm:

> What shall I render to the Lord
> for all his bounty to me?
> I will lift up the cup of salvation
> and call on the name of the Lord.[79]

What ought I to do for Christ? Brethren, what must we do? To the one who is open to God's plan of Christian salvation and spiritual growth the answer is clear. I should unite myself to Christ my Savior—through knowledge, love, imitation, and assimilation, a grace or gift of God, so as to accomplish through him and with him the divine work of salvation, the universal, priestly, and sacrificial mission of Christ, a mission which the Church assumes on its pilgrimage through time. This is the mission to which St. Peter invites every Christian, by his image of a living Temple whose cornerstone is Christ:

> Come to him, to that living stone, rejected by men but in God's sight chosen
> and precious; and like living stones be yourselves built into a spiritual house, to

---

76 Heb. 12:2. Also Acts 14:22 and Ephes. 5:1-2. On this stripping of self to put on Christ, and this death to self to live to God, see J. Galot, *Le coeur du Christ* (1953), p. 101; S. Stehman, *Le voyage à l'ancre*, pp. 54ff; M. Zundel, *Le poème de la Sainte Liturgie* (1934), p. 255.

77 John 20:21.

78 John 15:20.

79 Ps. 116:12.

be a holy priesthood, to offer spiritual sacrifices acceptable to God through Jesus Christ. . . . But you are a chosen race, a royal priesthood, a holy nation, God's own people, that you may declare the wonderful deeds of him who called you out of darkness into his marvelous light.[80]

c. Synthesis: the Discourse of the Eternal King

The presentation of the divine plan of salvation corresponds only to the first point ([95]) in the second part of the meditation on the Kingdom; the remainder is related to the retreatant's offering. But although brief and schematic, this exposé contains the principal elements of the mystery being proposed. Two ideas recapitulate the core of the doctrine to be developed concerning the Christian vocation, which is the topic of the discourse of the eternal King: the amplitude of Christ's mission and, consequently, of our own sharing.

From the very beginning Christ no longer appears only as the one who saves me, which was the predominant note of the experience of the First Week. Here he is presented as the eternal Lord controlling the movement of the universe in its journey toward God. For everyone and everything he is the way that leads to the Father, that communicates the Father and life in the Father.[81] His divine call goes beyond the summons expressed in the creative act of the Word, and is contained in the act of Christ saving us. Nothing is to be excluded from this plan and mission of the Lord; even whatever appears to be an enemy is the object of his desire, which is to lead everything "to the glory of the Father." Thus the retreatant is invited to see Christ our Lord, the eternal King, and before him, all of mankind, whom he calls, as well as each one in particular. His divine intention is the one we have just described: "It is my will to conquer the whole world and all my enemies, and *thus to enter into the glory of my Father*" ([95]). Ignatius says no more. He has presented the essential core for a long contemplation. Now we must spend some time contemplating it. Our task is to help the retreatant understand the grandeur of the mystery of this divine call and of universal salvation in Christ. In him the world once again sets out on the way that leads to its destiny, to God and its happiness.

---

80 1 Pet. 2:4-5, 9. The priesthood of all Christians, of the faithful in Christ, is also the object of the song of the twenty-four elders around the Lamb in Apoc. 5:9-10. See also Ex. 19:6.

81 In the first Directories, Christ is often presented, in connection with the Kingdom, as being the Way, the Truth, and the Life, as he described himself in the Gospel; e.g., in Polanco's Directory (*SpEx*MHSJ, p. 812-813), the Directory of G. Dávila (p. 916), the Directories of 1591 (p. 1045), and of 1599 (p. 1147).

However, to "follow" Christ on this road, as the Gospel will tell us, to be his disciple, that is, a Christian, we must be united to him, be with him, which means to enter into the unfathomable plan of his mission, to share the "pain" and the "glory." Nothing is excluded from what the plan of salvation proposes to man. Christian participation, as we have seen, means taking a part in the universal mission of Christ, which is priestly and sacrificial. "Whoever wishes to join me in this enterprise must be willing to labor with me, that by following me in suffering, he may follow me in glory" ([95]). This is the paradoxical character which Christ's mission takes on in the ontological conditions of its accomplishment, and this characteristic of the mission remains manifestly true whether we speak of the Master or of the disciple. Suffering and glory, death and resurrection, in order to accomplish a grand and universal salvation—this is the proclamation of the "glorious cross" which the Savior proposes to us if we wish to follow him and go with him through the world which is to be saved, toward the glory of the Father. "There is a balance between the cross and the glory in the spirituality of Ignatius just as there is in the spirituality of the Gospel where Christ, each time he predicts his Passion, announces his Resurrection!"[82] "This role of the crucified Christ drawing the world to his Father," writes Hugo Rahner, "in the Ignatian mysticism calls for a logic which obliges the retreatant to follow him without reserve. Once the retreatant has understood that the Father is the end and that Christ is the way, he realizes that carrying his cross after Christ is a rigorous necessity. This is the mystical meaning of Ignatius' 'with me' *(mecum)*".[83]

In the beginning of the Exercises the retreatant had caught a glimpsed of something which was a fundamental difficulty for him or her—the meaning of existence, of life, and of the universe in movement toward its Creator. What he had glimpsed then, he now finds accomplished in Christ, the mediator and head of a redeemed world. At the same time the person, who has been called from the beginning to collaborate in this entry into the divine glory, now takes up again this unique way which enables him here and now to bring about its progressive completion. This call to the Father along with the whole universe, in Christ is already the transfiguration of the world of this person's life. This is the Christian's privileged situation.

---

82 J. Lewis, *Notes de cours,* p. 33.

83 H. Rahner, "La vision de saint Ignace à la chapelle de La Storta," *Chr,* no.1 (1954), 63–64. See Nadal's thought on this subject in the texts translated and published in *Chr,* no.1 (1954), 93.

3. *The Personal Offering*

It seems, according to Ignatius, that there could be two ways of answering the call of the eternal King: that according to which one has "judgment and reason" ([96]), or the other in which one wishes "to give greater proof of his love" and "to distinguish himself in whatever concerns the service of the eternal King and Lord of all" ([97]). The difference between the two responses has never been made very clear by the commentators. Either they minimize the first, reducing it to a simple acceptance of what is already of obligation, somewhat like the knight in the parable; and then they cannot explain the conclusion of this attitude, namely to offer oneself totally to the task.[84] Others more or less consciously assimilate this response to the second ([97]) and then try to make more precise the terms of this response which concludes with a prayer of self-oblation ([98]).[85]

Only Clémence, as far as we know, proposes in the article we have cited an interpretation which takes into account the difference between the two responses which Ignatius proposes for meditation.[86] Here we borrow the principal elements of his interpretation, in order to integrate them into our context of God's salvific plan. In fact, however, this only confirms the conclusions he himself reached.

---

84 L. Ambruzzi, for example, considers the first response as flowing from good common sense, while only the second is the fruit of generosity and love. It is perhaps difficult to proceed in any other way when one distinguishes between these two responses by considering, not their object, but their interior dynamism (see L. Ambruzzi, *A Companion to the Spiritual Exercises* [Mangalore, 1952], pp. 72–74). Similarly J. Hardon distinguishes two aspects of the commitment: "The first is a willingness to go beyond mediocrity in the service of Christ, the Son of God; the second a projection of personal love into the world outside, so that other souls may also yield a higher than ordinary service to Christ their King" (in *All My Liberty,* pp. 24–33).

85 This is somewhat the position of La Palma, Calveras, and Iparraguirre who, having posed the problem of the call ([95]), then consider the response in terms of [97] and especially analyze the very exact requirements of the offering ([98]). J. Lewis spends more time on the first response ([96]); but he attaches the word "task" to what follows. "The task," he states, "is the program of abnegation which becomes mandatory; it is the gospel message of renunciation" (*Notes de cours,* p. 34). He orients his commentary in the same direction. Let us note that the "task" consists, first of all, in uniting oneself to the work of universal salvation: to lead the world back to the glory of the Father ([95]), which will necessarily imply renunciation ([97–98]).

86 See "La méditation du Règne," *RAM,* 32 (1956): the first response, pp. 154–160; the second, 160–172.

a. A Problem of Exegesis: the "Task" of Christ

However, before considering the solution we are adopting in line with Clémence, we must resolve a problem of Ignatian exegesis which directly influences the interpretation of the passages studied. On three occasions in his text, Ignatius uses the same word, although in different forms, both the verb and the noun. In [95] he writes "has to labor with me" (*ha de trabajar conmigo;* in [96] "will offer their entire selves for the work" *(ofrecerán todas sus personas al trabajo);* and in [97] "not only will offer their persons for the work" *(no solamente ofrecerán sus personas al trabajo).* The French translations use a much more diversified vocabulary. For the verb *trabajar* we find *travailler* (to labor, work, toil), *travaux* (works), *peine* (penalty, pain, labor), *tâche* (task, job), *besogne* (work, business, job), *service* (service). We found only two French translations using the same vocabulary as the original Spanish. In an article for *Christus* François Courel chose to translate the word *trabajar* by *peiner* (to labor) and *peine* (pain, labor). In his commentary Clémence uses the words *travailler* (to work) and *travail* (work). In themselves the expressions *travailler avec moi* (to work with me), *peiner avec moi* (to labor with me), *s'offrir au travail* (to offer oneself for the work), *ä la peine* (for the labor), can be synonymous in French. The difficulty comes from the context in which similar and closely related words—in the same sentence—ought to be clearly distinguished in order to express very definite realities, or to be united in an interplay of complementary nuances. This is the case in [95], where man, being called to *trabajar conmigo* will do so *siguiendome en la pena* (by following me in the pain). The translation used by Clémence better distinguishes the realities implied: *travailler* (to work) with me, so that following me in *la peine* (pain); the translation of Courel expresses rather the nuances contained in these same realities and says: *peiner* (to labor) with me, so that following me in *la souffrance* (suffering). These two expressions, not only taken in themselves, but considered in the whole of the context, lead to rather different interpretations and affect the meaning given to the responses ([96 and 97]) in which we again find these words *travail* (work) and *peine* (labor or pain).

The Spanish noun *trabajo* (work, labor, toil, fatigue, hardship, occupation) means primarily a work (in French *un travail*), a task *(tâche),* a job *(besogne).* It may also be used figuratively in the sense of pain *(peine),* that is, a painful work *(travail pénible),* a labor *(labeur).*[87] It is this second meaning which Courel chooses, and this causes no difficulty in [95] where the

---

87 The plural *trabajos* is often found ([116]).

mission of the Lord *(trabajo)* ends in glory *(gloria)* through *pena* (suffering). The work which the King proposes is necessarily a task entailing pain—a sacrificial mission, as we have seen. But in [96], this choice no longer orients the offering toward the work itself in general *(travail en général)* which the discourse of the King proposes—the universal work or mission of salvation—but rather, toward *what is a characteristic* of that work: to offer oneself for the pain *(la peine)* which so often goes with it. Now in the context where there is already a question of suffering *(pena)*, that reinforces the interpretation suggested by the translation adopted.[88] This reading of the French text as thus presented makes us consider the difficult aspect of the work to be undertaken and turns us immediately to the third point [97]. This final element, which can seem an advantage, in reality distracts us from what is essential: the contemplation of the sublime mission of the King which above everything else has to be accepted in all its breadth. Clémence's interpretation focuses better on that which is the essential, by drawing our attention not to what is to come ([97]) but to what has previously been stated ([95]); the call of the King with its two propositions, the magnificent mission or work of universal salvation *(trabajo)* and participation in the suffering *(pena)* in view of the glory *(gloria)*.[89]

In choosing the words *travailler* (to work) and *travail* (work),[90] Clémence avoids any equivocation and opts for an interpretation which is clearly defined. For him the retreatant is invited to take part himself in the work *(travail)* or task *(tâche)* of the universal Lord which will be accomplished through *peine* (pain) and difficulty but in view of the glorifying the Father

---

88 Furthermore a note of F. Courel removes all doubt which might remain, when there is question of "the means" which Christ "offers us in the *labor (peine)* of his Passion." Labor *(peine)* which he uses to translate *trabajo* is placed in a direct relationship with the Passion *(Exercices,* trans. Courel) p. 67, note 1).

89 We asked several Spanish Jesuits what the expression in [96], "will offer themselves entirely for this work" *(ofrecerán . . . al trabajo)*, meant to them. They replied spontaneously that it meant to offer oneself *for everything the King had previously proposed:* his work, his mission, his conquest, his program, with all that implies. Furthermore, the term chosen by Courel in his translation involves a slight mistranslation in French in [93], where *trabajar en el día y vigilar en la noche* is given as "to labor *(peiner)* during the day and watch *(veiller)* by night." Since the call is addressed to the same knight, it seems that if he must work *(travailler)* during the day and watch *(veiller)* during the night, he will have to labor day and night *(peiner jour et nuit)*, not only during the day as the translation proposed.

90 These are the words used by the Latin translations: The *Versio prima* and the version of Roothaan use *laborare et labor,* and the *Versio vulgata* uses three words, *laborare, labor, et servitium.*

([95]).[91] As a consequence of these linguistic distinctions we can say that the first response ([96]) envisages the full acceptance of this work or labor *(trabajo* or *tâche)* of salvation which calls for our full cooperation.[92] Then Ignatian discernment[93] suggests a further step ([97–98]) which makes more precise the exigencies that follow from this vocation. It also deepens the awareness and the realism of the commitment envisaged.[94] Finally, the offering will come to crown the acceptance of both the first ([96]) and the second ([97]) responses, and the two of them finally become only one larger and more comprehensive response. This interpretation too, however, gives rise to some problems, which we shall now examine more closely.

b. *The Nature of The Two Responses ([96 and 97–98])*

The unity of the meditation on the Kingdom is not clear at the first glance. It confronts us with its limping parallelism, its concise directions, and even its paradoxes concerning the nature of the activity which, in the second part, reduces the contemplation to the hearing of a call or invitation. Not rarely one point or aspect is treated extensively but at the expense of another. Nevertheless, all the important items are contained in this text; and they progress according to a logic which here also is based on experience. To subtract anything from this text would be a pity. In it we have one of the most concise and carefully labored texts of the Ignatian corpus. In it, too, the author's intentions are explicit: He intended the parable to help the retreatant to contemplate; the contemplation itself consists in the hearing of a call or invitation; and the response to this invitation evolves with realism toward a definite climax, an offering which fosters the contemplation of the divine salvific plan and which is simultaneously a response born of love. One ought not, without a truly sound reason, to sacrifice either part of this exercise which structures all the work of the three Weeks about to come.[95] An insecure foundation is a danger for the edifice about to be built.

As we have seen, the parable does not convey logical or intellectual help aimed at illustrating or clarifying the doctrine about to come, in such a way that it can be omitted as a favor to an exercitant who is well instructed and

91 J. Clémence, "La méditation du Règne," *RAM,* 32 (1956), 152–153, where he gives a very significant opinion of Y. de Montcheuil found in some unpublished notes on the Kingdom.
92 Ibid., pp. 154–160.
93 Ibid., p. 167.
94 Ibid., pp. 160ff.
95 See *SpEx*MHSJ, pp. 694–696, on the Kingdom as the true starting point of an interior Christian reform.

able to comprehend that doctrine without further human help. Instead, this parable is an active preparation for the contemplation which is the hearing of the Word, the Eternal King and his message. Therefore, as the second prelude indicates ([91]), it disposes the retreatant to hear the King's call, and consequently to accept it.[96] It does this by mobilizing all the human resources of our being through the dynamics of the spiritual desire which the First Week has focused on Christ.

The call of the King is the contemplation properly so-called. In a few words, simple and rich, what is proposed is God's salvific and sanctifying plan in its essential elements: salvation for all humankind, oneself included; death and resurrection in Christ; and all to the praise, service, and glory of God. That plan is transformed here into a call to participation addressed to every person. The person is invited, not only to share in salvation (this is the object of the First Week), but also to share in the mission of salvation: to associate himself or herself with Christ in leading the whole world, and even that part of it which still carries on the work of the Enemy, back to the Father.

The first response ([96]) of the retreatant who with the requisite dispositions[97] contemplates the wonders of Christ's plan for salvation and spiritual growth is marked by a desire to take part in the universal apostolate. Whatever his or her state of life, his occupations and other circumstances (health or sickness, poverty or wealth, and the like), his life henceforth will become one of associating himself with Christ in his salvific mission, collaborating wholeheartedly in this task which leads the world, made for God, back to the Father, in Christ. Contemplating Christ evokes a great desire "to lose one's life" for "the salvation of many." "The final point of the highest perfection," writes Lallemant, "is zeal for souls."[98] Other saints too who belong to different traditions,[99] in their rightly ordered desire for perfection, sought to realize the same ideal; they used various means but always travelled along the unique

---

96 The prelude in question actually distinguishes two times: not to be deaf to the call (i.e., to hear it, to understand it), and to respond diligently.

97 With "judgment and reason," an upright spirit enlightened here by faith, by the content of Revelation.

98 L. Lallemant, *The Spiritual Doctrine* (1946), p. 294.

99 From the men of action like Ignatius and Alphonsus Liguori ("I love Jesus Christ, and that is why I am on fire with the desire to give him souls") to the masters of the contemplative life like Teresa of Avila (see *Le chemin de la perfection*, Fides, Montréal, p. 24) and the Little Flower, "universal patron of the missions." On the apostolic character of every contemplative life, read *Sponsa Christi* of Pius XII, *AAS*, 43 (1951), 5–21, and the extract quoted by J. Moyersoen, in *Ign*, 1956, p. 77.

way of union with Christ the Savior. This is the meaning of the first response ([96]), which Ignatius asks the retreatant to ponder in this second point, the response to the call. Clémence explains it in this way. Attention is first directed to "the work proposed by Christ." "Certainly," he writes, "the work and the person cannot be separated—the third point will make this clear—but a sound spiritual pedagogy obliges one to distinguish certain stages, in which one aspect never excludes the other, and never prescinds from the other, but simply predominates over the other, appears on one level while the second remains on the other level."[100]

We would say even more. This distinction arises spontaneously; it springs less from a care for sound pedagogy than from a spontaneous movement of the exercise, that is, a movement which has been aroused, directed, and enlightened by the light of the universal. That universal is here the preceding contemplation ([95]), which consists in a call to participate, above all, in the salvific mission of Christ. Such a contemplation stirs up a desire from then on to give oneself fully "to the work." It is highly important to attend to this movement. As it matures it will bear its fruit, also spontaneously, in the following point of the meditation. On the contrary, if the director, by the way he proposes the matter, encourages the retreatant to pass almost directly from the contemplated salvific plan to the second response, he runs the risk of concentrating too rapidly the exercitant's whole attention on an asceticism which is cut off from this dynamism which confers on any renouncement a motivation now expanded and deepened, the motivation which springs from God's sanctifying plan.[101] Then the meditation of the divine plan would have served merely as an introduction to a message of moral self-denial to which a generous retreatant would give himself or herself, while forgetting the true meaning and purpose of this abnegation. The work of salvation is in its nature sacrificial; hence, it necessarily counts on abnegation. But abnegation is not by itself the road to perfection; it must be

---

100 J. Clémence, "La méditation du Règne," *RAM*, 32 (1956), 159.
101 This is all the more true because of the terms of the offering which follows; they do not express half-measures. The retreatant will immediately come up against a very austere reality in this prayer, a reality which he should not alter or distort. Everything which precedes must truly prepare him for it, not only from the point of view of psychological dispositions but also spiritual understanding: The true indifference, a spirit of self-renunciation, springs from the contemplation which engenders a higher desire. Here this contemplation is the call of the King: a grand mission and participation in it. This call in [95] is continued in [96] with a view to leading the retreatant to an acceptance of the difficult implications of [97–98].

entirely ordered to union with Christ for a work which infinitely surpasses it. That is why the exercitants should long contemplate at least the general significance, full and positive, of this vocation in Christ—that they may adhere to it, as Ignatius says, "in order to offer themselves entirely for the work" ([96]).[102] Then the time will soon come which makes the exigencies more precise, and which will bring to the ardor of charity the discretion which takes account of the divine ways.

The second response ([97–98]) has been the object of attentive study by many commentators who have distinguished and analyzed in it the various requirements of the Christian vocation to evangelical perfection.[103] Here, at the end of the movement we have described, let us recall only the overall meaning of this "more generous" response. Christ's way of life is what is proposed to a generosity which sets no limit to one's commitment. It is a way of contempt, humiliations, and poverty, a way which moves toward the opposite extremity from sin. Thus this last response gathers together the two component elements in the history of our salvation, of which the preceding exercises have now made us aware. The first is sin, the evil which is the only obstacle in the person's heart which can thwart the accomplishment of God's wonderful plan: the universe in movement toward the divine glory through the intermediary agent of the heart of the man or woman who has turned to God. Before any specific apostolic tasks, the first co-redemptive collaborative work of anyone will have to be achieved in one's own heart, by offering one's nature with its affections into a direct relationship with the work of universal salvation.[104]

102 The following contemplations on the life of Christ will go much deeper in this direction, by furthering a parallel deepening of the response to be given. This is a case of the Ignatian dialectic which has already been described.

103 See L. de La Palma, *Camino Espiritual* (Madrid, 1944), pp. 202–210; J. Calveras, *Práctica de los Ejercicios de San Ignacio* (Barcelona, 1962), pp. 207–210; and "Qué ofrece el ejercitante en la oblación del Reino de Cristo?" *Mnr*, 5 (1929), 8–18; I. Iparraguirre, *How to Give a Retreat*, pp. 123–126; J. Lewis, *Notes de cours*, pp. 34–36; J. Clémence, *RAM*, 32 (1956), esp. 170–172. On the subject of the universal call to evangelical perfection, L. Mendizábal gives an excellent bibliography in his *Annotationes in theologiam spiritualem* (Rome, 1962), pp. 71–74; see also the bibliography in his later *Dirección espiritual* (Madrid: BAC, 1978), pp. 12–14.

104 See Luke 17:21; Rom. 14:17; Phil. 3:7–16; Ephes. 6:13–17. L. Lallemant, in *The Spiritual Doctrine*, pp. 80–107, has a long development on this theme of purity of heart which prepares the perfect apostle of the Lord. See also S. Weil, *La pesanteur et la grâce*, p. 29: "Offering: One cannot offer anything other than oneself, 'I'; and everything called offering is nothing other than a label placed on a projection of the self, the 'I'."

The second element considered is the necessity of laboring with Christ *(conmigo, mecum)* toward accomplishing the personal and universal work of salvation. "Without me you can do nothing."[105] This is the union with Christ the Savior, the mediator of our own divinization as well as the head of the Mystical Body, the head of the new creation in movement toward its own fulfillment. This response of the third point now unites these component elements of the work of salvation as it is applied to our own lives: to desire the accomplishment of Christ's mission together with Christ who calls us to it, but according to his manner of proceeding, that is, to offer oneself "to imitate him in bearing all wrongs and all abuse and all poverty, both actual and spiritual," in accordance with God's ways for us ([98]). The Exercises to come, by intensifying our union with Christ through the contemplation of the mysteries or events of his life, will envisage a more perfect imitation of Christ, and will also dispose us to enter more deeply into that opposite extremity from sin, that is, into that Christlike attitude which has been lived out by our Savior. Finally, these two movements link themselves together harmoniously in an attitude of perfect indifference, in which our desire for God tends toward the "third kind of humility," especially in the contemplation of the crucified Christ. It is in this context, we think, that Ignatius' vocabulary, which was the cause of some difficulty in the past, can be best understood. Not only does the universal work of salvation come to a point in a person's living heart in which it seeks its fulfillment, but it also gives birth and growth to an attitude of openness and commitment which unites the soul more intimately and unreservedly to the redemptive desire of the Lord. Who would be surprised that this should demand a renunciation even to the point of going "against their sensuality and carnal and worldly love" ([95])? To be truly "with Christ" as one of his followers, opposing evil, who would not accept all the sacrifices, however costly, that could be demanded of him or her? "Jesus' teachings are contrary to the sentiments of nature. Without the help of grace, it would be impossible, not only to put them into practice, but even to understand them."[106]

The offering of the Kingdom is not reserved to a privileged few. It is open to every Christian who will have made himself or herself aware of the full meaning of his vocation in its fullness, according to God's designs for him.

---

105 John 15:5.
106 Theresa of the Child Jesus: *Manuscrits autobiographiques*, C 18.

C. *The Kingdom in Its Reality, the Church*

A point very delicate for the dynamic structure of the *Exercises* is what we must take up now. There is no question of our yielding to the temptation of an intellectual logic which would allow us to take the consideration of the mystery of salvation in Christ and then add to it some reflections on the complementary mystery of the Church. For to the mind which contemplates and deeply understands the reality, the Church does in fact appear as the realization of the Kingdom of Christ.

But while one is making the Exercises, is it necessary to take this customary prolongation into account? And if so, from what principles must we start and in what perspective? Once again, a person who does not know what he wants, nor how to accomplish it, will yield to the temptation to multiply these "complementary developments" which can abound during the Exercises. These "considerations" with which some overload the time of an Ignatian retreat can be harmful to the movement of the Exercises. What we propose, therefore, in this last section of our study on the Kingdom goes beyond the problem of this meditation. In that problem itself we shall find the very reason for a consideration of it within the context of the Exercises, and the conditions of its employment.

1. Principles

First of all, we must not forget that the logic of the Exercises is one grounded on experience rather than merely intellectual, a logic of intelligent exercises rather than well-organized instructions. Consequently, if one should add to the matter proposed by Ignatius in order to have the intellectual satisfaction of a fuller, more complete development, he might very well find himself somewhat in opposition to the movement fostered by the Exercises. As we have said, the time of the Exercises is not the place for doctrinal exposition as such and for its own sake; the objective (the message) is always proposed in view of the subjective (the experience), while this subjective experience evolves under the light of the Truth being contemplated. The amount of material to be given on those points where the "extension" of the subject being meditated upon can go in different directions must be carefully judged: Either one perfects the intellectual exposition of the message being presented in view of completing the instruction of the retreatant, or one updates the truth being proposed in order to make the exercise, now being prolonged, more for the exercitant in present circumstances. In other words, a prolonging of the exposition is needed only in the measure in which the prolongation of the exercise itself and the updating of the content demand it. We are far from opposing an integral exposition of the truth; but we wish to safeguard the movement or experiential logic of the Exercises without which they no longer exist as "exercises." In this sense we think it is preferable to give up a development of a complementary aspect of a reality being meditated, even an important one, if we cannot integrate it into this essential movement of the Exercises properly made. Such integration is not always a matter of course!

In the present case, on the level of "exercises" as well as on the level of ideas, we think that the present reality of the Kingdom should be extended as a part within the whole of the movement of the *Exercises*.[107] They from the very beginning have aimed to confront a real, concrete person with the fullness of the truth and to make him or her realize that his life ought to evolve in dependence on this truth: the presence of the divine plan of creation, of the ordering of all things to God, and of personal salvation in the whole Christ. The retreatant has understood the direction of his own life through a consideration of the history of sin; then under the action of grace he has mobilized all his human powers to offer himself to take part not only in the salvation offered by Christ but also in his mission of salvation. The whole of the Second Week right up to the Election will aim precisely at the realization of the commitment aroused by the Kingdom. Therefore, this experience of commitment (the offering) is not the viewpoint on which we should exclusively focus here. In regard to this experience of commitment, the slow movement of the Exercises, adjusted to the rhythm of each retreatant, is much more desirable than our impatient actions. We should remember that the contemplation of God's plan of salvation is the foundation of this commitment, an engagement which should mature with the passing of time. That is why Ignatius places, before the final response and offering of greater love and distinguished service in [97] the more general and global response in [96] which, from a lofty and more detached point of view, examines the reality to be embraced. This provides a vision which alone is capable of making us accept and even desire supernaturally the demands which the concrete commitment will present in detail ([97–98]). We believe that it is in this objective line of the message that the updated presentation of the Kingdom can be considered with profit, and also be integrated into the very movement of the

---

107 It is conceivable that this reality can be sufficiently emphasized during the contemplation of the call of the King itself ([95]). But not to overload the tableau, one can also resort to a further consideration which prolongs the thrust of this exercise on a particular point. Ignatius used to present his rules "for thinking with the Church" ([352–370]), but at a different time. The *Directorium Granatense* states that these rules should be given, like the others, "when it seems best" (*SpEx*MHSJ, p. 962).

Exercises. In other words, we want a better understanding of the present-day character of the plan of salvation. This is what fundamentally channels our energies towards the generous offering of our entire being—both on the level of the Lord's mission and on the level of our Christian participation. This is absolutely in the spirit of Ignatius' *Exercises*. [108]

First, on the objective level of the Lord's message, we ought to observe that this mission of salvation which the King proposes through his "call" is today lived out and realized in and through Christ's Church. Second, on the level of our participation, we should deepen our understanding, within the ensemble of the divine salvific plan which develops into the present ecclesial mission, of the role played therein today by a concrete human being, whether man or woman, priest or lay person, simple Christian or professed religious.

2. Mission

The present-day reality of Christ's Kingdom, on the level of the mission of salvation, is his Church. The Church "is the historic concretization of the salvific will of God now become a reality in Christ."[109] How can we integrate this reflection into the dialectical procedures proper of the *Exercises?* Our response just above was: by presenting it as bound into the destiny of the universe, as the Kingdom of the present day in movement, as the life and mission of Christ prolonged "in space and time." For Nadal, this integration is the fruit of prayer itself which embraces the whole truth of Christ. "The Word of God," he writes, "is eternal life in the Spirit; to feel him, to relish him, to receive him into one's heart, to embrace him is the principal fruit of prayer. From this flows, in all sweetness, union with the Catholic Church, with the Vicar of Christ, with religious rites and ceremonies, then obedience, and so forth."[110] In contemplating in this way the mission of Christ today, we turn our attention toward inserting ourselves into God's plan of Christian salvation, and toward accepting more consciously its paradoxical reality ([95]), that is, to surrender ourselves more, to "offer ourselves entirely for this work" ([96]). This manner of proceeding does not in any way withdraw us from the movement proper to the *Exercises*. On the contrary, it prolongs it

---

108 In other words, the matter to be considered is that of *SpEx*, [95–96]: of the *universal* which enlightens and deepens the personal (no. 95).

109 K. Rahner, *Mission et Grâce*, II, p. 30. On this theme of the Church, "present incarnation of Christ," read: J. Daniélou, *Approches du Christ* (Paris, 1960), pp. 174, 180–181; 0. Cullmann, *Christ et le temps*, pp. 105, 109–110, 133; A. Nisin, *Histoire de Jésus* (1961), pp. 52–53.

110 Nadal, Orationis observationes, in *MonNad*, IV, 717, [261]; also *Journal spirituel*, (trans. Laval), no. 244.

beyond the time of prayer, into the in-between times of the retreat, in which every activity ought to be made part of the same thrust.

It is not necessary for us to present in detail here the possible content of these reflections—or readings—on the prolongation of the Kingdom into the topic of Christ's mission today through the mystery of the Church.[111] It might, however, be helpful to trace the more important lines by which this can be done in accordance with the experience and spirit of St. Ignatius. Without feeling ourselves strictly bound by this content, perhaps we shall find some elements in his views which assure fidelity to his *Exercises* and further justify our integration of the theme of the Church into the rest of the Exercises.

For Ignatius, the Church was known and loved as part of the Divine Majesty's plan for salvation and spiritual growth, in the same experience which revealed to him the harmony of all the mysteries in God. Nadal affirms that Ignatius received "very vivid insights and feelings on the divine mysteries and on the Church."[112] For him the Church enjoys a lordship which is the very same as that of Christ. Consequently he presents her in the *Exercises,* at the very beginning of his Rules for Thinking with the Church ([352–370]), as the "true spouse of Christ our Lord."[113] As with the other themes in the *Exercises*—creation, man, Christ—Ignatius' interior knowledge of the reality of the Church had its starting point from above, by viewing things from God's viewpoint. That is why his faith is, first of all, respect, veneration, and obedience—but never adulation. When he asks us to "praise" what the Church praises, it is much more through grandeur of soul than submission; for in this sympathetic ecclesial attitude he found much more and broader insight than in a facile readiness which is content merely with condemning anything that goes against one's personal views.[114] Ignatius often met a great deal of misunderstanding on the part of the hierarchical Church and from many of its representatives, but he would never entertain the idea of blaming the Church herself.[115] For basically he accepted—as does

---

111 See J. Mouroux, *The Christian Experience,* ch. 7, pp. 185–218. This chapter 7 is excellent on "the Christian Experience as Experience within the Church."

112 See *MonNad,* V, *(Commentarii de Instituto S. I.),* p. 40.

113 On the Church considered as spouse see D. Mollat, *Chr,* no.1 (1954), 39; Young, *Finding God,* p. 83; and H. U. von Balthasar, *The Heart of the World,* (San Francisco, 1979), ch. 12, pp. 189–203.

114 See Pierre Charles, "L'esprit catholique," *NRTh,* 69 (1947), 225–244, an original commentary on the Ignatian rules for thinking with the Church.

115 Ignatius' reaction to a Church which was so patently in need of reform remains typical enough; it is that of an unfailing attachment which seeks to serve by

everyone who acknowledges his sinfulness and his solidarity with our common human poverty—that this reality of the Church, divine in her origin and her saving mission, should be lived out by men and women, by weak human beings such as we are.

Helpful for our reflections here is what Karl Rahner insightfully wrote in his "Ignatian Spirituality and Devotion to the Sacred Heart":[116]

> For the one who has really undergone the experience of the absolute transcendence of God (that experience which has God truly in view and not this sublime transcending of our own infinity), he in all humility will allow himself to be established by God within his own limitations, and he will accept with humility and simplicity the finite willed by God, but different from God, including the relative inequalities existing between things which God has willed and which, for the creature who does not pretend to be God, take on, in a certain sense, an absolute value. From this attitude flows the unconditioned aspect of the love of Ignatius for the humanity of Christ extended to the least details of his earthly life, and also to the Church, to the ecclesiastical hierarchy, to the pope, to the Rules for Thinking with the Church.

Furthermore, Ignatius loved and served the Church of Christ with a realism which was equalled only by his respect for it. He never disassociated the universal Church in Christ from the present-day Church in man.[117] For him, inflamed with the love and service of Christ from the very first day of

curing, supporting, and correcting to the utmost of his powers. On this subject see F. Richter, *Martin Luther and Ignatius of Loyola* (Westminster, Md., 1960), pp. 193–194. Respectful and active submission to the Church is perhaps the point on which the Society has been most faithful to the spirit of her founder; and the most striking example of this painful submission, which in no way diminished the Society's faith, respect, and service, is that of the universal suppression of the Society by Clement XIV in 1773. See J. Crétineau-Joly, *Histoire de la Compagnie de Jésus,* 2nd ed. Lyon, 1846, t. 5, p. 328, which contains the statements of Father General Ricci, written in prison, shortly before his death.

116 K. Rahner, "Spiritualité ignatienne et dévotion au Sacré-Coeur," *RAM,* 35 (1959), 151; English, "Ignatian Spirituality and Devotion to the Sacred Heart," p. 126 in his *Christianity in the Market Place* (New York, 1966), pp. 119–146; In the same vein, read: "Dieu s'est confié aux hommes." [For a chronological listing of 31 articles on the Sacred Heart published by Karl Rahner from 1934 to 1982, see A. Callahan, R.S.C.J., *Karl Rahner's Theology of the Pierced Heart* (Lanham, Md.: University Press of America, 1985), pp. 151–154. Ed.] See also Jacques Leclercq, *La vie du Christ dans son Eglise,* "Unam Sanctam" no. 12, (Paris, 1947), p. 72, and K. Adam, "Le mystère de l'Incarnation du Christ et de son Corps Mystique," *Et,* 237 (1938), esp. p. 45.

117 "The local Church is the very realization of the universal Church." This idea is developed by K. Rahner in *Mission et Grâce,* II, pp. 28–33.

his conversion, the Church took on the same complex appearance which he venerated in Christ. It is "our Holy Mother, the hierarchical Church" who communicates life and who directs us toward eternity, in the name of Jesus Christ ; she is also the daily, humble reality, the Church that must "gather together" the whole universe in Christ, the Church of the "souls to be saved." Damien Mollat writes: "In the thought of Ignatius the universe and the Church are joined together in Christ in their very being, under the double title of creation and redemption. Both of them are works of his love and his grace. They owe their existence to him, and they have no other end but him."[118]

The fervent and realistic ideal of the service of Christ made Ignatius "a man of the Church" in the fullest sense of that term.[119] It would be a betrayal of his thought[120] and experience to present "a Kingdom of God" which did not lead to the service of the Church of Christ. His first companions, formed in his school, knew that; and in their commentaries on the Kingdom they spoke explicitly of "the Church militant in which Christ continues to carry his cross today."[121]

3. Participation in the Work of the Church

On the level of Christian participation, the present-day reality of the Kingdom takes into account how we human beings, just as we are, are called

---

118 D. Mollat, *Chr,* no.1 (1954), p. 39; Young, *Finding God,* p. 83. Also M. Zundel, *Le poème de la Sainte Liturgie,* pp. 183–184.

119 This is the object of Hugo Rahner's special study, *The Spirituality of St. Ignatius* (Westminster, 1953). On this topic see also pp. 3–6 of his pamphlet *True Source of the Sodality Spirit* (reference above in fn. 15 of this ch. 5), as well as the reference there to W. Ong in *Review for Religious;* also H. Rahner's "Esprit et Eglise, un chapitre de théologie ignatienne," *Chr,* no. 18 (1958), 163–184; and H. R. Burns, "St. Ignatius and the Mystical Body," *WL,* 87 (1958), 107–114.

120 J. Lewis, *Notes de cours,* p. 3, whose brief exposition on the subject brings together the following references: *EppIgn,* VIII, 462–464; V, 220; I, 390; *SpEx,* [23, 60, 71, 95, 98, 106, 137, 151, 232, 236, 311]. See also in *Obras completas,* Index, pp. 992–993, s.v. "Iglesia," some forty references on Ignatius' different points of view on the Church as spouse, mother, Mystical Body, revelation and prolongation or progressive development of Christ, and the like.

121 See *MonNad,* V, 6, 293, 295; also, the texts translated and presented by M. Giuliani in *Chr,* no.1 (1954), 88, 90–92. For Nadal, the whole of the meditation on the Kingdom flows into the mystery or marvel of the Church: "What happened in the case of the temporal king and of the commitment to him has been and is occurring, in all reality, in the Church" (*MonNad,* V, 293). The *Directorium Granatense* clearly places Scripture and the Church among the means which the Second Week puts at our disposition in order to acquire "an

---

by the King to collaborate in his task. There is question here not of anticipating the meditations yet to come by an impatient leaping forward to the election, but of intensifying a present point in the movement of the Exercises. For this purpose, we should state at least something about the states or modes of life in which, and by means of which, a person can live out his or her Christian vocation. The aim is to enable each one to find the truth, the truth about his or her state of life. For every situation in which we find ourselves before God is incomplete, and can be understood only in the perspective or vision which includes the context of the complementary situations. The real question is, therefore, that of our understanding more deeply the mystery of our participation here and now, that is to say, by starting from what we are in fact.

The foundation for our consideration is the following. When God calls by showing us, in the Foundation, the purpose of his continuing act of creation and, in the Kingdom, his continuing work of salvation in both its universal and its particular aspects, he is addressing himself very personally to the person whom He creates and saves. His word, which "sounds the depths of hearts," is a call to each one and touches one in the deepest level of one's being. Furthermore, in every case, the call is made in view of a human community in which the creative and salvific acts insert us at different levels. Therefore our exposition will best be made by our looking upward to God's intention; in other words and in Ignatius' way, "by starting from God." God's intention is manifested through his act of creating each one of us and his plan of salvation—which includes creation and redemption.

In regard to both creation and redemption, God constituted man and woman, distinct and complementary, as collaborators with Himself. "So God created man in his own image, in the image of God he created him; male and female he created them."[122] The work in which they ought to collaborate, creation, is itself ordained entirely to the work of the heavenly Kingdom, that is, the eternal love which men and women attain through the life of faith and

experiential knowledge of God" (*SpEx*MHSJ, 962–964), and there Christ is presented as "Head of the Church."

122 Gen 1:27. In P. Ricoeur's *Philosophie de la Volonté*, I: *Finitude et culpabilité* (Paris, 1949), there are some interesting reflections on the "Adamic myth" where it appears that it is the "whole of human nature" *(l'être humain complet)*, i.e., man and woman, which sinned against God. It could be similarly stated that the one who is being called to love and serve God fully, and who is made in the image of God, is the whole of human nature, man and woman. They together are to continue God's work. And this collaboration in a work of creation that has become a work of salvation is precisely what we need to clarify here.

the work of salvation. In the same way the full collaboration of man and woman ought to be orientated toward the elaboration of the Kingdom of God—toward pursuing the creative work of God. Procreation and improvement of the earth have meaning only if we respect the purpose of the divine work which we take up, and if this work ultimately leads more chosen persons into the divine glory. We are speaking of God's own purpose which he imparted to all his creatures. We, participating in the divine powers, and creators by nature and redeemers by grace—we are all called to share in what expresses the total work of God: his fatherhood, which is found at the beginning and at the end of every life, of every form of existence, and "from whom every family in heaven and on earth is named."[123] God, the author of all life, continually brings us to this first life in view of eternal life and love in the heavenly Kingdom. We in our turn, as collaborators in this ultimate work of divine salvation through our Christian vocation, participate in it according to almost infinitely varying degrees as priests or lay persons.[124] Similarly, there are diverse ways of reaching this spiritual paternity of the Kingdom. Some achieve it through married love and physical motherhood or fatherhood, which they ought to carry forward in Christ through the education of their children in the faith. Others attain the same goal through their consecrated love which embraces, in the same Christ, the immediate work of salvation in which they realize their spiritual paternity or maternity.[125] For every Christian has one same vocation, in Christ and in his Spirit, because we all have the same unique end: to lead back to God the world and many elect for the eternal Kingdom of love, where the Lamb and his spouse, the whole Church gathered together, all will sing the glory of God.

In the Kingdom more than elsewhere, "the Eternal Lord of all things" calls "each one in particular" to collaborate "with his whole being" in the

123 Ephes. 3:15.
124 This collaboration in the work of creation takes account of the distinction and the complementarity of the sexes. On the supernatural level of the redemption, there is an additional distinction, that between the priesthood of the laity and that of the ordained priests. There is, first of all, "a question of degrees," but this variation in degrees is such that the Lord has elevated the ministerial priesthood to the dignity of a sacrament. The distinction between life in the world and life in a religious institute is established, not on degrees of participation, but on the ways (or means) by which this participation is lived out. On the subject of the perfection of the Christian vocation in our context and of sanctity "as viewed by faith" *(sous le regard de la foi),* see R. Latourelle, "La Sainteté, signe de la Révélation," *Greg,* 46 (1965), esp. pp. 48–52.
125 On the topic of spiritual paternity, see L. Mendizábal, *Annotationes de directione spirituali,* pp. 132–134.

building up of the Kingdom of God which, begun here below, will find its fulfillment in eternity. This task, with all its grandeur and its human and divine elements, is what we desire to accept today, "by starting from what we are," with full knowledge of the Savior's cause. And knowing all the "pain" which it will necessarily impose on us, we entrust ourselves to Christ, for only "with Him" will it be possible for us to acquit ourselves of this task "for the glory of God," and "according to his designs." That is why we repeat the humble and bold offering of St. Ignatius, "in the presence of Thy infinite goodness, and of Thy glorious mother, and of all the saints of Thy heavenly court, this is the offering of myself which I make with Thy favor and help" ([98]).

Chapter 6

THE ELECTION:
THE READJUSTMENT OF ONE'S SITUATION IN LIFE

A. The Interpretation of the Second Week

*1. On the Objective Level, a Message Aiming at
Readjustment and Commitment*

The retreatant has just pronounced the offering of the Kingdom ([98]).
The director must now lead him or her through the complex paths of the
Second Week. To begin with, we have at hand diverse elements with which
we should organize the work ahead. These elements always concern the
universal and the particular. In the Kingdom, the question is one of a universal mission of salvation in which we ought to take part, and of a struggle
against the concrete evil which encompasses our own life. This is a positive
commitment: to offer oneself completely for the work. It is also a specific
readjustment which touches certain negative factors in our lives. In a word,
the aim is both expansive apostolic zeal and asceticism properly so-called.

The positive aspect of the commitment in the Second Week is very clear;
both the call of the Kingdom which still rings in our ears and the work of
preparing for the election make this obvious. The grace we ask for throughout these days tends in the same direction: to know, to love, to serve, and to
follow. But this aspect should not be allowed to hide certain basic aspects of
the offering of the Kingdom: To live it out in practice will often require a
struggle against impulses from our lower nature. The ascetical character of
the commitment is not dropped. The Two Standards and the Three Kinds of
Humility will keep that fact before our eyes. Yet it sometimes happens that,
at the time of the election, the retreatants seek God's will about themselves
while remaining only on the margin of the concrete details of their interior
lives—lives unfortunately attracted by evil as well as good; or similarly, while
insufficiently aware of the demands which will be made on them by the
coming contemplations on the "mysteries" or events of Christ's life. Hence,
the first pitfall of the Second Week is that of becoming a person "positively
imprudent," one who can therefore fall victim to illusions. Ignatius warns the

retreatant to beware of temptations which come "under the appearance of good." In his earlier days at Manresa he was more intent on imitating the insufficiently understood example of the saints than in searching for God's will—which might perhaps be contrary to his own.

But should we, on the other hand, under a pretext of realism, adopt a negative attitude by which we exhaust our energy only in a struggle against the powers of evil? Would this be the whole outcome of the preceding experience, something which seemed so positive and inspiring, and was centered on a call of the eternal Lord to share in his universal mission of salvation for the divine glory? It is true that Ignatius does direct the work of the Second Week toward this struggle against Satan, who often seems to be at the side of Christ. The offering of the Kingdom, the Two Standards, the Three Classes of Men, the Three Kinds of Humility, and even the election itself, which can also be a "reform of life," are sufficient evidence that struggle against some natural inclinations is called for. The danger, then, would be that of limiting ourselves to this explicitly negative perspective, and of embracing an asceticism separated from its motivating source. This would soon become a short-sighted. moralizing asceticism, one in which only an extremely strong-willed or "voluntaristic" person could long persevere. How then, as we begin the contemplations of the Second Week, can we safeguard and reconcile these two paradoxical aspects of our commitment, the positive and the negative, the expansive universalism and the ascetical particularism?

A glance at what we have said thus far shows that our work can be summed up in our becoming more aware of two fundamental factors which have come to a head in the final point of the meditation on the Kingdom, the attraction to evil and that to the good. Such awareness focuses on those universal human situations which here and now affect us as retreatants in the very depths of our being. The first is a consciousness of our sinful condition, of our inclusion in the world of evil; and this reveals the immense poverty of our being and our need for divine salvation. The second focuses on the saving mission of Christ who through grace associates with himself everyone who has been redeemed. This twofold awareness gives rise to two important points which throw some light on the present situation of any man or woman: Through Christ, the Savior, God reveals himself essentially as merciful love which delivers man from evil and gives back to him his original capacity of love; and Christ, in the very act by which he reveals God and saves us, opens up for us the ways of love by calling us to collaborate with our whole being in the salvation of the universe as it is making its way toward its end of bringing glory to God, through our right use of our free wills. The offering of the Kingdom comes to its climax by bringing these two concepts together, when

215

the exercitant surrenders himself to the universal Lord without reserve and resolutely joins battle against the evil in his own life, in order to insert himself more fruitfully into God's entire plan.

The personal act by which the retreatant offers himself ought never to be separated from the universal dynamism which inspires it. One should not struggle against evil simply because it is evil, or only because of its relationship with Christ's sufferings. God is not seeking from us some sort of revenge for sin. What is sought remains our union with God as Savior and involvement in his work of Christian salvation. Thus the work which we have to do, at this point in the Exercises is simply this: to take inspiration from the above twofold awareness. That is, we ought consciously to prolong the offering we made in the meditation on the Kingdom, with its two paradoxical aspects, the positive expansive universalism and the ascetical particularism, something very personal.

In this chapter we shall stress intentionally the readjustment of the exercitant's present situation in life, to enable him or her to enter, we think, into greater conformity with Ignatius' spirit. But this readjustment is precisely that commitment which the genuine meeting with the Lord engenders. What appears to be in itself negative is entirely positive through the dynamism which inspires it, and through the immediate and panoramic end which attracts it. This conscious and generous readjustment, realized under the influence of grace and in the measure allotted by the divine will, is at one and the same time a grace of salvation, a movement of love, and a living incarnation of the gift of self.

2. On the Subjective Level, Commitment through Imitation

In the preceding paragraph we pointed out the direction to be safeguarded in the work to be done in the Second Week: an orientation which integrates the paradoxical elements in question. This orientation is based on the movement which engenders it and the end which attracts it. We must now treat with greater precision, within the limits of this sketch, the manner in which this work is to be accomplished. As a prolongation of the offering of the Kingdom which unites the two currents of thought mentioned, and to avoid sacrificing any of the constitutive elements of the synthesis which is to come, this work will necessarily focus on the objective mission of the Lord who is embraced by the response of faith and love, and on the subjective participation, personal and realistic, of the individual Christian.

The fusion of these two objectives is harmoniously realized in the theme of imitation, which occurs throughout the Second Week.[1] Just as it unites the levels of the universal and the particular, of the objective and the subjective, the theme of imitation concentrates the activity of the exercitant into one same movement and directs it toward one same end, on the levels of the intellect and the will. It subjects this personal activity directly, through contemplation, to the action of grace, that is, to the divine motion. These, then, are the elements of the Ignatian dialectic which we must master if we are to present the difficult exercises of the Second Week properly.

Ignatius introduces the theme of imitation in the offering of the Kingdom: "It is my earnest desire and my deliberate choice . . . to imitate Thee" ([98]). All through the Second Week this expression is nuanced by many formulations which repeat the grace to be petitioned: "an intimate knowledge of our Lord . . . that I may love Him more and follow Him more closely" ([104]); "beg for grace to follow and imitate more closely Our Lord" ([109]); "the desire to know better the eternal Word Incarnate in order to serve and follow Him more closely" ([130]); ". . . thereby to imitate Him better" ([147]); "in order to imitate and be in reality more like Christ our Lord, I desire and choose poverty with Christ poor, rather than riches"; ([167]); "the more to imitate and serve Him" ([168]).

Ignatius' language is unequivocal. He is not writing about a "kind of apparent conformity to be achieved by an external imitation,"[2] which human effort alone might achieve, with a little patience and to an astonishing degree. The imitation in his mind is the fruit of the grace which the retreatant has earnestly petitioned. It is closely bound to the interior knowledge of the Lord and to the love which flows from it; and it necessarily fructifies in the service and following of Christ. Under the divine action, it is an assimilation to the Christ who communicates his own life to the one whose enlightened offering He has accepted: "To be placed with Christ" corresponds to the Ignatian prayer "Take and receive" ([234]).

Theological reflection on God's plan of salvation expresses the same reality in a different way: to be son or daughter in the Son who is known and loved by the Father, in order to realize the divine work of salvation with and through Christ. It is the same becoming-like to *(adsimilatio)* the Christ of the Kingdom which the author of the *Exercises* desires. For Ignatius thus makes the genuine imitation of Christ and his life dependent upon the gratuitous gift

---

1 *SpEx*MHSJ, p. 697.
2 P. Galtier, "Notre croissance dans le Christ," *RAM*, 31 (1955), 4-5.

of God. But he wishes to further the acceptance of this gift, under the action of grace, through the faithful and attentive activity of the intellect and will, of knowledge and love through contemplation which gives depth to our understanding of God's plan of salvation through the paschal mystery of Christ, and through the work of the election which brings about the readjustment of the retreatant's situation in life in the light of the mystery which is contemplated.

Indeed the thrust of the theme of imitation is to unite the two levels of activity in the Second Week. This activity is exercised on the objective level of the Kingdom "according to the spirit of Christ": by contemplation of the Lord who is the way to be embraced and the life to be shared, with the help of grace, and without turning back. At the same time this activity is exercised on the level of one's intimate, personal self: by working the whole of one's life more and more into accord with the Truth of Christ, in the light of his revelation. "Until Christ be formed in you."[3]

Thus the imitation is a grace which transforms one into the image of Christ; it operates through interior knowledge and an increase of love. That is why, in the Second Week, the prayer of contemplation was chosen as the way to submit to the divine action the retreatant's spiritual activity and his or her efforts to correspond with grace. Contemplation increases the knowledge and intensifies the love in view of the readjustment which is measured and sustained by the grace of Christ who is encountered in this prayer. It is a strengthening confrontation of the particular retreatant, who is poor but open, with the demands of the transcendent universal which, because it is divine, is at the same time both the norm and the cause of the desired readjustment. For us Christ is the mediator of all our activity now set into contact with the supernatural. Not only does he deliver us from evil and show us the Father, but, through his Spirit, he is the source of that efficacious knowledge and love which we find at the origin of every authentic imitation. Hence arises the importance of this "transforming" contemplation of the mysteries of the life of Christ, which arouses and directs our efforts at readjustment, the free activity of the intellect and the will to cooperate with grace. For, ultimately, grace alone can restore the divine image in us and

---

3 Gal. 4:19. The same theme of imitation of Christ, variously expressed as assimilation to him (= "becoming like to" him), conformation to him, or configuration with him (= "becoming structured according to or modeled after him"), is met often in Scripture, e.g., in Gal. 2:19–22; 3:27; Col. 1:8; 3:10; 1 Cor. 11:1–3; 2 Cor. 4:7–12; Ephes. 4:15, 24; Rom. 13:14; Matt. 16: 24; Mark 8:34; John 12:26; 14:6; 15:1–9. See also Ignatius of Antioch (to the Philadelphians) and St. Augustine (Sermon 142, in PL 38:783–784).

efficaciously associate us with the universal mission of salvation. The fact that Ignatius considers knowledge and love as graces to be earnestly asked for throughout this Week, shows well on what level he situates these graces and how he subordinates to them the retreatant's humble but intelligent and faithful collaboration.

> To know the Lord is not within our power; it is a grace, and we should plead for it unceasingly. We should remain during the whole of our prayer in a posture of supplication. May the Eternal Father, through his Spirit, grant us to know his well-beloved Son and conform us to him.
>
> This conformity to Christ will be obtained only by a prolonged effort to be present to the mystery; and this is, properly speaking, the contemplation that is taught by the Exercises. It is a question, in an atmosphere of recollection, of coinciding, so to speak, with this "epiphany" of the Incarnate Word, who manifests the kenosis of God made man for our salvation.[4]

When the retreatant unceasingly asks for the grace of a more intimate knowledge in order to love more ardently, to follow more closely, and to imitate Christ better, then contemplation leads along this road to the election which it illuminates from above.

> As was the case with the apostles, increasing familiarity with the Lord goes hand in hand with movement forward, as a more profound adherence to his thought and reflections.[5]

3. Exegesis of the Gospel "Mysteries"

Each of the two levels we have been discussing poses its own very particular problem. Their solutions will give us a better understanding of the depth of the purpose envisaged at this step, and of the riches of the dialectical interactions of the Second Week, which has its roots deeply fixed in the fruitful mystery of the relations between nature and grace. On the level of Christ's mission and of contemplation, of intellect and knowledge, we shall study the problem of the exegesis of the Gospel events of Christ's life, the "mysteries" in the sense used by Ignatius in *Exercises* [261–312], the Annunciation through the Ascension. Then, on the level of Christian participation and of election, of will and of love, we shall consider the problem of the action of the Holy Spirit in the soul of the retreatant. At the end of these two

---

4   H. Holstein, "La contemplation des mystères du Christ," *Chr,* no. 8 (1955), 453.
5   Ibid., 455–456.

studies, our previous assertion about the unifying role of imitation through the paths of the contemplations and the action of grace will be even more confirmed. In all this, through reverent listening to the divine word, the exercitant submits to the Holy Spirit's efficacious action. In these conditions God accomplishes within retreatants, in Christ and through his Spirit, the marvel of his salvation which, without our being aware of it, embraces the entire community of humankind and the whole of creation.

a. The Problem

No doubt there are several ways of broaching the problem of the exegetical interpretation of the Gospel mysteries of the Second Week. Some authors or directors treat it indirectly, wondering if it is permissible to use "the data of history, archaeology, and biblical exegesis" in proposing these mysteries according to the mind of Ignatius.[6] Others start with the difficulties raised by the confrontation of the data from contemporary exegesis with the traditional use of Scripture in the Exercises. In particular, we know that the historical character of Christ's words and deeds as reported in the Gospels has been much nuanced through the more exact knowledge which has been gained from study of the literary forms, the procedures in composition, and the kerygmatic, catechetical, and sometimes apologetic objectives of the sacred writers. That "solid foundation of facts" which Ignatius wanted to be proposed for contemplation has in many a case been shaken and revised.[7] In

---

6 On this theme of imitation of Christ, assimilation to him, or configuration with him, see A. López de Santa Anna, "El uso de la historia y arqueología biblicas en las meditaciones de los Ejercicios según la mente de San Ignacio," *Mnr*, 1 (1925), 107–117. The author replies to our question by quoting Nadal, Borgia, the official Directory of 1599, La Palma, La Puente, P. Ferrusola, Roothaan, Meschler, Mercier, Diertins, de Pontlevoy, and Hummelauer about the "material to be prepared" and the need of introducing the retreatant to the meaning of the persons, the words, and the deeds. If he does not succeed in showing the possible harmony among these principles, the data of exegesis, and Ignatian usage, at least this article gathers a series of interesting opinions to which we shall have occasion to refer.

7 Two articles especially treat of these very contemporary problems which are of great relevance: that of F. J. McCool, which studies the historical concept which has been questioned—see "The Preacher and the Historical Witness of the Gospels," *TS*, 21 (1960), 517–543 (reproduced in *The Modern Approach to the Gospel and the Spiritual Exercises* [New York, 1961], pp. 167–199); and that of J. A. Fitzmyer, "The Spiritual Exercises of St. Ignatius and Recent Gospel Study," *WL*, 91 (1962), 246–274. The latter is more general and examines the various problems raised by the recent discoveries of *Formgeschichte* and *Redactiongeschichte* (more particularly of the "Sitz im Leben Evangelium)" in relation to the use of Scripture in the Exercises for contemporary

general, some will reprovingly accuse the author of the *Exercises*—or the director—of subordinating the Scriptures to the explicit purpose which he is seeking in preparing his retreatant for the Election; and this sometimes seems to go beyond or even contradict the objective interpretation of the revealed message. However, because many have never really understood the profound meaning of the Ignatian Election, they do not even think of asking whether this subordination might not have precisely the same objectives as the proclamation of the divine word and the transmission of the gospel message. Furthermore, because many have not understood the genuine dialectical interactions of the Exercises, they fail to notice that, in truth, this subordination does indeed coincide with the very same purposes which the Evangelists had in proclaiming the Gospel events; and that in fact the Election does evolve in total dependence on the revealed message. Finally, there are some who refuse a priori to believe in the possibility of an adequate solution to the problem, on the ground that an exact interpretation of the Scriptures requires knowledge of discoveries which have been made only rather recently about the intention or purposes of the inspired writers and about the circumstances which surrounded the writing of their Gospels. Ignatius, a man of his own time, certainly knew nothing of these preoccupations of contemporary exegesis, legitimate and fruitful as they are.[8]

b. The Ignatian Dialectic: Objectivity and Transcendence

Because these ways of posing the problem often limit us to particular points of view and weaken the significance of the solutions proposed, we shall omit them for the moment. We shall look instead at the entire dialectical movement which we have been studying.

The question at issue is, indeed, that of presenting, from the beginning, an objective message which should condition the spiritual experience of the retreatant. Let us recall that this was the nature of the spiritual journey which Ignatius made at Manresa. We have spoken of the proportioning required by

retreatants. [D. M. Stanley, *A Modern Scriptural Approach to the Spiritual Exercises* (Chicago and St. Louis, 1967), shows by example one way in which the problems treated by Fitzmyer can be handled. See also Stanley's *"I Encountered God!" The Spiritual Exercises with the Gospel of St. John* (St. Louis, 1986). Ed.]

8 It must be admitted that from the point of view of the Christian sense of scriptural interpretation, the end of the Middle Ages and the beginning of the following period are characterized by a great poverty of conception and by the elaboration of an intellectualism which is rather abstract. See R. Guardini, *La Figura di Gesú Christo nel Nuovo Testamento*, pp. 18–19.

the work which must be carried forward simultaneously on two levels, where the presentation of the gospel message should not become instruction for its own sake, but should be given in function of the experience to be aroused and directed in the retreatant. In the logic of the Exercises, the experience of the retreatant develops in dependence upon the revealed message from which it draws its light and force. From the first creative act, everything is dialogue between God and his creature; and the experience of the Exercises is something lived out "in the school of God," who operates at one and the same time through the interior action of the Holy Spirit and the presence of the Church which proclaims and interprets the message.[9] This respect for the Ignatian dialectic becomes even more important in the Second Week, where the objective message is immediately coincident with the divine Word. It is no longer a question merely of the economy of salvation which has been revealed, but of the very words and deeds of the Incarnate Word himself, who reveals and works out this economy or administration of salvation. "For the word of God is living and active, sharper than any two-edged sword, piercing to the division of soul and spirit."[10] Moreover, Ignatius exercises great discretion in regard to these scriptural words, a discretion dictated by the logic he adopted. During the first day of the Second Week he develops his method of contemplating ([101–126]). After this has been done, his manner of proposing the points for meditating on the mysteries of Christ's life could not be more laconic. From this point of view, Ignatius is in no way a man of his own age, nor of the eras of those who have abandoned his recommended conciseness to lose themselves in prolix and distracting commentaries.[11]

What is most important in this dialectical movement is the aspect of the subordination of the lower level, the subjective experience of the retreatant, to the preeminent message. This subordination should not be accepted on the logical level only, as if it worked all by itself and ought to produce its fruits by its own activity *(ex opere operato)*. It requires practical and delicate pre-

---

9 The Church is present to the retreatant, not only through her prayer and her sacraments, nor solely in the person of the director who proposes and directs, but also through her centuries-old understanding of God's revelation contained in the interpretation of the gospel message which is being presented—and that in proportion to the competence of her spokesman. Through him or her who transmits the message and its richness, the Church continues to bring the word of Christ to the ends of the earth.

10 Heb. 4:12.

11 There are scarcely any direct interpretations (or applications) of the mysteries in the *Exercises*. To this statement there are only three or four rare exceptions (Nativity, Jesus in the Temple, the Call of the Apostles, the Resurrection). We shall come back to these later.

sentation. Indeed there is a quite negative way of proceeding—most often unconsciously taken because of ignorance or because it is an easier way—against which we must be on our guard. This negative way of proceeding is all the more deceitful insofar as it falls into the "positive indiscretion" of which we spoke earlier. Here we are speaking about that way of proposing the points for contemplation which gives a long account of the facts of the mystery to be considered, explains in detail all the applications, lessons, and conclusions, and lengthily exploits the sentiments associated with the event contemplated. This method is very negative, in this sense that it exhausts, in concepts strictly human, what God desires to make understood through an inexhaustible mystery. As far as possible, it deprives the mystery of its transcendence. If it cannot do this directly by rendering the divine word inefficacious, it does so by exhausting the retreatant's ability to listen. Instead of opening up the mystery in which the soul will encounter God, it draws the mystery down to man's level and deprives it, through so many distracting commentaries, of its value as a sign, as a word spoken in the deep interior of the soul. Ignatius carefully avoids this first danger by soberly and faithfully proposing the "historical foundation" of the mysteries or events to be contemplated. In the Second Week he presents a choice of eighty-two points for contemplation (from [101 to 164] and [262 to 268]). Of these, forty-eight consist virtually of quotations from Scripture, thirty-one consider deeds as they are narrated in the Gospels, and three treat of matters not found in Scripture.[12]

c. The Necessity of Correct Interpretation

By his discretion Ignatius condemns some notorious abuses which are really the fault of the commentators and not of the Exercises themselves. The reason for this discretion seems especially worthwhile to us: to subject the retreatant's prayer more directly to the grace of the divine message, in ac-

---

12 If we consider the whole of the last three Weeks in which the contemplation of the Scriptures follows the same directives, we find the following figures: 145 points of contemplation, of which 89 are quotations, 51 are facts conformed to the data of Scripture, and 5 are details which have been borrowed from other sources, especially from Ludolph ([266, 273, 288, 299, 310]). To that should be added three or four minor details concerning gospel facts which cannot be verified with certainty in the texts or their possible translations: Jesus speaks "kindly" to the vendors of doves ([277]), our Lord eats in the house of Simon "together with Lazarus" ([286]), "when the supper was finished" Judas went forth to sell our Lord ([289]), and the apparition in Galilee takes place "on Mt. Tabor" ([307]).

cordance with what emerges from the Ignatian dialectic when faithful to itself.

However, if we press this attitude to its extremity, it exposes the exercitant to a kind of subjectivism, that of free interpretation. If God, through his revealed message, addresses himself to each person in particular, who would dare to interfere in this intimate and sacred dialogue? It is clear enough that Ignatius does not orient his principle toward such private interpretation. When he speaks of "the historical foundation of the facts" which are to be "faithfully" presented, he is insisting that *there is* an objective datum of revelation, *an objective truth from God which ought to be humbly received and contemplated in prayer.* It was in the completely objective light of the divine designs that Ignatius was ravished; and then, already at the time of the graces of Manresa, he understood himself better and also his place in the whole framework of God's plan. But what God asks for in return, the response which he expects from the one to whom his eternal Word is speaking today—this remains something secret in this communication between "the Creator and his creature" ([15]), and it should be respected.

Is Ignatius content, then, to avoid the extremes we have already mentioned by transmitting the message in a rather material way, in order to avoid changing it by various modes of interpretation? Certainly he does not expect the director to limit himself to the mere reading of the gospel text when he or she is giving to the retreatant the matters to be contemplated. Does he then put his trust in the inspiration of each director of the Exercises? Or does he somewhere give us some principles of interpretation, especially of his basic principle which connects the contemplation with the objectivity and the pre-eminence of the revealed message? If so, would these principles coincide in some way with those of contemporary exegesis of the Gospels? This last question brings us back to the difficulties raised above. We hope to give a solution in our treatment of the Ignatian point of view concerning the interpretation of the mysteries or gospel incidents of the Second Week.

d. A Theological Perspective

Many indications enable us to extract from the *Exercises* Ignatius' thought on the interpretation of the Gospel mysteries. What we are considering here is not only a problem of exegesis but a genuine theology of the revealed mysteries.[13] All the evidence shows that Ignatius possessed this the-

---

13 On the necessary relationships which must be encouraged and made explicit between exegesis and theology, even on the subject of the mysteries of the life of Christ, see the beautiful pages of K. Rahner in *Theological Investigations,* I,

ological outlook, and that to a lofty degree, in consequence of the exceptional intuitions and illuminations of Manresa. If we retrace this theology as revealed in his statements, we can extract from them precious directive principles, which the findings of modern exegesis will only enrich. One fact, however, cannot be ignored. Because of the meagerness of the material to be analyzed and the poverty of expression of his day, it was difficult for Ignatius to express clearly even to himself, and then to apply to each mystery, the principles which made up his vision of God and all creation. This was a very theological outlook bearing upon the words and deeds in the life of Christ. Contemporary exegesis, we shall see, through an objective analysis of the milieu in which the Gospels were formed, and also of the preoccupations of their authors, enters the same fertile field of interpretation, and gives us tools becoming ever more adequate to express the richness of what is contained there. The director of the Exercises who wishes to be faithful to Ignatius' vision, and to the interpretation of the mysteries which that vision authorizes, will have everything to gain by learning and mastering the positive data provided by modern exegesis. We shall also see what principles are necessary in regard to the use of these data—principles imposed by the very logic of the *Exercises*.

e. The Glorious Christ

The contemplation of the Kingdom, which inaugurates the spiritual journey through the Second Week, does not present us with a Christ other than the Christ found in Ignatius' other writings. We saw this in chapter 2 when speaking of the Ignatian world view, and in chapter 4 when we spoke of the Christ of the First Week. For Ignatius, Christ was viewed always in only one way—as the Lord of Majesty, whose grandeur he had perceived in his experiences at Loyola and Manresa (chapter 1). In the colloquy of the first exercise, before the cross, the retreatant is placed in the presence of the "Creator" who submits to temporal death, for him ([53]). Ignatius, we repeat, does not play a game of hide-and-seek to make us believe that he will first present a partial vision of Christ which will gradually lead us to the surprise of discovering a more glorious Christ at the time of his resurrection. With Ignatius, we are always in the presence of the same Lord, "Dios, nuestro Señor."

The interesting thing about the Kingdom is that it clearly relates this vision or world view to the contemplations to come, and makes it into "a

pp. 190–192. An article of C. Spicq is somewhat in the same vein, "Nouvelles réflexions sur la thólogie biblique," *Rev. de Sc. Ph. et Th.*, 42 (1958), 209–219.

foundation for the meditations on the life of Christ." The characteristics of the Lord which it emphasizes for this purpose call back to mind the essential mission of salvation,[14] a mission which is not only deliverance from evil but also a call to participation, imitation, and assimilation.[15]

Anyone who, during the Second Week, would regard the mysteries as a simple, linear, historical development would be making a great mistake. In this regard the views of Ignatius are truly in harmony with those which the best writers in the field of exegesis are highlighting today. It is clear enough that the evangelists did not write merely to narrate the life of Jesus. "It is not simply a question," writes J. Guillet, "of reviving memories, of being enchanted with a luminous past. Rather, there is question of finding again, in the words and deeds of Jesus of Nazareth, the glory which his resurrection caused to burst forth, that glory which remains for eternity what it was for thirty years in a visible and sensible form, the glory of the only Son" (John 1:12).[16] Their "memoirs," then, consist of a rereading of the events of Christ's life, but read this time in the prodigious light which the resurrection throws back on his previous life, in which they now suddenly discover the infinite dimension and unique value of a sign—a sign given by God to man. The same deeds of which they had been the frequent or privileged witnesses, and the same words they had heard so often, are offered anew to their enlightened intellects; and behind each of these events they see not only their extraordinary and well-beloved Master at work, but also God among us, the Lord of Glory. Such is the Good News they announce: God is forever among us. And that is also the point of view of Ignatius, for whom "the Eternal

14   "The Christ of the Kingdom is the one who has accomplished the whole of his work of salvation, he is the presently reigning King of the world, St. Paul's risen and eternal Lord, possessing in himself and disclosing the whole of his redemptive work" (J. Lewis, *Notes de cours,* p. 31.

15   "And Father Ignatius placed this meditation on the Kingdom of Christ in the beginning of the Second Week as the foundation of all the meditations on the life of Christ, in order that through this meditation we may be in a general way stirred up toward imitating him" (*SpEx*MHSJ, pp. 694–695). The same assertion is found in the Directories of Miró (ibid., p. 861), Dávila, (p. 917), and in those of 1591 and 1599 (pp. 1046 and 1148). On the subject of this foundation, Marín rightly recalls that the danger today is that of making no more use of it once it has been presented; for all the remaining contemplations should be presented with reference to it. See "Aportaciones biblicas a la contemplación del Reino," *Mnr,* 35 (1963), 333. See also, in the same number, p. 296, the thought of H. Rahner as given by Granero, on the purpose of the meditation on the Kingdom.

16   J. Guillet, *Jesus Christ Yesterday and Today,* p. 7. The same idea is found in R. Guardini, *La figura di Gesù Cristo nel Nuovo Testamento,* pp. 23, 38, 41–43.

Lord" of the Kingdom ([98]), the "eternal Word Incarnate" of the Second Week ([130]), continues to make his call heard, to invite "each one in particular" to enter into the inmost secrets of His life here and now being presented for contemplation. If one does not accept this way of presenting the "life of Jesus," one repeats the words of Ignatius but empties them of the vision which gave them life; one repeats the words of the Gospel without opening the heart of the retreatant to their inexhaustible meaning.[17]

That this perspective is the one which Ignatius applies to his interpretation of the mysteries is directly proved by his exercises on the Incarnation and Nativity ([101–126]), where he expounds his method of contemplation. For the other mysteries, the care of making this application is left to the director or to the retreatant himself. Now this plan which is outlined in the contemplation of the Incarnation goes far beyond the material or historical event which is embodied in this mystery. Indeed, it embraces the history of salvation in all its amplitude. The first prelude contains the essential elements of the drama, from the active presence of the Blessed Trinity—which includes the preexistence of the Word—and all the peoples on the face of the earth going down to hell, all the way to the lowly events of Nazareth when, as Ignatius repeats, "the fullness of time had come" ([102]). The following contemplation, on Bethlehem, projects this sacred history beyond all the contemporary circumstances which surrounded the material event: "to consider . . . [their] making the journey and laboring that our Lord might be born in extreme poverty, and that after many labors, after hunger, thirst, heat, and cold, after insults and outrages, He might die on the cross, and all this for me" ([116]). This general perspective on the whole scene will enable us to connect each event to the unique history of salvation—that of our Creator and Lord becoming man and dying for us. The facts and deeds of Christ—which Ignatius expressly calls mysteries[18]—took place only once, but with significance which endures for eternity; and the perspective proposed to bring out their meaning is certainly the most fruitful there is, since it proceeds from the light of God's revelation.

17　As J. Corbon says, the important thing is "to read the Gospel according to the Spirit and not according to the flesh," *L'expérience chrétienne dans la Bible,* p. 91.

18　On the different meanings of the word "mystery," see the Appendix below, in the Reference Matter; also M. Van Caster, "Le mystère du Salut, contenu du message chrétien," *LV,* 10 (1955), 523. In Ignatius' case it is less important to know the source from which he borrowed the term than to note the use to which he put it.

Before we move forward to the particular problems of application, we shall say one last word of explanation about this perspective which is both evangelical and Ignatian. Some persons cannot easily understand how, in practice, one can consider the Christ of the crib or of Nazareth, or the Christ of the public life and the cross, simultaneously with the glorified Christ. For them, the expression "glorified Christ" refers explicitly to the fact of the resurrection. How, then, can a person contemplate the risen Christ through deeds which are prior in time and even accomplished independently of that glorious event, his resurrection? Does not this procedure seem rather artificial? When Jesus performed one or another concrete act during his historical life, he evidently was not yet risen!

To understand this perspective—and this is absolutely necessary for the contemplations of the Second Week—we must separate in our minds the fact of Christ's glory from the fact of his resurrection. The resurrection permitted the apostles to become aware of Christ's glory, that is, of what he was in reality behind the human appearance which he had shown at the time. The glory of Christ is what he is from all eternity, in his divine majesty.[19] The resurrection does not procure Christ's essential glory; it reveals it. In the crib and on the cross it is the same glorious Christ, the Lord of Majesty, God among us, who is born and who dies. But human eyes could not see this glory before its full "revelation." The paschal event was needed to manifest the immediate presence of the divine in the person of Christ. "My Lord and my God" (John 20:28). Thus, to review, consider, and contemplate the whole life of Christ as the glorious Lord is to accept "God among us" in these humble deeds. From the Kingdom onward, it is no longer only a man whom we see walking through the villages of Palestine; it is "the eternal Lord of all things" who walks, speaks, loves, cures, accomplishes his immense mission, in which, with a divine respect, he invites us to take part.

f. "Interior Knowledge"

Corresponding to this perspective which dominates the Second Week is the manner of application which is proper to Ignatian contemplation. It is characterized, in relation to the mysteries it takes up, by certain precise

---

19 The biblical sense of the glory of God and of Christ has been the object of some excellent studies. Among which are: P. van Imschoot, *Théologie de l'Ancien Testament*, I, "Dieu," especially pp. 212–219 (Paris, 1954); J. Duplacy, "L'espérance de la gloire de Dieu dans l'Ancien Testament," *BVCh*, 8 (1954–55), 40–54, and "La Gloire de Dieu et du Seigneur Jésus dans le Nouveau Testament," *BVCh*, 9 (1955), 7–21; D. Mollat, "La gloire de Dieu et du Sei-

requirements and a great flexibility. Both of these characteristics should be known and respected if we wish to reconcile this traditional method of contemplating the mysteries with the new ways of examining the texts which express these mysteries.

What permits Ignatius' method to assimilate the continual discoveries of exegesis and theology is the fact that it is based, first of all, on knowledge. We have seen, in chapter 3 when we discussed the Ignatian dialectical procedures with their interacting mental processes, the role of the spiritual understanding both in the activity of the Exercises and in the experience of the saint at Manresa. The revealed message is addressed first of all to the intellect, and the graces for which the retreatant asks are light, knowledge, and interior penetration. Then, from within his or her interior depths and under the action of grace will arise the efficacious "spiritual sentiments" which will transform the soul. We might think that this would be more appropriate to the First Week in which the retreatant, through the meditations of that Week, would gain the sense of his or her own sinfulness so as really to participate in the gift of salvation. However, Ignatius insists just as much on this same procedure in the Second Week; and he does so spontaneously, we believe, because of his experience at Manresa, where the lights given to his understanding evoked and directed the effective readjustment of his life into the ways of love and the following of Christ. That is why, among the graces to be petitioned throughout this Second Week, the most important is "an intimate knowledge of our Lord, who has become man for me" ([104]). Ignatius goes further and asks his retreatant to fill his or her mind with "a desire to know better the eternal Word Incarnate" ([130]). These two expressions indicate that Ignatius is no longer writing about a mere historical knowledge of the events of Christ's life. His words are: "an intimate knowledge of the Lord" *(conosimiento interno)* ([104]). Going farther, he asks his retreatant to maintain "a desire to know better the eternal Word Incarnate" ([13O]). Behind the revealed data about the events, persons, words, and deeds is the mystery of the Christ of faith and his saving plan, all of which Ignatius wishes the retreatant to penetrate more deeply. In it the exercitant will discover and receive, with the help of grace, the interior dynamism which draws a person to follow Christ with no other limit than the divine will.

We might perhaps frighten some simple persons by telling them that, in the matter of contemplation, the activity of the intellect remains the best

gneur dans le Nouveau Testament," *Chr,* no. 11 (1956), 310–327; J. Guillet, on "The Glory of the Lord, in *Jesus Christ Yesterday and Today,*" ch. 2, pp. 26–41; [also, D. Mollat, *DBTh,* pp. 202–205, s.v. "glory." Ed].

means to initiate a genuine encounter with the Lord. They are not surprised, though, to hear that it is necessary to know one better in order to love him or her more. The reason for this is that these simple persons, mystified by those more sophisticated, often identify "work of the intellect" with "abstract speculation." In the *Exercises* Ignatius constantly appeals to the intellect, but he never falls into mere speculation. We must understand his point of view and see its value if we wish to give the Exercises "according to his spirit." Apart from prayer properly so called, there are two ways of describing the activity of the retreatant in the contemplation of the mysteries. On the one hand, Ignatius asks him or her to consider and reflect ([2, 106, 107, 108, 114, 115, 116, 123, 124, and passim]), or to explain and savor ([2]); and on the other hand, he wants the retreatant to "make myself . . . as though present" to the scene being contemplated ([114]). Many persons ordinarily stress this last phase as best describing the work of contemplation. But for lack of depth they often reduce this attitude to activity of the imagination which reconstructs the scene in order to try to be present to it merely in its historical aspects. As a result, imaginative persons become inventive, sensitive persons easily become emotional, and intellectual persons become bored. Even if the activity of the imagination aids toward mustering our interior energies and sensitizes them to the more human aspects of a subject of meditation or contemplation, it still does not give to prayer its deepest roots. The activity of the spiritual understanding is more important, for it orients toward the heart the matter which is bring presented as a part of Christ's salvific plan. The retreatant, then, becomes genuinely present to that dimension which goes far beyond the historical event and which confers on it an importance just as great as that of the deeds considered as situated in historical time. This presence to the mystery is far superior to that which is attained through any interior representation, no matter how imaginative or moving it might be.[20] The imagination ordinarily limits itself to the contemplation of the Christ of history through which we must pass; but the spiritual understanding disposes the exercitant for a more enriching presence, that to the Christ of faith reached through the indispensable intermediary of his Incarnation. It is our spiritual understanding, helped by grace, which grasps the timely importance for ourselves of the mysteries that were lived out in the

20 "The gospel becomes truly our history only when we consent to become present to it, to consider it, not as a narrative of past events, but as Christ present to our own personal existence. It is the reality of this encounter with our own life on the level of salvation that tends to make us succeed in Ignatian contemplation." (H. Holstein, in *Chr*, 8 (1955), 464.

past, and this allows us to participate more intimately in the mysteries we are contemplating.

In the *Exercises,* then, this activity of the intellect which aims at an interior knowledge of Christ is of outstanding importance. Ignatius neatly distributes it among the three persons involved: the director who "faithfully" proposes the subject for meditation ([2]), the retreatant who "reflects on it for himself" ([2]), and God, for whose help the retreatant begs as a means to a deeper interior knowledge ([104]), and which he receives "from the grace of God enlightening his mind" ([3]).

Grace (as one of the three factors involved here) accomplishes its work by itself and in ways which can be very different.[21] In this connection it is necessary to distinguish or "discern" the false consolations of the evil spirit appearing as an "angel of light," which are more frequent at this stage of the Exercises ([332]). The retreatant's participation should follow the directives drawn from the Ignatian interacting dialectical procedures which we analyzed above in chapter 3, B. What should be avoided here is to lose oneself in a search for the possible meanings in the scriptural texts—a danger especially pertinent to those trained in exegetical studies.[22] The purpose, attained through attentive listening to the Holy Spirit, is clearly determined: a more exact understanding of the mystery in order to contemplate the whole grand reality, of which the material events are only a sign, and which give, most importantly, a genuine "interior relish" for the things of God ([2]). Thus everything is oriented toward the love and imitation which make one like to Christ—as is shown with precision by the grace to be petitioned. And this ordered contemplation ordinarily culminates in the intimate prayer of adoration and oblation.

The role of the director becomes much more subtle at this level—the only level, practically speaking, where he can exercise some influence. (We

---

21 See The Rules for the Discernment of Spirits for the Second Week. In them Ignatius distinguishes the different forms of consolation: "without any previous cause" ([330]) or consolation preceded by "perception or knowledge of any subject" ([330]); see also [333, 336].

22 What characterizes the work of the retreatant in the Second Week, as Holstein rightly shows in the article just quoted, is the difference of the repetition of the First Week from that of the Second Week. In the first case, on sins ([62]), Ignatius asks the retreatant to go back over those points where he or she experienced greater consolation or spiritual "appreciation" *(sentimiento);* in the case of the contemplations on the Incarnation and Nativity, he speaks ([118]) of "greater understanding" *(conoscimiento).* The detail is important.

are not speaking here of spiritual direction.)[23] In general, the one who presents the points should, according to the spirit of Ignatius, be sober and precise. He or she ought to open the way for a deeper understanding of the preeminent mystery or plan of salvation, which gives the light enabling the retreatant to situate himself or herself within the wide expanse of God's truth. During the prayer which follows, and under the action of the Spirit, the rest of the work is accomplished in terms of "fruits and spiritual sentiments." This, though difficult, is practically the only rule to be followed. With regard to each particular Gospel mystery, this rule opens the way to an intelligent use of the data of exegesis. In fact, Ignatius and those who have been faithful to his perspective rightly strove to situate and interpret each mystery—or at least certain details of these mysteries—within the whole expansive vision suggested by the Kingdom.[24]

This task is now enormously simplified for us by the work and discoveries of exegesis and biblical theology. Present day-exegesis, through but also apart from the complications of its critical methods, ultimately gives us a simplicity of vision which all the psychological and moralizing or pious commentaries have never before attained. It opens the way to an understanding of the facts pertaining to the infinite dimensions of the mystery in question, in place of exhausting the topic in restrictive and often arbitrary applications. Later on when we separately examine the events of the infancy, the hidden life, and the public life, we shall indicate briefly how to apply to the mysteries contemplated, within the Ignatian perspective, what exegesis and theology have brought us about these realities. In principle, we should note, everything remains ordered to the spiritual purpose envisaged. In order to bring out the profound meaning of a text, it is not necessary to explain the

---

23 On this topic we refer the reader to ch. 3, in which the role of the director, in his proposing the meditations, is placed more clearly on the level of the intellect rather than on that of the will and feelings. On the discretion required to fulfill this role, which simply prepares the retreatant, according to the "principles of evangelical perfection," for the true encounter in which God himself accomplishes the work, read the reflections of spiritual writers such as John of the Cross and Thérèse of the Child Jesus—St. John in his commentary on the third strophe of "The Living Flame of Love," in *Collected Works of St. John of the Cross*, trans K. Kavanaugh and O. Rodriguez (New York, 1979), p. 628; for the context see pp. 621–634; and St. Thérèse in her *Manuscrits autobiographiques*, A, 129–130.

24 See the numerous opinions given by López de Santa Anna (above in fn. 6); on the subject of the introduction to the meaning of persons, words, and actions, the official Directory, XX, 5; on the "material to be prepared," L. de La Palma; and several others, including M. Meschler (who explicitly states that the director must use the "ancient and modern biblical commentaries").

details of its analysis; but to speak intelligently about these matters one would have to have a detailed knowledge of them. From the abundant discoveries of research, then, the director should choose what is strictly necessary to make the true sense of the mystery glow, and to lead the retreatant to an interior understanding of the reality being contemplated. When an event—for example, the wedding feast of Cana—is presented explicitly as a "sign," the director's desire to propose its true significance would be vain if the retreatant does not know what constitutes the element of sign in it, and what a sign does.

g. Exegesis and Contemplation

Here a practical question arises: How can one insert these commentaries into the points which one is proposing for the contemplations? The matter is very simple, we think. The "first prelude," which Ignatius ordinarily adds to his meditations, and of which the purpose is precisely to relate the history, is designed for that purpose. Right from the beginning the director ought to give the history of the event by revealing its relationship to the Kingdom, that is, to Christ and to his mission. Usually the director's work should be limited to this first time. That is, after all, what Ignatius does in the contemplation on the Incarnation ([102]), the Passion ([191, 201]) and the Resurrection ([219]).[25] In acting this way to the extent expedient, the director is following the mind of Ignatius, who devised the first prelude and placed it as a preparation for the contemplation itself—that is, even before the composition of place and the petition for the specific grace. This prelude allows for an explanation of the facts to be contemplated, and the director introduces the retreatant to them by opening them up carefully, soberly, faithfully, and in their richest meaning. Immediately after that, he determines the other preludes which directly start the contemplation. Then he leaves to the retreatant the task of applying the Ignatian method of contemplation: to look at the persons, hear what they say, and see what they do. The directors who give points by doing themselves what the exercitants should do (to see, to hear, and the like) often fatigue the retreatants' powers of attention in regard to this gospel event. Therefore, once the method has been taught (the first exercises of a series, as Ignatius does), the director should be content merely to introduce the exercitant to the mystery, especially during the first prelude, and to

25 However, between *SpEx* [111] and [116], i. e., between the first prelude and the third point, the contemplation on the Nativity focuses the reflection properly so called on the salvific and sanctifying significance of the actions. Therefore an accommodation is possible, according to the subjects.

indicate the direction which the exercitant ought to follow in contemplating the matter. It is the exercitant's task to commit himself or herself to encounter the Lord in the prayer.

As to the problem of the perspective proper to each evangelist, in the Exercises that problem is resolved in practice, we think, through its relation to the overall vision of the series of contemplations taken as one whole. Indeed, the particular perspectives, although truly distinct, are presented as realizations, under specific aspects, of the one general plan always centered on Christ and his salvific message; and all this is happily summed up in the vision of the Kingdom.[26] Thus the particular perspectives fit more easily into the general perspective of the series as a whole, especially when we keep ourselves within the practical plan of the Exercises. This always looks toward our becoming like to Christ, to acceptance of the salvation he offers, and toward sharing in his mission of salvation. This practical plan is also that of the Gospels themselves.[27] By respecting the perspective which an evangelist gives to the mystery he is reporting, we are not distracted from the ultimate end which determines and integrates the particular ends. Furthermore, we know that the choice of the mysteries to be contemplated and of the order to be followed remain flexible in the Exercises, by Ignatius' design. In this connection he tells us that we can lengthen, shorten, suppress, or choose other mysteries, and that "they serve here to afford an introduction and method for better and more complete meditation later" ([162]).[28] Hence, nothing prevents us from unifying, to a certain extent, our choice of mysteries for contemplation by using one or another Gospel and its particular perspective.[29]

26 In the study of the primitive kerygma (see the discourses of the Acts and the general plan of the Synoptics) and of the Christological hymns of the apostolic Church (a trace of which appears in the New Testament, e.g., John 1:1–18, Phil. 2:6–11, Col. 1:15–20, 1 Tim. 3:16, Heb. 1:2–4) some interesting points of reference may perhaps be found on the subject of this perspective which dominates the several points of view. See Robert and Feuillet, *Introduction to the New Testament* (1959), especially pp. 252–262, 342–352, 747–752; also D. Daube, "The Earliest Structure of the Gospels," *NTS,* 5 (1959), 174–187; S. de Ausejo, "Es un himno a Cristo el prólogo de San Juan?", *EstBi,* 15 (1956), 223–2,77, and 16 (1956), 381–427. For the perspective of each evangelist, see the Biblical Bibliography, below in the Reference Matter.
27 Read Andreas ab Alpe, "De imitatione Christi in Novo Testamento," *VD,* 22 (1954), 57–64, 86–90.
28 The same idea is expressed on the subject of the Passion in the Third Week, [209].
29 Here we refer to the suggestion of J. Fitzmyer, *WL,* 91 (1962), 266–267, which he draws from his reflections on the *Sitz im Leben Evangelium,* the "Gospel context" which makes possible a better understanding of the intentions of some

4. *The Action of the Holy Spirit*

In the Second Week there are two corresponding levels: the level of the mission of Christ and that of the Christian participation which interacts with it. The first level, Christ's mission, through the orderly contemplation of the mysteries in his life, posed the problem of exegesis as a support for the intellectual activity which disposes the exercitant for interior knowledge of the Lord. The second level, the sharing in his mission, gives rise to another problem equally important—that of the action of the Holy Spirit in the exercitant's soul where, through the spiritual movement of the will, the experience grows into an effective love which makes the exercitant more like to Christ. "God's love has been poured into our hearts by the Holy Spirit."[30] Ignatius is precise: "to ask for an intimate knowledge of our Lord who has become man for me, that I may love Him more and follow Him more closely" ([104]). Much has been written on this problem of the divine action in the Exercises.[31] We do not wish to treat it for the interest which it has in itself. Rather, we want to situate it anew within the dynamic perspectives of this Ignatian dialectic which is directing our analysis, so that we may better determine the movement to be followed in the Second Week to make sure that the election may be made under the "influence of a motion from God."

---

one evangelist. It is true that one then follows more closely the movement of the Gospel which has been chosen as the center of unity. We find the proposition interesting and promising. To take the infancy narrative as an example, Luke's Gospel is totally integrated into the perspective considered in the *Exercises.* (Perhaps the same holds true of Matthew's Gospel.) In this perspective, the midrashic genre poses no problem whatever for the contemplation; it serves the same purpose which the biblical author envisaged. As we shall see, the same is true for the public life, where the perspective of John, for example, coincides more closely than any other with the "view of faith" of the *Exercises.* However, we should not make this procedure inflexible. It is not a question of gradually painting a portrait of the Lord, whose characteristics would certainly be more unified if we followed only one author. The real question is that of *seeing a divine plan realized in Christ,* and no author, no text of the New Testament is a stranger to this plan. The complementarity of the different points of view of the evangelists should not be neglected either.

30 Rom. 5:5.
31 On the role of grace in the Exercises, consult any of the following articles: R. Orlandis, "De la sobrenaturalidad de la vida en los Ejercicios," *Mnr,* 12 (1936), 195–223; F. X. Lawlor, "The Doctrine of Grace in the Spiritual Exercises," *TS,* 3 (1943), 513–532; A. Steger, "La place de la grâce dans la spiritualité de saint Ignace," *NRTh,* 70 (1948), 561–575; in English, "Grace in the Spirituality of St. Ignatius," *WL,* 78 (1949), 205–224; J. C. Boyer, "La puissance de la grâce selon saint Ignace," *Greg,* 37 (1956), 355–365. For what refers to the Holy Spirit see the following paragraph.

a. Transcendence and Grace

Until now we have joined the matter of God's transcendence, during the Exercises, to that of the message, to foster scrutiny of and respect for the objective content of that message, and to make sure that the message itself will be the guiding principle of the retreatant's subjective experience.[32] In a sense, the revealed message ought to play in our lives the role of that cloud which, like our faith, was "dark on one side and luminous on the other"[33] and directed the march of the Israelites in the desert. By insisting on this we have been aiming to draw attention to this fundamental characteristic of the Ignatian method: It must be viewed in direct relationship with the privileged experiences of Manresa. Our remarks were then addressed to those who interpret the Exercises. On the side of the retreatant and of practice, this same fact is expressed in Ignatius' vocabulary by the word "grace." Far from seeing any difference or contradiction on either level, or in either mode of expression, we shall find only a necessary complementarity. This is especially true if we think of the efficacy of the divine word as described in Scripture, and of the grace which flows from it.[34]

Ignatius, it is granted, does not explicitly treat the topic of grace. But it is evident that he implicitly understands the action of grace throughout the *Exercises*. Great flexibility and attention are required to open the soul to its gentle movement. For the making of the Exercises, this is even a reason for the paradoxical characteristic of systematization which causes them to seem rigid to those who know them only from outside. In reality, however, this orderly systematization is looking toward a personal, faithful, and intelligent effort to correspond to this essential action of grace. This correspondence evolves through the retreatant's own interior experience, which is necessarily flexible, open, and often also feeling its way amid pain.

In the eyes of the retreatant, this relationship to grace takes on various forms. First of all, the Exercises are given to him or her in their totality as a work to be undertaken and completed with the help of God's grace; for they are a place for encounter and communication between the Creator and his creature ([15 and 16]). The effort which is demanded of the retreatant, right from the beginning, is to dispose himself or herself generously "to receive graces and gifts from the infinite goodness of . . . God" ([20; also, 2, 5]). It

---

32 ". . . to put order into one's personal life; and for this there is an objective norm which directs and functions as the backbone of the Exercises as a whole" (F. Marín, *Mnr,* 35 (1963), 333.

33 See X. Léon-Dufour, s.v. "cloud," *DBTh,* (2n ed., 1973), pp. 82–85.

34 See M. Zerwick, "Sacra Scriptura: mysterium gratiae," *VD,* 21 (1941), 3–8.

is in this light that the director will be able at least to some extent to judge the retreatant's cooperation with the Exercises and his or her progress as indicated by the graces which can be expected ([4, 6]). The method which the exercitant will use also aims to gain these gratuitous gifts which bring about the conversion desired. Beginning with the examen of conscience ([24, 43]) and throughout the meditations ([46, 55]) and contemplations ([104, 139, 146]) the "what I want" *(id quod volo)* which ordinarily expresses the advance of the exercitant's purified spiritual desire—all this formulates the continual petition that ascends from the depths of an open heart seeking to dispose itself to receive divine grace.[35] The colloquy too, into which every meditation grows, gives free reign to this spontaneous and personal prayer ([54, 64]). Ignatius' insistence that in the meditations the retreatant should concentrate on the matter at hand uniquely concerns the application of one's whole being to welcoming the divine gifts ([11]). During this journey, the particular points will be considered in their explicit relationship with grace. Sin is seen as a willful privation of grace ([50]); the Eucharist, on the contrary, helps to "retain the increase of grace which one has gained" ([44]); penances are performed "to obtain some grace or gift that one earnestly desires" ([87]); and finally, the offer of the Kingdom counts above all on "the favor and help of the Lord" ([96]).[36]

Nevertheless, the central work of the Exercises of the Second Week is above all the work of the election, the work of bringing the retreatant's life into conformity with the divine message which expresses God's will. This is achieved in dependence on God's grace earnestly begged ([175, 176, 180, 183, 184]), and also through the careful application of the rules for discernment, "for understanding to some extent the different motions produced in the soul" ([313-336]). Practically speaking, it is only in these rules that Ignatius departs from his usual "doctrinal reserve." And he presents a magis-

---

35 On the joint role of effort and grace in the Exercises, see our development in ch. 3, B, c above. Also read the numerous practical applications of F. Courel in his French translation of the *Exercises.* These notes occur precisely in those places where the effort demanded needs to be bound to its function of corresponding with grace. We consider them to be a helpful aid to the one giving the Exercises, at least as a reminder which is most often justified. For this reason, we separate them from the other notes and indicate them here in one place, by referring to the page and note number: see *Exercices,* trans. Courel, pp. 13, n. 23; 27 n. 1; 31,n. 1; 39 n.1; 44, n. 1; 47, n. 2; 56, n. 1; 65, n.2; 68, nn.1,3; 78, n. 1; 86, n.1; 90, n.1; 97, n.1; 101, nn. 1, 2; 168, n. 3; 169, n. 1; 177, n.1.

36 Even the rules "for thinking with the Church" refer explicitly to the problem of grace: [363, 366-370].

terial lesson drawn from the experiences of consolation and desolation which occur through the course of the Exercises, and through which there is brought about the genuine readjustment of the retreatant's personal life, in the presence of the divine light and truth: "God wishes to give us," Ignatius wrote, "a true knowledge and understanding of ourselves, so that we may have an intimate perception of the fact that it is not within our power to acquire and attain great devotion, intense love, tears, or any other spiritual consolation; but all this is the gift and grace of God our Lord" ([322]). This was a deep conviction of his, so that he began or ended his letters with these words: "May the grace and love of Christ our Lord be always ours to help and favor us." Likewise, the last prayer of the *Exercises* brings back again this humble and confident petition: "Give me Thy love and Thy grace, for this is sufficient for me" ([234]).

We have just described in Ignatian terms a simple fact, that of grace in the *Exercises*. In the history of their practice, this reality has often been contested by some who could not discern to what extent the effort asked of the exercitant not only aims at correspondence with graces, but counts above all on an initial impulse from grace, namely, that grace which was begged at the beginning of every exercise and every activity. That grace was waited for throughout each exercise and sought once more in the colloquy. In the Exercises, everything is in function of the reception of divine gifts, and everything is accomplished through the spiritual fruits which work in us. But for Ignatius, engaged in an interacting dialectic of exercises, the important thing is the fact, not so much of the divine action in us (God's fidelity poses no problem for him), but rather the generous and enlightened response to this activity of grace in the soul. For him this was an important, urgent necessity: to dispose oneself, within the limits of one's capacities, to this effective correspondence with grace, by removing the obstacles for which one is responsible—that is, for any complicity with Satan. Thus the accent is placed on this aspect of the problem: to submit oneself to the divine movement, "to come to a decision under the divine influence." On this subject we have eloquent confirmation on the part of Ignatius himself. He sometimes speaks, in discernment situations, about God's action in us and of his manners of acting. Always Ignatius' purpose is to clarify the correspondence to God's action which a person ought to have who is attentive to responding to God and in seeking to find his will. So tenaciously does he hold to this view that he follows a parallel when he is teaching the soul to avoid the actions of the "evil spirit," "the enemy of human nature" whose purpose is to lead one in the opposite direction into infidelity to God, through "hidden deceits" which are sometimes most subtle ([332–334]).

Finally, if we link this orientation of the retreatant's activity to the fundamental problem of "experiencing salvation," which is the framework of reference for all the forms taken on by the experience which is lived out in making the Exercises, we come back again to the background (already treated in chapter 5) of the absolute gratuity of salvation, and of the transcendence of the divine Word who does what he says. The Exercises were born from this experience of light and gratuitousness. They seek to prepare the soul for the same experience of purifying encounter in which love is attained through self-despoliation, and in which death to self opens the way to a resurrection to the Other, namely to the whole Christ.

b. The Ministry of the Spirit

We have been studying a perspective of "practical exercises" subordinated to an exalted vision of divine transcendence and immanence. This has enabled us to see Ignatius' discreet and precise viewpoint on grace in the Exercises. Can we affirm that there are present a similar perspective and language about the Holy Spirit, about whom Ignatius' little book speaks with even greater caution? In replying to this question we intend to show the extent to which the *Exercises,* despite the reserve in their expositions, are eminently a "ministry of the Spirit," at the same time that they are "a ministry of the Word." The intelligent proclamation of the Word is accompanied during the Exercises by a great and applied concern to submit to the Spirit himself of the Christ who acts in us. This brief assertion strikes us forcefully as a conclusion from the statements which preceded it. Moreover, it makes explicit to the director the procedure to be followed when helping the exercitant. When he or she is contemplating the events of Christ's life, the director ought to help the retreatant to find the divine will *which the Spirit points out* and allows him or her to embrace. It is important to establish this point which is too often disputed or is not very clear in the mind of the director.

If Scripture does not tell us very much about the nature and the person of the Holy Spirit, if it does not show us his face to contemplate, it is nevertheless true that everything having a salvific value is subject to his action. Already in the Old Testament, as Guillet writes,

> From one end of the Old Testament to the other, the Spirit and the Word of God never cease to act together. If the Messiah can observe the Word of the Law given by God to Moses and achieve its justice, it is because He has the Spirit. If the prophet gives testimony to the Word, it is because the Spirit took hold of him. If the Servant is able to bring to the nations the Word of Salvation, it is because the Spirit rests upon Him. If Israel one day is able to keep the Word in

her heart, it will be only in the Spirit. Though inseparable these two powers have nevertheless very distinct characteristics. The Word penetrates from the outside, as a sword lays bare the flesh; the Spirit is fluid and infiltrates imperceptibly. The Word makes itself heard and known; the Spirit remains invisible. The Word is revelation; the Spirit, an interior transformation. The Word stands erect, upright, holding forth; the Spirit falls, spreads itself, submerges. This division of roles and their necessary association are found in the New Testament: the Word of God made flesh through the operation of the Spirit does nothing without the Spirit, and the consummation of His work is the gift of the Spirit.[37]

On our journey toward the Father our own spiritual destiny in Christ necessarily develops, in its turn, in dependence upon the guidance of the Spirit of the Father and of the Son.[38] Thus the unity of God's plan of salvation and sanctification is brought about by the Holy Spirit. The apostle Peter explains it this way in his first epistle:

> The prophets who prophesied of the grace that was to be yours searched and inquired about this salvation; they inquired what person or time was indicated by the Spirit of Christ within them when predicting the suffering of Christ and the subsequent glory. It was revealed to them that they were serving not themselves, but you, in the things which have now been announced to you by those who preached the good news to you through the Holy Spirit sent from heaven, things into which angels long to look.[39]

In the *Exercises* we find an attitude in regard to the Holy Spirit which is similar to that of the Scriptures. Not often is he mentioned directly; the objective remains this Way which must be accepted in the Son who reveals it to us, in order that we may enter with the whole of creation into the glory of the Father (1 Cor. 15:24). But this salvific work and the "exercises" which foster it are accomplished entirely under the indispensable notion of the Spirit; and they demand the constant attention of the director and the retreatant if they are to submit to his divine influence. The difference between the Scriptures and the *Exercises*—and this is the stumbling block for those who oppose Ignatius on this point—is reduced to a matter of language which nuances the matter being expressed but does not truly alter it.

---

37 J. Guillet, s.v. "Spirit of God," in *DBTh*, p. 573. The entire article, pp. 571–576, is of great interest.

38 Ibid., pp. 573–576.

39 I Peter 1:10–12. On the subject of the coincidence of the spiritual life and the life of the Spirit, in God's carrying out of his plan of salvation (the "economy" in Ephes. 1:10 and 3:9), see L. Mendizábal, *Annotationes de Directione spirituali*, pp. 8–34, 89–95, 142.

When we were describing Ignatius' world view in chapter 2, starting with the initial experiences which produced it and the works that expressed it during his lifetime, we saw that he preferred to remain in the presence of the Holy Trinity, whom he addresses most often by the name of the "Divine Majesty." In fact, he designates a divine Person by his proper name only when some evident reason requires it; otherwise—even when there is question of creation, salvation, or sanctification—he prefers to refer to this Divine Majesty, God our Lord, whose action is understood by him to be one and inseparable. When he speaks about God's working out on earth of his plan of salvation gradually evolving in history, Ignatius will specify the role of Jesus Christ, "the eternal Word Incarnate"; otherwise, our salvation is attributed to "God our Lord." Thus he unites the three divine Persons to the same divine task. Similarly in regard to the third Person, whenever there is question of precise and revealed facts attributed to the Holy Spirit, Ignatius expresses this explicitly; for example, speaking of Elizabeth at the time of the Visitation ([263]), of Jesus' baptism ([273]), and again at the time of the apparitions in which the Lord communicates the Spirit ([304, 307]), and of the Ascension, when he tells them to wait for the promised Spirit ([312]). Elsewhere he prefers to speak of God, or of the divine action in us, and to put everything in readiness to enable the retreatant to surrender totally and concretely to Him. There is only one exception to this reserve which is so characteristic in the *Exercises*. It occurs where Ignatius expressly affirms that our life in Christ develops under the action of the Holy Spirit, who is simultaneously both the Spirit of Christ and the Spirit of his Church ([365]). But this reserve in no way alters the reality it expresses according to a vision or concept which finds its unity in the mystery of the God of Majesty, three Persons in one nature.

Carl A. Lofy, in his work on "the action of the Holy Spirit in the *Autobiography* of St. Ignatius," provides another proof of this point. Lofy has very appropriately compared the text of the *Autobiography*, where there is very often question of spiritual fruits attributed to the divine action, with other Ignatian texts—in particular, with three letters of spiritual direction addressed to Teresa Rejadell and Francis Borgia.[40] Here these same spiritual fruits, often designated by the same words, are explicitly attributed to the work of the Holy Spirit. Now these fruits and spiritual feelings are also those of the *Exercises*, which the retreatant insistently asks for and receives by

---

40 The letter to Teresa Rejadell (which goes back to the year 1536 when Ignatius was in Venice) is a document unusually rich in spiritual doctrine, esp. on the art of discernment. It is in *LettersIgn,* pp. 49–55.

disposing himself for the divine action and its motions in the soul.[41] Several other letters of Ignatius also present, on the occasion of different contexts, the Holy Spirit as the author of these gifts and graces: love, consolation, spiritual desires, lights, desires "inflamed and accepted," inspirations, virtue, unction, knowledge.[42] More strictly related to the *Exercises* is the Autograph Directory which, in speaking of the election, clearly and without any ambiguity states that "interior peace, spiritual joy, hope, faith, and love, tears and elevation of the spirit . . . are all gifts of the Holy Spirit *(todos son dones del Espiritu Santo).'*[43] Finally, some of the ancient Directories rightly remind the retreatant of his duty to exercise himself, but to do this without forgetting that the initiative comes from the Holy Spirit, with the fruits which he produces in a generous soul.[44]

We would like to close these few pages on the analysis of the action of grace and of the Holy Spirit in the Exercises by calling attention to the unique point of view which interests us here. These proposals were meant to enlighten us on the significance we attach, in the Ignatian logic of interactions in the Exercises, to subjecting the retreatant's experience to the preeminent guiding factor, God's message and plan of salvation. The divine revelation, on the objective level, guides the retreatant's work on the subjective level. Here we are not talking about a simple logical subordination which would be easily grasped by the intellect. It is a question of an existential subordination which must be part of the experience in its progress, and which particularly characterizes the stage of the Second Week, in which "the retreatant is to

---

41 Lofy has made a complete list of these fruits. The names which he gives them show clearly that these graces and fruits are the same as those treated in the *Exercises:* sorrow for sins, consolation, energy *(esfuerzo)* and strength *(forza),* tears, peace, ease, faith, hope, and charity, inflamed love, attraction for the things above, for eternal things, fervor, light and illuminations, devotion, true joy, spiritual relish, contentment, interior experience, resolutions, good desires, courage, work and suffering in joy, certitude and confirmation, "finding God," perseverance, gifts and graces. See his unpublished dissertation (listed in fn. 67 of ch. 1 above), Vol. II, pp. 7–32; and for exposition of his point of view, read esp. Vol. I, pp. 3–17, 50–64, 77–79.

42 *LettersIgn,* pp. 43, 45, 95, 100, 112, 189, 217–218, 246, 258, 268, 343, 390, 409, 417, 434.

43 *SpEx*MHSJ, p. 780.

44 "The director should take serious care that the exercitant does not urge himself on too much. For, even though he should not be lazy but should exert himself, nevertheless it is the Holy Spirit who has the first role. It belongs to Him to draw one to Himself and to inflame him with the sweet flame of His charity" (*Breve Directorium,* in *SpEx*MHSJ, p. 974). See also ibid., *Directorium Anonymum B3,* pp,. 935–936; *Directorium Granatense,* p. 961; Directory of 1591 and of 1,599, pp. 1077 and 1176.

make a decision under a divine motion" or impulse, and to make that choice through contemplation. To listen to the divine word, to contemplate the plan of salvation accomplished through Christ is, according to the spirit of the *Exercises,* to submit oneself attentively with the whole of one's being, through humble and vigilant prayer, to the very action of the Spirit of Christ who, through these living realities, is united to our own spirit and effects in us the desired work of assimilation and configuration to Christ, to the glory of the Father. Through this experience, in which the human and the divine meet, that labor of readjustment, which is imposed on the exercitant by the absolute demands of the revealed message and God's particular will for us, is elaborated and perfected. That is why the work of election and of readjustment of the Second Week goes infinitely beyond the levels of natural, psychological, and moral activity. It is a divine work of grace in us, to which only the most attentive application of generous and enlightened human effort can correspond.

B. The Ways of Readjustment

We shall now see how Ignatius applies the principles which flow from his dialectical procedures to the complex journey of the Second Week. Although he recommends that we should accommodate ourselves to the rhythm of the retreatant, by shortening or lengthening its duration as the case requires, this cannot be done at the expense of the objective data which flow from the principles we have already studied. Hence, we shall examine more closely the division of the matter of this Week, not to conform ourselves to it blindly, but to observe the proportion suggested by its proper interpretation. Perhaps we shall find some extremely precious indications about the procedure which ought to be followed in the Second Week.

1. The Matter of the Second Week

Ignatius divides the matter of this stage into two well-defined blocks, [101–134] and [135–189]. The second block is composed of two groups of different elements, properly Ignatian and truly evangelical. That is why we choose to call them here "three time-periods," even though the last two are concerned with one same stage of the retreatant's development. For a Week of twelve days, such as Ignatius proposes it, let us notice the time he reserves for each of these diverse stages and let us look briefly at the content of each one.

The first time-period, ([101–134]), is devoted exclusively to the contemplation of the mysteries of Christ's infancy and hidden life. This stage lasts for three days, with two mysteries being contemplated each day.

The second time-period ([136–157, and 164–168]) is one of introduction to the election. It lasts only one day and, at first glance, it embraces an imposing amount of matter: The Two Standards, The Three Classes of Men, The Three Kinds of Humility, The Introduction to "the Matters about Which an Election Should Be Made." Further on we shall justify this grouping of the matter for the fourth day as we propose it here: ([135–157]) and ([164–168]).

The third time-period ([158–163 and 169–189]) takes up contemplation again, and focuses it on the public life of Christ. It also includes the concurrently progressing work properly so-called of the election ([158–163 and 169–189]). This time-period covers the last eight days, on which, moreover, Ignatius proposes only one Gospel mystery a day for contemplation.

Thus in the Second Week we have the following distribution of the subject matter of the twelve days twelve days:

Three (days 1,2,3,) are devoted to the mysteries of the hidden life, one (day 4) to the introduction to the election, and eight (days 5–12) to the public life and the election itself.

Of these twelve days, eleven are devoted chiefly or largely to the contemplation of Gospel scenes:[45]

Fourteen mysteries are proposed by Ignatius. Of these, six, in three days, bear on the hidden life, and eight, in eight days, on the public life (the ministry of Christ). The stages, as is evident, are variable: three, one, and eight days.

The rhythm or pace itself is more or less intensive. There are two mysteries a day at the beginning, and after that only one, but between these two stages there is this fourth day ([136–157]) crammed with all the Ignatian meditations! The division of the matter according to Ignatius is clearly determined and seems to follow laws other than those of chance. We have only to remember the First Week, in which he was satisfied to propose five exercises

45 As Iparraguirre states (*História de los Ejercicios de S. Ignacio*, II, 322), Miró's "cry of alarm" against the "tendency to adapt the *Exercises* too freely" is quite understandable. He was protesting against J. Blondo's proposal to add, during the Second Week, some considerations on the virtues and on the rules. Miró, who had known Ignatius personally from 1550 on, recalls that Ignatius insisted that one should be satisfied with contemplating the mysteries of Christ, from which all profit comes. An ardent defender of the Ignatian points of view, Miró has left us some beautiful reflections on the subject of the contemplation of the Gospels in his "Defense of the Exercises" (*SpEx*MHSJ, pp. 684–698, esp. pp. 696–697, no. 22).

on sin without indications as to how long they were to last, except for "the time required" to obtain the desired fruits ([4]).

Consequently, we shall study these three time-periods in order to see what characterizes the organization of the Second Week according to Ignatius. Even though it is quite permissible for us to choose other mysteries, to shorten or lengthen this stage, the Ignatian distribution of the matter remains for us a valuable indication which can direct our own work.

2. The First Time-Period:
Contemplations on The Hidden Life ([101–134])

The first stage lasts for three days and considers six mysteries spread over fifteen prayer periods. The organization of the work is simplified: Everything is reduced to contemplation without any other concern—which will not be the case in the two following time-periods. Each day the retreatant first contemplates two mysteries, each of which is related to the other (Incarnation and Nativity; Presentation in the Temple and Flight into Egypt; Jesus at Nazareth and at Jerusalem); then these two mysteries taken together are twice repeated in "the repetitions" as in ([118–120]); and finally, the day ends with an application of the senses ([121]) on this same matter.[46] It is clear that Ignatius wants to keep his retreatant in the presence of the eternal Word Incarnate for three days ([130]), to plunge him or her into this mystery so that he or she may in no way be distracted. Before listening to the "official" call, which will come from the Lord himself preaching to the crowds and to the disciples and expressing his "demands," one should take up again the attitude of the first response of the Kingdom and gaze on or contemplate at length what is characteristic of the mystery of the Word Incarnate: mystery of the eternal God, despoiled and given over to the poverty of our human condition from the crib to the cross ([116]), in order to save us. Ignatius asks the retreatant "to call to mind frequently the mysteries of the life of Christ our Lord from the Incarnation to the place or mystery I am contemplating" ([130]).[47]

---

46 The importance of the repetitions, which prolong one's contact with the Lord through the mystery in which he manifests himself, is well known; they allow grace to do its work. Within the day, the Ignatian method follows a curve which proceeds from the first contemplation through repetitions to the more intuitive and passive application of the senses. See *Exercices,* trans. Courel, [76], note 1. We especially recommend the article of J. Maréchal (listed above in fn. 72 of ch. 3), which shows the value of the application of the senses; also Iparraguirre's note 88 on *SpEx,* [121], in *Obras completas,* 4th ed. (1982), p. 236.

47 To be more convinced that this is the Ignatian way of considering the mystery of the Incarnation, in addition to the rather clear directions contained in the *Exer-*

Matthew and Luke wrote their infancy narratives to show that in Jesus the promised salvation is accomplished in the history of the People of God and in the history of humanity.[48] We who wish to welcome Christ coming to fulfill his mission, his Kingdom, shall easily be able to find the signs of this mystery in the scenes of the two Gospels written for this precise purpose. To the extent that we go back with Matthew and Luke to the prophesies which have been evoked and fulfilled through the literary form they have chosen— whether it be Daniel, Malachi, Isaiah, Joel, Zephaniah, or even the history of Moses—we shall receive this light which makes the mystery take on new splendor, by means of the subtle reference points which the evangelists wished to retain in the historical life of Jesus.[49]

However, the "Introduction to the Consideration of Different States of Life" ([135]), which introduces us to the following stage, tells us in what sense Ignatius presented these last two mysteries of the first time-period: the life of Jesus at Nazareth and the visit to the Temple when he was twelve years of age. It will be worthwhile for us, in our turn, to pause here for a moment; for it seems that in the Ignatian perspective this last day of contemplation on the hidden life has a particular intention or significance.[50] The first two days kept us face to face with the mystery of the Incarnation in all its depth, and this reveals to us the real sense of Christ's mission among us: God made

cises themselves, we might cite several texts where the reference to the "Creator and Lord who has chosen to be poor and to become the Son of the Virgin" is often repeated: e.g., *Cons.* [79]; *Examen*, [4, 11]; *LettersIgn*, pp. 19, 31–32, 44. All this can be reduced to the thought of St. Paul in 2 Cor. 8:9. On the theology of the Incarnation, see K. Rahner, *Theological Investigations*, I, pp. 163–168; on the definition of Chalcedon, pp. 174–179; 189–192; on the theology of the Incarnation, IV, pp. 105–120; on dogmatic and biblical theology, V, 95–97; on the necessity and also the limitations of traditional Christology, XVII, 24–38.

48 A very good introduction to the mysteries of the Infancy of our Lord according to St. Luke, is R. Laurentin, *Structure et théologie de Luc I–II* (Paris, 1957); [also, F. Prat, *Jesus Christ: His Life, His Teaching, and His Work*, trans J. Heenan (Milwaukee, 1950), ch. 3. Ed.].

49 Even the importance attributed to Mary in Luke's Gospel serves our plan of contemplation on the Kingdom, just as it serves Luke's plan through the midrashic genre. As R. Laurentin shows, Mary makes real the presence of the Daughter of Zion to God's mystery or plan of salvation which is being accomplished in her. She is there called upon to fear not, to rejoice, and to receive the one who is bringing salvation. This too is the immediate topic of the People of God and of our own participation, which is here at issue and is offered to our contemplation throughout God's whole revelation (see R. Laurentin, *Structure de Luc I–II*, ch. VI, pp. 148–161).

50 Note that this is one of the rare places where Ignatius suggests so positive an interpretation of a mystery.

man, born of the Virgin, amid the poverty and indifference of our world; his cultic offering to the Father at the presentation in the Temple, where we find ourselves present at the fulfillment and consecration of the divine promises; then the mystery of division, of persecution, linked to the mystery of glory and adoration when Christ offers himself for the salvation of all mankind. The whole drama of salvation is evoked and its realization is presented amid a scene of humility and despoliation.

But next the life of our Lord will unfold in an obscurity which effaces the very traces of glory and persecution which we saw in its first manifestation. It is the life of man which the Son of God is going to live day after day, like ourselves; and through this he will render to his Father the homage which will save us.[51] Ignatius saw Nazareth as the sign and the reality of filial obedience which the life of every creature ought to reproduce in its turn—the fundamental submission which is part and parcel of our being as creatures. For in the mind of Ignatius, to obey is essentially to love, to respect, to accept God's will through all the ways in which it is communicated. To obey is to adore by means of one's life. Thus it is the opposite of sin, the sin of the angels, of Adam, and of all persons condemned because "they did not want to make use of the freedom God gave them to reverence and obey their Creator and Lord, and so falling into pride, were changed from grace to hatred of God, and cast out of heaven into hell" ([50]). At Nazareth, that is, in the humble prolonged life of the Incarnate Word, in his slowly developing human life—where human becoming and time do not attempt to encroach upon eternity—the Lord lived in obedience ([135]), lived simply in our human condition. That is how his incarnation was offered to the Father in the perfect homage of the gift of self—a homage which no one before Jesus could offer as an adequate response to the eternal and perfect fidelity of God.[52] Christ saves us, first of all, by the perfect human fidelity which he integrates into his continual offering to his Father. As the worshiper beyond compare *(cultor excellens)*, he is the opposite extreme of the first Adam, the father of infidelity. That is all that Christ had to do to save us; but he did it during a

---

51 On "Christ and every day life," read the beautiful pages of G. Salet, *Trouver le Christ*, pp. 9–31; also "Jésus à Nazareth" of Péguy in his *Mystère de la charité*, pp. 107–111: "For he had worked as a carpenter, in his trade"; [also, Prat, *Jesus Christ: His Life*, ch. 3. Ed.].

52 On the perfect homage *(obsequium)* of Christ to the Father, through the obedience of the Son, see J. Guillet, *Jesus Christ Yesterday and Today,* , pp. 93, 102–103, 106, 108, 226–229; also H. U. von Balthasar, *Théologie de l'Histoire*, pp. 32–34, 48–50, 61–62; E. H. Schillebeeckx, *Christ, the Sacrament of the Encounter with God* (New York, 1963; Dutch original, 1957), ch. 1, esp. pp. 29–32, where Christ is presented as the "supreme worship rendered to the Father."

lifetime of about thirty years. At the end of so great a love, the Spirit of God will demand of this perfect fidelity "the greatest proof of love," the sacrifice which will "consummate" the work of salvation. "Being obedient unto death, even death on a cross." The life of Jesus, that of these long years of Nazareth, invites us humbly to unite our whole being to this "mission of the eternal King," which is lived first of all through the perfect homage of the gift of self, in union with Christ, to the divine glory.

The mystery of Jesus in the Temple, at the age of twelve, comes in to interrupt this long meditation. It reveals its deep meaning and opens the way to his offering of "himself exclusively to the service of his eternal Father," as Ignatius states in ([135]). This mystery interrupts the continuity of this theme. It allows us for a moment to see the term of this fidelity which is an expression of love and of gift. From Luke's point of view, this scene with its three days of anguish for Joseph and Mary at the time of the Passover and in Jerusalem, prefigures the Passion which will crown this homage of a God to God.[53] To contemplate these mysteries, to unite oneself with Christ in them, is to enter, more than through any meditation on particular virtues, into the way proposed by the Second Week in its relationship with the Kingdom. It is the way which demands the most exacting purification of one who would follow Christ. The purified heart will then be able to receive with a humble, respectful, and confident love, the word which is presented as "a two-edged sword" and which will resound throughout human history, on the occasion of this public life which continues even to our own day.

Ignatius, therefore, sees in these two mysteries of the last day the possibility of a call to a greater perfection. This call is necessarily there; God never proposes a lesser perfection: "Be perfect as your heavenly Father is perfect" (Matt. 5:48). Ignatius knows this. He has been implying it since the last part of the contemplation on the Kingdom. He will repeat it cryptically right up to the consideration on the Three Kinds of Humility. Indeed, it is a call to "evangelical perfection," as he states ([135]), but understood in a much richer sense than is often thought. It is somewhat like the case of the rich young man in the Gospel. For the Christian the call to evangelical perfection culminates in union with the Christ of the Passion; and this mystery is sketched in "the pure service" of which one catches a glimpse here. In the same [135], where he alludes to this mystery, Ignatius states expressly that

---

53 On this mystery of Jesus in the Temple, see R. Laurentin, *Structure de Luc I-II*, pp. 106, 111–112, 142–146, 168. The same meaning is given to this mystery (put in a relationship with the Passion) by F. X. Durrwell, "La transfiguration de Jésus," *VS*, 85 (1951), 122–123.

the purpose, which goes beyond the choice of a state of life, is ultimately "to prepare ourselves to arrive at perfection in whatever state or way of life God our Lord may grant us to choose." Because he has not clearly distinguished, in his choice of vocabulary, between the search for God's will concerning one's state of life and the perfection of the life embraced, Ignatius has exposed himself to minimizing interpretations. If we keep clearly in mind what he is aiming at, in the procedure of the *Exercises* (see chapter 3 above) and in every person he addresses, the confusion will soon disappear. What truly counts for Ignatius is that the exercitant should come to know the Lord interiorly and well, in order to be more completely with him, and for him, and unto him, along with all things on the face of the earth and for the glorification of the Father (Rom. 11:36). To reach this level, sacrifices will be necessary, and these sacrifices are not optional. It is for this that the Lord, our companion, is preparing us and is calling us."[54]

3. The Second Time-Period: The Ignatian Meditations ([135–157 and 164–168])

a. A Problem of Structure

For an understanding of the structure of the Second Week, three sections the *Exercises* are very important: ([135, 163, and 164]). The first, the introduction to the consideration of states of life, effects the passage from the first to the second time-period of this Week, by specifying the purpose of the fourth day. Indeed, right from the start Ignatius there establishes a relationship with the mysteries which were contemplated on the preceding third day, a relationship that throws some light on their interpretation. He then goes on to declare that the retreatant will now follow twofold or concurrent paths. "While continuing to contemplate His life," the retreatant must seek to know God's will concerning his or her state of life, if there is place for that, and ultimately concerning, in any case, his or her "service of the Divine Majesty." In this way Ignatius presents the parallel procedures of the last stage (the third time-period), in which the election-readjustment will be worked out in the light of the mystery being contemplated and under the action of the Spirit.

---

54 It seems preferable, in some cases, to substitute for the expression "evangelical perfection" some other phrase, such as "Christian vocation to holiness," "spiritual growth," "self-fulfillment," "sanctification," or "spiritual development," all of which terms cover the same reality. On the subject of the Ignatian application to the mystery in question, see G. Fessard, *La dialectique*, p. 63.

Nevertheless, before this task is taken up, Ignatius places the retreatant in an intermediate time period. "As some introduction to this" he proposes the very Ignatian matter of the Fourth Day which makes precise the general perspective in which we ought to situate the mysteries of Christ's life, the work of salvation and of our own spiritual commitment, the election. This is the way in which he announces the subject matter of the two following meditations, the Two Standards and the Three Classes of men. The intention is clear: to dispose ourselves better and explicitly to seek the perfection which the Lord expects of us, "in whatever state or way of life God our Lord may grant us to choose." That is why we have divided the entire stage of the Second Week into three time-periods: the hidden life (first three days), introduction to the election (fourth day), and the public life along with the election (last eight days).

However, things become complicated anew when Ignatius announces ([163]) a second introduction to the election; and he does not seem to leave this to one's choice. If the beginning of the election is well determined by Ignatius, the second introduction will be so too. For in [163] he writes: "The treatment of the matter dealing with the Choice of a Way of Life will begin" with the first contemplation of the public life which includes "our Lord's departure from Nazareth for the Jordan." Thus right from the start this new procedure is moving on parallel paths, one of considerations disposing us for a sound election, the other of contemplations of mysteries of the life of Christ. If the introduction already proposed ([135]) for the second time-period (that is, for the fourth day in [135]) had been sufficient, there would have been no problem. But this [163], which asks the retreatant to take the matter of the election in hand, adds: "as is explained later." These explanations are found in the method of election elaborated throughout [164–189]. At the beginning of them is this one in [164]: "Before entering upon the Choice of a Way of Life, in order that we may be filled with the love of the true doctrine of Christ our Lord, it will be very useful to consider attentively the following Three Kinds of Humility" ([165–168]). This, therefore, is the problem: From the fifth day on we follow the twofold paths of the election and of the public life; but the election itself demands a new introduction, in addition to that of the fourth day, an introduction which "considers" the Kinds of Humility. According to Ignatius' explanations, precisely where should we situate this work of the second introduction to the election itself?

The problem is not solved simply by distinguishing between the two expressions used: "to treat the matter cf the election" as if it were in one case a question of the complete election and in the other of its object alone. The question is not that of beginning to consider, on the fifth day, that about which one will make an election when the time comes (which time ought then to be preceded by a new introduction: the Kinds of Humility), as if the matter of the election meant nothing more than the objects with which it is concerned. If a certain ambiguity has slipped in here in the French translation, this ambiguity does not exist in the Spanish. Courel, in his translation into French, uses the term "matter of the election" *(matière de l'élection)* in [163], and "the matters of the election" *(les matières de l'élection)* in [170], where the objects of the election are certainly in question. Then it is easy to be caught in a play on French synonyms and to say, as Courel himself adds in a note: "starting with the fifth day ([158, 163]) the retreatant envisages the matter of the election, that is to say, the object of the choice."[55] But where the French uses the same word "matter" *(matière),* the Spanish Autograph uses the different words: first, "the matter dealing with the elections will begin" *(la materia de las elecciones se comenzará)* in [163], and in [170] "to get knowledge as to what matters an election ought to be made about" *(para tomar noticia de que cosas)* and "all things about which we want to make an election" *(todas cosas, de las cuales queremos hacer elección).* Therefore it distinguishes between the matter or topic of the election and the things about which the election should be made. This word "matter" *(materia)* is applied in two other places to the election, and in them it is not used to signify the object about which the election turns, but the sum total of data or matters pertaining to the topic of the election. One begins to examine the matter of the election as one begins the treatment of any subject.[56] There is question, therefore, of beginning the work of the election, onward after the morning exercise of the fifth day.

The second introduction is, in Ignatius' tenor of thought, something added to the first, and it fits perfectly into his plan, as we shall see. The progression of the three Ignatian texts—the Two Standards, the Three Classes, the Three Kinds of Humility—has often been emphasized. Nevertheless, it would be difficult to combine these two introductions into one. The introduction to the fourth day already contains five exercises determined by Ignatius ([148–149]). Furthermore, we should not delay entrance into the contemplations on the public life which ought to accompany the entry into

---

55 See *Exercices,* trans. Courel, p. 91, note 1.

56 Furthermore, in both cases Courel's translation is a more exact interpretation when he writes in [18], "not to go into questions—*en materias*—of the election" (ne pas s'engager dans *les questions (en materias)* "de l'élection," and in [338], "to consider four things of which there was a question partly in regard to the *object*—*en la materia*—of the election" (de considérer quatre choses dont il a été question en partie au *sujet [en la materia]* de l'élection).

"the matter [or topic] of the election." That confirms our point of view: The parallel paths of the election and of the contemplations coincide exactly, and they are interrelated in a real way. The message is proclaimed and received—just as was the case when it was first proclaimed by the evangelists—to foster a greater adherence to Christ, and greater likeness to him among those who received it.

Hence, right from the start of this new time-period, the morning of the fifth day, the work of the election should be taken up, by means of the consideration on the Kinds of Humility, with concurrent dependence on the contemplations. In particular, this consideration on humility should not constitute an isolated exercise. The director ought to explain this in his meeting with the retreatant, and to ask him or her "to consider attentively the following Three Kinds of Humility. These should be thought over from time to time during the whole day" ([164]). The retreatant should also make the colloquies that will be indicated further on, (namely in [168]).[57] It is important to help the retreatant see this perspective which highlights the necessary fundamental attitudes; and also to invite him to return, of his own volition, during these following days when the tasks of contemplation and election will be proceeding side by side, to reflection on this "true doctrine of Christ our Lord" in order to become "more filled with love of" it ([164]).

Ignatius sets no prescribed time to be devoted to this consideration. The same will be true for the election which evolves in dependence on contemplation and the divine action. That is why we think Casanovas' remark is correct when he speaks about the division of the mysteries in the Second Week: "During the second part of the Week (that is, starting with the fifth day), only one mystery is taken as the subject for prayer, whereas during the first part of the Week two mysteries ware used each day. The reason for this difference might be the following. In this second part of the Week the retreatant is involved in the question of the election. That is why the saint wishes the retreatant to take some time for the election and, in a special way, for the

---

57 On this subject keep in mind the directives of the Directories, starting with Polanco, namely that the kinds of humility are given on the fifth day after the first contemplation (Nazareth-Jordan), which takes place normally "at dawn"; thus the retreatant has the entire day to come back to it "from time to time." See *SpEx*MHSJ, Directory of Polanco, p. 816 (no. 77); Directory of Miró, pp. 870 and 872; *Directorium Granatense*, p. 966; Directories of 1591 and of 1599, pp. 1064 and 1163. We should remember especially that in no way should this consideration encroach on the time set aside for prayer (contemplation) properly so called.

three Kinds of Humility."[58] Having carefully fixed this point of departure which will direct the last part of the Second Week, Ignatius will ask only one thing: to contemplate day after day. During these days at the moment willed by God, the work will go on: to begin, while contemplating the life of Christ, to seek and beg where and in what manner the Divine Majesty wishes us to serve him ([135]).

In order to determine more clearly the characteristics of this immediate preparation for the last time-period, "public life concurrently with election," we shall group together here our reflections on the exercises of the fourth day and on the introduction to the election through the Three Kinds of Humility. We shall reserve for the last stage the election properly so called and the parallel contemplations.

b. The Two Standards

On the occasion of the first exercise of this series, Ignatius infers in advance and expressly states what the next contemplations will permit us not only to see and contemplate as spectators, but what they will permit us to assimilate through prayer. It is in this unique drama, intimate and universal, which is played from the hidden life onward in the eyes of the world and through the ages, that we take our place as disciples of Christ. It is the drama of two lineages which is found at the beginning of the history of sin, and also of the consequent division which God himself, in some way, maintains in the heart of a person in order to keep him or her aware of it and to protect him against a false peace which lulls him to sleep and brings him to hell. "I will put enmity between you and the woman, and between your seed and her seed."[59] Christ says in a similar vein: "I have not come to bring peace, but a sword."[60] "Henceforth in one house there will be five divided, three against two and two against three; they will be divided, father against son and son against father."[61] This profound division symbolizes the division of all existence itself. From Cain and Abel, Chanaan and his brothers, Ishmael and Isaac, Esau and Jacob, Joseph and his brothers, Edom and Israel, the drama of "brothers at enmity with one another" is presented on the stage of sacred

---

58 I. Casanovas, *Ejercicios de S. Ignacio,* I, 254. We should note that in the Third and Fourth Weeks the retreatant will contemplate two subjects each day. See [190, 204, 208].
59 Gen 3:15.
60 Matt. 10:34.
61 Luke 12:53.

history in order to help us understand better that in man's heart two kingdoms confront each other and that man is invited by God to choose "at the risk of losing his life."[62] "No one can serve two masters; for either he will hate the one and love the other, or he will be devoted to the one and despise the other. You cannot serve God and mammon."[63] In our desire for tolerance we would like to conciliate these two exacting masters. But this is where we fool ourselves and hold on to the secret desires which bind us to ourselves. The service in question here involves the whole of man and his destiny. No compromise is possible between these two masters and these two worlds, each of which demand man's whole self. This state of affairs is not of our own doing. Who would even think of choosing between life and death? Two irreconcilable worlds contend for the destiny of men and women and the motions of their hearts. "For I do not do the good I want, but the evil I do not want is what I do."[64] Such is the reality, in line with the gospel and the most authentic Christianity, which Ignatius envisages with all the audacity and confidence of one who has placed his entire faith in Jesus the Savior: "For I know whom I have believed."[65]

In the Two Standards ([136–148]) Ignatius presents us with a meditation which is entirely spiritual and compelling. Anyone who would see in it only the opposition of two camps contending for the forces of the world, together

62 On these two "lineages" which are a way of death and a way of life, a way of hate and violence and a way of pardon and peace, one can find in the biblical genealogies of Genesis and of 1 Chronicles many details which will allow one to illustrate and deepen the theme of enmity. In particular, see the symbolism of the personage-types of these lineages: Cain, Abel and Seth, the two Enochs, the two Lamechs.

63 Matt. 6:24.

64 Rom. 7:19. See also Rom. 7:14–25 and Gal. 5:17. On the theme of the fleshly being and the spiritual being, see 1 Cor 2:14–3:11; 15:44, and note *a* of the Jerusalem Bible. On the dangers of riches and the deceits of Satan linked with them: the Beatitudes, the episode of the rich young man and the poor Lazarus, and also Hab. 2:5; James, 1:9–11; 2:5–9; 4:4–10. The theme of the two ways or two cities, announced already in Ps. 1 and Phil. 3:18–21, has been developed often in spiritual literature: e.g., in the beginning by the *Didache* (the two ways), ch. 1, 1; 3, 7; 6, 1, and later by St. Augustine (the two cities as ways of living) in *The City of God,* especially Book XIV. Finally, an article by L. Teixidor examines the subject as treated by St. Ignatius by comparing it to the prior developments of Scripture, St. Augustine, and St. Thomas. See "El desorden de mis operaciones," *Mnr,* 4 (1928), 97–119. On this law of division within us, read Fessard, *La dialectique,* pp. 54–56; R. Guardini, La figura di Gesú Cristo del Nuovo Testamento. p. 76; L. Lallemant, *The Spiritual Doctrine (1946),* pp. 114, 128; A. Frank-Duquesne, *Cosmos et Gloire,* pp. 35–38; J. de Vaux, s.v. "Good and Evil," *DBTh,* pp. 213–215.

65 2 Tim. 1:12.

with an exposition of their programs, not only stops at appearances, but contradicts the intentions of the author. This meditation should be closely connected with the contemplation on the Kingdom. Furthermore, Ignatius drew it too from his mystical experience at Manresa. It takes up again the idea of "universal conquest," but, as in the case of the oblation of the Kingdom and with the same clairvoyance, it goes directly to the heart of man and begins the process of purification, humility, and union with Christ the Savior.[66]

Ignatius first denounces the ruses of Satan, "the deadly enemy of our human nature" ([136–142]).[67] In the exposition of his stratagems we find the very basis for the Satanic action in the world. This action is bound to man's instinct for possession and in his hunger to be, which he tends most often to satisfy by possessing. "The love of money," writes St. Paul, "is the root of all evils."[68] Matthew uses one word to designate both the kingdom and the master that in us are opposed to God, money, "mammon."[69] On the other hand, the entire experience of the First Week culminates in the most evangelical imperative—that of the absolute spiritual poverty of our condition—emphasized so forcefully by the contemplations on the mystery of the kenosis in the Incarnation—and this makes us aware of the poverty of our being before preaching to us poverty of possessions.[70] Hence Ignatius will speak of the coveting of riches ([142]). Cupidity, the instinct to possess, power and ambition, money, lust for riches: so many words which express the first trick of Satan, "the root of all evils" in the world and in us. By nature man is poor, through the contingency of his being which is experienced at all levels of his existence. Occasionally struck by a sentiment of this real poverty as a threat to his being, man has the "existential" impression of getting lost, an impression of breaking up, of sinking. He avidly (and often unconsciously) attaches

---

66 See M. A. Fiorito, "La opción personal de San Ignacio," *CyF,* 12 (1956), 27–40.

67 See the biblical meaning of this expression according to S. Lyonnet, in "La méditation des deux Etendards et son fondement scripturaire," *Chr,* no. 12 (1956), pp. 435–456. Linked to the meaning Ignatius gave to sin, this expression is found, not only in the *Exercises,* but also in *LettersIgn,* pp. 17, 19, 51, 56–57, 162, 184.

68 1 Tim. 6:10. On this subject see C. Bernard, *De theologia orationis christianae* (Rome), 1963–64, pp. 65–66.

69 Matt. 6:24.

70 This is the first poverty, which makes us tend toward the second, through a spontaneous spiritual desire which is measured by the divine will alone, either through a direct invitation to effective poverty or through the circumstances of life which impose it.

himself to "the goods" he encounters. He rises to being and to life in an artificial manner, starting with those "tangible goods" which give him the impression of permanence. In the background of every movement which does not aim at the gift of self—"to love one's life"—is an instinct, one might say a mechanism,[71] which is exploited by the spirit of evil: to bind man and his existence to any good whatsoever, one's good name, activity, body, strength, beauty, talents, achievements, art, ideas, friendships, or even one's integral observance of the law.[72] These are "one's riches." Such is the drama lived out by individuals and societies, by all the men and women who seek their own exaltation by some "disordered use" of creation. And this exaltation, both in their own eyes and in those of others,[73] is what Ignatius calls "the empty honors of this world" ([142]): honors which are vain and worthless and which easily attach themselves to anything other than what one truly is, or which identify with one's person any good which gives a basis for one's pretensions to the esteem and recognition of others. Whence follows, Ignatius concludes, "overweening pride" ([142]). Starting from a good which confers a "false value" one—through an unwarranted identification—the man or woman devotes himself to his or her own cause (self-seeking), chooses his own views (self-sufficiency) and prefers himself to everything else. If he does not prefer himself to God directly, he does so at least with regard to his laws and demands, on the ground that they are opposed to his point of view or are not in agreement with the unique character of his condition. Then one has become one's own norm; he or she eats "the food of the gods."[74]

Empty honors—we said—which attach themselves to anything other than what I myself really am! Perhaps we bring ourselves to believe there is an ordered honor which can be drawn from this modest personal substratum, the "what I myself am." But ontologically we are poverty, dependence. All we have, we hold it as coming from God, constantly, through pure gratuitousness: "What have you that you did not receive? If then you received it, why

71 Perhaps this is simply the instinct for self-preservation, but disordered, turned away from its true function, under the effect of sin. It is the reign of concupiscence!
72 On the seeking for "consideration" even through the world of religion, read the reflections of Lallemant, *The Spiritual Doctrine* (1946), pp. 134–135, and Teresa of Avila in her autobiography (see *Collected Works*, I, pp. 211–212). Think esp., too, of the case of the Pharisees, "doctors of the law," in the Gospels.
73 "Others": They can be either society, one's immediate friends and circumstances, or one person to whom one is very close.
74 It suffices that this happens in regard to one point alone through which one's whole being loses the divine favor, "the state of grace."

do you boast as if it were not a gift?"[75] Should anyone admire in us a "talent" of any sort (strength, beauty, art, ideas, priesthood, or the like), that person would be quite right, for all these realities proclaim God's praise.[76] But to give greater value to the creature as such, detached from the divine gift which it mirrors forth by its creaturehood, that is an attempt to turn creation from its movement toward God. "Why do you call me good?" Jesus asks the rich young man in Luke's Gospel. "No one is good but God alone."[77] Everything good in us comes from God; we should acknowledge this and honor God. Hence, Ignatius writes, "In a similar way, we are to picture to ourselves the sovereign and true Commander, Christ our Lord" ([143]). He exhorts "all men" by helping them to find "that supreme spiritual poverty" which is recognition and acceptance of one's own finiteness, of one's contingency and limitations.[78] From this recognition, through putting aside every "empty honor of the world," he leads one on to the desire "for insults and contempt" ([146]), as an inverse form of this Satanic desire to be considered someone of great worth. This spiritual desire even envisages the fact of being despised, provided God's interests are not impaired (discreet charity, [147]). From this "highest spiritual poverty" and the desire for an effective renunciation of the world's honors will result, says Ignatius, "the humility" which leads "to all other virtues" ([146]). It is a question here of true humility, that fundamental attitude based on self-knowledge and self-acceptance, which situates man in his true place in the order of creation, opens him up to God's gratuitous gifts whose benevolent Source he honors, disposes him to follow the divine will, submits him to the movement of the divine Spirit, and conforms his life to that of Christ for the glory of the Father. Humility is poverty, renunciation, acceptance of and total openness to God.

This Ignatian meditation ought not to be reduced to an analysis of the two systems that are opposed to each other, with an evaluation of their forces and tactics. It is a profoundly existential meditation which engages our responsibility by revealing to us the present character of that sundered situation in which our spiritual destinies must be played out.[79] The third prelude has us

---

75 1 Cor 4:7. See the third sermon of St. Bernard on the "Song of Songs" in *Oeuvres mystiques* (ed. du Seuil), pp. 182–185.

76 Nothing in one's being ought to be withdrawn from this participation in the universal harmony which proclaims God, from the very vital forces of one's sexual life to the highest aspirations of the human spirit.

77 Luke 18:19.

78 On detachment considered in this perspective, see John of the Cross, *Collected Works*, pp. 96–99, 112–113, 617–634.

79 On conceiving awareness of this dramatic and traumatic situation, read S. Stehman, *Le voyage à l'ancre*, p. 98.

ask for "knowledge" and help to avoid "the deceits of the rebel chief" and graces "to imitate" the life of the "sovereign and true Commander" of our lives ([139]). It is a grace of light and strength sought through the prayerful consideration of this mystery; it invites us to insight into the movement of the opposing forces which are at work within us, and also to a complete commitment of ourselves to the powers of the One who alone can conquer in us and for us. Here Ignatius asks us to envisage an unrestricted challenge to our whole lives, beyond their particular desires and choices. He asks us to look at the only two choices we really have: to offer ourselves to the Light who saves us from ourselves, or to abandon ourselves to the powers of that Darkness who veils and deceives.[80] For of these two masters, one flatters the tastes of nature (cupidity, exaltation of self, and pride); the other sacrifices them to a greater love in imitation of Christ who leads one to completely unrestricted interior despoliations.[81] No one but the person himself or herself can make this choice. In 1536 Ignatius wrote to Teresa Rejadell:

> I am not going to save myself by the good works of the good angels, and I am not going to be condemned because of the evil thoughts and the weaknesses which the bad angels, the flesh, and the world bring before my mind. God asks only one thing of me, that my soul seek to be conformed with his Divine Majesty. And the soul so conformed makes the body conformed, whether it wish it or not, to the divine will. In this is our greatest battle, and there the good pleasure of the eternal and sovereign Goodness.[82]

Ignatius attached much importance to this consideration: "This exercise will be made at midnight and again in the morning. There will be two repetitions of the same exercise, one about the time of Mass and the other about the time of Vespers. The same three colloquies, with our Lady, with her Son, and with the Father, will close all these exercises" ([148]).

c. The Three Classes of Men

When those who are familiar with the *Exercises* hear the title "Three Classes," they immediately think of that psychological attitude described by Ignatius, which goes from simple and ineffective velleity, through a sincere but weak attitude prone to compromise, to a firm decision of commitment.

---

80 See John 3:19–21 and 1 John 1:5–7.
81 "But keeping the commandments is usually a tragic business for the Christian. It is an obligation laid upon a being who is sinful and divided, and it brings war and sword. . . . Every Christian experience involves an absolutely clear awareness of the fact of sin" (J. Mouroux, *The Christian Experience*, pp. 352–354).
82 *LettersIgn*, p. 25.

But is this all that Ignatius had in mind in providing the retreatant with this meditation, in which willfulness and generosity are somewhat mingled together? Let us examine the matter a little more closely before treating the meditation on Three Classes of Men ([149–157]).

From the very beginning of the Exercises, we have been observing at a curious upward movement, a movement which is focused on the theme of imitation of and attachment to Christ, and aims to bring these attitudes into practice.But at each transitional step of this ascent there is also a fall, more or less frightening, a downward movement toward the renunciation which lies beneath the problem of union and identification with Christ. During the First Week, at the same time when the retreatant is perceiving that God is delivering him or her from evil by showing him the face of his mercy in Christ, he also realizes that he must withdraw from evil in order to be with God ([63]), and so he desires "exercises" which will guide him on the way. In the meditation on the Kingdom our attention is at first brought to bear on the winning call of the Lord to share in his universal mission of salvation, but it is in regard to following Christ that the offering commits the disciple to the demanding paths of imitation ([98]). The contemplation of the infancy and the hidden life of Jesus places the retreatant in the presence of the Christ of majesty, the "eternal Word Incarnate" ([130]); but his coming among us reveals, nevertheless, the mystery of the greatest possible self-despoliation there is—precisely there where the human and the divine unite in the most perfect act of humility. There we see that already the shadow of the cross dominates this life of oblation, service, and love.

In other words, from the very beginning, the experience of purification which opens the way to love, and also the contemplation of the Kingdom and the Gospel mysteries, have filled the heart of the retreatant with the desire to imitate Christ, and to be associated with Him with his or her whole being, for the grand work of saving the world, unto the glorification of God. But the relationship to the human substratum of this experience, in which availability is gradually identified with the acceptance of despoliation of self, has been maintained throughout, but discreetly up to the present. A profound need for purification, a source of availability, always precedes the reality of an authentic communion.

On the day before the retreatant begins to travel this twofold path of contemplation-election during which, under the influence of the Word and the Spirit, he or she will desire to accept God's will, Ignatius reverses the perspective of his considerations. The movement of ascent is brusquely interrupted and the retreatant's attention is focused on this fundamental necessity of self-despoliation which is entailed by the authentic imitation of Christ and the sharing of his life. Four times during this day he would have the retreatant contemplate its reality, in the way in which he presents it in the Two Standards without any disguise. To our desire for riches and our natural attachment to the things of this world which become "values" for us and tie us to ourselves, Christ opposes the highest spiritual poverty and the desire for humiliations which hand us over to the Lord.[83] To the soul who yearns for Christ, Ignatius presents the fullness of the mystery of Christ. The meditation of this day brings to light a frightening law of the Gospel: "If your eye causes you to sin, pluck it out and throw it away."[84] Thus the deepening of our sincere spiritual desire, the fruit of grace, inevitably encounters the contrary reluctance of our sensitivity which gives in to the inclinations of nature. Satan deceives us by the desire for riches, by the search for empty honor and the pride of life. At this moment the retreatant will certainly feel the lively reaction of the flesh, as has been the case since the offering of the Kingdom. This is true especially if he or she humbly and sincerely begs, three times in each of the four exercises of the day, during the colloquies of the Two Standards, for "the grace to be received under His standard, first in the highest spiritual poverty, and should the Divine Majesty be pleased thereby, and deign to choose and accept me, even in actual poverty; secondly, in bearing insults and wrongs, thereby to imitate Him better, provided only I can suffer these without sin on the part of another, and without offense of the Divine Majesty" ([147]).

In the evening of this day which so forcefully shows the opposition between our spiritual desire and our sensitivity, Ignatius presents a meditation which he wishes to be very affective and prayerful. Indeed, as Courel notes, "this exercise, the last of the day ([148]), substitutes for the application of the senses. It should allow for a repetition of the Two Standards to obtain, not precisely better knowledge ([139]), but rather an adherence of the heart which brings about an acceptance of God's will" ([155]).[85] If we desire to be firmly set in the truth, we ought to give this meditation a shade of color quite different from the one we pointed out in the beginning: Shall I be among the group of those content with velleities, the half-willed persons who play with compromise, or shall I be among those decisive persons who ac-

---

83 Note, for example, that in the Kingdom the retreatant offers to imitate Christ by enduring humiliations, while in the Two Standards, he asks contrariwise to be allowed to bear insults and wrongs "thereby to imitate him better."

84 Matt. 18:9.

85 *Exercices,* trans. Courel, p. 86, note 1. Also J. A. Hardon, *All my Liberty,* pp. 45–46. See the progression emphasized by Fessard, *La dialectique,* pp. 57–62, from the Kingdom to the Three Classes of Men, as a growth in freedom.

cept the challenge? We are not treating here of a question to which I desire and ought to give myself an answer. This meditation comes here in order to consider the conflict which it has emphasized on this day, or at least has brought to a greater awareness in the retreatant. As I make myself more attentive to the word addressed personally to me, I make this fervent prayer in order to obtain the grace which will permit me to overcome the resistances and repugnances of nature, and to accept in its entirety God's will which I seek to discover. Let us now examine the interacting dialectical elements, spiritual desire and the resistances of nature, which make up the structure of this humble meditation of petition.

First of all, the meditation is introduced as follows: "Three Classes of Men. This is a meditation for the same fourth day to choose that which is better" ([149]). In the second prelude, and with this intention, Ignatius writes: "Here it will be to behold myself standing in the presence of God our Lord and of all His saints, that I may know and desire what is more pleasing to His Divine Goodness" ([151]). In the third prelude he states: "Here it will be to beg for the grace to choose what is more for the glory of His Divine Majesty and the salvation of my soul" ([152]). As we see, the meditation follows a path where there is question of spiritual desire intensified by the presence of God and his saints, and of begging for grace in order to make a good election, to choose as God wishes me to choose, to embrace what is best. For the retreatant at this point in the Exercises, these preludes contain all the elements of his or her concrete situation. To desire to recognize and accept, with the help of grace, what will be for the greater glory of God, expresses his or her awareness of the difficulty posed by this question of choosing what is better. It is a difficulty which springs only from the profound resistances of our sensitive nature which seeks itself—and not from well-ordered "judgment and reason" ([96]) enlightened by faith. The proof is the first prelude, which sets up the problem, centers the difficulty of commitment experienced by the three classes of persons on one factor alone, "the attachment to the sum acquired" ([150]). That, Ignatius states, is the obstacle. "The love of money is the root of all evils."[86] If we pass immediately to the third class consisting of those who overcome the obstacle, we see that they have achieved the simple attitude of indifference ([155 and 157]). The question there is no longer about the imitation of Christ in poverty and humiliations. One might suppose that Ignatius has abandoned this line of thought and gone backward. As a matter of fact, he returns to the fundamental atti-

---

86   1 Tim, 6:10.

tude of indifference which is necessary for the genuine acceptance of this mystery, which will be one of imitation in poverty and humiliations, in accordance with the divine will (the triple colloquy of the same exercise). From the first day until now, all the work done has been aiming to arrive at this indispensable indifference, the fruit of grace, which proposes, beyond the inclinations of nature, a superior, powerful, reflective, and enlightened motivation, a revelation from God Himself. Thus nothing is abandoned of what had been envisaged in the theme of imitation and attachment to Christ. It is as if Ignatius were saying to us: Do you experience this confrontation between the desire which comes from above and the desire which comes from below? Then beg earnestly, through a grace of perfect indifference, that the desire which comes from above may become more intense. The indifference, which is a grace, will enable you to overcome all repugnances and direct your desire to the unique search for the divine will, for the glory of His Majesty—no matter what the cost in pain may be to these same sensitive inclinations of your nature.

If we examine closely the example of the three classes or categories of persons, we see immediately that in all of them there is a sensible attachment which is in conflict with their desire for God, their desire for salvation and peace in God ([150]). To resolve this conflict, Ignatius in no way states that the will is at fault; but he clearly shows, by means of the third class who attain the objective, that the lack of indifference is the reason for their weakness ([155 and 157]). Ignatian indifference is not a matter of the will as understood in the natural meaning of that term. In it the will does play its modest and important role, that by which it collaborates toward the person's cooperation with grace.[87] But the grace alone accomplishes the supernatural work in us, the work of sanctification. Ignatius states that it is God who "will put in the will" of those of the third class the "desire to be better able to serve God our Lord" which will enable them to overcome the affections in the sensitive part of their nature for this created good—affections which will perhaps remain throughout life. It is not stated that the affection for the created good is less strong in those of the third class than it is in those of the other classes. Neither is it stated that they possess a stronger natural willpower than the others. But it does appear that a superior spiritual affection, the fruit of grace, comes in to reestablish some sort of equilibrium between

---

87 See Cantin's article, "L'indifférence dans le Principe et Fondement des Exercices spirituels," *ScE*, 3 (1950), 114–145. He gives a good explanation of how "indifference disposes the will" (p. 128). We shall return to this problem when we treat the second kind of humility.

the initial desire for "peace in God" and the instinctive repugnance to the "ridding themselves" spiritually (and effectively if God so asks) of the good that is loved. That is why Ignatius concludes that with them, "the desire to be better able to serve God our Lord will be the cause of their accepting anything or relinquishing it." The force of this new attitude ought to be placed entirely on the side of the grace which adds a new weight ("my weight is my love; by it I am carried wherever I am carried"[88]) to the inclination of the will itself; and the human voluntary effort adds to this great grace the simple contribution called for by fidelity and cooperativeness.

On this evening of the Fourth Day, I as a retreatant will and desire more than ever to be with Christ; and this desire is greater today the more keenly I experience myself, through an urge of my lower nature, as an enemy of Christ and a partisan of Satan's standard. So I beg for that initial, humble, fundamental indifference which will make me open to an even greater grace measured out by God—that of the imitation of Christ and of the service of the Divine Majesty.

In a note Ignatius adds that for one for whom indifference is still very hard to accept (in spite of the intensification of his or her desire to serve and imitate Christ—which has been the object of constant petition since the beginning of the Second Week and the normal prolongation of the experience of the First Week)—such a one should act against his or her natural repugnances in order to offer a sacrifice which will make one more open to grace. Such a one may well ask not only for the necessary spiritual poverty, but also for an effective poverty. In making this last petition, perhaps it would be preferable in many a case to think less of the effective poverty of religious life than of the poverty which deprives one in fact of the precise good to which one is attached, such as health, success, wealth, or the like.

d. The Three Kinds of Humility

As is true also of many other particular details of the *Exercises,* much has been written on the topic of the three "manners" *(maneras)* (called also "kinds" or "modes" *[modos]* or "species" *[species]* or "degrees" *[grados]*)[89] of "humility" ([164]). To gain some idea of the extensive discussions and varying opinions about this knotty topic, we have merely to refer to the articles of Cantin and Delépierre. There we can trace the opinions of Suárez,

---

88 St. Augustine, *Confessions,* XIII, 9, 10.
89 For instances of this varying terminology in the Autograph, Versio prima, and Vulgate texts of the *Exercises,* and in the Ignatian Directories, see *SpEx*MHSJ, pp. 368-369 and 781.

de la Palma, Le Gaudier, Roothaan, Denis, Meschler, Pydinkowsky, Prat, de Pontlevoy, Nonell, Valensin, Calcagno, Pinard de la Boullaye, Gaultier, Boyer, and others. We have consulted these, and also the commentaries of Calveras, Iparraguirre, and Carl A. Lofty.[90]

We shall base our treatment on these investigations of our predecessors. But once again we shall situate the problem anew, by viewing it within the context of the unfolding thought in the biblical interpretation which we have been presenting.

The first question which arises concerns Ignatius' advice in his preliminary Note III ([164]), to the effect that "it will be very useful to consider attentively the following Three Kinds of Humility." He does not prescribe a meditation on them. Added to this is the fact that these degrees of humility are presented as a "consideration" which does not require an exercise properly so called. This consideration takes place on the morning of the Fifth Day, after the first contemplation. It introduces the retreatant more immediately to the "matter of the election." At the end of the Note the retreatant is invited to return to this subject "from time to time during the whole day, by making colloquies in the manner indicated"—colloquies which refer only to the Third Kind ([168]). What function, then, does this important and manifestly relevant consideration have in the unfolding of the Second Week? We shall reply to this question by examining what these "three manners and degrees of humility" mean.

Doctor Ortiz, the professor of Scripture at Salamanca, made the Exercises under Ignatius' personal direction at Monte Cassino during the forty days of Lent in 1538. He is the one who in the notes he has left us best expresses, it seems to us, in a few words what these "kinds" of "humility" are: "three manners and degrees of love for God and of desire to obey, imitate, and serve his Divine Majesty."[91] In the way that Ignatius enunciates

90 The following are the chief references where additional bibliography on the subject will be found: J. Calveras, *Práctica de los Ejercicios de S. Ignacio*, pp. 287-294; I. Iparraguirre, *How to Give a Retreat*, 149-154; J. Delépierre, "Note sur les trois degrés d'humilité," *NRTh*, 70 (1948), 963-975; R. Cantin, "Le troisième degré d'humilité et la gloire de Dieu selon saint Ignace de Loyola," *ScE*, 8 (1956), 237-266; C. A. Lofy, "The Third Degree of Humility," *WL*, 88 (1959), 366-375.

91 Pedro Ortiz, legate of Charles V to Paul III, made the Exercises for 40 days under the direction of Ignatius at Monte Cassino in 1538. He made some notes on the experience and afterwards put them in order in his own way. Nevertheless in them we find much that is of great interest. They bear principally on "the doctrine on choosing a state of life, or another good thing." The first of the four preludes to this method of making an election is the equivalent of the present *Exercises* [164-168] on the Kinds of Humility. On eight occasions Ortiz

the three "manners" or "degrees" of humility, they are considerations of the fundamental attitude on which they directly focus. Ortiz' way of expression, however, draws attention rather to the dynamism of these diverse manners of being humble. In all three cases there is question of love of God which brings with it a desire to be obedient, to imitate, and to serve. All this is certainly in the line of the affections and spiritual fruits sought for from the very beginning of the Exercises, and especially during the Second Week. Now to the intensity of this love, and of the consequent desire to act in accordance with it—to this intensity corresponds the more or less profound attitude of being humble which is simultaneously self-renunciation, spiritual poverty, Ignatian indifference to anything created, and openness to the divine will or good pleasure. How can I be more pleasing to Him?

The first degree of humility is the easiest to interpret. It is a fundamental and indispensable attitude of obedience to the law of God. Here Ignatius is saying: ". . . as far as possible I so subject and humble myself as to obey the law of God our Lord in all things" ([165]). The whole logic of the Exercises, according to the manner in which Doctor Ortiz expresses himself, states rather: My love of God is now such that I have a great desire to be faithfully obedient to the divine law.

In the second degree we lift ourselves to the attitude of perfect indifference. But here we are speaking of Ignatian indifference as it is found in the Foundation ([23]), and which persons of the third class ([155]) obtain as a particular grace in order to overcome the disordered attachment to the goods they have acquired. Ignatius states: "I possess it if my attitude of mind is such that I neither desire nor am I inclined to have riches rather than poverty, to seek honor rather than dishonor, to desire a long life rather than a short life, provided only in either alternative I would promote equally the service of God our Lord" ([166]). The logic progression of the Exercises, according to Ortiz, explains it more in this way: My love of God (or my attachment to Christ) is such that I put my search for the service and glory of God above all my desires and personal attachments. I find myself disposed to accept his entire will, whatever it may be and whatever it may cost. In this sense, we have an important precision in St. Ignatius' Autograph Directory, one which was repeated later in the Directory of González Dávila. It expressly directs

uses the well-known expression "Three kinds and degrees of love of God and desire to obey and imitate and serve His divine Majesty" (tres maneras y grados de amor de Dios y deseos de obedecer y imitar y servir a su divina Majestad). See Camilo M. Abad, "Unas anotaciones inéditas sobre los Ejercicios de San Ignacio compuestas por el Doctor Pedro Ortiz y su hermano Fray Francisco," *MiCo*, 25 (1956), 25–114 (esp. pp. 28, 38, 41–43).

that "one who does not have the *indifference* of the second degree" ([166]) should not be permitted "to engage in the elections." Here Ignatius replaces the word "humility" with "indifference," which he presents as an indispensable disposition for the election, because indifference is a disposition of being open to the divine will which is preferred over all other inclinations. When a retreatant does not have the indifference of the second degree, Ignatius adds in the Autograph Directory, it is preferable to keep him occupied in other exercises until he reaches this point."[92]

We have now completed a first stage in our interpretation of the degrees of humility. It has enabled us to know what is essential to the first two degrees. It is important to notice above all that these two envisage a progress already acquired, without which the work may not be continued. The consideration of the third degree is a separate matter. It will move toward a fruit to be obtained, which is not necessary at this point in the making of the Exercises although it is desirable. That is why Ignatius asks ([168]) anyone who desires it to make colloquies for this purpose throughout the day. There is question then, for the time being, of verifying his or her complete availability and openness to the divine will, the object of the election. That necessarily implies the desire to avoid any further sin and to be faithful and obedient to God. But also necessary is the indifference of the third class of men, that indifference for which the work of the whole previous day has been disposing the retreatant through a long process of purification of affections, and of attachment to Christ in the contemplations. In the same Autograph Directory in which Ignatius requires that the retreatant should, with God's help, be in the second degree of humility before undertaking the election, in order to have a will entirely open, he adds only this, that it is desirable that the retreatant "should, if possible, arrive at the third degree." In the same way González Dávila clearly describes the journey toward the first goal (the indifference of the second degree), through the preceding exercises (the Two Standards, the Three Classes of Men), and a readiness to go beyond into the third kind of humility:

> The director must see to it *(procurar)* (as our Father told me), that the retreatant arrive at the third degree of humility, or at least the second, the purpose of the Two Standards and the Three Classes of Men; and the retreatant who has not reached this second degree is not in condition to make the election, and it would be better for him to wait and mature through other means and meditations.[93]

92 *SpEx*MHSJ, pp. 781 and 921.
93 Ibid., p. 921.

Our interpretation, which has limited itself so far to throwing light on what is essential in the first two kinds (obedience and indifference), has in the meantime left in the shade a difficulty which must now be examined. We have intentionally held it until this moment. For many have begun their analysis of the problem by starting from its negative aspect, that which causes trouble in the two sections in question ([165, 166]). Now these points, which are difficult to resolve, do not precisely concern the nature of the kinds of humility as we have defined them. As a result, many have often tried to define the meaning of the first and second kinds of humility by starting with a secondary element (which by that very fact becomes ambiguous). We are referring to the clause in each of the sections which deals with the sin to be avoided: mortal sin in the first case ([165]) and venial sin in the second ([166]). Further still, in these two instances some commentators have dwelt on only one aspect, important but partial, of the problem: the statement about accepting death rather than committing a mortal sin, which is then repeated about deliberate venial sin. To define the kinds of humility by using these "conclusions" as a starting point is to walk backward without seeing where one is going.

To explain ourselves, let us begin with what we have learned. In both these cases, Ignatius begins by defining positively what these two kinds of humility are: an attitude of obedience to divine law, then indifference to created goods which is dictated by a greater attachment to Christ. This brings it about that the retreatant will prefer God's will to any other attachment. "If any one comes to me and does not hate [that is, have less love for] his own father and mother and wife and children and brothers and sisters, yes, and even his own life, he cannot be my disciple."[94] These two attitudes require a humility which is a self-renunciation supported by a love of God and a desire to serve his Divine Majesty despite one's fears and weaknesses. But Ignatius desires that at the time one puts oneself into the work of making the election, one should verify the sincerity of one's love. For this purpose the two kinds we have just defined contain a short phrase, a sort of criterion which will

---

94 Luke 14:26. On the meaning of the Hebraism of "hating" one's life, see note *d* on this verse in the Jerusalem Bible. To become convinced of the fact that Ignatian indifference depends on the superiority of a spiritual desire which reorders human and earthly attachments, we should observe how the men of the Third Class find in this grace the strength to surmount any "obstacle" they might encounter ([155]). Read the article of R. Cantin (*ScE,* 3 [1950], pp. 134–139), where he shows that the second part of the description of indifference in the Foundation ("Our one desire and choice should be what is more conducive to the end") is, according to Ignatius, an integral part of this virtue.

allow one to judge his or her sincerity. It is a requirement of lofty gospel demands which we will never completely fulfill, and which challenges us ever onward, even to the giving up of our very lives. Furthermore, there is not here a question of a life-long commitment which should be evaluated for firmness and perseverance—an attitude of mind not at all in conformity with Ignatius' manner. Instead, there is question of the present moment, that which controls our entering into the election, (in Ignatius' thought, the "introduction to the matter of the election"). This is the moment which engages us to search for and to accept God's will for us. Now, at this time, an attitude which poses no limit to love, to grace, to the divine will is not surprising. Therefore the attitude of obedience and indifference (and that of the love, self-renunciation, and desire to serve and imitate which support them) demands at this point that I would not envisage the diverse sinful possibilities enumerated by Ignatius. The question here is indeed that of examining, of considering, deliberately, within the perspective of an election, the possibility of preferring anything at all which would be a deliberate offense to God. "Not even were I made lord of all creation," Ignatius writes, "or to save my life here on earth, would I consent to violate a commandment" that binds me under pain of mortal or venial sin. If therefore at this moment of opening myself to the divine will I am in a disposition such that I cannot even envisage putting into the scale anything, even the whole world, to outweigh obedience to God, because I desire to prefer Him above all else, then I am ready to hear his voice, to accept his expression of his good pleasure, and to make an absolutely disinterested election. One, therefore, who has attained the indifference of the second kind ([166]) is ready to take up both the contemplation of the public life and "the matter of the election."

Once the first two kinds of humility have been understood, the third no longer causes difficulty. On the contrary, the retreatant sees how much grace it supposes if it is to be attained in one's life, and he or she can humbly plead for it. As Ignatius writes, if he has a desire for it, he "should beg our Lord to deign to choose him for this third kind of humility, which is higher and better, that he may *the more imitate and serve him,* provided equal or greater praise and service be given to the Divine Majesty" ([168]). Very often, however, it has been wrongly concluded from this that the third kind aims positively at imitation, while the other two seek only a more perfect fidelity and indifference. We should not forget that the second kind contains everything the Exercises have proposed up to this point. Let us recall what we said earlier about the Three Classes of Men. We saw that after speaking of imitation through the endurance of poverty and humiliations, from the Kingdom to the Two Standards inclusively, the meditation on the Three Classes confined itself to the problem of attachment, not by way of turning the thought backwards but rather with a view to assuring that indifference which is indispensable to this higher attachment signified by the service and imitation of Christ. This, too, is what is begged for in the colloquy ([156]) of this meditation. In that indifference we find the whole object or aim of the second kind of humility; and that is why it is indispensable for anyone who desires to make an election.

The third kind speaks of imitating and serving Christ better ([168]), of being in reality more like him ([167]). It opens the door, therefore, to a more perfect humility, to a greater love of God which increases the desire to obey, imitate, and serve his Divine Majesty. But how is this desire expressed? In what way is this love greater? In an *offering* which is an expression of a preference, a desire to be with Christ effectively poor, humiliated, made a fool of. In that is the whole of the third kind, and we must not weaken it. Not only do I prefer the divine will and the service and imitation of Christ above anything else (the second kind), but I positively offer myself, in the measure consonant with God's greater praise or glory, to be with Christ in poverty, dishonor, suffering, and death. This offering cannot be, for Ignatius, the result of a mere act of the will. It is all too clear that there is question of the perfection of love, of self-renunciation (humility), and the fruit of grace; and this cannot come merely from a more or less generous effort of the will. But the retreatant who seriously and interiorly tends in that direction, as the Ignatian Directory desires him or her to do, with the generosity and the renunciation which correspondence to grace demands, will enter just that much more completely into the divine intention for himself or herself in making the election. In so doing, the retreatant disposes himself or herself to receive those greater divine graces from which God will draw ever greater praise or glory to Himself. Thus it is an opening of the way to a mystery of union, of a more perfect identification, which supposes the most complete humility on the part of the one who wholeheartedly desires "to be with Christ."

Let us add that through its object the third kind of humility presents, more or less briefly, a preview of the mystery of the Passion which we shall be considering later. For the moment the Passion is not referred to. Ignatius is content to define the third kind of humility by starting with the elements at hand; he makes no mention of sufferings or the cross. His words are: "Whenever the praise and glory of God would be equally served, . . . I desire and choose poverty with Christ poor, rather than riches; . . . insults with Christ loaded with them, rather than honors." However, to these elements already known from the data of the Second Week he now adds this conclusion which generalizes the object of the election by extending it to every aspect of God's plan of salvation through Christ, the "folly of God" which is opposed to the "wisdom of this world." This is the opening into a path which entices the retreatant to give himself or herself to the love of God without any limits other than those imposed by God's glory and his Kingdom developing on earth.[95] "I desire to be accounted as worthless and a fool for Christ, rather than to be esteemed as wise and prudent in this world. So Christ was treated before me [167])."[96] In addition to the purification of the interior sentiments and the authentic detachment from self, the third kind of humility introduces a social dimension, an upside-down way of living which is with God's grace effectively carried out in face of the world. For it is a life which only the Spirit of God can draw from the cross, the life so profusely poured out there. In the case, therefore, of this person who has desire, it is a passage from the fundamental attitude of the third kind to its concrete, visible, social realization through one's self-oblation and the grace for which one has humbly begged. This grace is one which the Lord gives *to whomsoever he calls* to this third kind of humility. It is only after I have been chosen that it will be given to me to choose in my turn. To sum up, we see in what sense the third kind of humility is above all an interior attitude or a more complete and perfect disposition of charity and of humility. But to this disposition there corresponds, in the measure chosen by God, a carrying over into practice which is imitation of Christ poor and humiliated.

4. The Third Time-Period:
The Public Life and the Election ([158–163, 169–189])

The last stage of the Second Week, in Ignatius' arrangement, consists of eight days. It is a stage which is at once the easiest to interpret and the most delicate to live through. It is simple from the point of view of interpretation because all the retreatant has to do is to follow the parallel paths of contemplation and election. But it requires very delicate management because of the

---

95 This subject is related to that of "discreet charity" (caritas *discreta*); it is also treated by Cantin, who gives a good explanation of the controversial expression "equal or greater praise and service." See "Le troisième degré," *ScE*, 8 (1956), esp. pp. 246–266.

96 The first part of the expression could lead one to believe that Ignatius is thinking of precise facts in the life of Christ, in his Passion; the second part opens onto a more universal sense which reminds one of St. Paul's 1 Cor. 1:22–25, where the wisdom of this world is opposed to the folly of God (which includes and explains the particular episodes of the life of Christ where derision openly manifests this "separation" from the world).

many factors which come into play, and because of the relationship linking together the different levels of activity which should be respected now more than ever. Therefore, one should bring to this stage great attention and prudent discernment. Let us, therefore, review these various elements, in order to gain quickly a more precise concept of what they are and what they demand.

The road on which the retreatant enters on the morning of the fifth day is clear and unobstructed. The only task directly in view will be contemplation; but indirectly, the work of the election will be carried on, in the light which God will give. Ignatius gives no further precise directions as to the route to be followed. He knows that every good election must come "from above." "The love which moves and causes one to choose must descend from above, that is, from the love of God" ([184]). The retreatant who is already disposed to accept the divine will should set about listening very attentively to the divine word, and should respond to the action of the Spirit in himself or herself. Then, through the prolonged contemplation of the mysteries of Christ, choices will be brought to mind at the moment when the retreatant's soul will be mature enough, with God's grace, to handle them responsibly. "While proceeding with his meditations on the mysteries of Christ our Lord," writes Ignatius, "the retreatant should consider, when he is in consolation, in what direction God is moving him; and likewise when he is in desolation."[97] Experience shows that the retreatant, following this method, sometimes discovers more than the decision he or she must make. The very object of the election can be determined by this interior movement and can correspond to the demands of a need for a readjustment of life that is much more authentic and inspired from above. From this point of view, we cannot foresee exactly when the work of the election itself will take place. Or rather, we should say that the work of the election continues throughout this stage (from the morning of the Fifth Day onward); but it is impossible to set a time for the final act of choosing by which the retreatant will commit himself or herself to the following of Christ—the act that obliges one, today, to follow Christ, and thus allows one to gather the fruit of the election. In this last stage, therefore, the director ought to introduce the retreatant to this task in accordance with Ignatius' directives ([169–189]), and to follow the person step by step so as to apply to the interior evolution in progress the criteria for discernment which bear either on the action of the spirits in general, or on one or another of the different Times for making the election in particular

---

97 *SpEx*MHSJ, p. 781.

([175–178]). It is precisely here that the task becomes more delicate. The director and the retreatant will be attentive, each one, to the signs of the Spirit which experience will reveal. The purpose is not only to reject those false ways or solutions offered to the retreatant's generosity or pusillanimity, but also to discern, by starting from the word of God and its universal demands, the particular and present demands or invitations from God's will in regard to oneself.

Seen in this way, this stage of contemplation-election entails particular demands which we reduce to three: More than ever the retreatant ought to establish himself or herself in a climate of interior silence and prayer; the message proposed should be completely respectful of the truth which it has the mission to transmit; and finally, the attention paid to the motions in the soul, those impulses which may be graces, is of capital importance.

a. Silence and Prayer

St. Ignatius desired that the period of election should be the object of special care. We notice immediately that he made this a time of intense contemplation—eight days during which no other exercise properly so called is prescribed save contemplation of the mysteries of Christ's life. A director should make sure beforehand that the retreatant has the necessary dispositions, and should engage him or her in other exercises, such as the Two Standards and Three Classes of Men, as long as the desired indifference has not been acquired. Then the retreatant, full of desire and attention, applies himself or herself to the contemplation which is a personal encounter with Christ. In his Autograph Directory Ignatius asks explicitly that "when entering the election, the retreatant should keep himself in special solitude, without seeking to see or feel anything which is not from above."[98] The reference here is not only to the taking of certain material precautions, but rather to an interior solitude so as to achieve in all their fullness the conditions for a good election. These conditions are at the same time those for a personal encounter with the Lord. This is what Ignatius in Annotation 15 firmly calls to the director's attention, from whom he expects fully complete discretion:

> The director of the Exercises ought not to urge the exercitant more to poverty or any promise than to the contrary, nor to one state of life or way of living more than to another. Outside the Exercises, it is true, we may lawfully and meritoriously urge all who probably have the required fitness to choose continence, virginity, the religious life, and every form of religious perfection. But while one

---

98 Ibid., p. 779.

is engaged in the Spiritual Exercises, it is more suitable and much better that the Creator and Lord in person communicate Himself to the devout soul in quest of the divine will, that He inflame it with love of Himself, and dispose it for the way in which it could better serve God in the future. Therefore, the director of the Exercises, as a balance at equilibrium, without leaning to one side or the other, should permit the Creator to deal directly with the creature, and the creature directly with his Creator and Lord.

These cautions with which Ignatius surrounds the election show to how great an extent he considered it to be a work which is truly both divine and human, and which demands our respectful, patient, and recollected attention. The word of God will not be refused to the servant who listens.

b. Objectivity of the Message

However, the revealed message must also be very much respected. God's word is efficacious; the word of the one who has the mission to transmit it ought not to impair it. That is why the principles enunciated above in A,1 of this present chapter, on the objectivity and the transcendence of the revealed message (which contemporary exegesis and a sound biblical theology enable us to hear again) are entirely applicable to the contemplation of the mysteries of the public life. One can, then, discuss the Pauline and the Johannine perspectives which in different ways play their parts in Ignatius' world view, his frame of reference in which God's plan of salvation and sanctification is so great a part. Traces of both these perspectives are easily found.[99] But what

---

99   In Ignatius the historical perspective of salvation is typically Pauline, as we see in the First Week (drama of sin) and certain features of the Kingdom and of the mystery of the Incarnation. Elsewhere the person of Christ is contemplated according to a Johannine perspective. This is a consequence of the conversion experience of Ignatius himself, in which the influence of the transcendent and the presence of the Son in relation to the Father predominate. (The same is true for the place which the mystery of the Incarnation occupies in this vision.) These perspectives, however, are somewhat complementary to the idea of a new beginning for the world which is expressed there, and to the fulfillment of the messianic promises, about which the perspectives of Paul, John, and the Synoptics coincide. If we limit ourselves to these essential elements of the message, which are also proposed by the Kingdom, we are on the way to contemplating the Gospels without any distinction of authors, but with the sole intention of being incorporated into Christ and living in him—and it is for this purpose that he has been proclaimed to humanity. We say this without diminishing the value and the interest of the opinion which suggests that we should unify, as much as possible, the presentation of the mysteries or events in Christ's life by using one same evangelist. In this way we would propose Luke for the Infancy and John for the Public Life, but we would insist on a certain flexibility. On the Pauline

273

is most important is to pick up the thread which allows us easily to follow the theological call of the Kingdom and the perspective initiated by the mysteries of the infancy. This is to make ourselves present to Christ who is accomplishing his mission of salvation, delivering us from evil, freeing the world from the yoke of Satan, restoring the divine image in all things, attaching us to his followers, and restoring the unity of the world created for God and his glorification. With this panorama as our goal, we can contemplate every word or deed of the Lord from this higher point of view; and in it the preoccupations particular to each of the sacred writers fit together and become a part of the panoramic sum total of God's truth.[100]

c. Discernment of Spirits

The last element to be considered is that which is properly the unifying factor in these concurrent procedures of contemplation and election, in which the actions of the human person and those of God meet and collaborate. We are referring to the motions from the Holy Spirit. Ignatius always supposes that some of these come to those making the Exercises.

---

perspective, see L. Levie, "La méditation fondamentale des Exercices à la lumière de saint Paul," *NRTh,* 75 (1953), 815–827; J. Adúriz, "La 'Primera Semana' y toma de consciencia del hombre adamita," *CyF,* 12 (1956), 61–62. (This article also treats the Johannine perspective.) Read also: A. Feuillet, "Le plan salvifique de Dieu d'après l'Epître aux Romains," *RB,* 57 (1950), 336–387, 489–529; S. Lyonnet, "L'histoire du salut selon le chapitre VII de l'Epître aux Romains," *Bib,* 43 (1962), 117–151.

100 We know that Ignatius does not impose a definite choice of mysteries to be contemplated; he states that we can add to or subtract from his suggestions. which are given to serve as "an introduction and method for better and more complete contemplation later" ([162]). If we examine the mysteries that have been proposed during these eight days ([158–161]) and those which he adds as options for the same period ([273–288]), we shall notice some preferences which orient the proclamation of the word: There are the mysteries which inaugurate the messianic mission of Christ and commit him to the struggle against Satan; those which concern the call of the Apostles, their formation, and their being sent on mission; there are some miracles which have special sign value for education in faith; then the more or less direct explanation of the gospel doctrine, the demands of Christ, with the sermon on the Beatitudes and the preaching in the Temple; finally, there are the great signs of the divinity in relation with the central mystery of the Passover, of death and life: the transfiguration and the resurrection of Lazarus. A practical necessity will oblige the director to propose only those mysteries whose religious significance he or she will have understood well through study and prayer—mysteries which are related to God's plan of salvation. This is the reason why we propose, below in our Biblical Bibliography, an extensive list of books likely to enlarge this area of possible readings.

The word "motion" is taken here in its meaning of an impulse or inclination of the mind or will; these motions are the *inclinaciones y mociones* of Ignatius' *Constitutions* ([92, 144]) and *Exercises* ([6, 227, 313, 329]). They may come from God, or a good angel, or a devil, or from the urges of our physical human nature ([32, 313-317]). They may be graces or they may be temptations.

To borrow some expressions of Hugo Rahner, the time period of the election—whether it is a period of activity which is mystical, or ascetical, or of theological reasoning—is always a time in which the "love that moves and causes one to choose must descend from above" (*de arriba*, [184]). A right choice is especially dependent on this divine action in the soul. Ignatius states, "I should beg God our Lord to deign to move my will and to bring to my mind what I ought to do to promote His praise and glory with regard to the matter in question" ([180]). It is in the Spirit, through prayer, that the meeting between the living word of God and the soul open to the divine will takes place. Step by step, we have seen, as the objective revelation of the message progresses, there is a parallel maturing in the spiritual experience of the one who receives it in faith and love. The dialectical passage from the universal to the particular is made in the Spirit; for it is through his Spirit that Christ meets our spirit and vivifies it. However, there is a drama which unfolds here, the drama of the "spirits." The Spirit of God is not the only one who operates in us. There is also the subtle art of deceit. On the Fourth Day of the Second Week, on the eve of the election, Ignatius directs the retreatant to ask for "a knowledge of the deceits of the rebel chief and help to guard myself against them" ([139]). Here more than ever, the most important experience is one of discernment. To this end Ignatius has composed some rules for the Second Week ([328-336]) which have a particular application to the different "Times" ([175]) during which an election might be made.[101] Although the director ought not to intervene in this dialogue between the retreatant and God during this privileged time of election, he or she is nevertheless the sentinel who keeps watch over its secret. But his weapon will be only the discernment which requires on his part a spiritual understanding of God's ways and a great spirit of prayer.

---

101 We shall not try to explain here in greater detail the significance of the "Three Times" for making an election, the conditions of their realization, and their relationship to the Second Week. The matter is important but it has already been treated at length by others. Some references on particular points are these: on the election in general, see E. Hernández García, *La Elección en los Ejercicios de San Ignacio*, (Comillas, 1956); H. Rahner, "*Notes on the Spiritual Exercises*," *WL*, 85 (1956), 321-327; Fessard, *La dialectique*, pp. 70-103; M.

It is along this path of interior attention that the concurrent work of contemplation and election will be accomplished. The proclamation of the word, which makes the public life of Christ come alive, is grasped in proportion to the measure in which this interior attention is converted into acceptance and receptivity. But the Spirit, who accompanies the word and makes it bear fruit, also requires attention to his unforeseeable motions which particularize, according to the Father's will, the universal demands of the Word who gives life. Each exercitant, in accordance with his or her own individual personality, takes into his or her heart the total mystery of Christ, that is, His plan of salvation, sanctification, and beatitude.

"I am the light of the world," says Jesus, "he who follows me will not walk in darkness, but will have the light of life."[102] Every one of us—whoever we are—is the prodigal son of the earth who turns toward the Father. We are all, too, the rich young man who carries his pack of good things which must be renounced in order to follow the Master. Whether the retreatant of the Second Week follows Christ as a "simple Christian" or as a "consecrated person" is of little importance. Each one will hear Christ dictate His suggestions which tear him or her from himself, magnify the poor and the persecuted, and put him on guard against the leaven of the Pharisees. But each one will also see His signs of power and of infinite love and tenderness. These reveal the heart of our older brother, the firstborn of a new race. When we approach the Lord "in truth" to embrace his universal task of goodness and salvation, we shall receive his lot of the cross to be carried today, under the concrete form of this or that renunciation of self, or this or that readjustment of life which is required in order to be "with him," and to learn how to serve and praise the divine Majesty in all things. But there is a love, "stronger than death," which binds us to Christ and his life. The retreatant will beg him day after day for this love, with the confidence which is inspired by him who is

---

Giuliani, "Se décider sous la motion divine," *Chr,* no. 14 (1957), 165–186; J. M. Le Blond, "Que ta volonté soit faite," ibid., pp. 150–164; the three Ignatian Directories, *SpExMHSJ*, pp. 778–794. In particular see, for the "First Time," L. González Hernández, *El Primer tiempo de Elección segun San Ignacio* (Madrid, 1956); for the "Second Time," K. Rahner, *The Dynamic Element in The Church,* pp. 89ff; for the "Third Time," G. Fessard, *La dialectique,* pp. 255–304 (esp. 271–283), and K. Rahner, *The Dynamic Element,* pp. 89ff. [See also J. Toner, *A Commentary on Saint Ignatius' Rules for the Discernment of Spirits: A Guide to the Principles and Practice* (St. Louis, 1981); H. Coathalem, *Ignatian Insights,* pp. 243–278. Ed.]

102 John 8:12.

forever "God among us." And along the whole road to be traversed in order to be "with him" completely, the retreatant will know the desire to hold nothing back—even if this means the way of the cross!

Chapter 7

THE THIRD AND FOURTH WEEKS:
OUR EXPERIENCE OF THE PASCHAL MYSTERY

A. The Paschal Mystery and the Exercises

Many reasons can be offered to justify the existence of the Third and Fourth Weeks of the Exercises. Directors or writers often rightly point out that these Weeks provide confirmation of the preceding election. But all too often they mention only this; or, by stressing the need for confirmation too much, they justify these Weeks too exclusively from a psychological point of view.[1] For many exercitants, consequently, the entry into this last stage requires a considerable effort lest one give in to an impression that "the problem has been resolved" and one has little left to do but wait until the retreat is over.[2] In truth, however, the full justification for a stage beyond that of the election and commitment is to be found on the level of God's plan of salvation and sanctification. For the person who has lived through the genuine and deep spiritual experience of the Second Week,[3] a new stage is called for by his or her spiritual desire which springs from grace. The Third and Fourth Weeks satisfy this desire, especially because they are an opportunity to develop empathy with Christ in that "paschal mystery" in which the God-man works out the divine plan of salvation through his Passion and Resurrection. "For if we have been *united with him in a death like his,* we shall certainly be *united with him in a resurrection like his*" (Rom. 6:5). On this level too there will be "confirmation," and that in a more profound sense.

---

1 As an example of a rather psychological interpretation, see the commentary of J. Nonell, in his *Analyse des Exercices spirituels* (1924), p. 86.

2 That is why many Ignatian retreats reduce the time allotted to these two Weeks to a minimum. This is done to the detriment of the authentic experience of the Exercises.

3 Here we allude to the fact that the election ought to be converted into a deeply personal conviction. It starts from an identification with the divine will, an identification which is progressive and necessarily demanding, and then it moves through the contemplation of Christ, guided by motions from under his Spirit.

1. In regard to the Passion Events and Christ's Plan of Salvation

"He became obedient even unto death, even death on a cross (Phil. 2:8)." The mystery of Christ which the Christian retreatant now wishes to experience with an enlightened spiritual awareness is above all the paschal mystery: his going through His passion and death and resurrection, his "going up to Jerusalem." Everything else in his life is his journey toward this hour of Christ which consummated the work of salvation. In the economy of the Incarnation through which the Word became one of us in order to save us, this had to be true, "so that by the grace of God he might taste death for every one."[4] His whole life on earth, from its first moment on through its unfolding, consisted in this filial act which was opposed to the sin of Adam. To the disobedience and the revolt of the creature, Christ—God become a creature—opposed obedience, respectful homage, and the fidelity of love.[5] The state of perdition, that inevitable consequence of sin, was replaced by the sanctification of the humanity which he took on. This was the fruit of his obedience and perfect homage to the Creator. In Christ, humanity simply turned toward God and to adoring him in truth; and that was the road to salvation. But this perfect homage of the human conversion had to embrace the entire amplitude of the first turning away from God. Beyond the innumerable gifts contained in creation, man had above all received from God the very special gift of life. His sin, which snatched him away from God on the pretense of making him "the master of his life and his destiny," had changed this life into death. "To dust you shall return." And through that death destruction was spread throughout creation. The perfect homage of worship which Christ by himself gives to the Father will attain its end only by the reversal of all the consequences of sin. In Him, death will again become life. "Death is swallowed up in victory."[6] Christ will transform temporal death by integrating it into his "creaturely homage" to the Father. Thus he makes of it an act of perfect obedience which is both adoration and an expression of the greatest love. Instead of guarding it jealously in order to save that life which he too had received as a gift, Christ will lose it and give it freely: "Father, into thy hands I commend my spirit!" (Luke 23:46). And through this act, man's death in Christ becomes life again. It is a *passage* from the servitude of sin and death to the eternal liberty of the divine life.

---

4   Heb. 2:9.
5   The fact that Christ saves us as a creature like ourselves brought about a necessity that he should die. This order which God chose remains purely gratuitous; it is an expression of a mystery of love and of transcendence which nothing can diminish.
6   1 Cor. 15:54.

2. *In Regard to the Retreatant and His or Her Spiritual Experience*

The retreatant making the Exercises started from the deepened knowledge of sin and one's powerlessness to reverse it. He or she with God's help made acts inserting himself into the salvific plan of Christ. Now he ought to embrace the full amplitude of the divine salvation which Christ proposes to him, and to live out this experience to which his "deliberate choice" in the offering of the Kingdom has already disposed him ([98]). He or she ought to follow Christ to the very heart of death, in a spirit of adoration and love, in order to meet this Life in a genuine way. Such is the lot of every Christian, which too often is accepted in its fullness only with the final grace which comes at the "last moments" of this earthly life. But during the Exercises the retreatant wholeheartedly embraces this destiny, without reservations, for each moment of his or her life. The election will have been, in the light of the divine plan of salvation and sanctification, the present, definite step which "places him with Christ" in this plan. It is a road which contains both death and life, and which as a result immediately attaches him, as a disciple, to following the "Lord who is going to His suffering for my sins" ([193]). It is there that I shall realize with him my salvation, and that I shall be associated with him toward achieving the salvation of the world. To will to accomplish this truly Christian ideal—and therefore it is an apostolic, communitarian, and universal ideal—by any other way would be to want to change the divine order of things. The act of personal sanctification exists only as a participation in the saving act of the Christ who lovingly embraces the whole of humanity which was created to glorify the Father.[7] On the other hand, to aspire in truth to this Christian and communal participation without passing through the personal and committed sanctification which grafts one onto Christ, is to perform a work merely natural and cut off from the divine. For salvation is not an enterprise with only a natural dimension—no matter how spiritual, social, or altruistic this dimension might be.

To have made an election in order to be truly associated with Christ in the accomplishment of his mission of salvation—this was simply to prepare oneself conscientiously, with God's grace, to live the Christian experience in a preeminent way, that of the paschal mystery. This is what one can do in the Third and Fourth Weeks; and one's life of ardent faith and ordered love will prolong it each day for the rest of one's life.

---

7 On this subject see F. Bourassa, "Verum Sacrificium, "Part II, in *ScE,* 4 (1951), 98ff.

The Christian religion is not simply a doctrine: it is a fact, an action, not of the past, but of the present, where the past is recovered and the future draws near. Thus it embodies a mystery of faith, for it declares to us that each day makes our own the action that Another accomplished long ago, the fruits of which we shall see only later in ourselves.

Here is the meaning of the pasch: It points out to us that the Christian in the Church must die with Christ in order to rise with Him. And not only does it point out, as one might indicate with the forefinger something beyond one's reach (that is what the pasch of the Old Testament did), but it accomplishes the very thing it points out. The pasch is Christ, who once died and rose from the dead, making us die in His death and raising us to His life. Thus the pasch is not a mere commemoration: It is the cross and the empty tomb rendered actual. But it is no longer the Head who must stretch Himself upon the cross in order to rise from the tomb: it is His Body, the Church, and of this Body we are the members.

This death with Christ and this resurrection with Him, giving us the life hidden with Christ in God, who will appear when Christ Himself will appear, is the whole mystery that St. Paul tells us God had reserved for these later times—our own. . . .

At this time, together with its changeless Head, the Mystical Body, ever renewed, partakes of the Last Supper, is stretched upon the cross, and descends into the tomb to rise again on the third day. This is the paschal mystery.[8]

B. The Conditions of the Spiritual Experience

1. The Fundamental Attitude

What do we mean by the expressions "to be disposed to follow our Lord in his Passover," or "to be 'with him' in his Passover?" We are tempted to reply by making a distinction between "following Him," (1) by contemplating the events or mysteries of his life, during the Third and Fourth Weeks, and (2) by the Christian practice of concrete everyday life. Then we perceive that no one experiences real difficulty in answering the invitation to the first way, whereas the second leaves many behind, following him only from afar. "The spirit indeed is willing, but the flesh is weak."[9] However, if the privileged days of the Exercises have not succeeded in bringing into our lives a convergence between the ideal which we pondered and our practice, then the existential value of the preceding experience—in particular, of the election—

8 L. Bouyer, *The Paschal Mystery*, pp. xiii, xiv, xvii.
9 Matt. 26:41.

will be of little worth; and there will be scarcely any "confirmation" except on the logical level of knowledge, the only level on which one is truly engaged.

a. *The Present Moment of the Retreatant's Experience*

At the moment when the exercitant enters the Third and Fourth Weeks of the retreat, the two levels come into contact in a particular way, especially in a retreat well made. The contemplation of the paschal mystery on the objective level and, on the subjective plane, the experience of living as a genuine disciple of Christ teach the retreatant during the Third and Fourth Weeks how to make the contemplation of these great truths truly effective in daily Christian living. Through the contemplation of these truths on the objective level and through the purification of the retreatant's own soul on the subjective plane, the time devoted during these final two weeks to reflection and to the readjustment of oneself to the requirements of the divine will (which are universal and simultaneously particular because applicable to the retreatant's own life)—this time transforms the present moment of the retreatant into a period of the Christian experience fully alive.

Also, to speak of the basic dispositions for the entry into the Third Week is truly to bring together at this point in time those paths which seemed to be separating into the ideal and the practical. There will be, assuredly, attitudes proper to the flow of the Third Week; we shall see this soon. But these particular "states of soul" are only actualizations of a fundamental attitude now acquired and adapted to one's personal life as a result of the preceding experiences. Otherwise, there is danger that these states of soul, aroused by the contemplation of the Passion, will become only emotional reactions which do not seriously affect the movement of the creature in his or her union with God through grace. (One becomes very much like the "good Christian" who, during Holy Week, weeps copiously at the memory of the Passion, and for the rest of the year scarcely gives it a thought!)

Further still, the stage which is beginning might otherwise become separated once more from the present moment of Christian experience which, over and above all imaginative and even spiritual reconstructions, ought to be lived out in practice. Immediately after the election, the exercitant begins, or begins anew, his or her concrete Christian life, but its present reality has been greatly deepened. It is no longer adjusted to interests merely immediate and visible. It is the insertion on one's own life, here and now, into that divine saving plan as something to be lived out continuously in daily practice—in other words, into that mystery which is the essence of the Christian life in act.

While making the Third and Fourth Weeks, Ignatius' retreatant is not doing exercises in view of some particular and functional result. He or she is already living out profoundly the Christian commitment accepted under the action or motions from the Holy Spirit. The only "functional" aspect we see there is that one "learns" how to live it fully, without bias or false complacency with oneself, so as to be more humanly faithful to it throughout one's life. But this is already and preeminently the life style of "Christian practice" which every Christian, whether active or contemplative, man or woman, rich or poor, lives in his or her own way for the glorification of God. We are dealing, then, with the basic Christian experience in the strongest sense of this term, without which there is nothing Christian in our lives except the name; also, with carrying it out in practice, rather than with an experience which is merely promise barely sketched and lived out with the minimum of attention.

It is to this basic Christian experience that the fundamental attitude which we now take up corresponds. In describing it we shall be answering our first question: What does it mean "to be disposed to follow our Lord in his Passover"? We shall do this by reuniting closely the two levels we mentioned above, those of the ideal and its practice. We are referring to the final stage of the Exercises, and consequently to the whole of the Christian life—of which this stage is only an existential point, that of the present moment, which is one truly precious, strong, and privileged.

b. Indifference, the Source of Commitment

On the level of the subjective experience, the Exercises up to this point have been above all a cooperation with grace toward establishing and developing that fundamental attitude which generates the genuine Christian experience fully alive. However, there are two special points of this long process which can gather its many data together and help us understand this fundamental attitude. These two points, which orient our description here, are the Three Kinds of Humility ([165–168]) and the Election ([169–189]).

Before undertaking the election, that is, at the beginning of the contemplations focused on the public life of Christ, Ignatius expects that the retreatant will have reached the second kind of humility. We have already seen the extent of this manner *(manera)* of being humble, (which we have measured more by its positive content than by its negative criterion and corollary, "I would not commit a venial sin"). It is, in reality, perfect indifference with regard to everything created. In other words, it is a preference, through an attachment to Christ, for the service of Christ to the glorification of the Father, over any merely human attachment—whether it be to health, life, wealth, or any other merely personal benefit whatever. The person of the second kind of humility is one numbered among the third class of men. He or she is a person of the Second Week who has chosen, while overcoming his own preferences, attachments, or repugnances, to be "with Christ," no matter what it costs. Consequently, he or she is preeminently a person of the election. If God speaks, he or she will accept his full will. Now this attachment to the Lord, born of grace through the initial experience of mercy and then borne onward through the expansive contemplation of the Kingdom and the mysteries of the Incarnation, the Infancy, and the Hidden Life, will ordinarily have deepened during the Second Week proportionally to the purification of one's natural affections—which can be an "obstacle" ([150]). This attachment to Christ will have increased during the transforming contemplations of the public life. For these latter contemplations are indeed a more personal and intimate encounter with the Christ of Majesty, of power and goodness, whose demands are seen to be immense but whose yoke is seen as sweet and his burden light. In other words, the attitude of the second kind of humility—which is already a victory of grace over personal attachments at the moment of entering this stage of contemplation and election—can only be strengthened through a meeting with Christ and his inspiring plan of salvation throughout those days when every desire of the retreatant remains open to the divine good pleasure. This person of the second degree, the third class, and the election made with complete liberty and generosity; this person who is becoming attached more and more to the salvific and sanctifying strategy of Christ, now finds himself or herself ready to follow the Lord in his Passover. "He became obedient, even unto death."

The fundamental attitude of the authentic Christian experience, therefore, is this initial indifference, in the Ignatian sense, which is entirely open to the will of God in an ever increasing attachment to Christ. It is a counterbalance which enables us little by little to overcome and to purify our human attachments to created things. This pressing or "controlling" love (2 Cor. 5:14) keeps us ever walking in the footsteps of Christ all the way to the end. "Lord, to whom shall we go? You have the words of eternal life."[10] "No one who puts his hand to the plow and looks back is fit for the kingdom of God."[11] We have become like the man who found a treasure hidden in a field; he covers it up; "then in his joy he goes and sells all that he has and buys that field."[12]

10 John 6:69.
11 Luke 9:62.
12 Matt. 13:44.

2. The Proximate Conditions

a. The Distinction of the Levels

During the Third and Fourth Weeks St. Ignatius adds two kinds of "notes" to the subjects of his contemplations. Some are concerned with the interpretation of the Gospel mysteries,[13] while others deal with the subjective dispositions or moods of the retreatant. Very often in the history of the Exercises the mistake was made of confusing these two aspects and, through starting with the subjective attitudes which Ignatius considered to be normal at this stage, of regarding this procedure as the objective presentation of the Passion.

This confusion of levels is seen in some interpreters (especially exegetes), who think that the spiritual significance of the Passion narratives is thereby weakened. But we see this confusion more frequently in the practice of many directors of the Exercises who, by their manner of proposing the mysteries, easily fall into the trap already mentioned. The result tends to be that the objective presentation of the message is aimed primarily at arousing sensible and spiritual affections, rather than at opening the intellect to the sacred meaning of the mystery or salvific plan and thereby fostering an interior transforming prayer. We shall return to this problem of interpretation in the following paragraph of our study. But already now we felt obliged to point out this distinction, in order to situate these fundamental attitudes of the retreatant, and through this to describe the "proximate conditions" of the paschal experience.

b. Bringing the Fundamental Attitude into Reality

The subjective disposition of soul about which Ignatius speaks—especially when he insists that the retreatant remain in sorrow, grief, and tears ([195, 203, 206])—can best be explained in the context of their relation to the fundamental attitude described above. The grief on which Ignatius insists is the grief of a great love which is turned, all of a sudden, to the object of its love to contemplate it in the self-abasement of the Passion. These subjective states are thus the actualizations of the fundamental attitude described above, that of a love eager to welcome the total mystery of Christ, God's whole plan of salvation and spiritual growth in the Mystical Body. The Christ of this Passion then transforms this receptive love into a purifying and

---

13 See esp. *SpEx,* [199, 204, 209, 226–229]. In fact, Ignatius is here emphasizing some "points of view" on the objective mystery or salvific plan. We shall see the value of this later.

redemptive compassion. For Ignatius there is question of something far more than the mere arousing of pity through a spectacle of physical, psychological, and moral pain in the sense of the medieval Passion plays, which for so long have inspired Catholic exegesis. "Ask," states Ignatius, "for sorrow, compassion, and shame because the Lord is going to His suffering for my sins" ([193]). Right from the beginning the relationship of the drama of the Passion to its historical and ontological causes is made explicit. The Passion events of the Third Week are going to unfold the tragic scenes of this drama which the first colloquy of the *Exercises* already evoked in theological terms: Because of sin, my sins, notice ([53]) that the *Creator* has made himself also a *creature,* and from eternal life has come to death here in time.[14] It is also the drama of the Two Standards which is taken up again and fully actuated, when the Lord submits freely to the powers of Darkness in order to undo all their ruses, to deliver us from their malice, and to give back to our lives and to the universe the meaning which God had intended.

Thus when Ignatius asks us to make every effort to remain sorrowful with Christ sorrowful and suffering, he wants us not to abandon too quickly our chosen way of being associated with him in his saving mission all the way to its end. He wants us to stay with him, behind him, as best we can, for this descent into the heart of death and of hell, knowing that it is the way "out of this world to the Father."[15] It takes a faithful love and a living faith to inspire and nourish these dispositions of the Third Week. They dispose us to be more completely conformed to Christ, and to receive the spiritual fruits which his grace freely produces in us.

It is necessary, therefore, to see behind Ignatius' language an extraordinary attachment to Christ, which he supposes is shared by the person who undertakes the last stage of the Exercises: a particular love for the Christ of the Passion who saves us "at the price of his blood and of his life."[16] What Paul proclaimed Ignatius proposes for the contemplation of the person who will "desire nothing other than Christ and him crucified, in order that, cruci-

---

14 On this subject read J. Lewis, *Notes de cours,* p. 38.

15 John 13:1. On this descent of the whole Church into hell with Christ, read H. U. von Balthasar, *Heart of the World* (San Francisco, 1979), p. 199: "This, O Church, is both the need and the promise. Attach yourself to me so irrevocably that I may be able to make you descend to the very depths of hell; then I shall attach you to myself so irrevocably that you may be able to ascend to the heights of heaven."

16 *LettersIgn,* pp. 121, 351, 425. On the dispositions of the retreatant when beginning the Third Week, see J. Lewis, *Notes de cours,* p. 39; G. Fessard, *La dialectique,* pp. 124–125; I. Iparraguirre, *How to Give a Retreat,* pp. 168–177.

fied in this life, he or she may be raised to the other."[17] Ignatius knows very well that there is no true joy of the resurrection which does not first know the grief-stricken passage through the cross. That is why he does not spare the person who is called to contemplate the mystery or plan of salvation which is death and life.[18] Soon we shall see this still more clearly. Throughout the Third Week it is the object which we contemplate, and which gives meaning to the sentiments we seek in this stage of the Exercises.

C. *THE THIRD WEEK: The Mystery of the Cross*

Here we shall group our remarks about Ignatius' point of view on contemplation during the Third Week. These remarks refer to all the events from the Last Supper to the burial inclusively ([190–209]). They pertain especially to the dialectical interactions of the spiritual experience which find here their ordinary prolongation. They determine, where pertinent, the orientation which in Ignatius' view arises from the religious signification of the narrated Passion events. Through this we shall see how the perspective of each evangelist is integrated, that we may conform ourselves to it in the best way possible for improving the Christian experience at which this stage of the Exercises aims.

1. *The Ignatian Dialectic*

Ignatian retreat directors rather generally think that the exposition of the Passion events has always been somewhat difficult in itself—even without the

17 *LettersIgn,* p. 69.
18 We find the same realistic preoccupation in the 26th letter of St. John of the Cross to a spiritual son: "If ever . . . a religious, whatever his rank, superior or not, tries to teach you a doctrine that is lax and easy, do not believe him, do not accept it, even if he should confirm it by miracles. But reach out to penance and still more penance, to the point of complete detachment; for if you wish to possess Christ, you will never find him without the Cross" (see *Collected Works,* p. 702). On the equivalent of the Gospel theme of the "narrow gate" (Luke 13:24), some interesting reflections may be found in the following authors: John of the Cross, *Collected Works,* pp. 76–79; 585–595; Teresa of Avila, (*Collected Works,* pp. 337–338); J. Galot, *Le coeur du Christ,* p. 101; J. M. Tézé, "La lutte de Jacob avec l'ange," *Chr,* no. 33 (1962), 69–77; L. Mendizábal, *Annotationes de Directione spirituali,* pp. 217–218, 222; M. Zundel, *Le poème de la Sainte Liturgie,* pp. 96–97, 255; S. Stehman, *Le voyage à l'ancre,.* pp. 53–54; S. Weil, who has explored this theme in *La pesanteur et la grâce,* pp. 16, 17, 30–31, 45, 84, 86, 104–105, 107. Still more can be found in Scripture: Matt.10:37–39; 16:24–26; Mark 8:34–37; Luke 9:23–25; John 12:24; 1 Peter 4:1–3, 13–14; Rom. 12:14–21; 1 Cor. 2:2–16, 22–25; 2 Cor. 12:7–10; Gal. 2:19–20, 6:16; Phil. 1:19–24, 2:6–11, 17–18; 2 Tim. 3:12.

addition of some particular theoretical problem. The difficulty stems, perhaps, from overlooking a fundamental theoretical problem which concerns two factors: the dialectical procedure of the *Exercises* with its special application to the Third Week, and the objective interpretation of the Gospel events. If this problem of theory is neglected, the purpose envisaged in these topics remains vague and fails to indicate a definite line of direction to be followed. We alluded to this when we were speaking of the "subjective dispositions" of the retreatant, of the moods of soul which the experience of the Third Week ordinarily supposes. From them directors have very often mistakenly drawn their criteria for their interpretation and presentation of the mysteries to be contemplated. However, as Hugo Rahner notes regarding [208], in this stage Ignatius surprises us more than ever by his increasing economy of words: "The stronger the tension becomes in the gospel history of salvation and in the soul, the more sparing of words and silent Ignatius becomes."[19] He only asks the exercitant to continue "to labor" in a state of interior pain and deep distress ([195]), and to beg even to an extreme, as the grace proper to this Week, grief and affliction as well as sorrow and shame ([193, 203]). Here we meet again the first aspect of the Ignatian interpretation, which finds the origin of these subjective dispositions not merely in the pity one feels upon seeing intense physical and psychological pain, but also and beyond that in one's awareness of sin and its consequence, death. The wages which sin pays to the sinner is death (Romans 6:23). We might add, drawing example from the first colloquy of the *Exercises* ([53]), "even the death of the Creator . . . become man."

It is important, then, to place oneself within the context of the movement of the Exercises, at this time in the experience when the objective and the subjective levels are especially converging. It is always the fundamental experience of the Kingdom which we must keep in mind to guide ourselves in our interpretation. During the whole of the Second Week, the Lord, who came to fulfill his mission by calling us and associating us with Himself, now in the Third Week lives out that mission at its summit. It is the long-awaited "hour" when he "consummates" his redemptive work; when, by uniting us to himself in our humanity which he assumes personally, he "passes from this world to the Father." It is in this that salvation essentially consists. In the perspective on the *Exercises* which regards the Kingdom as their axis, as also in that which regards God's plan of salvation as their framework of reference, the moment of the Passion is the most meaningful in the Christian experi-

---

19   H. Rahner, "Notes on the Spiritual Exercises," *WL*, 85 (1956), 301.

ence. We must keep this spirit in mind if we wish to meditate on the Passion *"in the context of the Exercises,"* and not to isolate the Passion and make it into a simple contemplation which is not much more than respectful onlooking. "The Exercises," Jacques Lewis states, "are in truth merely the Kingdom which has been met, embraced, and fulfilled; met in the Principle and Foundation and the colloquy of mercy, embraced during the Second Week, fulfilled in one's association with the Cross and the Resurrection."[20]

For that reason, and also because he situates himself within the preeminent truth of God's plan of salvation, during the Third Week Ignatius spontaneously brings into convergence the two lines of force which have structured the making of the Exercises up to this point: that of the First Week, which directly considers sin in our lives, and that of the Second Week, which seeks to know, love, and follow Christ our Savior—in one phrase, the history of sin and the history of salvation. This intention comes out especially in the preludes which indicate "the grace we should ask for." They also present, as the motive for our grief with Christ, not so much the suffering in itself, but rather the fact that we should recognize the cause for it as being in ourselves, in our sins. When we meditated on evil in the First Week, we saw ourselves as beings of extreme poverty and interior suffering. Christ comes to embrace this sorrowful human condition in order to change it into life and joy. Hence, we are invited to unite ourselves intimately with this suffering of Christ which is really our own, and which he carries, so to speak, "cosmically." Our suffering for him is added to that of the universe, to overwhelm the Savior of the world. But above all, it is united to a redemptive suffering of infinite worth which delivers us from evil in the love which supports it.

> Surely he has borne our griefs
> and carried our sorrows;
> yet we esteemed him stricken,
> smitten by God, and afflicted.
>
> But he was wounded for our transgressions,
> he was bruised for our iniquities;
> upon him was the chastisement that made us whole,
> and with his stripes we are healed.
> All we like sheep have gone astray;
> we have turned every one to his own way;
> and the Lord has laid on him the iniquity of us all.[21]

20   J. Lewis, *Notes de cours,* p. 17.
21   Isai. 53:4–6.

In the same way, the struggle of the Two Standards is taken up and experienced by Christ in his Passion. The universal level of the conflict between man and Satan, and that of our own subjection to the snares of the Enemy are brought together. On the one hand, for Christ the perspective of the Kingdom and the Two Standards leads directly to death on the cross—the Kingdom of God being built up against the powers of Darkness. On the other hand, our own personal, present insertion into the history of evil is efficaciously taken over by Christ "made sin" for us, in order that it may also be efficaciously transformed through insertion into the living and universal history of salvation. In this way the double movement of the First and Second Weeks effectively reaches us, in Christ, to snatch us from evil and immerse us in a love which is at one and the same time indivisibly personal and universal. Because of the Lord and his mission, because of Satan and his ambitions, the sorrowful drama unfolds in union with the whole world where everything invites us to participate—love as well as hate, death as well as life. The one who situates himself or herself within the truth of God's saving plan, as the logic of the *Exercises* so forcefully presents it, will feel himself touched very intimately in his most inward self. He or she will perceive himself as called "in particular" by the King of the Kingdom and as saved by name in His love. However, in Jesus, Creator and universal Lord, the retreatant will make this "passage" which snatches one from self and ushers one into the cosmic march of all creation, in Christ, toward salvation and the glorification of the Father. Hence, if the retreatant takes his or her place in the truth of this divine salvific plan and in the authentic perspective of the *Exercises,* his or her experience of deliverance, which is profoundly intimate and personal, will be accomplished in Christ and in "the others"—all the others whom Christ attaches to himself by saving them, in order to form his Body, both mystical and real.[22]

2. Contemplation in the Third Week

There are two principles which seem to underlie the contemplations of the Third Week: first of all, the importance of a simple and genuine contemplation which can unite us to the mystery of the Passion, and second, the necessity of arriving for this purpose at the religious signification of this mystery—that is, of viewing it in its whole comprehensive truth. The contemplation no longer seeks only the light from above which enlightens our

---

22 If the experience does not evolve in this direction, there will be no meaning "existentially" in the universal character of the contemplation "to Attain Love of God" ([230–237]).

darkness to show us the way to God in accord with all the demands he makes of us. It functions also as a union with a mystery, God's plan, which is lived out today as well as during every instant of our Christian existence. But that it may serve in this way we must grasp the meaning of the plan, open ourselves to its true expanse, and unite ourselves to its vital core where the salvific power of the Lord is operative. We must make ourselves truly "with him" at this interior turning point where reality is achieved through failure, and where death is transformed into glorious life. If the Lord goes through his Passion alone, then I do not eat of the Tree of Life; but by freely becoming one with him in the death he offers me, I pass over into life.

Through keeping these two principles in mind, our interpretation of the Gospel events of the Third Week will fit in with Ignatius' laconic terseness and the particular points of view which orient his considerations ([195–197]). In this way we shall not waste time repeating facts which are already known—something which too often only exhausts the retreatant's interior perception, as we have mentioned before. We shall recall these facts only in the first prelude; but with Ignatius we shall evoke the primary signification of the mystery by presenting its principal aspects, universal and personal. For this purpose we have first of all, in the *Exercises*, the perspective of the ensemble recalled above. It is the perspective which is extracted from the Kingdom and the Two Standards and from the general movement of the Exercises, and which draws a person away from sin and carries him or her along on the way of love toward glorifying the Father through participation in God's plan of salvation and sanctification through Christ. This perspective corresponds rather closely, as we shall see, to that of the evangelists in the general drift of their Gospels and especially in their Passion narratives. Finally, to this perspective Ignatius adds a few indications which are immediate to each contemplation and facilitate its insertion into the vision of the ensemble—a vision centered on Christ who is going to his Passion for my sins ([195–197]).[23]

If we keep these two points clearly in mind (perspective of the whole and immediate applications), which are also emphasized by the religious signification of the Gospel narratives, our exposition of the mystery of the Passion will be relatively easy as well as suggestive. It will be an invitation to contemplative prayer which is far from complicated, and which by that very fact is more conducive to insight into God's revealed and comprehensive plan of

23 On this subject see J. M. Granero, "Las contemplaciones de la Tercera Semana (Notas de teología Soteriológica)," *Mnr,* 27 (1955), 35–41.

salvation. Neither the convergence of the objective and subjective levels of action about which we spoke, nor the universal aspects of the Passion will have to be a preoccupation for us. When the Passion is presented simply just as it is, everything happens spontaneously. The soul welcomes the narrative and the message when it sees that Christ, who saved the world by leading it to his Father through his Passover, embraces the soul itself with a most intense love, even though it has turned its back to its Lord by its sins. Care must be taken, simply, not to deprive the Passion narrative of these broad aspects which snatch the soul from self-love and place it in the current of a universal and personal love which forcefully draws one onward. "For the love of Christ controls us."[24]

3. The Last Supper ([190–199])

The contemplations of the Third Week begin with the Last Supper. The Eucharistic mystery is presented in its sacrificial rather than in its sacramental aspect. For Ignatius, the Last Supper is the Lord's entry into his Passion. This is the immediate occasion which moves him to instruct us to ask for grief, emotion, and confusion "because it is for my sins that the Lord is going to his Passion" ([193]). We shall spend some time on this first contemplation because it gives to those which follow their immediate signification in the context of the divine salvific plan. It reveals in particular the meaning of this death on the cross, which will be a free gift of self ([195–196]) and a redemptive sacrifice ([197]). In other words, by offering his body and blood, Jesus made them into a sign reminding us of the redemptive covenant established once for all for the salvation of many.

"His free gift of self." This freedom with which the Savior disposes of himself during the course of the Passion, through the intervention of his accusers and executioners, in order to surrender himself to the love and the will of God—this is what Ignatius contemplates from this first exercise onward ([195–196]). In his eyes, too, that is why the Last Supper, inaugurates and anticipates the unfolding of the Passion events. As Bouyer writes:

> On Holy Thursday we shall see in the Eucharistic supper the voluntary act of oblation of the Word Incarnate: that offering to God of the humanity which the Word had assumed to himself, accepting in advance the bloody immolation that this sacrifice entailed. On Good Friday we shall observe the concrete realization of the God-Man in the immolation of the cross.[25]

24 2 Cor. 5:14.
25 L. Bouyer, *The Paschal Mystery*, p. xxi.

Fessard, writing about the dialectic of the free act within the making of the Exercises, shows well the importance of this gesture which offers the victim to the divine will. It is an act of supreme freedom; and with God's grace the retreatant, who is now disposed to make his or her own offering, will associate himself with it. The truth which Fessard documents by using an Antiphon of St. Ephraem emphasizes, under a verbal paradox, an essential aspect of this mystery: "Transubstantiation and Passion are linked together like the interior and the exterior of one same conversion. The interior, like everything spiritual, takes place in an instant, whereas the exterior, the Passion, requires time to become true."[26] But this free act which offers the self "in an instant" is primordial in that it becomes, in a sense, the "true cause of the Passion." It is because he surrenders himself—"kills himself" according to the words of St. Ephraem's antiphon—that his enemies will be able to arrest him and effectively immolate him.[27] "This is my body." This sacred phrase, through the power imparted to it by Christ, the Word of God, accomplishes and will continue to accomplish the Son's free offering of himself to the Father. It also gratuitously associates us with him.

However, the most important thing about the drama of the Passion which the Last Supper reveals to us is this sacrificial character which makes it the main element in God's plan of redemption. Indeed, it is a "new Passover" which the Lord accomplishes and institutes, and in which he himself becomes the Lamb who is immolated for the sins of the people. And if he thus offers Himself freely, Ignatius notes, it is "for my sins." Such is the last point of his contemplation, in which the history of salvation is brought into contact with my lowly self at this point in time and invites me to insert myself into it, by enduring with Christ my own personal sufferings ([197]). We should therefore ponder anew these ideas on the Last Supper as a redemptive sacrifice, in order to perceive more clearly the ever present realization of the

26 G. Fessard, *La dialectique,* p. 114. To verify the analogy of these notions with those of "interior sacrifice" and "exterior sacrifice," both in the world religions and in the case of Christ, see F. Bourassa, "Verum Sacrificium," *ScE,* 3 (1950), pp. 146ff. The idea of the "moral transubstantiation" of our lives in Christ is also developed by M. Zundel, *Le poème de la Sainte Liturgie,* p. 255.

27 To these gestures which make more explicit the relation of the Last Supper to the mystery of the cross, one can well join the words of Christ's farewell address and those of the priestly prayer found in St. John. These words are, so to speak, "the very heart of the Passion." See J. Guillet, *Jesus Christ Yesterday and Today,* pp. 121–122; also pp. 131, 156, 176. Likewise on the subject of Christ's liberty in the face of death, made clear by the three resurrection miracles during his life, see R. Guardini, *The Lord* (Chicago, 1954), pp. 367–373, esp. 371–373.

divine plan which saves us by inviting our own participation in bringing it to fulfillment.

To the words "this is my body" which offer the victim, Christ adds a ritual gesture which anticipates his own immolation. In the divine blood "poured out for many," at the very hour when the commemorative Passover reached its climax, Christ entered into a new covenant, the "New Testament." The act, his death on Good Friday, which was intended merely to do away with a Jew who was "inciting the people to revolt," was through his anticipation made into a sacred act, a sacrifice, "something made holy"; and he further handed this rite on to his nascent Church. In the Last Supper, the mission of salvation already finds its accomplishment, in such a way that each time it will be "commemorated" in the future, it will be the whole work of salvation tending toward its greatest fulfillment in the living Church of Christ.[28]

> Because Jesus, in full possession of his liberty, gave his disciples his own body and his blood, he reveals to them that his death is something other than an execution organized by the Roman and Jewish police. Because Jesus, still free to come and go, has delivered himself publicly to death, he made it clear in advance that at the hour when men would arrest him and bind his hands, each of his movements, apparently dictated by the Satanic powers unleashed against him, would actually constitute the unfolding of a ceremonial minutely provided for by the will of the Father. Between the ritual of the Last Supper and the unfolding of the Passion there is much more than a symbolic prefiguration, there is an immediate connection. The Last Supper makes the Passion into a sacred action, the progress of the victim to the final immolation.[29]

This, then, is the crowning of the work of salvation, of the mission which led Christ to this hour when, with the world to be redeemed and with

28 "The Last Supper taken by Christ with His disciples has had a twofold effect: a real action accomplished once for all, and a ritual action perpetually renewable. The mystery is that the two are only one." L. Bouyer, *The Paschal Mystery*, p. 42. On the Last Supper and the anamnesis or "memorial," which in the Christian liturgy embrace the whole history of salvation from the creation to its perfect accomplishment in Christ (see the content of the prayers), read the very interesting article of L. Ligier, "Autour du sacrifice eucharistique. Anaphores orientales et anamnèse juive de Kippur," *NRTh*, 92 (1960), 40–55.

29 J. Guillet, *Jesus Christ Yesterday and Today*, p. 156. On the same subject, read F. Bourassa, "Verum Sacrificium," *ScE*, 3 (1950), esp. pp. 159–165, and R. Guardini, *La figura di Gesú Cristo nel Nuovo Testamento*, pp. 47–52. On the separate consecration of the Body and the Blood, the theme which constitutes the background of our reflections, see St. Thomas, *Summa theologiae*, III. Q. 76, a. 2, ad 1; Q. 78, a. 3, ad 2; Q. 80, a. 12, ad 3; Q. 82, a. 4, ad 1;3, a. 10c; Q. 83, a. 4.

humanity united to him through the Incarnation, he "passes from this world to the Father." Consequently, we shall find here the goal of our configuration, of our being made like to Christ, to him who thus freely offers himself and dies in order to rise again. To the extent in which we are united with him in his Passion, and of our participation in his death, we already participate in his glory. The divine plan of the covenant is what he brings to fulfillment in the Last Supper, "the mystery of faith" for us! "The vital factor in faith is the possibility for the Church and for each Christian in her to be drawn by Christ near to himself and to share in his sacrifice (just as Christ shared in our poverty and in our guilt, 'being made sin for us')." What faith believes is that Christ has an efficacious will to establish an inconceivable union between himself and us. "The Church believes that Christ will make of her and of Him two beings in one flesh. Thus, she believes that the death of the one grain of wheat will communicate to numberless grains on the awn the power to live and to die in their turn until the final harvest."[30]

To sum up, let us remark that Christ accomplished this mystery by making use of the ritual elements of the commemorative Passover of the Old Testament: first of all, on the evening of Holy Thursday, (or to be more precise, of the Last Supper), and on the following Friday. He conferred on these rites a divine, sacramental power; and the "memory" of it extends its efficacy all the way to ourselves in order to complete the universal work of salvation. But to bring about this transmission of divine salvific power to a humble eucharistic rite, he himself will live, "in the name of the people," the solemn rite of the Great Passover, offering to the Father the perfect and immaculate victim which his infinite love demanded. "Sacrifices and offerings thou hast not desired, but a body hast thou prepared for me. In burnt offerings and sin offerings thou hast taken no pleasure. Then I said, 'Lo, I have come to do thy will, 0 God.' "[31]

That is why near this ninth hour when, according to the liturgical prescriptions, the Jews had to immolate the lamb of the Passover in the temple, Christ will die on the cross, laden with our sins, in order to offer to God the homage of his obedience, his love, and his perfect adoration.[32]

---

30 L. Bouyer, *The Paschal Mystery,* p. 45.
31 Heb. 10:5-7; see also Ps. 40:7-9.
32 On this subject read the very beautiful text of L. Bouyer, *The Paschal Mystery,* pp. 63, 72-75. We have intentionally limited our treatment to the religious signification of this gesture of Christ, who accomplishes and freely institutes a new Pasch, thus giving his redemptive meaning to the Passion and to our participation in God's plan of salvation. It would certainly be interesting to probe other aspects, as for example, the "eucharistic communion" in the sacrifice of Christ through the intermediary of the Last Supper as a sacrament. It would also be

4. The Religious Signification of the Passion Narratives

a. In the Evangelists

The principles which based the interpretation of the Gospel events in the *Exercises* on objectivity and transcendence—that is, on the faithful transmission of the Gospel message and on the action of the Holy Spirit (see chapter 6, above, especially nos. 1 and 4)—these principles now lead us to seek the chief signification of the events presented in the Passion narratives, in order to understand better the purpose at which they are aimed.

In accordance with the history of their literary formation, these narratives spring from a preoccupation purely theological which was somewhat influenced by the framework of the "liturgical celebration of the Passover."[33] For all practical purposes we should recognize that the evangelists did not intend to write ordered history or to present a psychological portrait of the drama of the Passion. For them, the facts are undoubtedly important; but the evangelists' chief interest is directed toward relating these facts to the divine plan of redemption and salvation. "For them," Martin Dibelius writes, "an understanding of the historical and psychological development of the events of the Passion was a matter of indifference. Only one thing mattered: to understand what God had willed to accomplish by means of these events."[34] Thus in their eyes "the history of the Passion was directed more toward proclaiming salvation than toward reporting human details, no matter how interesting we find them."[35] Xavier Léon-Dufour, who has analyzed at length the different opinions found in the history of the literary criticism of these Passion narratives, agrees that "the events are not reported in themselves and for themselves. . . . Habitually the events are presented theologically."[36] This theological perspective causes these events to be viewed in the light of "paschal faith."[37] "That was the primary object of faith, the condition of salva-

---

fitting, especially at this point in the Exercises, for us to give a particular importance to the celebration of the Eucharist. It is good to remember that Ignatius asked his retreatant to assist every day at Mass and Vespers, which represented practically the whole of the liturgical life of his time.

33 For this part of our work, we have drawn our inspiration largely from X. Léon-Dufour's excellent article in *SDB*, s.v. "Passion," col. 1420–1492; also from a conference given by M. Dibelius, "La signification religieuse des récits évangeliques de la Passion," *Revue d'histoire et de philosophie religeuses*, 13 (1933), 30–45.

34 M. Dibelius, ibid., 32.

35 Ibid., 34.

36 X. Léon-Dufour, *SDB*, col. 1428.

37 Ibid. See also M. Dibelius, "La signification," p. 44: "There everything is contemplated from the point of view of faith in the Passover."

tion. It was necessary to recognize that God had snatched his Son from the darkness of death."[38] In this perspective "the evangelists did not report the story of a failure in a cold and detached manner; rather, they invite the reader to believe in a victory that goes beyond failure. Hence arises the implicit presence of the glory in the most humble facts, that glory which shines forth from the Transfiguration on to the narrated details of the way of the cross."[39] They have, therefore, proclaimed Christ crucified "not to appeal to sentiment, but to announce the gospel of salvation."[40] This proclamation of a salvation accomplished by the mystery of the Passion will surely arouse those profound spiritual sentiments which enlightened faith engenders. "When they heard this they were cut to the heart, and said to Peter and the rest of the apostles: 'Brethren, what shall we do?' "[41]

In these Gospel narratives, this presentation of the message is based on objective and transcendent data, and it is particularized according to the aspects of the God's salvific plan which are emphasized by each evangelist. Two quite different traditions can be observed. In both cases there is primarily question of "highlighting the accomplishment of God's will. This will is shown concretely in the person of Christ; and in regard to this there is evident a twofold tendency focused respectively on his human and his divine aspects."[42] In contemplating the same sacred events, some evangelists will focus more on the figure of the "suffering servant"; others on the "Son of Man," or the Son of God, or the King who comes to give witness to the Truth. In fact, literary criticism has established the existence of a primitive narrative before the redaction of the Passion narratives. This narrative, which perhaps was never written,[43] would have been composed in an ecclesial and liturgical milieu, and would have contained the principal elements which were to serve as a basis for the more developed narratives of the two subsequent tendencies: the conspiracy and paschal meal, the garden of olives, the judgment, the crucifixion, and the burial; and to this, it seems, the account of one apparition was added. As to our canonical narratives of the Passion, it is clear enough today that they are "mutually independent, but from time to time they represent different but similar editings of a common source. Matthew and Mark seem often to depend on a common document, Luke and John

---

38   X. Léon-Dufour, *SDB*, col. 1428.
39   Ibid., col. 1428–1429.
40   Ibid., col. 1430. The author quotes 1 Cor. 1:17–18, 2:8; Phil. 2:7–8.
41   Acts 2:38.
42   X. Léon-Dufour, *SDB,* col. 1430.
43   Ibid., col. 1454.

on a common tradition."[44] Thus the Passion narratives, in relation to the tendencies just pointed out, and within the common purpose which unites them, are grouped together two by two. The first pair, Matthew and Mark, look rather to the suffering Christ who saves us by fulfilling the prophecies of the Servant of Isaiah,[45] while the other two, Luke and John, aim to transcend the suffering in order to see more clearly the glory of the Son of God, of the King who from his 'throne' on the cross founds his Kingdom of life. With John, we even gaze upon "a triumphal procession of Jesus toward the Father."[46]

b. *In the* Exercises

In the *Exercises* Ignatius groups his topics for contemplation into fairly complete units. After the Last Supper come Gethsemani, the religious and political trials, the way of the cross, the crucifixion and death, the burial, and the three days of death. This question arises: To which narrative or theological tradition is the Ignatian perspective in the *Exercises* most open? The ultimate purpose which aims at the transforming contemplation of the divine plan of salvation and sanctification coincides perfectly with the perspective "of faith" found in the Gospels. For this reason we are already inclined to affirm that the particular perspectives of the Passion narratives can be integrated into this overall perspective of faith, each in its own way.

But we can go even further. At first glance it is evident enough that Ignatius followed the first tradition which considers profoundly the sufferings and failure of Christ sorrowful and torn. This insistence is in conformity with the care used in the *Exercises* to bring one to consider the pain and the struggle which the Lord undergoes in our place, in order to save us. The ideal of imitation, of becoming like to Christ, must be linked to the reality of our condition as torn between good and evil, and exposed to the snares of the Enemy. Right from the offering of the Kingdom, the retreatant is alerted to

---

44 Ibid.
45 Ibid. The reference in general is to Isai. 53 and to Ps. 21; see also Ps. 31, 38, 69, and 78.
46 X. Léon-Dufour, *SDB,* col. 1478. Space does not allow us to give more details here on the particular perspectives of the evangelists in their Passion narratives. What distinguishes them, divides them into sub-groups, and reunites them in a common purpose is very well described by Léon-Dufour, *SDB,* col. 1478: for Mark, col. 1472–1474; for Matthew, col. 1474–1476; for Luke, col. 1476–1478; and for John, col. 1478–1479; also M. Dibelius, art. cit., for Mark, pp. 35–36; for Matthew, pp. 37–38; for John, pp.41–42; regarding Luke, the author's point of view seems to be incomplete; it should be completed by Léon-Dufour's treatment (col. 1476).

this mystery of the cross, and there he or she contemplates its complete realization in the flesh of Christ. Hence we must be with the Lord in his suffering; we are invited to follow him unto his death. Otherwise, we are simply spectators at a Passion event which may be very touching, even to tears, but which in no way disturbs the egotism of our lives.

However, to think that Ignatius saw this aspect alone would be to diminish considerably the signification of the Third Week. It would be to detach this Week from its Ignatian context, that is to say, from that overall vision of the whole which brought about its birth and furnishes its orientation, and to deprive it of an important part of its interior dynamism. With Ignatius we are always before the Christ of majesty, the Creator and Lord, the eternal King of the Kingdom who fulfills his mission here on earth by passing through the painful death from which he delivers us.

This is the overall perspective cf the *Exercises,* which imparts its own paschal optimism to the sorrowful content of the Third Week, just as it does to every form of asceticism, and to the very mystery of the Passion. To overlook this here would be to truncate the experience of the Exercises, and even the experience of Christian faith.[47] When Ignatius asks us "to consider how the divinity hides itself" during the mysteries of the Third Week, he does not state that we ought to prescind from it and to eliminate the divinity from the mystery. Rather, when writing the statement he was precisely drawing attention to it in order to emphasize the free "emptying of himself" *(kenosis)* by the Lord of majesty who submits his humanity to the terrible sufferings of the Passion. After having asked the retreatant "to consider how the divinity hides itself," he adds: "For example, it could destroy its enemies and does not do so, but leaves the most sacred humanity to suffer so cruelly" ([96]). Therefore, whether we hold to Matthew or Mark, who see the accomplishment of messianic salvation in the suffering of the condemned; or whether we pass—directly or in the repetitions—to Luke, who has the Lord engage in an eschatalogical combat in order to triumph completely over Satan, thus uniting us to His victory; or whether with John we contemplate the majesty of the Word Incarnate who is freely founding his Kingdom, to the glory of the Father, through the ignominy of the cross—in all these ways of proceeding, if we keep our attention fixed on the essential and religious

---

47 It would be useless to object that Matthew and Mark both have centered their narratives on the Suffering Servant. For all that, the paschal aspect is not absent (see the two articles indicated above): In Matthew and Mark Christ is strongly proclaimed as the Messiah and King, but it is as a Suffering Servant. crushed by grief and death, that he wins victory and life for us.

perspectives of the inspired narratives, we insert ourselves directly into the movement of the experience proper to the Third Week. And in proportion as prayer unites us to the Lord who attaches us irrevocably to himself in his struggle and his victory, we shall achieve the true purpose of the contemplations on the Passion.

c. In Theological Reflections

To sum up, we must, first of all, keep in mind the twofold aspect which pertains to the divine and human person of the Lord, the eternal King of the Kingdom given over to the salvific ignominy of the Passion. Let us take up again the initial perspective which arose in our dialectical analysis of the experience which ought to be lived out within this mystery of grandeur and of suffering. The structure into which the Passion event to be contemplated and the foreseen experience to be lived would be inserted, can be reduced to these three principal points which can be expressed in three phrases: the wages of sin, the gospel of penance, the ministry of reconciliation. These will give us headings under which we can formulate our theological reflections, by grouping them when we have occasion to propose one of the Passion mysteries. We can do this by aiming our presentation of the drama of the Passion at a spirit of communion in the expiation which interiorly justifies us and also accomplishes universal salvation.

"The wages of sin is death" (Rom. 6:23). The first aspect characteristic of this presentation is its connecting the drama of the Passion with the "mystery of lawlessness" (2 Thes. 2:7), of sin, of evil—all that the exercitant pondered in the First Week and the Two Standards, and which was raised by the last point of the contemplation in the Third Week: "All this for my sins" ([197]). The wages paid out by sin to the sinner is death: That is the theological signification of the Passion event being contemplated; and it includes our own death and the death of the God-man in order to change into life the failure to which humankind has subjected its own existence and that of creation. Fessard considers that "the *Exercises* are a rigorous commentary on this statement of St. Paul: 'For our sake he made him to be sin, so that in him we might become the righteousness of God.' "[48]

The Gospel of Penance. The second aspect we have to examine is the penitential suffering by means of which the "passage" which saves us is accomplished. With Matthew and Mark Ignatius insists on this. On our part, we should avoid the escape route of being content with words and beautiful

---

48   2 Cor. 5:21, and G. Fessard, *La dialectique*, p. 199.

sentiments. Ignatius asks that we strive to share in some way the painful destiny of Christ who humbles himself to share our destiny in order to save us. To this end he provides seven days for the Third Week ([208]), and he notes ([209]) that it can be longer. "The contemplation of the Christ of the Passion was of enormous importance in the eyes of the one who . . . had learned, in Ludolph's *Vita Christi* and Jacopo's *Flos Sanctorum,* that the whole of the spiritual life is in the crucified Lord."[49] The gospel of penance—this is indeed a characteristic of the authentic proclamation of God's plan of salvation through Christ, and of the imitation to which it commits us through the truth contained in this divine plan.

The Ministry of Reconciliation. Finally, deeply inside the drama of the Passion is a universal aspect which, through participation with Christ, necessarily introduces us into the universal love which animated the Redemption and brought it to realization. This was stressed in connection with the Kingdom, in the section on the theology of our Christian participation, and we touched on it again when we spoke of the dialectic of the experience of the Third Week (chapter 7, C, 1 above). We are dealing with a "ministry of reconciliation" exercised by every Christian in virtue of his or her union with Christ, the Savior. To become aware of this here in terms of the explicit relationship of the contemplation of the Passion to the Kingdom, its real foundation in the *Exercises,* is to go even further in our response to the invitation of the eternal King. That response already contained these elements mentioned just above. It is also to be more completely "with him" in order to accomplish his universal mission of salvation to the glory of the Father ([95]). The prayer, therefore, ought simply to make the retreatant present to this great salvific plan which is presented to the Christian understanding in its essential dimensions. Instead of merely repeating and treating in great detail that Christ suffers, that he endures such or such a torture, the director ought to present the signification of the drama and its episodes, by revealing the greatness of Christ who suffers, in what circumstances and for what motives he endures, remains silent, and dies. Then the preeminent sign which God gives us in the infinite love of his Son will penetrate more profoundly into our hearts, together with the efficacious grace of the salvation which we received with humility. "They shall look on him whom they have pierced."[50] They will look and they will understand what love and death really are, and also the gift of life through love. And they will desire, in their

---

49 J. Lewis, *Notes de cours,* p. 39.
50 Zech. 12:10; John 19:37.

purified love, to unite their own death, which is realized a little each day, to the death of God crucified for us in his love. "We are," Simone Weil writes somewhat harshly, "what is farthest from God, at the extreme limit, from which it is absolutely impossible to come back to him. In our very being, God is tormented. We are the crucifixion of God. God's love for us is passion. How could the good love the evil without suffering? And the evil also suffers by loving the good. The mutual love of God and man is suffering."[51]

Christ, the Word of God expressed for us in the visible flesh which manifests his glory, utters to us on the cross the last and supreme word of his revelation of the Father. He shows that the Father is love, and that he saves man because He loves him!

D. THE FOURTH WEEK. The Resurrection: the New Life

1. A Note on the Ignatian Exegesis

Ignatius' attitude in his handling of the Resurrection is rather surprising. How does it happen that, although for the thirty-day retreat he proposes as many as twelve exercises on the apparitions of our Lord, there is not even one exercise on the mystery of the Resurrection considered in itself? But it would be a hasty mistake, we think, to affirm that the mystery of the Resurrection has been excluded from the text of the *Exercises*, or has received too little attention. We say right off that from one end of the Fourth Week to the other Ignatius leads the retreatant to contemplate almost exclusively "the risen Christ."

Furthermore, in the fourth Annotation, this final Week is described in these words: "The Resurrection and Ascension." If in [218] he opens the Week with the words "First Contemplation: The apparition of Christ our Lord to our Lady" ([299]), he places this same apparition as the first in the list of topics to be contemplated, and above it he puts a title for them all: "The Resurrection of Christ our Lord—the First Apparition." In Ignatius' mind, these two mysteries, the apparition to Mary and the Resurrection, seem to be closely connected, and this connection should not be attributed to chance. Another indication of this close connection is the manner in which he proposes them by going from one to the other almost indifferently. In [299] he writes: "The Resurrection of Christ," but he joins it to these words: "First Point. He appeared to the Virgin Mary." The words "first point," are also striking; it is the only instance of its kind, since there is no second or

---

51   S. Weil, *La pesanteur et la grâce,*. pp. 104–105.

third point. We are dealing, therefore, with one topic, a unique tableau! By contrast, in [218] he writes: "The Apparition of Christ our Lord to our Lady" and in [219] he devotes the whole first prelude—that is, the history of the event to be contemplated—to Christ's passage from death to hell and then to the risen life, a journey which ends with his appearance to "his blessed Mother." The second prelude ([220]) well unites these two subjects, by juxtaposing the two places where they occurred; we have the impression of going from the sepulcher directly to our Lady's house. Finally, the third prelude ([221]) focuses anew on the risen Christ, on his glory and joy which we beg to share with him; there is no further mention of our Lady. But once these preludes, which should serve to reveal the meaning of this mystery, have been formulated, the entire contemplation focuses anew on the Lord rising and appearing to our Lady.

What should we retain of all this in order to understand the paschal mystery? Would it be better to sacrifice the Ignatian setting and be content with the mystery of the Resurrection itself, which is so rich and so important? Are we not at the heart of the Christian experience, where we must hold on to what is essential?

To these problems of Ignatian exegesis and the questions they raise about the appropriateness of the procedure which introduces us to the Fourth Week, we have found only one satisfying response: to accept the functioning of Ignatius' own mind. He is always alert to dominate from above *(de arriba)* the present object of attention, in order to insert it into a larger context of some productive movement. Hence, we prefer to pursue the Christian experience according to Ignatius' own procedure, by giving it its full existential value. In this light we shall be able partly to justify his stubbornness in proposing the mystery in a way that is, to say the least, unusual. But better still, we shall have a deeper understanding of the meaning of this stage (the Fourth Week) and of the nature of the fruits expected from it: "the joy of the Resurrection" ([48, 221]), the "true and most sacred effects" of this mystery in which the Lord manifests his divinity ([223]), and the consolation he brings to those who are the recipients of his apparitions ([224]). Finally, our spiritual awareness receives a "confirmation" coming from above and surpassing all human hope. We even dare to add that this authentic Christian experience, lived in its fullness, is what led Ignatius to this way of presenting the Resurrection of the Lord in close relationship with His apparitions and, first of all, with the apparition to our Lady.[52]

52 Several times Ignatius has introduced details for contemplation which are not mentioned in the Scriptures. He does it with a certain reserve: (e.g., in [310]):

2. The Joy of the Resurrection

a. The Risen Christ

In no way can the "joy of the Resurrection" be explained on a level merely psychological. Christ's joy is not the joy of a man who has regained his health, nor that of an ambassador rejoicing in the success of a mission accomplished in the face of tremendous difficulties. The joy of Easter is of a character entirely religious. It is the joy of the Kingdom of God made real in all the amplitude of the divine plan which had this new reality as one of its factors.

> After the Great Sabbath of the descent into Limbo during the paschal night, we shall witness finally the exaltation of the new Man, the glory born of opprobrium, the life rising from the sepulcher.
>
> And in all this, we shall be only contemplating God as He reconciles all things unto Himself in Jesus Christ.[53]

"as may be piously believed," "as is read in the Lives of the Saints." Nevertheless on the subject of the apparition to our Lady he sets aside his reserve, makes no mention of any "pious tradition," but simply appeals to the "understanding." We think that he is referring to spiritual understanding which, enlightened by faith, grasps the cohesion and harmony of the mysteries of revelation. Our purpose here is not to furnish a "proof" in favor of this opinion which Ignatius accepted, but to show the sense of his position, and especially the basis for *his manner of contemplating the mystery of the Resurrection.*

We should note that Ignatius was not at all the first to suggest the possibility of Jesus' having appeared first to Mary. Ludolph the Carthusian, who speaks of it in ch. 70 of his Life of Christ, records the more or less explicit testimony of Sts. Ambrose, Anselm, and Ignatius of Antioch. Similar opinions are attributed to George of Nicomedia (9th c.) and John the Geometrician (10th c.), according to the article of J. Galot on "the earliest assertion of the co-redemption of Mary" (in *RScR*, 45 [1957], pp. 202 ff). St. Teresa of Avila, in her IVth spiritual report *(relación)* from Salamanca, April 18, 1571, states that the Lord assured her that he appeared to our Lady after the Resurrection (*Oeuvres complètes,* éd. du Seuil, p. 502). Finally, a brief article in the *Osservatore Romano* (April 23, 1954), "La Résurrection et l'Immaculée," lists the names of those who have held the opinion: St. Ambrose, Sedulius (5th c., in his commentary on the *Carmen Paschale),* St. Paulinus of Nola, George of Nicomedia, Simeon of Metaphrastes, Eadmer of Canterbury, St. Albert the Great, St.Bernardine of Siena, St. Ignatius of Loyola, St. Peter Canisius, Maldonatus, St. Lawrence of Brindisi, Cardinal Baronius, M. Olier, and even the "very prudent Benedict XIV," who stated "that this pious opinion is based not only on fitness, but also on the tradition proclaimed equally by ancient architectural and liturgical monuments, starting from Jerusalem itself."

53 L. Bouyer, *The Paschal Mystery,* p.xxi.

The Resurrection of the Lord is the infinite possibility of the divine life offered to a humanity again made capable of receiving the gift of God. "Out of his heart shall flow rivers of living water."[54] At this point in time, during the early hours of Easter, when Christ comes forth from the tomb and destroys the night of death, he opens his arms to a new creation. His heart, overflowing with tenderness, welcomes a humanity regenerated in himself. The strongest images of the Bible cannot express this joy of the eternal Love, concentrated in the heart of the Christ who today takes possession of the object he has loved and which is at last free to give itself back to him. It is the unfaithful spouse of the Old Testament, the figure of Israel and of all straying humanity, pursued with infinite divine patience, who suddenly turns to her Lord, adorned with all the grace and divine life which the Lord's surveying glance sees through the centuries culminating in this point of time. It is the prodigal son—as immense as humanity and as undefined as the centuries—who returns to the Father so full of joy after waiting so long for this return. The joy of Easter is the embrace of the Father and his son who meet again, of the biblical husband and wife who have been reunited. For Jesus our Lord it is the joy, in the name of his Father and his human brethren, of suddenly crossing over the centuries of separation, with the wall of sin overturned like the gravestone. It is the joy of finding again the immense multitude of his redeemed brothers and sisters, now redeemed. "Go and tell my brethren to go to Galilee, and there they shall see me."[55]

b. Our Lady

However, two notes should be added to this contemplation of the Resurrection, the passage from the grave to the fullness of life, in the context of the universal mission of the Lord: one concerning our Lady, the other regarding the retreatant. The joy of Christ resides in God's glorious plan of the deliverance of a world once subjected to Satan which suddenly recovers, in power, the divine mark of the life of grace. For at this precise moment in time in which this new Pasch was accomplished, the possible consent of redeemed humanity, which was now free to receive Love and to respond to Love, was found in the humble "Let it be done to me" *(fiat)* of Mary, "full of grace." It is Mary who represents and makes present this new humanity, which the

---

54   John 7:38.
55   Matt. 28:7, 10. In the New Testament Christ's prayers of jubilation are always strictly related to the divine plan of salvation which finds its fulfillment in souls disposed to receive it. On this see C. Bernard, *De theologia orationis christianae*, pp. 15–16, 20, 55.

Lord receives and embraces in his triumphal joy because it says yes to the divine gift from the Life; it is represented by Mary—made present by her, the humble and joyful lady who can offer it to the divine embrace. For Christ the joy of being raised from the dead is not the joy of breathing again, but rather the joy of bringing to the new and liberated humanity his own life now capable of being received in its fullness. In his victorious love Christ could not offer his life to nothingness, to inanimate or irrational beings incapable of love, nor could he give it immediately to those whose faith had not yet overcome the final obstacles. Mary alone awaited the divine manifestation; in her, the Daughter of Sion, the new "Mother of the living," the risen Christ appeared to all of the new creation, to the universal Church born on that day.

In Ignatius' contemplation, if to come to life again means to take possession, by right of being the eternal King of the Kingdom, of the new humanity redeemed by the divine blood, the Resurrection of Christ and the apparition to our Lady constitute only one Resurrection event, one "mystery"—just as Ignatius represents them in his contemplation ([218–225, 299]). At the head of this beloved humanity, which is figuratively called the spouse of the Messianic Christ, is Mary, the first and indispensable link between Christ's humanity and our own. She is before him as our humanity's first representative. It would be impossible, theologically, that redeemed humanity should fail to follow the Virgin expressly willed as part of the divine plan. It would be impossible that Mary, "Mother of the faithful," would not be the first of all the redeemed souls, and at their head in the movement toward the heart of the glorified Redeemer, toward the arms of Christ open to receive into his love the humanity won at the cost of his blood. A love has endured from all eternity and today, at this point in time and in the person of the humble Mary as representing all of us, receives a response of love:

> Arise, my love, my fair one, and come away;
> for lo, the winter is past,
> the rain is over and gone.
> The flowers appear on the earth.[56]

---

56 Cant. 2:10–12. On the interpretation of the apparition to our Lady as the person representing redeemed humanity, see what M. Olier states in *Osservatore Romano*, April 23, 1954, p. 2; Fessard, *La dialectique*, pp. 132, 137–140, and M. Giuliani, "Le mystère de Notre-Dame dans les Exercices," *Chr*, no. 3 (1954), esp. 38–39.

c. The retreatant

Behind Mary—and this is the second note to our Ignatian contemplation—and beyond the present moment, we see the whole of humanity, past and future, included as the object of the immense joy of the risen Christ. In this immense crowd of redeemed souls moving toward the love and joy of the Lord, I shall see me, my own self, as the "least," in St. Paul's words "as one untimely born," who comes painfully along, who falls and rises again, and who today runs to the Lord's open arms. This is the grace I ask for: to enter into the joy of the Lord, which is a joy of love, and for us the joy of being the object of his love and joy, as one delivered from evil and infallibly moving toward his eternal Heart.[57]

Freely Christ laid down his life, freely he comes to take it up again. The one who has followed him through his Passion will have no trouble in grasping the significance of this immense joy of the Love who is "strong as death," and who calls to life, in order to lose in himself and save in himself the soul desirous of the eternal Lord. That is the whole of the Christian life: "That I may know Christ and the power of his Resurrection, and may share his sufferings, becoming like him in his death, that if possible I may attain the resurrection from the dead."[58]

3. The Apparitions

We shall not give here a theology of the "forty days," on which much has already been written.[59] We are content to show how, during the Fourth

---

57 On the resurrection, birth, and movement of a new world centered on the glorious heart of the Risen Christ, read the magnificent 10th chapter of H. U. von Balthasar, *The Heart of the World* (San Francisco, 1979), pp. 157–173. Also J. Corbon, *L'expérience chrétienne dans la Bible*, pp. 205–208, 229. On the Resurrection considered as the birth of the Church, the new humanity "gathered together" because of the divine life offered from this moment on to every redeemed soul, see F. X. Durrwell, *The Resurrection: A Biblical Study*, trans R. Sheed (New York, 1960), ch. 5, esp. pp. 166–194. On the "new creation" in Christ, see the last part of the article "Creation," by P. Auvray, s.v. "The New Creation," *DBTh*, pp. 101–102. Finally, on the universal character of Christ's victory in his Resurrection, which embraces the whole of creation, see O. Cullmann, *Christ et le temps*, p. 132.

58 Phil. 3:10–11.

59 J. Corbon, *L'expérience chrétienne dans la Bible*, p. 234; G. Fessard, *La dialectique*, pp. 140–145, 200; A. Nisin, *Histoire de Jésus*,. pp. 31ff; H. U. von Balthasar, *Prayer*, pp. 220–224, and *La théologie de l'Histoire*, pp. 88–100; R. Poelman, "La Foi, croissance intérieure," *LV*, 11 (1956), esp. pp. 635–636; R. d'Ouince, "Mort et résurrection en Jésus-Christ," *Chr*, no. 31 (1961), 343–354.

Week, the contemplation of the apparitions prolongs, for whatever time is necessary, the contemplation of the Resurrection and the meeting with the risen Christ. It also intensifies our union with the Savior, our joy in his love, our consolation which strengthens our life of faith, and the confirmation of our concrete attachment to the Lord and to his mission of salvation.[60]

In Ignatius' language, as in that of the primitive Church,[61] the Christ who appears is the risen Christ. Every manifestation of his glory ("God among us") becomes a divine sign. It is posited once and for all and addressed not only to those for whom it is immediately intended, but also to those who will be able to contemplate it and welcome its consoling and strengthening signification. When He appears, before any concrete application of the message to particular persons and circumstances, Christ first of all manifests the economy of salvation in the love of the Father which saves from death. He is the communication of the divine life with its power and freedom. Also, every contemplation of an apparition takes us back to the eternal Resurrection; it is, first of all, a visit from the risen Lord who is forever alive. Through an increasing purification we shall welcome this wondrous sign and its beneficial communication.

But within this mystery and this manifestation with its universal and cosmic range, each one meets the Lord personally, in the depths of his or her own being. First of all, we note that Christ did not appear to those who did not have the faith.[62] To those to whom he did manifest himself, he did so more or less spontaneously according to the measure of their faith, which is essentially the measure of acceptance and surrender. "But to all who received him, who believed in his name, he gave power to become children of God."[63] Christ manifested himself as he is now and as he will be for all eternity, in his glory and his divinity, the source of life. To each one in accordance with his or her state, starting from the personal act of faith and love which attached that person to Christ, the risen Lord grants a personal and present deliverance and an intimate sharing in his divine life which has gained the victory

---

60 It is during the complete experience of the paschal mystery of the Third and Fourth Weeks that the confirmation of one's choice in the Lord takes place: to become strong in the way of life chosen for following Christ. See Fessard, *La dialectique*, p. 200.

61 It is wise to remember that in general the first narratives of the Passion terminated with the episode of an apparition. See the articles of M. Dibelius and X. Léon-Dufour indicated in fn. 33 above.

62 See G. Fessard, *La dialectique*, p. 134, who on this subject refers to St. Thomas, *Summa theologiae*, III, Q. 55, a. 4.

63 John 1:12.

over evil and death. Appearing to them, that is, communicating to them himself with the holy fruit of his Resurrection, the Lord delivers them forever from the death which oppresses them and he confers on them the joy of love. Magdalen, Peter, Thomas, the disciples of Emmaus, and all the others will live forever in Christ. For in him they have cast off that sorrowful burden which the Lord has changed into life—a load of sadness, of remorse and of tears, of fear and of doubt, of pessimism and of despair. "They have seen the Lord" and have contemplated in him an infinite mystery of love. Nothing will ever again be able to separate them from him.

> Who shall separate us from the love of Christ? Shall tribulation or distress, or persecution, or famine, or nakedness, or peril, or sword? For I am sure that neither death, nor life, nor angels, nor principalities, nor things present, nor things to come, nor powers, nor height, nor depth, nor anything else in all creation, will be able to separate us from the love of God in Christ Jesus our Lord.[64]

We shall always have the testimony of those who have seen; through it the power of the sign is not dulled. Instead, it comes down to ourselves today in the Church of Christ. The Lord blesses the faith which believes without having seen, the faith animated in us by the divine love of which the life, death, and Resurrection of Christ remain as the unshakable foundation and the everlasting sign presented for our recognition.

4. *The Return to the Father*

On three occasions ([4, 226, 312]) Ignatius would have us understand that the last contemplation of the Fourth Week ought to be about the Ascension. Even if one were to contemplate the apparition of Christ to St. Paul ([311]), still the last contemplation of the cycle of resurrection apparitions should be the Ascension ([313]). This way of transcending the historical dimension so expressly, when Ignatius is so faithful to history, is on his part very significant. It confirms the line of interpretation we have followed up to now, namely, that the narrative facts are considered in their relationship to the revealed mystery, the divine plan of salvation.

The Ascension is the event, the sensible sign manifested to our understanding and proposed for our contemplation, of our return to God through the mediation of the Incarnate Word. Christ came for this unique mission of salvation, to reunite scattered humanity, the mysterious creation of "things in

---

64 Rom. 8:35, 38–39.

heaven and things on earth" of St. Paul,[65] and "thus to enter into the glory of his Father" ([95]). In Ignatius' mind, where the contemplations of the Fourth Week (like those of the Passion) find their foundation in terms of the Kingdom, the mystery of the Ascension is expressed along the same line as it is in St. John. Placed at the termination of this salvific movement whose goal was already assigned (and expressed by the same words, "return to the Father") during the meditation on the Kingdom, the Ascension is the event-sign which here proclaims its crowning. For John, Christ speaks (for example, throughout his farewell discourse) of a "return to the Father" as soon as there is question of his Passion; for Ignatius too, the point of departure of this salvific mission is already expressed along the line of the "return to the Father." Thus the spiritual signification of the mission of the Word is emphasized: to assume our sinful humanity through the Incarnation and with it to pass from this world to the Father (so that we too may be "with him"). The Son is always in the Father, and he who sees the Son has already seen the Father.[66] But the world which Christ attaches to himself has not yet returned to the Father. That is why it is important that Christ go, that he return to the Father through the sign-event of his death, resurrection, and ascension. It is in Christ that prodigal humanity rises and goes toward the Father. Then, in the embrace of the Father and of the whole Christ, the pouring out of the Spirit will become possible and will animate us—an effusion which another mystery-event, Pentecost, will signify to our minds and make into a reality in our lives.[67]

In the unique mystery of this return of Christ to the Father, begun in the Incarnation and crowned through the event of the Ascension, we return to God and receive the promised spirit of divine life. The entire universe, carried up by Christ, finds itself invited to this sublime triumph; and there is no moment more fit than the Ascension to reveal to us what has arrived among us, the Kingdom of God. All that remains for us to do now is to catch hold of

65 Col. 1:16, 20; Eph. 1:10.
66 John 14:6–10.
67 On the joining, in a common understanding, of the three mysteries (death, resurrection, and ascension) which constitute "one inseparable unity," see R. Guardini, *La figura di Gesù Cristo,* p. 51. Polanco has in his Directory a statement which even joins Pentecost to this trilogy (*SpEx*MHSJ, pp. 825–826). On the return to the Father and the pouring out of the Spirit, a unique reality, see J. Guillet, *Jesus Christ Yesterday and Today,* pp. 90–193. See also F. Bourassa in "Verum Sacrificium," *ScE,* 4 (1951), 104ff., where the communication of the Spirit is presented as "the term of the sanctifying movement, the fruit and consummation of the sacrifice."

this world set in motion toward God that we may, in imitation of Christ and against the subversive action of the Enemy, unceasingly endeavor to guide it along to its original and divine orientation, namely, the positive direction which the glorious mystery of the Ascension always indicates to us as a going up, an "ascension" toward the Father, toward the life of the Spirit and the Kingdom of Love.[68]

The foundation of our hope is Christ, who has returned to his Father's home and who, seated at the right hand of God as the firstborn of a new race, is the everlasting and loving intercessor. "He always lives to make intercession for us."[69]

---

68 Refer to our "Conclusion to Part I" above, where the Ignatian global vision and spirituality are summed up in this intuition of our spiritual destiny in Christ: "God's Part in One's Self-Development."

69 Heb. 7:25. On the deeply spiritual meaning of the Ascension, which inaugurates a new kind of presence of Christ among us, read L. Evely, *That Man Is You* (1960), pp. 256–262.

Chapter 8

THE CONCLUSION OF THE EXERCISES:
THE CONTEMPLATION TO ATTAIN LOVE,
AND
EVERYDAY LIFE AFTER THE EXERCISES HAVE ENDED

A. The Problem of the Contemplation to Attain Love

Many different opinions, sometimes contradictory, have been expressed about this contemplation aimed at increasing our love for God ([230–237]). It is not always easy to see the basis for these interpretations and the direction in which they have evolved.[1] Right from the start we must put aside the theories of Miró and Hoffaeus; their Directories represent on this point a position that is extreme and unacceptable.[2] They propose this contemplation as something auxiliary, like the Three Methods of Prayer ([238–260]) and the different Annotations and Rules. Consequently, according to them this meditation, because it has a very practical purpose, can be given even to those who are only making the First Week. This opinion can appear to be based on the advice of Ignatius, who prescribes that the director should explain to this category of retreatant the way to make the examen, propose one or more methods of prayer, and submit them to some exercises aimed at purification. For this reason these Directories which place the Contemplation to Attain Love in the same category as the Methods of Prayer are at least consistent with themselves. We may add that we are not opposed to the idea of propos-

---

1 If we take the time to put some order into the better-known interpretations, our aim is to define with precision the orientation of our own commentary. We think this necessary because we shall be obliged to disagree with several opinions. We wish to clarify our own position in relation to these others in order to avoid wasting time by trying to reconcile our position with those opinions which we positively reject.

2 See *SpEx*MHSJ, pp. 860, 871, 872, 874. As for these two authors and the majority of those we shall quote, there is a good exposition of their thought in the well-documented article of J. M. Díez-Alegría, "La Contemplación para alcanzar amor en la dinámica espiritual de los Ejercicios de San Ignacio," *Mnr,* 23 (1951), 171–193.

ing this contemplation before, during, or after the Exercises, any more than we are to meditating on the Passion of our Lord at any time. But here the question is that of judging the proper function of this contemplation within the complete context of the *Exercises* and according to the primary intention of its author.[3]

The *Breve Directorium* represents another tendency, rather vague as a type of interpretation. This document simply affirms that one can meditate on the Contemplation for Love at any time, beginning with the Second Week. It even specifies "in the Second, Third, or Fourth Week," and recommends that it be done only "if there is need of it, and with prudence on the part of the director."[4] However, the author's idea which led him to this conditioned use of the contemplation is difficult to discover. A note of González Dávila in his Directory could be a partial explanation of this opinion; some *(algunos)* have the habit of presenting this contemplation at the beginning of the Second Week because they feel that it disposes the exercitant for the election.[5] If the motive for including it at this point in the Exercises corresponds to a certain reality (the profit to be drawn in order to dispose), this does not mean that such was its original purpose. Again, one can gain from this same exercise fruit corresponding to varying needs in different circumstances; for example, it can help to attain greater contrition in the First Week in view of all God's gifts to us, or to stimulate a greater attachment to Christ when one is meditating on the Kingdom, or to dispose one for a better election in the Second Week, and so on. But again, in doing this we are not necessarily respecting the original signification of this contemplation. We are in the area of "accommodations"; and to indulge in this too freely is to neglect the premises of the Ignatian thought process; also, to sacrifice for immediate gain a benefit which can come only from a slow and careful development.

The majority of commentators attach the Contemplation to Attain Love to the unitive way. This is the basis for the opinion which holds that one can begin this meditation in the Third Week. This theory (if we omit the *Breve*

---

3 We should note, with J. M. Díez-Alegría, that Polanco's commentary on the same subject (the Exercises given to those who are making only the First Week) makes no reference to the Contemplation for Attaining Love, even though it does mention specifically the following points: foundation, examens, exercises on sin, confession and Communion, additions, rules for the discernment of spirits for the First Week, first or third method of prayer, and, if necessary, rules for the distribution of alms, rules on scruples, orthodoxy, and temperance. See *SpEx-MHSJ*, p. 800.

4 Ibid., p. 985.

5 Ibid., p. 933.

Directorium which on this topic does not distinguish between the Second, Third, and Fourth Weeks) should be attributed to Achille Gagliardi, who quite simply attaches the Third Week to the unitive way.[6] Consequently, this tendency which joins the movement of the Exercises to the "ways" or stages of the spiritual life allows one to meditate on this Contemplation for Love simultaneously with the Passion of Christ. Such reasoning, it seems to us, hardly goes beyond the level of theory.

The most authoritative authors who restrict the Contemplation to Attain Love to the Fourth Week are Nadal, Polanco, González Dávila, the *Directorium Granatense,* and the Directories of 1591 and 1599.[7] The reasons given to support this more common and traditional opinion are not clearly spelled out. Nadal binds the Contemplation for Love directly to the unitive way which he considers to be proper to the Fourth Week.[8] González Dávila, after rejecting the opinion that would use the Contemplation as a preparation for the election, adds simply: "its place is in the Fourth Week, which is devoted totally to joy and love, and to those considerations which beget a relish for heaven." He quotes the well-known texts of St. Paul on the life of those risen in Christ who seek the things that are above.[9] Polanco notes very concretely that "the contemplation to attain love of God" is closely tied to the Fourth Week and "that it can be proposed after the first or second day of the Fourth Week, when the exercitant is engaged on the mysteries of the resurrection." In parentheses he adds: "But under the heading resurrection, include also the mysteries of the Ascension and Pentecost."[10] According to this opinion, the retreatant could begin this contemplation immediately after the Resurrection, hence at the end of the first day of the Week, or on the following day, because of its strict connection with all the glorious mysteries. In this way Polanco proposes his interpretation of the Contemplation by an explicit reference to the Resurrection, Ascension, and Pentecost. Thus he starts from the content of the Fourth Week rather than from a reference to the unitive way. Díez-Alegría notes that Polanco's idea of attaching the Contemplation to Attain

---

6 A. Ambruzzi, who expounds Gagliardi's opinion, shows that, on this subject, it has been followed by only a few of the commentators. See "The Third Week of the Exercises and the Unitive Way," *WL*, 50 (1921), 161–167.

7 J. M. Díez-Alegría joins to this group the names of Suárez and La Palma, to whom he refers several times in his article (pp. 179ff).

8 *MonNad*, IV, 673. J. M. Díez-Alegría in his article (pp. 173–174) quotes several texts of Nadal along this line.

9 Col. 3:1; Phil. 3:20, 19. See *SpEx*MHSJ, p. 933.

10 Ibid., p. 825.

Love to the Resurrection ("to the mysteries of the Resurrection") passed over into the *Directorium Granatense* and to the Directories of 1591 and 1599.[11]

However, even though one accepts the opinion which is almost commonly accepted today, that the Contemplation to Attain Love pertains by right to the Fourth Week of the *Exercises,* that does not solve the problem of its interpretation and function within them. For example, one could ask whether its role is such that it could be omitted without harming the total experience of the Exercises. Is it not a fact that it was a later addition to the principal core of the *Exercises,* as was the Foundation?[12]

Furthermore, would not the absence, at least apparent, of Christ in the body of the contemplation, make of it an exercise of a truly separate and different nature? If the answer is yes, then how is it related to the rest of the *Exercises?* And further, how can we conciliate this fact with the affirmations of Polanco and his followers who place it in the Fourth Week?

First of all, we must reject the opinion which situates this Contemplation outside the Exercises and makes it by its nature a kind of entry into the mystical life in the strict sense of this term. This opinion exaggerates the reality and can lead to errors which have nothing to do with the spiritual teaching of Ignatius.

Díez-Alegría quotes, as representative of this opinion, A. Denis (1893), who considers the Contemplation for Love a "new and more sublime way" than the Exercises.[13] According to this author, the newness and the sublimity of this way reside, it seems, in the sudden passage from the Christocentrism of the *Exercises* to a more elevated theocentrism where the spiritual thrust reaches God independently of the humanity of Christ, which has suddenly vanished. One is then committed to a way which is little conformed to the spirit of Ignatius and still less to that of the gospel or revelation.[14]

Today commentators take more account of the exercise under consider-

---

11 Ibid., pp. 970, 1072, 1171. See also J M. Díez-Alegría, "La contemplación," p. 174, notes 10 to 14.

12 See *Obras completas,* pp. 183–184; G. Fessard, *La dialectique,* p. 147.

13 See the article of J. M. Díez-Alegría, pp. 176–177, 183–186, which refers to the work of A. Denis, *Commentarii in Exercitia Spiritualia S.P.N. Ignatii* (1893), t. 4, pp. 130–133.

14 After having given several texts of A. Denis which follow this line of thought (see the preceding note), Díez-Alegría replies (*Mnr,* 23 [1951], 184 ff.) quite at length to this way of looking at the problem. He also quotes the example of Osuna and his *Tercer Abecedario* which, for a period of time, had led Teresa of Avila into error, by trying to make her neglect the humanity of Christ as if it were an inferior way of reaching God.

ation and of its immediate content, and in this way they try to discover its precise significance and purpose in terms of its function in the *Exercises* as a whole. Díez-Alegría, who follows this approach, reaches some interesting conclusions. His study is based, first of all, on an analysis of the second prelude ([233]), "the grace to be asked for"; and it singles out the movement of the exercise which goes from the "to love more" of the preceding Weeks to the "to love in all things" of the Contemplation for Love. In this sense this Contemplation directly concerns the Fourth Week, in which it is presented as a "final synthesis and the ultimate term of the Exercises" which introduces the retreatant, "who is already prepared," to the contemplative activity.[15]

Similarly Fessard, in his *Dialectique,* focuses his attention on both the structure and the immediate content of the exercise, but he errs by choosing too freely, and in regard to the matter at hand somewhat gratuitously, a few items favorable to his application to this Contemplation. He took them from the schema which he found so helpful in analyzing the ensemble of the Weeks. In doing so he neglects at times some essential, more synthetic, and spiritual aspects of the meditation. Consequently his idea of the "circularity" of the *Exercises* expresses a very rich reality corresponding to the Contemplation for Love.[16] But, based on insufficient data, his analysis of the points of correspondence between the three powers of the soul and the four points of the meditation, and between the four points of the meditation and the four Weeks of the *Exercises,* falsifies, we think, the original meaning of the Ignatian meditation. Finally, it leaves the Contemplation for Love impoverished—deprived, in part, of its most precious dynamism which enables the retreatant, after his or her authentic experience of the divine transcendence, to grasp the exact and inexhaustible meaning of the true divine immanence in the created world. In our view this Contemplation corresponds in its totality with Ignatius' manner—which is the Christian manner par excellence—of viewing the world and of living the life. But this vision of faith and of love presupposes the experience of the Exercises, which is, after all, the Christian experience, "the experience of God's plan of salvation through Christ."[17]

15 Ibid., especially pp. 189–193. As for the problem of theocentrism and christo-centrism, Díez-Alegría treats the matter rather well when he speaks of the interpretations of Nadal, Polanco, La Palma, and Suárez. He shows, in fact, that the *Exercises* are both theocentric and christocentric, as the very nature of the mystery of the Trinity so familiar to St. Ignatius requires. However, we feel that these elements of the solution might have been better integrated into his ultimate solution.

16 We shall take this idea up again at the end of our treatment.

17 See Fessard, *La dialectique,* pp. 147–164. In the schema of the free act, which he takes from Hegelian philosophy, Fessard has found an interpretation which

Transcendence and Immanence

B. Transcendence and Immanence

The point of view proper for the Contemplation to Attain Love is that of the immanence of God in the created world as an expression of his preeminently benevolent love for us. It is not our knowledge of God which starts *from* the created world, but the knowledge of and the encounter with God *in*

seem to us to come out well. In it "the before" and "the after" of the position of being which make up the free act are reproduced in the interior evolution covered by the Weeks of Ignatius. Considering the four points of the Contemplation for Attaining Love, Fessard thinks that he has discerned in the "triad" of the powers (memory, intellect, will) the principle of a relationship permitting him to use the preceding reasoning. Once the edifice is newly built on this terrain, whose fragility he himself recognizes (p. 150), he concludes to a convergence which would derive from the equation between the two relationships of "three to four" explained by the same schema of the before and after (three ways, four weeks: three powers, four points). Whence a new relationship arises of "four to four," i.e., of the four points of the meditation, taken one by one, to the four Weeks of the *Exercises.* However, the basis for this reasoning is weak, that of the three powers whose activity (through the intermediary of the schema of the before and after) is unequally spread over the four points of the contemplation. Our opinion is that this contradicts the habitual method of Ignatius, which we find intact throughout this contemplation; that is, within each point we see the normal progression of the three powers, to such a degree that each point can become the subject of a complete meditation in itself according to the ordinary movement of the *Exercises* (which opinion tradition supports). The second stage of the reasoning (four points : four weeks) is expressed in a series of correspondences between the two terms being compared which are often secondary and of little value as proofs, e.g., "to call to mind one's sins" which is only one exercise of the First Week, and "the many blessings received" in the Contemplation for Love; the God who "dwells in creatures" in the second point is just as present in the mysteries of the Third and Fourth Weeks as in those of the Second; the interpretation of the "God labors," which for Fessard evokes the Passion, rests on another interpretation, that of the Spanish *trabajar* which we have already questioned when we analyzed the Kingdom. Fessard is quite right in finding the attitude of the Fourth Week in the fourth point; however his long demonstration does not succeed in proving to us that such is not the case for the other three points which, taken one by one, are just as much attached to the same Fourth Week. The Hegelian schema, which seemed helpful in explaining the four Weeks, does not allow us to support the interpretation of the Contemplation for Love to which Fessard concludes in the end of his analysis.

[The Contemplation to Attain Love can be considered also from another approach, namely, as an initiation to a life of love, or as a way to love *(via ad amorem)*. In this procedure the four points become four degrees of deepening of the life of faith and love in everything. For further development on this topic, see G. Cusson, *Conduis-moi sur le chemin d'éternité: Les Exercices dans la vie courante* (1973), pp. 188–192, and "La contemplación para alcanzar amor y la oración del Jesuita" in *Ejercicios-Constituciones. Unidad vital?* Congreso Ignaciano, Loyola, 2–7 Setiembre, 1974 (Bilbao, 1975), pp. 324–329. Mary Angela Roduit.]

creation;[18] for in it God reveals himself essentially as one in a continual act of love for man. Everything is full of the presence and of the love of the Creator for his creature. This knowledge or awareness of a divine love which is concrete, present, active, and fulfilling ignites in the human heart a flame of intense gratitude and of adoration of the eternal Creator and Lord. Thus it attaches the person unreservedly to the dynamic service of his interests and his glorification in this world created for his praise. The Contemplation to Attain Love is simultaneously a respectful attention to finding God present to us in all things and a loving application of one's whole being to serving his Divine Majesty, his Sovereign Goodness. It is the loving and untiring action born of a continual contemplation of God, of God as present to us in all things. But in what does this correspond to the substance of the Ignatian conception of the Christian life? How is this integrated into the experience of the Exercises—which is the experience of God's saving plan, the mystery of Christ?

We have already replied to the first question when we examined extensively Ignatius' conception of God, the universe, and man with his or her vocation, above in chapter 2, B. Let us recall merely the chief items which find here their application to the Contemplation to Attain Love.[19] Ignatius' experience at Manresa, with all of it centered on the harmony of all the mysteries in God, blossoms forth in an attitude of apostolic openness and of humble respect for the earthly realities, in which man suddenly discovers everywhere the vivid traces of the living Lord, streaming from the divine transcendence over his created universe. We recall that God manifested himself to Ignatius, through Christ, as one always acting in favor of man whom He calls, together with the whole universe, "to enter into his glory." At the same time, as he opened himself to God's truth, and because of this, Ignatius learned to discover and revere everything which produced the grandeur of the created world: its origin from God and its being destined to return to him by contributing to his glorification. And as Ignatius himself will say later on, it is in "the light of the Creator," and by starting "from a love that comes from

---

18 "To know God in a creature is to know his presence and influence in the creature; to know God through a creature is to be raised from knowledge of the creature to knowledge of God by a kind of ladder in between" (St. Bonaventure, *Sent.*, I, d. 3, art. unic., q. 3, resp. (Vol. I, p. 74). See also St. Thomas, II *Sent.*, d. 23, quaest. unic., a. 2, c).

19 We shall reply to the second question in the following paragraph, in which the *Exercises* will be the direct object of our study. As in the Exercises, it is by starting from the Ignatian experience in relation to the divine transcendence that the retreatant's experience of the Contemplation for Love is clarified.

above," that he will view the whole of reality as animated by the divine dynamism of this creation which is on its way to God. In this new light he will gaze on the world, interpret it, love it, make use of it. "May our Lord give us the light of His holy discretion, that we may know how to make use of creatures in the light of the Creator."[20]

We have likewise seen that this light from the experience of God the Creator, the ever active source or principle and also the beatifying goal or "final cause" of all creation, has clearly revealed and made evident the two principal aspects of all created things which nourished Ignatius' contemplation: their subsistence in God from whom they draw their beauty and goodness, and the precious dynamism of their being ordered to mankind, ourselves. They reveal God's beauties to us (Ps. 19:1; Rom. 1:20; 11:26), that we may know him better and praise him more. This is the fact which aids us to attain our end, to know and praise God ([23]) in all things ([233, 235, 236]; *Constitutions,* [250, 288]). At the term of God's knowledge shines forth the divine glory or power, resplendent and active in the smallest atom of the created world. Ignatius writes, "All the good which is looked for in creatures exists with greater perfection in God who created it."[21] "May his holy name be praised and exalted in all and by all creatures, he who has ordained and created them for this end which is so just and proper."[22]

We have seen, however, that this knowledge of the Lord as alive in the bosom of his creation in order to sustain it in its movement toward the glory of salvation, is the term or object of a way of knowledge and of contemplation in Christ, the eternal and incarnate Word. For Ignatius, the meeting with Christ was really an entry into God, into this majestic and adorable God from whom all things flow, starting from existence and the multitude of benefits accompanying it. Through the experience of the Christ of Revelation—he who manifests the Father and reveals man to himself in the depths of his being which is both poor and magnificent—Ignatius became open to the world "of souls to be helped" and to the whole of creation which should be venerated because in it he found the One he was seeking and loving. In 1545 he wrote to Francis Borgia this very significant spiritual reflection:

> As to the consolation of my letters of which your lordship speaks, I find it easy to persuade myself . . . that you have been consoled by my letters, considering that those who leave themselves behind and *enter into their Creator and*

---

20 *LettersIgn,* p. 421.
21 *EppIgn,* V, p. 488; see also *LettersIgn,* pp. 18 and 309.
22 *LettersIgn,* p. 83.

Lord have an abiding awareness of and loving attention to him, and experience consolation. They *perceive how our whole eternal Good is present in all created things,* how he gives existence to all creatures and conserves them in himself by his own infinite being and presence. . . . For those who have a wholehearted love for the Lord, all things help them and serve them for an even greater reward as they draw near and find union in a most intense charity with their creator and Lord."[23]

Therefore, we infer, it was as a result of such experience that Ignatius reached the point where he loved the world because he loved God, and because the world would not exist without God. He also loved the world in proportion to his contemplation of God present in it; and he used it in order to "serve the divine Majesty in all things," and to praise and proclaim the grandeur of the Lord who condescends to live in it unceasingly, in a way that is multiple, diverse, and adapted. Consequently too, as we saw above in chapter 2, he was acting in the light of this conception of creation when he wrote: "The soul should find relief, even in things that are earthly or base, when one does not make oneself earthly or base, but love them all for God our Lord, and insofar as they are directed to His glory and service."[24] It is in the light of this perception, too, that we should interpret Ignatius' insistence on the use of human means "not to put our confidence in them, but to cooperate with the divine grace following the order of the sovereign providence of God our Lord."[25]

Our conclusion on this topic is this that this experience of the transcendence of God, of the "Divine Majesty," of the "Most Holy Trinity,"—a perception which comes through Christ as found in the truths of his mysteries of creation, Incarnation, and Redemption—gave Ignatius a vivid perception of the divine immanence in the created world.[26] It is not false to say that

---

23 *EppIgn,* I, 339–340, trans. of James Walsh; italics supplied. The entire letter is also in *LettersIgn,* pp. 83–86.

24 *LettersIgn,* p. 131. See also 1 Cor. 10:31: "Whether you eat or drink, or whatever else you do, do all to the glory of God."

25 *Constitutions,* [814]. See also *LettersIgn,* p. 240.

26 "The fact that Ignatius can find God whenever he wishes leads us to infer to a habitual union with God in the depths of his soul; the life of the three divine persons is in him. For Ignatius, to find God whenever he wished simply meant concentrating all the forces of his soul toward this union. In addition to this discovery of God which the saint could bring about at will, the deep-seated union of the soul with God is accompanied from time to time by passing mystical visions—something which it was not in his power to give to himself. On the other hand, the saint was capable of concurring in this discovery of God in his interior, this reaching out of his soul toward God, by his exterior work. In all things and in every activity he found God, and this was due above all to a projection onto his

Ignatius lived in a "divine milieu." Any small creature could put him into contact with God, because he unceasingly and concretely perceived that nothing exists or subsists without the active and loving presence of God; and that in return every creature becomes, in its own way, a reflection and proclamation of the divine grandeur. In spite of the evil that surrounded him, Ignatius had a deep interior life; and because of his spirit of contemplation and of openness to the presence of God in all things, he truly lived in "a divine milieu." The Contemplation for Love expressed with much discretion this manner of seeing and of loving God, of "finding him in all things," to use his own phrase. To find him in them is necessarily to contemplate him, to love him, and to serve him in or by means of them. There, for Ignatius, resides the source of peace and happiness for every creature who has entered and lives "in his or her Creator and Lord." He writes in May, 1547:

> While we should not give up tasks which we have received and are fulfilling for God's honor, it is possible that the greatness of love which overwhelms the soul should find relief even in things that are earthly and base, when one does not make oneself earthly or base, but loves them all for God our Lord and insofar as they are directed to His glory and service. This is something which necessarily has to do with our last end, who is Himself perfect and infinite goodness, and who ought to be loved in all other things. To this end exclusively the whole weight of our love should be directed.
>
> May it please our Lord by His infinite and supreme goodness to increase these desires of yours to love Him above all things, so that you will place not only a part but the whole of your life in the same Lord, and in all creatures for His sake.[27]

C. *The Presupposition of the Christian Experience*

In the preceding paragraph we have described, rather than explained, how Ignatius passed, during his Christian experience, from his perception of God's transcendence to a sense of His divine immanence in the created world. This description, which found its dynamic center in Christ, the heart of revelation, corresponds to a description of the Christian experience in general: in Christ and by him we are "drawn" to the Divine Majesty who

vision of things and onto his activity, of the light and the radiance of the divine union within the depths of his soul. St. Ignatius lives in the divine persons. But he never excludes the world from his love. For him it is sufficient to see God and to live with the world in God." K. Truhlar, "La découverte de Dieu chez saint Ignace de Loyola," in *RAM*, 24 (1948), p. 337.

27 *LettersIgn*, pp. 131, 50 (italics supplied). See also *Cons*, [288], and *LettersIgn*, pp. 236, 240.

reconciles us to the cosmic movement of the created universe which discovers its face renewed. If we now wish to explain this journey, with the help of human means enlightened by faith, we must return to the that interaction or dialectic of the Christian experience which guided us in our analysis of the spiritual movement of the Exercises. What immediately strikes us is once again the transcendence or preeminence of God's plan of salvation (from which the objectivity of the gospel message arises), along with the close relationship it has to the subjective experience that it arouses and directs in ourselves. In this context we find a similar explanation of the powerful theocentrism in the vision of the Contemplation for Love, through the route of an ordered Christocentrism. It is a route of revelation and of mediation.

1. The Evolution, on the Objective Level, of Our Understanding of God's Plan of Salvation in Christ

The evolution of our understanding and embracing of this mystery of Christ has been made sufficiently clear in the course of our study. Before our eyes the development unfolds from the contemplation on the Kingdom, which serves as a sort of foundation or bird's eye view for our understanding of God's plan, to its glorious accomplishment in the victory of the Resurrection, meanwhile going through the different steps of the events or mysteries in which the Word Incarnate assumes our human nature with its development, its struggles, its cross. It suffices now to set forth this glorious fulfillment in its relationship with the whole world, the object of the salvation which the Lord brought us. In its historical evolution this world enters only progressively into the history of salvation and into the work of "divinization" which this signifies. We easily see that this relationship of the risen Christ to the evolution of creation mounts far above the level of a simple intercession with the Father at whose right hand Christ is seated, now alive forever. Or better still, our concept of Christ's intercession needs to be purified and stripped of representations which weaken it, by reducing it to a sort of compassionate plea in the ethereal realms on our behalf. The true plan of salvation through Christ is expressed by St. Paul in his letter to the Ephesians: "He who descended is he who also ascended far above all the heavens, that he might fill all things."[28] The final point in the mystery of Christ, and of his victory over that death which is destruction, is his eternal and real presence which embraces the universe and draws it to the Father by snatching it from evil. "And I, when I am lifted up from the earth, will draw all men to myself."[29]

28 Eph. 4:10; see also Col. 3:11.
29 John 12:32.

The work of salvation, accomplished once in the person of Christ is, in a sense, only begun for us on Easter morning; it is actualized progressively in the extent to which God, through the mediation of the whole Christ, subjects the world to himself and fills the universe. "When all things are subjected to him, then the Son himself will also be subjected to him who put all things under him, that God may be everything to everyone."[30] Christ has centered the first fruits of a new life in himself, the foundation of a new world of which he is the "cornerstone." All history and all creation, being liberated from themselves, enter step by step into this "light of life." In the train of Christ, and in him present to the world "to the end of time," the world moves toward the Father, at the center of the divine trinitarian life, and the whole of creation enters into God by mounting above itself. This is an ascension which in no way alters its nature but fulfills it beyond all hope.

> At the time of creation, all was created by Christ.
> At the time Christ's death and resurrection,
>   all was reconciled by him.
> At the time of the eschatological fulfillment,
>   all will be submitted to God, who is everything
>   to everybody.[31]

By way of a concluding summary, the final fulfillment of God's revealed plan of salvation, which is a mystery of love expressed in the gratuitous calls to creation and salvation, is the progressive movement of the world toward God, through the coming of the Christ who assumed the totality of our human condition; of the world which, now renewed, finds again on itself the divine mark of its origin and the sublime ordination which God's creative act had imprinted on it. Man, now purified, is united to Christ, toward accomplishing this work for the glorification of God, of his Majesty and Goodness. As Karl Rahner states, "The Credo of the Christian avows that, in the end, there is only one history, only one fulfillment for all things; and that all things attain their finality only when they participate in the reality of God himself."[32]

---

30 1 Cor. 15:28.
31 0. Cullmann, *Christ et le temps*, pp. 127–128; also p. 132.
32 K. Rahner, *Mission et Grâce*, II, p. 66. See his interesting treatments on the same topic, ibid., p. 56, and in his *Theological Investigations*, on Christology and Biblical Theology, I, 65; VI, 95–97; and, on the necessity but also the limitations of traditional Christology, XVII, 24–38.

2. *The Evolution, on the Subjective Level, of the Retreatant's Experience in Christ*

The progressive growth of the Christian experience has also been the object of our study. We have seen that a continual effort at awareness of one's need for God, guided by the light of his revealed plan of salvation and sanctification, and accompanied by a desire to attach oneself ever more closely to him who is our Life, has enabled the retreatant to abandon himself or herself to the forces of grace in Christ which free him from evil and commits him— here and now through the procedure of the election—to the divine work of salvation. But it is at the moment of the Resurrection that we, united to Christ who shares his victory with us, enter effectively into the new world of divine life into which our present life is being integrated. The final attitude of the retreatant who has gone through the detailed course of the Exercises can be viewed as the first fruits of eternity sown in his soul, and also as the renewed exercitant's now dynamic and firmly willed orientation toward the future. This state of soul comprises unshakable faith in the salvation offered us by the Savior, and love which embraces, in Christ, the entire universe in its journey toward its fulfillment with the Father. For the person who has gone through this experience, the whole face of the earth has a renewed power. Everything is effectively seen as an element in a movement, in a divine work of construction. This movement begins from what is human; and it makes its way by means of what is human and created, at the cost of all the sacrifices entailed, toward the praise or glorification of God. The Contemplation to Attain Love is particularly harmonious with this attitude of the retreatant, risen in and associated with Christ, and to the dynamic vision which ought henceforth to occupy the center of his or her consciousness and direct his or her life.

The whole of creation, thus oriented and open to the progress of Christian salvation, now aspires to this grand deliverance in Christ, now manifested in the glory of the children of God, sons and daughters who in the Son bring to perfection the life-giving work of the Risen Christ.[33] The salvation brought by Christ affirms, by its very nature,[34] that everything returns to

---

33 Rom. 8:19–23.

34 It is good for us to recall that salvation is by its nature divinization, and that Christ achieves this divinization by taking on himself our human condition. The Pauline texts on the recapitulation of all things into Christ, and on the groaning or aspiration of the whole of creation for salvation, force us to enlarge our concept of salvation, to such an extent that it can embrace the whole of creation which God could not have called into being in order to annihilate it. "It is not extravagant," Karl Rahner cautiously writes, "to conceive the evolution of the

God, in Christ, in a way which is proper to itself. The dynamism which will accomplish this mystery is love, as we have seen. This immense "ascension" of the universe in association with Christ is a movement born of love, and on the way to love. This is its ultimate purpose; and Teilhard de Chardin is the one who was able to discern that fact in this evolution of the created universe toward its sublime end in Christ, when he wrote of the complete enamoring of the universe. Love alone! As a result, the experience of deepening our insight into the work of Christian salvation, and of fitting one's total self into its present and universal evolution, makes one more aware of the many aspects of that dialogue of love which takes place between the Creator and His creature. It is in these two senses that "all created things on the face of the earth" become the milieu and the expression of this exchange of love. The whole of creation is an expression of this urgent love of God and brings it to man's contemplative knowledge. But this creation, in its turn, is called by Christ through his grace, who through his Passover restored the orientation of the world, to become a means for the expression of human love, which is both contemplative and active, and which is directed to God—at every moment of our life. Here we come back to the two notes which Ignatius placed at the beginning of the Contemplation to Attain Love ([230–231]), about a love "which manifests itself in deeds," and which is a free and grateful offering back to God of that very gift which the Lord is showering upon us at every moment. Thus in Divine Providence's guidance of his plan of salvation, his "economy" or governance in which everything must be subjected to the Father in the Son, and must enter through Him as this unique Way into the divine life, the human effort of response becomes a reverent acceptance of the many-faceted gift of God, and simultaneously a response to his infinite love. It is, in the whole Christ, "the cooperation, vibrant with love, which we offer to the divine hands which are occupied in preparing both us and the world, through sacrifice, for the final union."[35]

world as oriented toward Christ and then to see the degrees of its ascent find their summit in him. We must be careful to avoid thinking that in this ascent the inferior being has within itself the forces capable of realizing this movement. If what St. Paul says in Col. 1: 15 [and, we add, in Rom. 8:19–23] is true and is not watered down by a moralizing interpretation, if the world as a totality, thus in its physical reality as well, historically attains (in a history which is essentially spirit, freedom, value), in Christ and through him, this state in which God is all in all, then the reflection we pursue cannot be fundamentally false" (*Ecrits théologiques*, I, p. 136; see also *Mission et Grâce.*, II, pp. 56, 66).

35 P. Teilhard de Chardin, *Le milieu divin: An Essay on the Interior Life* (London, 1960), pp. 69–73, esp. 70–71.

Through Christ and in the whole Christ, the Mystical Body which we make up, the world moves toward love, is transformed into love. But this love is precisely that love which a free person gives to God by means of this world, while united with Christ to the extent one has made oneself capable. In this way the theocentrism of the Contemplation to Attain Love springs from the Christocentrism of the *Exercises*. It takes place in proportion to the extent to which he or she is able to see the Lord's presence in the created universe, to respect and venerate it, and to praise and serve the Divine Majesty ever present and loving. That is why the one who is risen with Christ, and in union with him, will be able continually to exercise this effective love of God which takes its origin from every element in creation.[36] This is a love which is lived out in practice because it is the praise and service of God known and contemplated in all things, and always found in all things, found in each one of them. This is the meaning of the Contemplation to Attain Love; and this, too, is the reason why it ought to be placed after that on the Resurrection. It adds nothing to the *Exercises* themselves, but it makes their finality more explicit—from the point of view both of the objective divine plan of salvation and from the exercitant's subjective experience through which God accomplishes that plan within him. Consequently it can well be repeated over and over again. For it is an attitude of contemplative action acquired, through the exercitant's personal experience of faith in Christ, for all his or her future life.

D. Everyday Life after the Exercises Have Ended

We now turn our attention to the exercitant who returns from the experience of the Exercises back into ordinary daily life. He or she does this as a man or woman of the Exercises, an authentic Christian, a disciple of Christ in any place he or she can be found. We see a complete change of perspective which has been engendered by his or her intense faith—a vision which is now to be lived out in practice.

1. The Life of Faith

This faith is a birth, in Christ and the Spirit, to the world which comes from above. It gives rise to a change of values which one accepts and lives in

---

36 "The more we advance on the road to perfection, the more penetrating does our spiritual gaze become. It avoids 'idolatry,' because it is capable of recognizing the presence of the Creator in his creatures. This is the habitual outlook which the Contemplation to Attain Love ([230–237]), will aim to improve" (*Exercices*, trans. Courel, p. 37, note 1).

this new order: one saves one's life by losing it. The one who wishes to become great in the Kingdom must become little and serve others; the first is the last. Suffering and death, like failure, retain their character painful to nature. But in all these circumstances, a new supernatural instinct now more spontaneously discovers an irreplaceable seed of life for eternity. While human life is progressing inevitably toward death, the Christian is advancing toward eternal life—pressing on, like Paul, "to make it my own, because Christ Jesus has made me his own."

When we as exercitants return to the ordinary routine of our daily lives, we find that our way of knowing, loving, judging, and acting is new, because it is now permeated through and through by a vision of faith.[37] It is an active and dynamic faith—a faith "in act" to all possible extent, and not merely that basic "habit" (the *habitus* of scholastic theology) which comes to the full growth which only the great proofs and trials of life activate fully. This living faith places, as much as possible, all the moments of our lives on this privileged plane to which the initial act of faith normally elevates us. It now keeps us in our new direction on that level to which our "contemplation" during the Exercises has brought us. It is this life of faith—embraced and made more conscious and effective—which leads to this love which is capable of "finding God in all things"; which is united to him, serves him, and prays to him in everything that happens during the day. One is a "contemplative in action" *(contemplativus in actione).*

We have seen how the Exercises, through an intelligent deepening of the Christian experience, play a realistic and very spiritual part in this growth of the vision of faith which commits our lives and orients them toward a future so positively envisaged in the risen Christ. From this experience of grace, light and strength, we may draw a lesson of spiritual wisdom. This wisdom too is a gift of the Spirit and the fruit of an experience of discernment. Together with this final lesson we should now analyze the problem of the prolongation of the Exercises—which is also termed their "circularity," namely, from God to a human person whom they guide back to God.

2. *The Circularity of the* Exercises: *"From Him, and through Him, and unto Him All Things Are. To Him Be the Glory Forever." (Romans 11:36)*

The idea of circularity, as it is presented to us, contains two chief thoughts. One is the idea that the end of the experience in Christ is only the

---

37 See L. Mendizábal, *Annotationes in Theologiam spiritualem,* pp. 180–183.

beginning of a new life. The other is the thought of the active presence of Evil in the world. When the Christian thinks that the end has been reached by his or her accepting the gift which Christ offered, and when he or she discovers all the aspects of charity, he suddenly realizes with some shock that this is but the beginning of a new path on which everything must be begun anew. This path is the path of Christ's overflowing grace, but it is also simultaneously and necessarily a time for testing. Good comes into contact with evil, and the disciple of Christ is still the target for all of Satan's ruses. Here we have the "eschatalogical combat" in which everyone called to be a Christian must engage—while fortified, of course, with the strength of the Christ whom nothing can overcome. We carry within ourselves the persecution which the world brings. It is the result of each one's division within himself or herself. In our hearts two worlds confront each other, and this struggle gives rise to persecutions, judgments, the sword and death.

> Remember the word that I said to you,
> > "A servant is not greater than his master."
> > If they persecuted me,
> > they will persecute you too. . . .
> In the world you have tribulation;
> > but be of good cheer,
> > I have overcome the world.[38]

Such is, indeed, the Christian paradox: to be already risen in Christ and yet to remain exposed to a death that watches for us from ambush; to have the firm assurance of victory in Christ who is invincible, and at the same time to have with humility the certitude of being able to do nothing without God's all-powerful grace. "Apart from me you can do nothing" (John 25:5). Christ's peace springs from the integration or unity within our being, and is made existent through love. How then can we reconcile and live out these seemingly extreme attitudes—assurance of victory in Christ but helplessness without him—without letting that peace become a false security or self-abandonment which drops the continual vigilance asked for by the Master? "Watch and pray" (Matt. 26:41).

To the problem of how to live out in practice, through one's entire life, that Christian attitude of faith and love which is supposed by the final contemplation of the *Exercises,* there is only one solution: to be with Christ, to "live in Christ." We have had already experience enough of our own helplessness, whether in trying to snatch ourselves from the grip of evil, or in

---

38   John 15:20; 16:33.

counting too much on our own strength to accomplish the divine work of our sanctification. But we have also experienced absolute victory in the case of Christ, who draws us from sin and death. With Him what should we fear? What obstacle can resist us? What work is impossible to accomplish? With him, what mountain will be impassable? What sea will be unable to bear our feeble steps? What lame man will not begin to dance? What dead man will not return to life at the summons of his all-powerful and efficacious divine word? To be in union with Christ, at each moment of our lives, is to share His absolute victory over sin and death. It is, already in this world, to be alive with his divine life. Nothing has the power to separate us from Christ— neither hunger, nor nakedness, nor persecution, nor the sword, nor death. No, nothing has the power in itself to separate us from Christ and from the love of God manifested in him. It is in this sense that the Christian is, according to St. John, by nature unable to sin.[39] To be a Christian, in the strongest sense of that term, is to be with Christ, that is, to remain in fellowship with him. No failure, sin, or death has any grip on the Lord. But such is the power of our freedom that, if we isolate ourselves, or if we pursue the struggle against the powers of darkness and against ourselves alone, or if we want to be the source of our own sanctification and to do good, then our strength, our rock falls to nothing. We have tossed aside the support of him who "lives in us"; and detached in spirit from the One whose presence makes us Christians, we are doomed to failure, sin, and death.

The problem we face at the end is that of a new beginning. It is the question of knowing how to keep ourselves always attached to Christ in order to overcome, with his grace, the many resistances of our nature. These spontaneously pull us toward a false autonomy, an isolation which destroys. Our sole counterattack lies in renewing our experiencing of Christ's saving

---

39 "No one who abides in him sins. . . . No one born of God commits sin; for God's nature abides in him, and he cannot sin because he is born of God" (1 John 3:6, 9). For a detailed exegesis of these verses which many have tried to minimize by weakening the expression "cannot sin," see I. de la Potterie, *Adnotationes in exegesim Primae Epistolae s. Joannis*, pp.73–77. "The principle or source of impeccability and victory over sin is in the word of God which through faith remains and operates in us. In other words, it is the constantly exercised life of faith" (p. 75). St. John not only affirms that the "one born of God" does not sin, but that he "cannot sin" while he is abiding in God: "This incapability of the believer arises, not alone from the presence of God's word in us or (in other words) from faith alone, but only if the Word of God [the Son incarnate], abides in him or her (v. 9). . . . There is in us, in an active and efficacious way, a principle or source of moral and holy life, namely, the presence of the word in us" (pp. 76, 77).

power—of that same salvation through Christ which is fostered by the sequence of the Exercises, and which needs to be repeated over and over during our lifetime. As God's saving plan in Christ unfolds itself toward the exchange of love that is its term, and as Christian experience, within God's preeminent plan, moves toward the same goal of love, the Christian—in the continual renewal, at his or her life's every breath, of the process of purification, election, and commitment through the action of the Spirit—lives by his victorious faith, and thus unceasingly dies to himself in order to be resurrected in Christ to the life of God. Ever open to questioning from God, one lives more and more completely in God's presence, in the spirit of the Contemplation to Attain Love. One conforms oneself continually to the divine will and participates unceasingly in Christ's victory over the world.

In our opinion, this is the circularity of the Exercises. It is the Christian experience lived out in practice, over and over again in its totality every moment of our lives.[40] It is the continual "yes" which such Christians, by their living faith and burning love, offer to God while they are finding him in all things; and it presupposes the uninterrupted renewal of the process which snatches a person from evil and reconciles him or her to God in Christ under the action of the Spirit.[41] As an inevitable result of this experience, the person pursues his or her journey of openness to the created world; and the world, in and through this person and his or her union with the living Church of Christ, continues its painful but sure movement toward final salvation.

---

40 On the "circularity" of the Exercises, see Fessard, *La dialectique*, 164–177. In the same vein, Nadal writes in his Spiritual Journal that every religious and "even every Christian" ought unceasingly, "every day," to pass through the three spiritual ways, even after he thinks he has reached the unitive way in contemplation (see *MonNad*, IV, 690, [41]; VI, 56 [94], and passim; also, trans. of Laval, nos. 22, 23, 24, 46, 47, 52). See also the early *Directorium anonymum B 1* in *SpEx*MHSJ, p. 886, no. 6.

41 Here we touch on a characteristic of Ignatian spirituality which is essentially "experimental." The detailed methods of examination of conscience and of making an election have no other purpose than the more conscious and more generous submission of oneself to the action of grace and the Holy Spirit, in order to bring the details of one's life continuously into greater harmony with God's will. On this subject read: A. Delchard, "L'élection dans la vie quotidienne," *Chr*, no. 14 (1957), 206–219; F. Marty, "L'examen, prière de l'apôtre," *Chr*, no. 20 (1958), 494–511; R. J. Howard, "Examination of Conscience: Prayerful Election in Everyday Terms," *WL*, 88 (1959), 24–36; J. M. Le Blond, "Présence de Dieu," *Chr*, no. 22 (1959), 147–162; R. Hostie, "Le cercle de l'action et de l'oraison d'après le P. J. Nadal," Chr, no. 6 (1955), 195–211; [G. Aschenbrenner, "Consciousness Examen," *Review for Religious*, 31 (1972), 13–21. Ed.].

Through this person, too, the world is fulfilling its purpose: the praise, by intelligent beings, of the God who made it.

E. Concluding Reflections: The Starting Point of Ignatian Spirituality

As a conclusion of the study presented in this book as a whole, we shall point out what seems to us to be the aspect most characteristic of St. Ignatius' spirit and spirituality: a steady gaze on God and his preeminence over his creation, his "divine transcendence."

1. Various Approaches

More than a few spiritual writers have attempted to base the spiritual life according to the Ignatian school on the "indifference" of the *Exercises,* which progressively assures the retreatant's openness to God's will and thus generates a freedom and ready availability *(disponibilité)* for service. This manner of reasoning is not false. But it considers the problem from the wrong end, in regard to both the theoretical and the practical aspects of the spiritual life which it is describing. What is true or important of someone at a point of arrival is not always equally so at the starting point. To put the emphasis on this indifference as the foundation without which the edifice cannot be built is to run the risk of concentrating all one's spirituality on effort. As history has often shown, it interprets Ignatius in a voluntaristic sense. Indifference is indeed an integral part of the spirituality of the Ignatian Principle and Foundation ([23]). But it comes there only as a consequence of the affirmation and the consideration of the divine plan of creation, spiritual development, and salvation in the beatific vision, all for the glorification of God—St. Paul's complete "mystery of God." This plan includes the whole destiny of men and women, now reunited through Christ to their proper place in the created universe; that both they and it may achieve the purpose for which God created them: to contribute to the praise of God, by his intellectual creatures who freely come, by means of this universe, to know and love and praise him, and to be fulfilled and happy by doing this.

2. The Preeminent Guiding Factor: God's Plan of Salvation

The true point of departure of Ignatian spirituality, therefore, is situated in a steady gaze on the divine plan or purpose whose prodigious light informs and animates the whole subsequent process of thinking. Ignatius' spirit or tenor of thought, because it is so intimately interwoven with this originating divine illumination, is above all a spirit of contemplation—that is, an opening to the irresistible truth of God who liberates and sanctifies. This is the meaning behind a statement by Nadal: "The spirit of the Society is a clarity which takes possession of us and leads us."[42] We shall never understand Ignatius' spirituality, or its genuine nature, unless we start our study from this highest vantage point of Ignatius' spiritual journey, and then descend from there to those more common notions which have often been proposed as the starting point: the spirit of indifference, or that of service.

Ignatian contemplation is an intelligent and respectful opening of oneself to the divine truth and the radiant splendor of glory expressed there about the Father, the Son, and the Holy Spirit. Such loving contemplation engenders spiritual desire, which is itself a gift from God. This desire in turn raises the person above his or her entangling natural attachments (and thus arises indifference, the freedom from disordered attachments); and then it plunges him or her into the following of Christ with an interior thirst for fidelity and union, for imitation and service (and hence arise the three kinds of humility). Through exercises like those of Ignatius, the retreatant, with attention now centered on the divine salvific plan, St. Paul's "mystery of Christ," and on the mediation of Christ, disposes himself or herself with understanding and generosity sustained by grace, to welcome these divine gifts: the light which enlightens and the desire which draws and commits. In this way he becomes interiorly docile to the motions of the Holy Spirit, who now leads such a person, closely associated with Christ, to move with discernment through the possible ways of service, self-gift, and charity—all set in order according to the divine good pleasure. And the rest of life becomes an effort to make oneself a part of this same circular movement: God down to creation and back up again to God. This is a meaningful effort, based on the action of grace and fidelity to it; and it is pursued through a life attentive to seeking God in all things, to contemplating his radiant power and goodness, and to honoring and serving his Divine Majesty. It is a life all to the greater glory of God.

---

42 Nadal, in *MonNad*, IV, 690, [41]; a frequent idea in Nadal. See, e.g., ibid., 618, [37]; V, 724–725, [97]; VI, 55, [86]; *Journal Spirituel*, trans. Laval, no. 50.

REFERENCE MATTER

APPENDIX:
Some Background Aids

ABBREVIATIONS:
the Complete List

GENERAL BIBLIOGRAPHY,
from the French Book

BIBLICAL BIBLIOGRAPHY,
from the French Book

SUPPLEMENTARY BIBLIOGRAPHY,
on Biblical Theology in English

EDITORIAL NOTE
on the Term "Spiritual Exercises"

INDEX I:
of Authors Cited

INDEX II:
of Topics Treated

DETAILED TABLE OF CONTENTS

SOME BACKGROUND AIDS
toward a Deeper Understanding of This Book

1. *The Meanings of* Mystère, *Mystery*

In the experience of the American readers who read portions of Sister Mary Angela's first draft and misunderstood some terms and even the central message of the book (as was mentioned above on pages xix and xx), most of the difficulties arose from the word *mystère*. It occurred with great frequency in the French original, had different meanings in different contexts, and was always translated by the English "mystery,"—which assuredly was accurate but gave no hint about its varying meanings in its many occurrences. Hence in the shifting contexts these American readers either unwittingly attached to this term an erroneous or incomplete meaning (usually some degree of unintelligibility), or missed its rich connotations and nuances. Since the chief message of Cusson's book hinges largely on having fresh in one's memory considerable background knowledge of this term, an overview of its many meanings and history seems to be for these readers the best remedy for their difficulties and also the key to the spiritual inspiration which the book can bring.

Background

This word "mystery" has a complicated history, both in the Old Testament *(raz)* and in Greek antiquity *(mysterion)*. By our own day it has acquired so many meanings that no one dictionary lists them all; "the complete history of the word has yet to be written."[1] To find the right meaning in varying contexts we must move from dictionary to dictionary. Unfortunately, a word which has acquired so many meanings becomes a poor means to communicate thought with precision, particularly to the uninitiated. In doubt, since every mystery is something of a marvel, one can choose "marvel" as a conjecture sure to be correct, somewhat like

---

1 *New Catholic Encyclopedia*, s.v. "mystery," 10:151.

"whatyoumaycallit." But such a word communicates no precise information.

Our aim here is not to supply the missing complete history of this fascinating word with its elusive or enigmatic meanings, which since Vatican Council II has been appearing with ever increasing frequency in theological and spiritual writings, as also in the documents of Popes Paul VI and John Paul II. Our modest hope is, instead, to compose an essay to bring out, against a wider background, the chief meanings necessary for a deeper understanding of the inspirational message contained in Cusson's book.

To begin our survey in the thought world familiar to American readers, we cull (with modified numberings and some supplied examples) the following definitions, relevant to our purposes, from *Websters Third International Dictionary, Unabridged* (1981).

> I,a, a purely spiritual . . . interpretation (obsolete); b, a religious truth revealed by God that man cannot know by reason, and that after it has been revealed cannot be completely understood; e.g., the Trinity or Incarnation; c, a Christian rite or sacrament, e.g., baptism: . . . (1) the Eucharist; (2) any of the fifteen "mysteries" of the rosary, e.g., the Visitation; 3, . . . the events in the life of Christ, e.g., a healing; (d) secret pagan rites marked by the showing of sacred objects only to duly initiated worshipers, e.g., the Eleusinian mysteries; II, a secret; something that has not been or cannot be explained, that is unknown to all or concealed from some and thereby evoking curiosity or wonder, or that is incomprehensible or uncomprehended, e.g., "the mystery of his disappearance has never been solved," or, "it's a mystery to me."

Most noteworthily for us, not even this unabridged dictionary lists St. Paul's special use of mystery *(mysterion):* God's plan, kept comparatively unrevealed for past ages, to save all humankind, Jews and gentiles, through Christ's life, death, and resurrection.[2]

Websters' definitions reflect the habitual thinking of Americans. Therefore its omission gives us a clue as to why so many American readers so often missed this meaning in the first draft of this book. They did not know it, or at least did not have it fresh in mind. Instead, they drew from the term obscure or erroneous ideas, or unwittingly read into it one of the other meanings familiar to them and listed above in Websters— usually those meanings denoting unintelligibility. Satisfied with this sim-

2 Used with great clarity in, e.g., Rom. 16:25; Ephes. 1:8–10; 3:4–12; Col. 2:2,3.

ple but deceptive and negative aspect of "mystery," they missed the rich positive affirmations and the allusions which produce the central thrust of the book. This is probably the chief reason why some of these readers failed to find the inspiration which this commentary can bring if it is correctly read. That same reason, too, is what led to this second translator's decision to turn the word usually by "divine plan of salvation," varied according to contexts.

The Term "Mystery" in Scripture

To understand the basic meanings and also the richness of "mystery" in Scripture, or its rich connotations in St. Paul, we must consult biblical dictionaries and commentaries or theological works.[3] A few considerations important for our overview follow.

In the first half of the present century many scholars claimed that Paul's concept of *mysterion* arose chiefly from influence of the Greek mystery religions. This view is now discredited. The New Testament usage of the term, especially in Paul, stemmed principally from Judaism—particularly from the Apocalyptic tradition exemplified in Daniel 2:18-19, 27-30; 4:6. There the "secrets" or "mysteries" of God are references to his saving plan which is to be realized in "the last times" (the *eschaton*). In Wisdom 2:22 they are his designs for the immortality of the just, which are hidden from the impious who blaspheme God's providence.[4]

In the Gospels (Mark 4:11,12; Matt. 13:11), the "mysteries of the Kingdom" are those doctrines and truths pertaining to the Kingdom or reign of God which Christ made clear to his disciples, but which to others were scarcely intelligible and remained obscure, taught only in parables.[5] Paul too used the term with this meaning in 1 Cor. 13:2.

But the chief and special meaning of *mysterion* throughout Paul's writings is God's plan of salvation, sanctification, and eventual fulfillment of human beings in the happiness of the beatific vision. This design of his

---

3 Such as, to cite a few examples, G. W. Bromiley, *Theological Dictionary of the New Testament* (Grand Rapids, 1985); Léon-Dufour, Dictionary of Biblical Theology (1973); *The Jerome Biblical Commentary* (1968); J. L. McKenzie, *Dictionary of the Bible* (1965); *The New World Dictionary-Concordance to the New American Bible* (1970); W. A. Van Roo, *The Mystery* (1971), esp. pp. 7, 180, 184, 189; *De Sacramentis* (1957), pp. 3–18.

4 *The New World Dictionary-Concordance,* s.v. "mystery," pp. 467–469; McKenzie, *Dictionary,* s.v. "mystery," pp. 595–598.

5 Bromiley, *Theological Dictionary,* s.v. *"musterion,"* p. 617.

love was for ages kept comparatively secret, but was revealed clearly in Christ, specifically was achieved through his life, passion, death, and resurrection.

Further still, in God's plan Christ's redemptive action was to be the means through which the rest of the created universe could fulfill the purpose for which God created it; that is, not merely to mirror forth to men and women his existence, love, and power or radiant glory (Rom. 1:18-23), but also to allure them to achieve freely their supernatural goal, the beatific vision in union with the other members of God's Kingdom (1 Cor. 1:24-25; 13:8-12; Rom. 8:18-23; Ephes. 4:8-10). In this way all the created universe, through the human beings redeemed by Christ, can be said to be (in Cusson's often repeated phrase) "in motion" toward its fulfillment in God (1 Cor. 15:22-28; Rom. 8:18-23).

Through slight variations in various contexts, *mysterion* takes on in St. Paul nuances and connotations which are extremely rich. The "mystery of Christ" means or implies the good news or whole gospel which he was commissioned to preach (1 Cor. 1:23; 2:1,7). Paul's apostolic office is the "economy" *(oikonomia)*, the administration or stewardship of the mystery, and also the proclamation *(kerygma)* of it.[6] Paul calls for full knowledge of "the mystery of God, of Christ, in whom are hid all the treasures of wisdom and knowledge" (Col. 2:2-3), the loving design of God the Father to save all men, without distinction of races. Here the juxtaposition in "the mystery of God, of Christ" reveals that in Paul's mind "mystery of God" and "mystery of Christ" are synonymous phrases, each bringing out a different aspect of the same reality. In Ephesians 3 he speaks enthusiastically of his insight into this "mystery of Christ." Clearly, he regarded the mystery as the divine plan, not for salvation alone at some minimum level, but for spiritual development indefinitely large:

> For this reason I bow my knees before the Father . . . that he may grant you to be strengthened with might through his Spirit in the inner man, and that Christ may dwell in your hearts through faith; that you, being rooted and grounded in love, may have power to comprehend with all the saints what is the breadth and length and height and depth, and to know the love of Christ which surpasses knowledge, that you may be filled with all the fullness of God. Now to him who by the power at work within us is able to do far more

6 Ephes. 3:2; 7-12; 1 Cor. 1:21-24; Bromiley, *Theological Dictionary*, pp. 619, 679.

abundantly than all that we ask or think, to him be glory in the church and in Christ Jesus to all generations, for ever and ever. Amen (Ephes. 3:4, 14–20).

In Later Christian Writers

Christian writers in later centuries also used *mysterium* with both the old and increasingly new meanings, such as: (1) secret religious ceremonies known only to the initiated; (2) a secret; (3) God's plan for governing the world; (4) a symbol, allegorical sign; (5) a revealed doctrine; (6) the redemptive work of Christ; (7) rites, whether pagan or Christian; the sacraments; (8) the Eucharistic prayer, the ceremonies of the Mass.[7] "Mystery" was also used to designate any of the events in the life of Christ, such as those presented in the "mystery plays" of the Middle Ages.

As Catholic theological and spiritual writing gradually became more biblical after 1943, Paul's terminology also came into more general use. Not surprisingly (except perhaps to some whose theological training antedated 1943, and to whom its precise meaning was often an irritating puzzle), it occurred with great frequency in the documents of Vatican Council II. For example, the "mystery of Christ" appears in the decrees on the Church, no. 8; on Revelation, no. 24; on the Liturgy, nos. 2, 16, 102; on Bishops in the Church, no. 12; on the Ministry and Life of Priests, nos. 4, 22; on Priestly Formation, no. 16; on the Church's Missionary Activity, nos. 13, 21, 24.[8] Another term, ancient and somewhat forgotten but by then also new to some, came into frequent use, the "paschal mystery." The Council makes its meaning clear within the context of God's plan of salvation: ". . . the work of Christ our Lord in redeeming mankind and giving perfect glory to God. He achieved his task principally by the paschal mystery of his blessed passion, resurrection from the dead, and glorious ascension" (On the Liturgy, nos. 5,6).

The theme of the *mysterion* as God's salvific plan unfolding in history runs through and unifies all the writings of St. Paul—just as it also does for all the books of the Bible. Even though not explicitly stated or called by the term "mystery," it fulfills the same unifying function, with variations of personal approach, for the thought in many a classic work of

---

7 See Blaise, *Dictionnaire des auteurs chrétiens* (1954), pp. 547–548; Bromiley, *Theological Dictionary,* pp. 619–621).

8 J. M. de Aldama et al., *In Christo: El misterio de Dios. Cristología y soteriología* (Madrid: BAC, 1976), pp. xvi–xvii; see also "The Mystery of Christ: The Message and the Spirit," The Living Light, I, no. 4 (1965), 8–17.

other great Christian authors, such as St. John's Gospel and First Epistle, St. Augustine's *City of God,* St. Thomas Aquinas' *Summa of Theology,* and St. Ignatius' writings including his *Spiritual Exercises,* right down to Cusson's present commentary which interprets these *Exercises* in this light. All these authors were communicating God's salvific plan, each according to his own personalized concept of it and in his own way for his circumstances. Each person who makes Ignatius' Exercises, too, can use them as a channel through which God communicates himself to the exercitant and accomplishes his plan of salvation within her or him.

St. Ignatius' Use of the Term ''Mystery''

In all of St. Ignatius' writings, God's plan of salvation and spiritual growth is present as the background and frame of reference of his thought. In other words, the reality designated by St. Paul's term mystery is abundantly present, only a little beneath the surface. However, in his *Exercises* and *Constitutions* (or any other works as far as this writer knows), he does not use the term "mystery" to designate the divine salvific plan. He does employ the word mystery thirty times in the *Exercises* and twice in his *Constitutions* ([65, 345]), always with the medieval meaning of an event in the life of Christ.[9]

It is helpful to be aware that Cusson's terminology is, legitimately, partly the same and partly different from that of Ignatius. At times in *Pédagogie* he presumes terms such as mystery as already known—a procedure fully suitable for the readers (especially those in Rome) for whom he first wrote this treatise as also for many others but, as our experience showed, not for all our prospective English-speaking readers. In *Pédagogie,* the French original of the present book, *mystère* occurs with great frequency. Often it means an event in the life of Christ. Sometimes it means a truth revealed by God which we cannot fully understand. Most frequently, though, it means some aspect of the divine plan of salvation through Christ.

9 See esp. *SpEx,* [261–312], "The Mysteries of the Life of our Lord." For a complete list of occurrences, see *SpEx*MHSJ*Te,* p. 766. On one occasion of interior experiences of the Trinity, Ignatius exclaimed, as Nadal informs us (*FN,* II, 123), "I saw, I experienced interiorly, I penetrated into all the mysteries of the Christian faith." Here "mysteries" is used in the sense it has in Matt. 13:11 and Mark 4:11, 12, the truths of the Christian faith.

2. *A Bird's-Eye View of the History of Salvation,*
   by means of Scriptural Texts for a "Prayerful Reading" (Lectio
   Divina)

To have a synthetic concept of God's plan for salvation and spiritual
growth fresh in memory when one takes up the present book is a great aid
toward gaining a deeper and even a more prayerful insight into its rich
message. To provide such a synthesis (as a brief review for some, as
something perhaps new for others), as our conclusion here we present,
immediately below, a collection of Scriptural texts which summarize the
most relevant features of this plan of God's love, St. Paul's mystery of
Christ.

These texts, and the seven headings which introduce them, can well
be read in the spirit of the "prayerful reading" *(lectio divina)* commended
in chapter 48 of *The Rule of St. Benedict*. The headings stem from the
very structure of St. Thomas Aquinas' *Summa of Theology* (all things
come from God and through Christ are means to lead human beings back
to God), or from any of the manuals of theology since his day, all of
which mirror the Church's long theological reflection on the deposit of
faith found in Scripture. Biblical Theology as an academic study[10] rightly
restricts itself to what could have been known by those authors who composed the Bible. While this approach has its own great importance in our
times, for our purposes it is wise to keep in mind also the fruits of the
Church's reflection through twenty centuries on the deposit of faith, un-

---

10 Biblical theology of the New Testament, a division of positive theology, takes up
the whole reality of Christianity as it finds it attested and interpreted by the New
Testament authors in accordance with the revelations they received. It endeavors
not only to assemble from the Bible and to interpret the data relevant to any topic
on which it focuses, but also to make syntheses which the sacred writers did not
formulate. It aims to supplement systematic theology, not to supplant it. But
usually it avoids use of the terms and categories of dogmatic theology, since they
arose much later than the Biblical era. Different theologians, such as Corlui (in
1884), Lemonyer (1928), Lebreton (1947) Bultmann (1948), Lyonnet (1956),
Léon-Dufour (1962) Bonsirven (1963), McKenzie (1965), and A. Richardson
(1978), have each produced such syntheses on various topics, each according his
own nuanced notion of this evolving academic branch. (See, e.g., D. M. Stanley,
Christ's Resurrection in Pauline Soteriology [Rome, 1962], p. 2; Robert and
Feuillet, *Introduction to the New Testament*, pp. 746–752 and, for sketches of
various topics treated according to the methods of biblical theology, pp. 753–762,
the reign of God; 781–798, the Church, Actualization of the Reign of God; 820–
865, Pauline Soteriology, or any of the topics in Léon-Dufour, *Dictionary of
Biblical Theology*).

der the inspiration of the Holy Spirit who was guiding her "to all truth" (John 16:13).[11] The synthesis of all the truth gleaned from both Scripture and the later theological reflection is what will ultimately be of greatest value to us. Many elements for such a synthesis are found in Ignatius' *Exercises,* as also in Cusson's interpretation of them.

In a literal translation of St. Benedict's phrase "divine reading" *(lectio divina),* the adjective divine is wisely interpreted to refer, not to the reader's activity of reading, but to the nature of the text read. Hence the translation "prayerful reading" is accurate and clearer.[12] In traditional practice this *lectio divina* has been used especially on Scripture, but also on other spiritual treatises. To apply it to God's word in Scripture is to read the text reflectively, trying to comprehend what the inspired author intended to state, and with the purpose of stirring up faith and the affections in ourselves—devotion. "What is the loving God through this text saying to *me* here and now? And with what gratitude and love should I react?[13] Such reading can convert the reading or even the study of Scripture and other treatises of a spiritual nature into prayer.

GOD'S PLAN FOR THE CREATION, REDEMPTION, AND SANCTIFICATION OF HUMANKIND

1. God in his love created the material universe to reveal his existence and goodness to human beings, and to give them an opportunity, to achieve their fulfillment or happiness, in this world and the next, by knowing, loving, and praising or glorifying him forever:

> Ever since the creation of the world, his invisible nature, namely, his eternal power and deity, has been clearly perceived in the things that have been made. So they [the pagans] are without excuse; for although they knew God they did not honor him as God or give thanks to him, but . . . (Rom. 1:20-21).
>
> For from him and through him and unto him are all things. To him be glory forever. Amen (Rom. 11:36; see also 1 Cor. 13:9-12 just below).

11 On the relation between Biblical Theology and Dogmatic Theology, see Karl Rahner, *Encyclopedia of Theology: The Concise Sacramentum Mundi,* s.v. "Biblical Theology," pp. 138-140.

12 *RB 1980: The Rule of St. Benedict in Latin and English with Notes,* ed. T. Fry, (Collegeville, 1981), p. 248.

13 See D. M. Stanley, *"I Encountered God!": The Spiritual Exercises with the Gospel of St. John* (St. Louis, 1986), pp. 316; also pp. 312-313, 319.

2. To give human beings opportunity for a more intensive happiness, one undue or "supernatural" to them, he gave them a special means (termed "life" by St. John and "justice," "grace," "justification," and "life" by St. Paul). Thus they could know him not only dimly on earth through the creatures which reflect his attributes, but also by direct vision eternally in heaven:

> For [here below] our knowledge is imperfect; but when the perfect comes, the imperfect will pass away. . . . For now we see in a mirror dimly, but then face to face. Now I know in part; then I shall understand fully, even as I have been fully understood (1 Cor. 13:9–12).

> See what love the Father has given us, that we should be called children of God. . . . Beloved, we are God's children now; it does not yet appear what we shall be, but we know that when he appears we shall be like him, for we shall see him as he is (1 John 3:2).

> I came that they may have life, and have it abundantly (John 10:10).

3. That supernatural life, the necessary means to humankind's supernatural destiny, was lost to the human race through original sin; but God gratuitously restored it:

> Sin came into the world through one man and death through sin, and so death spread to all men. . . . As one man's trespass led to condemnation to all men, so one man's act of righteousness leads to acquittal and life for all men (Rom. 5:12, 18, 19).

4. God worked this restoration of supernatural life through the Incarnation and Redemption:

> The Word became flesh, and dwelt among us, full of grace and truth (John 1:14).

> God so loved the world that he gave his only Son, that whoever believes in him should not perish but have eternal life (John 3:16).

5. In Paul's concept of "the mystery," the Redemption was achieved by Christ's life, passion, death, and resurrection; and through baptism "into" him we become closely associated with him in his life, death, and eternal life:

> Do you not know that all of us who have been baptized into Christ Jesus were baptized into [fellowship with him in] his death? We were buried therefore with him by baptism into [this close fellowship with him in] his death, so that as Christ was raised from the dead by the glory [or resplendent power] of the Father, we too might walk in newness of life [with him]. For if

we have been united with him in a death like his, we shall certainly be united with him in a resurrection like his (Rom. 6:3–5).

6. At the end of the world Christ will present to his Father the Kingdom of all those who believed in him and served God faithfully, and thus they will attain the purpose for which God created them:

> For as in Adam all die, so also in Christ shall all be made alive. But each in his own order: . . . Then comes the end, when he [Christ] delivers the kingdom to God the Father after destroying every . . . authority [of his enemies] . . . For God has put all things in subjection under his feet. . . . When all things are subjected to him, then the Son himself will also be subjected to him, that God may be everything to everyone (1 Cor. 15:22–28; see also Rom. 8:19–23; Ephes. 4:8–10; Apoc. 21:1–4).

7. Similarly, the whole material universe will then fully attain the purpose for which God created it: to mirror forth God's perfections to men and women, and thus be a means enabling them to cooperate freely with his plan by meriting on earth their supernatural end, the beatific vision. However, since they were incapable of reaching it after Adam's fall, the material universe too was by that fall made incapable of helping them to their supernatural destiny. In St. Paul's words, it was subjected to futility—the futility which Christ's Redemption removed:

> I consider that the sufferings of this present time are not worth comparing with the glory that is to be revealed to us. For the creation waits with eager longing for the revealing of the sons of God; for the creation was subjected to futility, . . . [But] the creation itself will be set free from its bondage to decay and obtain the glorious liberty of the children of God (Rom. 8:18–21).

George E. Ganss, S. J.

A COMPLETE LIST
of those used in the footnotes

Ex   *Exercices spirituels,* translated by F. Courel

Lettres   Saint Ignace, *Lettres,* translated by G. Dumeige

Jr. spir.   Saint Ignace, *Journal spirituel,* translated by Giuliani

RP   Récit du pèlerin, St. Ignatius' *Autobiography,* trans. A.Thiry.

AHSJ   *Archivum Historicum Societatis Iesu.* Periodical, Rome

Ass.S   *Assemblées du Seigneur* (St. André-Bruges)

Autobiog   The *Autobiography* of St. Ignatius

Bib   *Biblica* (Rome)

BJ   The Jerusalem Bible

BVCh   *Bible et Vie Chrétienne* (Paris)

CBE   Collection de la Bibliothèque des Exercices (Enghien)

CBQ   *The Catholic Biblical Quarterly* (Washington)

Chr   *Christus.* Periodical (Paris).

Cons   *The Constitutions of the Society of Jesus,* by St. Ignatius

ConSJComm *The Constitutions,* translated with Commentary by G. E. Ganss

CyF   *Ciencia y Fe.* Renamed *Stromata,* 1965 (Buenos Aires)

DBTh   Léon-Dufour, *Dictionary of Biblical Theology* (1970)

DeGuiJes   *De Guibert, The Jesuits: Their Spiritual Doctrine and Practice*

DirSpEx   *Directoria Exercitiorum Spiritualium (1540–1599)* (1955). In the series MHSJ

DTC	*Dictionnaire de Théologie Catholique* (Paris)
EppIgn	*S. Ignatii Epistolae et Instructiones,* 12 volumes in MHSJ
EstBi	*Estudios Biblicos* (Madrid)
EstEc	*Estudios Ecclesiásticos* (Madrid)
Et	*Etudes* (Paris)
ETL	*Ephemerides Theologicae Lovanienses* (Louvain)
FN	*Fontes Narrativi,* 4 volumes in MHSJ
Greg	*Gregorianum* (Rome)
GuL	*Geist und Leben* (Würzburg)
Ign	*Ignis* (Ranchi, India, 1955–1956)
LettersIgn	*Letters of St. Ignatius,* translated by W. J. Young
LetV	*Lumière et Vie* (St. Alban—Leysse, Savoie).
LV	*Lumen Vitae* (Brussels)
MD	*Maison-Dieu* (Paris)
MiCo	*Miscelanea Comillas* (Comillas and Madrid)
MHSJ	Monumenta Historica Societatis Iesu, the series of primary sources, critically edited, of historical sources of the Society of Jesus, 129 volumes (Madrid, 1894–1929; Rome, 1929–)
MI	Monumenta Ignatiana. The volumes of MHSJ which present the writings of St. Ignatius of Loyola
Mnr	*Manresa* (Madrid)
NRTh	*Nouvelle Revue Théologique* (Louvain)
NTS	*New Testament Studies* (Cambridge)
RAM	*Revue d'Ascétique et de Mystique* (Toulouse)
RB	*Revue Biblique* (Jerusalem, Paris)
RDdT	*Revue Diocésaine de Tournai* (Tournai)
RScR	*Recherches de Science Religieuse* (Paris)
RyF	*Razón y Fe* (Madrid)
ScE	*Sciences Ecclésiastiques* (Montréal)

SDB	*Supplément au Dictionnaire de la Bible* (Paris)
Th	*Thought* (New York)
TS	*Theological Studies* (Woodstock, Md.)
SpEx	The *Spiritual Exercises* of St. Ignatius
*SpEx*MHSJ	*Exercitia Spiritualia S. Ignatii . . . et Directoria* (1919), in the series MHSJ.
*SpEx*MHSJ*Te*	*Sti. Ignatii . . . Exercitia Spiritualia. Textus.* (Rome, 1969). A revision of *SpEx*MHSJ.
VD	*Verbum Domini* (Rome)
VS	*La Vie Spirituelle* (Paris)
VSS	*La Vie Spirituelle, Supplément* (Paris)
WL	*Woodstock Letters.* Periodical (Woodstock, Md.)

GENERAL BIBLIOGRAPHY

from the French Book

Listed here are the books, articles, and commentaries which the author found most helpful when writing the French text of this book.

EDITORIAL NOTE: In cases where English translations exist, an effort has been made here to *substitute* their titles for the original French. This was found possible in most cases, but not in all.

Balthasar, H. U. von. *Heart of the World* (San Francisco, 1979; German, 1954; French, 1956).

A Theology of History, (New York, 1963; German, 1950; French, 1955).

Bourassa, F., "Verum Sacrificium," *ScE,* 3 (1950), 146–182; 4 (1951), 91–139.

Bouyer, L., *The Paschal Mystery* (Chicago, 1950; French, 1945).

Calveras, J., *Práctica de los Ejercicios de San Ignacio,* Barcelona, 1962.

Cantin, R., "L'indifférence dans le Principe et Fondement des Exercises spirituels," *ScE,* 3 (1950), 114–145.

"L'Illumination du Cardoner," *ScE,* 7 (1955), 23–56.

"Le troisième degré d'humilité et la gloire de Dieu selon saint Ignace de Loyola," *ScE,* 8 (1956), 237–266.

Clémence, J., "La méditation du Regne. Une pédagogie de la foi selon l'Evangile," *RAM,* 32 (1956), 145–173.

Coathalem, H., *Ignatian Insights,* Kuangchi Press, Taichung, Taiwan, 1961.

Corbon, J., L'expérience chrétienne dans la Bible. Coll. "Cahier de la Pierre-qui-vive," no. 21, DDB, 1963.

Dibelius, M., "La signification religieuse des récits evangéliques de la Passion," *Rev. d'Hist. et de Phil. rel.,* 13, (1933), 30–45.

Díez-Alegría, J. M., "La 'Contemplación para alcanzar amor' en la dinámica espiritual de los Ejercicios de San Ignacio," *Mnr,* 23 (1951), 171–193.

Dupont, J., "Repentir et conversion d'après les Actes des Apôtres," *ScE,* 12 (1960), 137–173.

Fessard, G., *La dialectique des Exercices Spirituels de saint Ignace de Loyola* (Paris, 1956).

Fitzmyer, J. A., "The Spiritual Exercises of St. Ignatius and Recent Gospel Study," *WL*, 91 (1962), 246-274.

Giblet, J. and Grelot, P., "Repentance/Conversion," *DBTh*, pp. 486-491.

Guardini, R., *La figura di Gesù Cristo nel Nuovo Testamento*, Brescia, 1959.

Guillet, J., *Jesus Christ Yesterday and Today. Introduction to Biblical Theology* (Chicago, 1965; French, 1963).

Iparraguirre, I., *Práctica de los Ejercicios de San Ignacio de Loyola en vida de su Autor (1522-1556)*. (Rome: Bibliotheca Instituti Historici S. J., 1946).

Líneas directivas de los Ejercicios Ignacianos (Bilbao, 1946); English trans. *A Key to the Study of Spiritual Exercises*, (Bombay, 1960).

Dirección de una tanda de Ejercicios (Bilbao, 1962); English trans. *How to Give a Retreat* (Bombay, 1959).

Adnotationes initiales de spiritualitate sacerdotali et Exercitiis sancti Ignatii (Rome: Gregorian University, 1964).

Laurentin, R., *Structure et théologie de Luc I-II* (Paris, 1957).

Léon-Dufour, X., "Passion," *SDB*, VI (1960), col. 1420-1492.

Les évangiles et l'histoire de Jésus (Paris, 1963).

Leturia, P., *Estudios ignacianos*. Revisados por el P. I. Iparraguirre (Rome, 1957).

Lewis, J., *Notes de cours sur les Exercises spirituels*. (Texte polycopie, l'Immaculée-Conception. Montréal, 1960.

Conduite d'une retraite ignatienne (Montréal, 1963).

Lofy, C. A., "The Third Degree of Humility," *WL*, 88 (1959), 366-375.

The Action of the Holy Spirit in the Autobiography of St. Ignatius of Loyola. Unpublished Gregorian University Dissertation (Romae, 1963).

Ludolphus de Saxonia, *Vita Jesu Christi, ex Evangelio et approbatis ab Ecclesia catholica doctoribus sedule collecta*. Ed. L. M. Rigolot. (Paris, 1870).

Lyonnet, S., "Le péché," *SDB*, VII, col. 481-567.

Mollat, D., "Le Christ dans l'expérience spirituelle de saint Ignace," *Chr*, no. 1 (1954), 23-47.

Mouroux, J., *The Christian Experience* (New York, 1954; French, 1952).

D'Ouince, R., "La formation de la liberté par les Exercises," *Chr*, no. 13 (1957), 91-105.

Peeters, L., *Vers l'union divine par les Exercices spirituels de S. Ignace,*

Louvain, 1924; English and adaptation by H. Brozowski, *An Ignatian Approach to Divine Union* (Milwaukee, 1956).

De la Potterie, I., *Adnotationes in exegesim Primae Epistolae S. Joannis* (Rome: Gregorian University, 1963).

Rahner, Hugo, *The Spirituality of St. Ignatius Loyola: An Account of Its Historical Development* (1953; German, 1949);

"Notes on the Spiritual Exercises," *WL*, 85 (1985), 281-336;

True Source of the Sodality Spirit. A pamphlet (St. Louis, The Queen's Work, 1956; French, 1954);

"La vision de saint Ignace à la chapelle de La Storta," *Chr*, no. I (1954), 48-65.

Rahner, Karl, "The Logic of Individual Knowledge in Ignatius Loyola," in *The Dynamic Element in the Church* (1964);

"Ignatian Spirituality and Devotion to the Sacred Heart," in his *Christianity in the Market Place* (1966), pp. 149-146.

Ecrits théologiques, (3 vols., Paris, 1963).

Mission et Grace, II, Serviteurs du peuple de Dieu (Mame, 1963).

This Biblical Bibliography is presented as a working tool for those readers who wish to apply to the various "mysteries" of the life of Christ the principles of interpretation which Cusson himself used while composing his book.

There are references concerning (1) the interpretation of Scripture in general; (2) the problem of evil, in the First Week of the *Exercises;* (3) all the mysteries of the hidden life and the public life, for the Second Week; (4) the Passion narratives, for the Third Week; (5) the glorious life, for the Fourth Week.

EDITORIAL NOTE: In cases where English translations exist, an effort has been made here to *substitute* their titles for the original French. This was found possible in most cases, but not in all.

I. THE INTERPRETATION OF SCRIPTURE

A. Generalities

Léon-Dufour, X., *Les évangiles et l'histoire de Jésus* (Paris, 1963), pp. 62–78, 101–220.
Etudes d'Evangile (Paris, 1965).
George, A., *Connaître Jésus Christ* (Guide de lecture pour les trois évangiles synoptiques), Paris, 1957.
Guardini, R., La figura di Gesù Cristo nel Nuovo Testamento (Brescia, 1959), pp. 26–28, 53–58, 88, 100.
Guillet, J. *Jesus Christ Yesterday and Today* (Chicago, 1965; French 1963), pp. 1–11.
Levie, J., "Le message de Jésus dans la pensée des Apôtres," *NRTh,* 93 (1961). 25–49.
Poelman, R., "En accueillant l'Evangile nous atteignons Jésus," *VS,* 109 (1963), 438–466.

Bea, A., *La storicità dei Vangeli* (1964), (contains the decree of the Biblical Commission of April 21, 1964).

Schoekel, L. A., *L'uomo d'oggi di fronte alla Bibbia* (1963), (Spanish original: *El hombre de hoy ante la Biblia* [1959]).

B. For Each Evangelist

Robert, A. and Feuillet, A.: *Introduction to the New Testament* (New York, 1965; French original, 1959). On Matthew, pp. 166–195; on Mark, pp. 196–228; on Luke, pp. 229–249; on John, pp. 604–666; on Biblical Theology, pp. 746–798; on Redemptive Incarnation in John, pp. 866–889.

Moule, C. F. D., "The intention of the Evangelists," in *Mem. T. W. Manson* (1959), pp. 165–179.

Gourbillon, L. G., "L'Evangile selon saint Marc, ou la bonne nouvelle annoncée par saint Pierre aux Romains," *Cahiers Evangiles*, no. 6 (1952), 23–36.

Deville, C., "L'Evangéliste de Sauveur (Saint Luc)," *Cahiers Evangiles*, no. 26 (1957), 5–73.

Brown, R. E., *The Gospel according to John I-XII*, New York, 1966.

Cullmann, O., *Les sacrements dans l'Evangile johannique*, (1951), ch. I: Le dessein de l'Evangéliste, pp. 9–28.

Léon-Dufour, X., "Actualité du quatrieme évangile," *NRTh*, 76 (1954), 449–468.

Léal, J., "El simbolismo histórico del IV° Evangelio," *EstBi*, 19 (1960), 329–348.

Dodd, C. H., *The Interpretation of the Fourth Gospel* (1960).

Feuillet, A., *Etudes johanniques* (1962).

II. THE FIRST WEEK OF THE EXERCISES

Antoine, P., "Sens chrétien du péché," *Chr*, no. 21 (1959), 45–67.

Beirnaert, L , "Sens de Dieu et sens du péché," *RAM*, 26 (1950), 18–30.

Dupont, J., "Repentir et conversion d'après les Actes des Apôtres," *ScE*, 12 (1960), 137–173.

Gelin, A et Descamps, A, *Théologie du péché* (1960).

Giblet, J. et Grelot, P., "Repentance/Conversion," *DBTh*, pp. 486–491.

Ligier, L., *Péché d'Adam et Péché du Monde. Bible, Kippur, Eucharistie.* Vol. I, *L'Ancien Testament;* Vol. II, *Le Nouveau Testament* (1960 et 1961).

Lyonnet, S., "Le péché," *SDB*, VII, col. 481–567.

De la Potterie, 1., "Le péché c'est l'iniquité (I Jn III,4)," *NRTh*, 78 (1956), 785–797.

Yurrita, J. M., "La 'Reconciliación' como experiencia religiosa," *RyF*, 164 (1961), 49–62.

III. THE SECOND WEEK OF THE EXERCISES

A. The Hidden Life

1. The Gospel Narratives of the Infancy

Léon-Dufour, X., *Les évangiles et l'histoire de Jésus*, pp. 343–351.

Laurentin, R., *Structure et théologie de Luc I-II*. (Paris, 1957). On the utilisation of this book within the framework of the Exercises, see M. A. Fiorito, "Notas para un estudio de los Ejercicios Espirituales," *CyF*, 531–558, esp. pp. 541–544 ("Midrash bíblico y reflexión ignaciana").

Bourke M. M., "The Literary Genus of Matthew 1-2," *CBQ*, 22 (1960), 160–175.

Cave, C. H., "St. Matthew's Infancy Narrative," *NTS*, 9 (1963), 382–390.

Racette, J., "L'évangile de l'enfance selon saint Matthieu," *ScE*, 9 (1957), 77–82.

Laurentin, R., *Structure de Luc I-II*. On Matthew, see pp. 94, 100, 105–109.

2. The mysteries of Christ's Life

a. The Incarnation

Barsotti, D., *Vie mystique et vie liturgique* (Paris, 1954), pp. 65–126.

Lemarié, J., *La manifestation du Seigneur* (Paris, 1957), pp. 135–229.

Brown, R. E., "The Theology of the Incarnation in St. John," *The Bible Today*, I (1963), 586–589.

b. The Annunciation

Allard, M., "L'Annonce a Marie et les annonces de naissances miraculeuses," *NRTh*, 78 (1956), 730–733.

Giblet, J., "L'aube du Salut: l'Annonciation," *BVCh*, 7 (1954), 96–108.

Laurentin, R., *Structure de Luc I-II*, pp. 26, 32, 35, 38, 64, 71.

c. The Visitation and Magnificat

Laurentin, R., *Structure de Luc I–II*, pp. 79–86.

d. Mary

Feuillet, A., "Marie et la nouvelle création" *VS*, 8I (1949), 467–478.
Hebert, A. G., "La Vierge Marie, Fille de Sion," *VS*, 85 (1951), 127–139.
Braun, F. M., *La Mère des fidèles*, (1954).
Guardini, R., *Die Mutter des Herrn*. Ein Brief und darin ein Entwurf. (Würzburg, 1956).
Thurrian, M., *Marie, Mère du Seigneur, Figure de l'Eglise* (Taizé, 1962).

e. Joseph

Bouton, A , "C'est toi qui lui donneras le nom de Jesus," *Ass. S.*, no. 8, 37–50.
Léon-Dufour, X., "L'Annonce à Joseph," *Mél. André Robert* (Paris, 1957), pp. 390.397, and *NRTh*, 8I (1959), 225–231.

f. The Nativity

Leaney, R., "The Birth Narrative in St. Luke and St. Matthew," *NTS*, 8 (1961–1962), 158–166.
Dupont, J., "La genealogia di Gesù secondo Matteo I, 1–7," *Bibbia e Oriente*, 4 (1962,) 3–6.
George, A., "La naissance du Christ Seigneur," *Ass. S.*, no. 10, 44–57.
Muñoz Iglesias, S., "Venez adorons-le!," *Ass. S.*, no. 3, 31–44. (Contains new treatments on the Magi.)
Lemarié, J., *La manisfestation*, pp. 67–132.

g. The Presentation in the Temple

Laurentin, R., *Structure de Luc I–II*, pp. 50–51, 58–63, 89–90, 115–116.
Lemarié, J , *La manifestation*, pp. 473–496.
Benoit, P., "Et toi-même, un glaive te transpercera l'âme" (Luc 2, 35), *CBQ*, 25 (1963), 251–261.
Neirynck, F., "Le Messie sera un signe de contradiction," *Ass. S.*, no. 11, pp. 29–42.

h. The Magi

Hodous, E. J., "The Gospel of the Epiphany," *CBQ,* 6 (1944), 69–84.
Denis, A. M , "L'adoration des Mages vue par s. Matthieu," *NRTh,* 82 (1960), 32–39.
Lemarié, J., *La manifestation,* pp. 239–281.

i. Jesus at the Age of Twelve

Dupont, J., "Jesus a douze ans," *Ass. S.,* no. 4, 25–43.
Laurentin, R., *Structure de Luc I–II,* pp. 106, 111–112, 141–146, 168–174.
Jésus au temple. Mystère de Paques et foi de Marie en Luc 2, 48–50. Coll. "Etudes bibliques" (Paris-Gabalda, 1966).

j. The Hidden Life at Nazareth

Lebreton, J., *The Life and Teaching of Jesus Christ* (1943), pp. 7–53.
Prat, F., *Jesus Christ: His Life, His Teaching, and His Work* (1953), ch. 3.
Salet, G., *Trouver le Christ* (1955), pp. 9–31.

B. The Public Life

1. The First Events

a. The Preaching of John the Baptist

Dupont, J., "Es-tu celui qui vient?" *Ass. S.,* no 4, 35–50.
Joüon, P., "L'Agneau de Dieu," *NRTh,* 67 (1940), 318–321.
De la Potterie, I., "Ecco I'Agnello di Dio," *Bibbia e Oriente,* I (1959), 161–169

b. The Baptism of Christ

Feuillet, A , "Le baptême de Jésus," *RB,* 7I (1964), 321–352.
Lecuyer, J., "La fête du baptême de Jésus," *VS,* 94 (1956), 31–44.
Legault, A., "Le baptême de Jésus et la doctrine du Serviteur souffrant," *ScE,* 13 (1961) 147–166.
De la Potterie, I., "L'onction du Christ. Etude de théologie biblique," *NRTh,* 80 (1958), 225–252.

Lemarié, J., *La manifestation*, pp. 287–378.

c. The Temptations

Charlier, C., "Les tentations de Jésus au desert," *BVCh*, 5 (1941), 85–92.
Dupont, J., "Les tentations de Jésus dans le desert," *Ass. S.* no 26, pp. 51–53.
    "L'arrière fond biblique du récit des tentations de Jesus," *NTS*, 3 (1957), 287–304.
    "Les tentations de Jésus dans le récit de St. Luc," *ScE*, 14 (1962), 7–29.
Lyonnet, S., "La méditation des deux Etendards et son fondement scripturaire," *Chr*, no. 2 (1956), 435–456.

2. Jesus' Meetings with Others

a. The Vocation of the Apostles

Goodier, A., *The Public Life of Our Lord Jesus Christ: An Interpretation* (1930), ch. V: The First Disciples, pp. 23–45.

b. Nicodemus

Bligh, J., "Four Studies in St John, II: Nicodemus," *Heythrop Journal*, 8 (1967), 40–51.
Mollat, D., *Initiation à la lecture spirituelle de saint Jean*, 1964, ch. 3, Jésus et Nicodème. Le mystère de la nouvelle naissance, pp. 21–26.
De la Potterie, I., "Naître de l'eau et naître de l'Esprit. Le texte baptismal de Jn 3, 5," *ScE*, 14 (1962), 417–443.
Roustang, F. "L'entretien avec Nicodème," *NRTh*, 78 (1956), 337–358.
Samain, P., "Nicodème," *RDdT*, 4 (1949), 143–148

c. The Samaritan Woman

Mollat, D., "Le puits de Jacob," *BVCh*, no. 6 (1954), 83–91.
    Initiation à la lecture spirituelle, ch. 4, Jésus en Samarie, pp. 27–35.
Pierron, J., "La source de l'eau vive," *Cahiers Evangiles*, no. 19, (1955). 7–80.

d. Casting the Sellers from the Temple

Cullmann, 0., Les sacrements dans l'Evangile johannique (1951), ch. 4, La purification du temple, pp. 41–44.

Van den Bussche, H., "Le signe du Temple (Jean 2, 13–22)," *BVCh*, no. 20 (1957), 92–100.

3. Christ's Teaching and Discourses

a. The Beatitudes

Dupont, J., *Les Béatitudes*, 1958.

Feret, H. M., "Introduction aux Béatitudes évangéliques," *VS*. 70 (1944), 223–234, 334–347.

Descamps, A. "Bienheureux les pauvres," *RDdT*, 7 (1952), 53–61.

George, A., "Heureux les coeurs purs! Ils verront Dieu," *BVCh*, no 3. (1956), 74–79.

Jeremias, J., *Paroles de Jésus—le sermon sur la montagne, le Notre Père*, Coll. Lectio divina, no. 38, (1963).

Tremel, Y. B , "Béatitudes et morale évangélique," *LetV*, 21 (1955), 83–102.

b. The Bread of Life

Feuillet, A., "Les thèmes bibliques majeurs du discours sur le pain de vie," *NRTh*, 82 (1960), 803–822, 918–939, 1040–1062.

Mollat, *Initiation à la lecture spirituelle*, (1964), ch. 5, Le Pain de Vie, pp. 37–45.

Ponthot, J., "Signification générale et structure du ch. 6 de saint Jean," *RDdT*, 11 (1956), 414–419.

Racette, J., "L'unité du discours sur le pain de vie (Jean VI)," *ScE*, 9 (1957), 82–85.

c. The Way, the Truth, and the Life

De la Potterie, I., "Je suis la Voie, la Vérité, et la Vie" (Jn 14, 6), *NRTh*, 88 (1966), 907–942.

4. Christ's Teaching: Parables

a. In General

Cave, C. H., "Les paraboles et l'Ecriture," *BVCh*, 72 (1966), 35–49.

George, A., Article "Parabole" in *SDB*, VI, col. 1150–1177.

Golenvaux, C., "L'intelligence des paraboles: la Foi," *BVCh*, 72 (1966), 50–54.

Fransen, 1., "Le discours en Paraboles (Matthieu XI, 2–XIII, 53)," *BVCh*, 18 (1957), 72.84).

Dodd, C. H., *The Parables of the Kingdom* (1935).

Jeremias, J., *Les Paraboles de Jésus* (1962).

Lebreton, J., *The Life and Teaching of Jesus Christ*, I, pp. 314–328 (parables of the Kingdom); II, pp. 86–98 (parables of mercy).

b. The Good Shepherd

Mollat, D., "Le bon pasteur (Jean 10, 11–18, 26–30)," *BVCh*, 52 (1963), 25–35.

Initiation a la lecture spirituelle, ch. 8, Le Bon Pasteur, pp. 59–64.

Robinson, J. A. T., "The Parable of John 10, 1.5," *(Zeitschrift fur Neutestamentliche Wissenschaft)*, 46 (1955), 233–240.

c. The Good Samaritan

Daniélou, J., "Le bon samaritain," Mél. André Robert (1957), pp. 457–464.

Derrett, J. D. M., "Law in the New Testament: Fresh Light on the Parable of the Good Samaritan," *NTS*, 11 (1964–65), 22–37.

Roi, J., "Qui est mon prochain?" *BVCh*, 70 (1966), 46–54.

Van den Eynde, P., "Le Bon Samaritain," *BVCh*, 70 (1966), 22–35.

Zerwick, M., "Homo quidam descendebat ab Jerusalem in Jericho (Lc 10, 30–37)," *VD*, 27 (1949), 55–59.

d. The Unjust Steward

Gaechter, P., "The Parable of the Dishonest Steward," *CBQ*, 12 (1950), 121–131.

Larroche, E., "La parabole de l'économe infidèle," *Bulletin de Littérature Ecclésiastique*, 54 (1953), 65–74.

Zerwick, M., "De Villico iniquo (Lc 16, 1–15)," *VD*, 25 (1947), 54–56, 172–176.

e. The Wise and Foolish Virgins

Feuillet, A., "La parabole des vierges," *VS,* 75 (1946), 667–677.

Zerwick, M , "Parabola de decem Virginibus," *VD,* 25 (1947), 56–57.

f. Other Parables

De Goedt, M., "L'explication de la parabole de l'ivraie (Mt. XIII, 36–43)," *RB,* 66 (1959), 32–54.

Dupont, J., "La parabole des ouvriers de la vigne," *NRTh* 89 (1957), 785–797.

George, A., "Le sens de la parabole des semailles (Mc 4, 3–9 parall.)," in *Sacra Pagina,* (1959), II, pp. 163–169.

Léon-Dufour, X., "La parabole des vignerons homicides," *ScE,* 17 (1965), 365–396

Swaeles, R., "L'orientation ecclésiastique de la parabole du festin nuptial, en Mt XII, 1–14," *ETL,* 36 (1960), 655–684.

Ternant, P., "Parabole du figuier stérile," *Ass. S.,* no. 72, pp. 36–47.

5. The Miracles

a. In General

George, A., "Les miracles de Jésus dans les évangiles synoptiques," *LetV,* 33 (1957), 7–24.

Cerfaux, L., "Les miracles, signes messianiques de Jésus et oeuvres du Père, selon l'Evangile de saint Jean," in *Recueil Lucien Cerfaux,* II, 1954.

b. Cana

Cadoux, C., "Les noces de Cana," *VS,* 81 (1949), 155–162.

Michaud, J. P., "Le signe de Cana dans son contexte johannique," *Lav. Theo. et Philo.,* 18 (1962), 239–285.

Charlier, J. P., *Le signe de Cana, Essai de théologie johannique* (1959).

Feuillet, A , "L'heure de Jésus et le signe de Cana," *ETL,* 36 (1960), 5–22.

Lemarié, J., *La manifestation,* pp. 381–426.

Mollat, D., *Initiation à la lecture spirituelle,* ch. 2, Les Noces de Cana, pp. 15–20.

c. Multiplication of the Loaves

Cullmann, O., Les sacrements dans l'Evangile johannique, ch. 10: La multiplication des pains, pp. 62–69.

Quievreux, F., "Le récit de la multiplication des pains dans le quatrième évangile," *RScR*, (Strasbourg), 152 (1967), 97–108.

Rose, A., "Les récits de la multiplication des pains dans les évangiles synoptiques," *Rev. diocesaine de Namur*, 4 (1949), 225–241.

d. The Calming of the Storm

Díaz, J. A., "Passage de la calma de la tormenta en el Evangelio segun Mateo," *Cultura Biblica*, 20 (1963), 149–157.

Duplacy, J., "La tempête apaisée," dans *BVCh*, 74 (1967), 15–28. et *NRTh*, 87 (1965), 897–922.

e. The Man Born Blind

Bligh, J., "Four Studies in St John, I: the Man Born blind," *Heythrop Journal*, 7 (1966), 129–144.

Mollat, D , *Initiation à la lecture spirituelle*, ch. 7, la guérison de l'aveugle-né, pp. 53–58.

f. The Paralytic

Dupont, J., "Le paralytique pardonné," *Ass. S.*, no. 73, pp. 34–46.

Van den Bussche, H., "Guérison du paralytique à Jérusalem le jour du sabbat (Jean 5. 1–18)," *BVCh*, 61 (1965), 18–28.

g. Peter's Mother-in-Law

Lamarche, P., "La guérison de la belle-mére de Pierre et le genre littéraire des évangiles," *NRTh*, 87 (1965), 515.526.

Léon-Dufour, X., "La guérison de la belle-mère de Simon-Pierre," *EstBi*, 24 (1965), 193–216.

h. Other Miracles

Léon-Dufour, X., "L'épisode de l'enfant épileptique," dans *La Formation des évangiles* (1957), pp. 85–115.

Moingt, J., "La guérison du lépreux," *Chr*, no. 1 (1954), 70–76.

Ternant, P., "La résurrection du fils de la veuve de Nain," *Ass. S.*, no. 69, pp. 29–40.

6. The Last Events

a. The Transfiguration

Durrwell, F. X., "La transfiguration de Jésus," *VS*, 85 (1951), 115–127.

Feuillet, A., "Les perspectives propres à chaque évangéliste dans les récits de la Transfiguration," Bib 39 (1958) 281–301.

Ramsey, A. M., "La Gloire de Dieu et la transfiguration du Christ," *Dieu-Vivant*, no. 5 (1950), 17–28.

b. Lazarus

Bouyer, L., Le quatrième évangile (1955), pp. 164–180.

Lebreton, J., *The Life and Teaching of Jesus Christ*, II, pp. 133–161.

c. The Ascent to Jerusalem

Fransen, 1., "Cahier de Bible: La montée vers Jérusalem," *BVCh*, no. 11 (1955), 69–87.

d. The Entrance into Jerusalem

Dupont, J., "L'entrée de Jésus à Jérusalem," *LetV* (supp. biblique de *Paroisse et Liturgie*), no. 48, pp. 1–8.

Maurice-Denis, N., "Le dimanche des Rameaux," *MD*, 41 (1955), 16–33.

Stanley, D. M. "Etudes mathéennes: l'entrée messianique à Jérusalem," *ScE*, 6 (1954), 93–106.

e. The Eschatalogical Discourses

Feuillet, A., "Le discours de Jésus sur la ruine du temple," *RB*, 55 (1948), 481–502; 56 (1949), 61–92.

George, A., "La venue de Fils de l'homme," *Ass. S.*, no. 3, pp. 29–38.

IV. THE THIRD WEEK OF THE EXERCISES

A. The Last Supper

1. The Washing of the Feet

Boismard, M. E., "Le lavement des pieds (Jn XIII, 1–17)," *RB*, 71 (1964), 5–24.

Spicq, C., "Le lavement des pieds, sacrement de l'autorité chrétienne," *VS*, 72 (1945), 121–130.

2. The Institution of the Eucharist

Benoit, P., "Les récits de l'institution et leur portée," *LetV*, no. 31 (1957) 49–76.

Bouyer, L., *The Paschal Mystery* (1950), pp. 71–94.

Delorme, J., "La Cène et la pâque dans le N.T.," *LetV*, no. 31 (1957), 9–48.

Dockx, S., "Le récit du repas pascal (Marc 14, 17–26)," *Bib*, 46 (1965), 445–453.

Dupont, J., "Ceci est mon corps, Ceci est mon sang," *NRTh*, 80 (1958), 1025–1041.

3. The Farewell Discourse

Behler, G. M., Les paroles d'adieu du Seigneur (S. Jean 13–17), "Lectio divina," 27, (1960).

Huby, J., *Le discours après la Cène* (1932).

Lebreton, J., *Lumen Christi* (1947), pp. 269–295.

B. The Passion

1. General Studies

Léon-Dufour, X., Article "Passion," *SDB*, VI (1960), col. 1424–1479.

Dibelius, M., "La signification religieuse des récits évangéliques de la Passion," *Rev. Hist. et Ph. rel.*, 13 (1933), 30–45.

Borgen, P., "John and the Synoptic in the Passion Narratives," *NTS*, 5 (1958–59), 246–259.

Osty, E., "Le point de contact entre le récit de la Passion dans saint Luc et saint Jean," *RScR*, 1951, pp. 146–154.

Vanhoye, A., "Structure et théologie des récits de la Passion dans les évangiles synoptiques," *NRTh*, 89 (1967), 135–163.

Mollat, D., *Initiation a la lecture spirituelle*, ch. 9, La Passion selon saint Jean, pp. 65–69.

Velge, N., "Le mystère du Messie souffrant," *BVCh*, 68 (1966), 76–89.

2. The Agony

Cantinat, J., "L'agonie de Jésus," *VS*, 88 (1953), 272–281.

Kenny A., "The Transfiguration and the Agony in the Garden," *CBQ*, 19 (1957), 444–452.

Descamps, A. "La structure des récits évangéliques de la Resurrection," *Bib*, 40 (1959), 727–741.

Jeauneaua E., "La fête de la nouvelle création," *VS*, 94 (1956), 353–361.

3. The Trial

Blinzler, J., Le procès de Jésus, coll. "In lumine fidei," (Tours: Mame, 1962).

Lebreton, J., *The Life and Teaching*, II, The Trial of Jesus, pp. 330–386.

Benoit, A., "Jésus devant le Sanhedrin," *Angelicum*, 20 (1943), 143–165.

Mollat, D., *Initiation à la lecture spirituelle*, ch. 10, Jesus devant Pilate, pp. 70–78.

De la Potterie, I., "Jésus, Roi et Juge d'après Jean 19, 3," *Bib*, 41 (1960), 217–247.

4. The Way of the Cross

Cantinat J., "Le portement de la croix de Jésus," *VS*, 80 (1949), 236–243.

5. The Crucifixion and Death

Cantinat, J., "Le crucifiement de Jésus," *VS*, 84 (1951), 142–153.

Lefebvre, G., "La Croix, mystère d'obéissance," *VS*, 96 (1957), 339–348.

Bonsirven, J., *Théologie du Nouveau Testament* (1951), "La mort de Jésus, preuve de sa messianité," pp. 187–189.

Lefèvre,A., "La blessure du côté," dans *Le Ceur*, Etudes Carmelitaines (Paris, 1950), 109–122.

Mollat, D., *Initiation à la lecture spirituelle*, ch. 11, Le côté ouvert, pp. 79–83.

"Ils regarderont celui qu'ils ont transpercé," *LetV*, 47 (1960), 95–114.

Samain, P., "L'eau sortie du côté de Jésus, symbole de l'Esprit," *RDdT*, 5 (1950), 318–321.

Vergote, A., "L'exaltation du Christ en croix selon le quatrième Evangile," *ETL*, 28 (1952), 5–23.

V. THE FOURTH WEEK OF THE EXERCISES

1. The Resurrection:

Durrwell, F. X., The Resurrection: A Biblical Study (1960; French original, 1950).
Barsotti, D., *Vie mystique et vie liturgique* (1954), pp. 191–240.
Von Balthasar, H. U., *The Heart of the World*, chs. 10 and 11, pp. 157–188.

2. The Apparitions

Lettey, C., "The Apparitions of Christ Risen," *CBQ*, 2 (1940), 195–214.
Menoud, P. H., "Pendant quarante jours (Ac I, 3)," Mél. 0. Cullmann (1962), pp. 150–152.
Von Balthasar, H. U., *The Heart of the World*, apparitions to Mary Magdalen, pp. 158–162; to Simon Peter, pp. 162–153; to Thomas, pp. 163–165.
Ehrhardt, A. A. T., "The Disciples of Emmaus," *NTS*, 10 (1964), 182–201.
De Giglielmo, A., "Emmaus," *CBQ*, 3 (1940), 293–301.
De Certeau, M., "Les pèlerins d'Emmaüs," *Chr*, no. 3 (1957), 56–63.

Dupont, J., "Le repas d'Emmaus," *LetV*, no. 31 (1957), 77–92.
Mollat, D., *Initiation a la lecture spirituelle*, ch. 12, Au bord du lac, pp. 85–89.

3. Ascension:

Benoit, P., "L'ascension," *RB*' 56 (1949), 161–203.
De Certeau, M., "L'Ascension," *Chr*, no. 22 (1959), 211–220.
Leclerc, J., "L'ascension, triomphe du Christ," *VS*, 72 (1945), 289–300.
Daniélou, J., "Les psaumes dans la liturgie de l'Ascension," *MD*, no. 21 (1950), 40–56.

SUPPLEMENTARY BIBLIOGRAPHY

Books and Articles in English

This is a Selected Bibliography of books and articles in English especially useful in connection with this book. For other books and articles in English to which references were given, see Index I: of Authors Cited, s.v. the respective authors.

Bromiley, G. W. *Theological Dictionary of the New Testament* (Grand Rapids: Erdsman, 1985).

Coathalem, Hervé. Trans. C. J. McCarthy. *Ignatian Insights: A Guide to the Complete Spiritual Exercises.* 2nd ed. (Taichung, Taiwan: Kuangchi Press, 1971).

The Jerome Biblical Commentary. Ed. R. E. Brown, J. A. Fitzmyer, R. E. Murphy. (Englewood Cliffs: Prentice Hall, 1968). See the index, e.g., s.v. "Biblical Theology," "*Mysterion* (mystery)," "Plan of God," and the like.

Encyclopedia of Theology: The Concise Sacramentum Mundi. Ed. Karl Rahner. (New York: Crossroad, 1975). On the relation between biblical and systematic theology, see s.v. Biblical Theology, pp. 139–140.

Guillet, Jacques. *Jesus Christ Yesterday and Today. Introduction to Biblical Spirituality.* Trans J. Duggan. (Chicago: Franciscan Herald Press, 1964.

Léon-Dufour, Xavier. *Dictionary of Biblical Theology* (New York: Crossroads, 1973).

McKenzie, *Dictionary of the Bible* (New York: Macmillan, 1965 and 1973).

The New World Dictionary-Concordance to the New American Bible (1970)

Robert, A. and Feuillet, A. *Introduction to the New Testament.* New York: Desclée, 1965; French original, 1959). On Biblical Theology, see especially pp. 747–751, in the section on Some Major Themes of the New Testament; also the following four chapters.

Stanley, David M., *Christ's Resurrection in Pauline Soteriology.* Rome: Biblical Institute, 1961. See especially pp. 2–4, The Concept of Biblical Theology, and pp. 232–23, Paul's Personal Experience of Christian Salvation (1 Tim. 1:15–16).

_____ *"I Encountered God!" The Spiritual Exercises with the Gospel of St John.* See especially pp. 311–327, A Suggested Approach to *Lectio Divina.* (St. Louis: The Institute of Jesuit Sources, 1986).

_____ *A Modern Scriptural Approach to the Spiritual Exercises.* (St. Louis: The Institute of Jesuit Sources, 1986; also, Chicago: Loyola University Press, 1986. (First printing was in 1967.)

on the Term "Spiritual Exercises"

Throughout this book, as was pointed out in footnote 3 on page 3 above, *Spiritual Exercises* (in italics) refers chiefly to Ignatius' book, and Spiritual Exercises (in roman type) to the activities of an exercitant within a retreat. This term "Spiritual Exercises" gives rise to many editorial problems. The procedures by which they are handled are shown by exemplification in the following paragraph.

Long before Ignatius various spiritual exercises, such as attendance at Mass or recitation of the Office, were common. He gradually composed directives for a sequence of such exercises. Before 1535 his companions Xavier and Favre made his Spiritual Exercises for a period of thirty days. Ignatius assembled his notes in his book *Spiritual Exercises,* which was (or were) published at Rome in 1548. To make references easier, in modern editions since that at Turin in 1928, a number in square brackets has been added to each paragraph of the text; for example, the purpose of the Exercises is stated in *Spiritual Exercises,* [21] or, in our abbreviation, *SpEx,* [21]. The Introductory Observations *(Anotaciones)* are in [1–20]. Important meditations or other exercises in his book are the First Principle and Foundation ([23]), the Call of the King ([91]), which is an introduction to the Second Week or division of the *Exercises,* the Three Modes of Humility ([238–260]). In references run into the text—for example, to the Call of the Temporal King ([91–100])—the parentheses ( ) indicate that the numbers are a reference, and the square brackets [ ] show that the numbers themselves are a modern addition to Ignatius' text. Since 1548 the *Spiritual Exercises* have been read or made by many persons. These Exercises are often a stirring spiritual experience.

Since the book, *Spiritual Exercises,* guides the making of the Exercises and, conversely, the making of them presupposes the book, the respective meanings of *Exercises* and Exercises overlap, and the decision about which meaning is predominant must be somewhat arbitrary.

INDEX I

of Authors Cited

*   *   *   *   *